# Problem Solving Survival Guide
VOLUME II: CHAPTERS 15-24

# INTERMEDIATE
# ACCOUNTING
## Thirteenth Edition

**Marilyn F. Hunt,** M.A., C.P.A.

**Donald E. Kieso,** Ph.D., C.P.A.
KPMG Peat Marwick Emeritus Professor of Accounting
Northern Illinois University
DeKalb, Illinois

**Jerry J. Weygandt,** Ph.D., C.P.A.
Arthur Andersen Alumni Professor of Accounting
University of Wisconsin
Madison, Wisconsin

**Terry D. Warfield,** Ph.D.
Associate Professor
Director, Andersen Center for Financial Reporting and Control
University of Wisconsin
Madison, Wisconsin

WILEY
JOHN WILEY & SONS, INC.

Cover Photo: Jon Arnold Images/SuperStock, Inc.

To order books or for customer service call 1-800-CALL-WILEY (225-5945).

ISBN-13   9780470380581

Printed in the United States of America

10 9 8 7 6 5 4 3 2 1

Printed and bound by BindRite Inc.

# CONTENTS

# PREFACE: To the Student

The purpose of this problem solving tutorial is to help you to improve your success rate in solving accounting homework assignments and in answering accounting exam questions. For each chapter we provide you with:

**OVERVIEW** — To briefly introduce the chapter topics and their importance.

**STUDY OBJECTIVES** — To provide you with a learning framework. Explanations of these ob jectives also provide you with a summary of the major points covered in the chapter.

**TIPS** — To alert you to common pitfalls and misconceptions and to remind you of important terminology, concepts, and relationships that are relevant to answering specific questions or solving certain problems. To help you to understand the intricacies of a problematic situation and to tell you what to do in similar circumstances.

**EXERCISES** — To provide you with a selection of problems which are representative of homework assignments which an intermediate accounting student may encounter.

**MULTIPLE CHOICE** — To provide you with a selection of multiple-choice questions which are representative of common exam questions covering topics in the chapter.

**PURPOSES** — To identify the essence of each question or exercise and to link them to learning objectives.

**SOLUTIONS** — To show you the appropriate solution for each exercise and multiple- choice question presented.

**EXPLANATIONS** — To give you the details of how selected solutions were derived and to explain why things are done as shown.

**APPROACHES** — To coach you on the particular model, computational format, or other strategy to be used to solve particular problems. To teach you how to analyze and solve multiple-choice questions.

This book will be a welcome teaching/learning aid because it provides you with the opportunity to solve accounting problems in addition to the ones assigned by your instructor without having to rely on your teacher for solutions. Many of the exercises and questions contained herein are very similar to items in your intermediate accounting textbook; the difference is, the ones in this book are accompanied with detailed clearly-laid out solutions. The use of the multiple choice questions in this volume and the related suggestions on how to approach them can easily increase your ability (and confidence in your ability) to deal with exam questions of this variety.

We are grateful to James Emig of Villanova University for his accuracy review, constructive suggestions, and editorial comments. Also thanks to Chelsea Hunt, James S. Hunt, Annabelle Specie, M.F. Specie, and Diane Henry for their assistance and support. Our appreciation to Mary Ann Benson who skillfully prepared the manuscript and performed the composition of this book.

Marilyn F. Hunt
Donald E. Kieso
Jerry J. Weygandt
Terry Warfield

# HOW TO STUDY ACCOUNTING

The successful study of accounting requires a different approach than most other subjects. In addition to reading a chapter, applying the material through the completion of exercises or problems is necessary to develop a true and lasting understanding of the concepts introduced in the text chapter. The study of accounting principles is a combination of theory and practice; theory describes what to do and why, and practice is the application of guidelines to actual situations. We use illustrations (practice) to demonstrate how theory works and we use theory to explain why something is done in practice. Therefore, it is impossible to separate the two in the study of accounting.

Learning accounting is a cumulative process. Therefore, it is imperative that you keep up with class assignments for every chapter. And because accounting is a technical subject, you must pay particular attention to terminology.

Accounting is the language of business. It is an exciting subject that provides a challenge for most business majors. Your ultimate success in life may well depend on your ability to grasp financial data. The effort you expend now will provide rewards for years to come.

We encourage you to follow the four steps for study outlined below to give yourself the best possible chance for a successful learning experience and to make the most efficient use of your time. These steps provide a system of study for each new chapter in your text.

**Step 1**
- Scan the study objectives in the text.
- Scan the chapter (or chapter section) rather quickly.
- Glance over the questions at the end of the chapter.

This first step will give you an overview of the material to be mastered.

**Step 2**
- Read the assigned pages slowly.
- Use the marginal notes to review and to locate topics within each chapter.
- Study carefully and mark for later attention any portions not clearly understood.
- Pay particular attention to examples and illustrations.
- Try to formulate tentative answers to end-of-chapter questions.

During this phase, you will be filling in the "outline" you formed in Step 1. Most of the details will fall into place during this part of your study. The remaining steps are necessary, however, for a keen understanding of the subject.

**Step 3**
- Carefully read the **Overview, Learning Objectives,** and **Tips** sections of this *Problem Solving Survival Guide* volume.
- Do the **Exercises** and **Cases** in the *Problem Solving Survival Guide* that pertain to the same learning objectives as your homework assignments. Review the relevant **Illustrations** in this book.
- Do the **Multiple-Choice Type Questions** in the *Problem Solving Survival Guide* that pertain to the same study objectives as your homework assignments.
- Refer back to the sections of the chapter in the text that you marked as unclear if any. It is likely that any confusion or questions on your part will have been cleared up through your work in the *Problem Solving Survival Guide*. If a section remains unclear, carefully reread it and rework relevant pages of the *Problem Solving Survival Guide.*
- Repeat this process for each assigned topic area.

**Step 4** • Write out formal answers to homework assignments in the text.

This step is crucial because you find out whether you can independently **apply** the material you have been studying to fresh situations. You may find it necessary to go back to the text and/or the *Problem Solving Survival Guide* to restudy certain sections. This is common and merely shows that the study assignments are working for you.

Additional comments pertaining to Step 3 and your usage of this *Problem Solving Survival Guide* volume are as follows:

- The **Learning Objectives** and **Tips** sections, along with **Illustrations** will aid your understanding and retention of the material. **Exercises** provide examples of application of the text material. These should be very valuable in giving you guidance in completing homework assignments which are often similar in nature and content.

- The **Approach** stated for an exercise or question is likely the most valuable feature of this *Problem Solving Survival Guide* volume because it tells you how to **think** through the situation at hand. This thought process can then be used for similar situations. It is impossible to illustrate every situation you may encounter. You can, however, handle new situations by simply applying what you know and making modifications where appropriate. Many students make the mistake of attempting to memorize their way through an accounting book. That too is an impossible feat. **Do not rely on memorization.** If this material is going to be useful to you, you must **think** about what you are reading and always be thinking of **why** things are as they are. If you know the reasoning for a particular accounting treatment, it will be much easier to remember that treatment and reconstruct it even weeks after your initial study of it.

- **Explanations** are provided for exercise and questions. These are very detailed so that you will thoroughly understand what is being done and why. These details will serve you well when you complete your homework assignments.

- Always make an honest effort to solve the exercises and answer the questions contained in this *Problem Solving Survival Guide* volume **before** you look at the solutions. Answering the questions on your own will maximize the benefits you can expect to reap from this book.

- The **Multiple-Choice Type Questions** are self-tests to give you immediate feedback on how well you understand the material. Study the **Approaches** suggested for answering these questions in the *Problem Solving Survival Guide.* Practice them when answering the multiple choice questions in the text. Apply them when taking examinations. By doing so, you will learn to calmly, methodically, and successfully process examination questions. This will definitely improve your exam scores.

- When you work an **Exercise** or **Case** in the *Problem Solving Survival Guide* or in the text, always read the instructions **before** you read all of the given data. This allows you to determine what you are to accomplish. Therefore, as you now read through the data, you can begin to process it because you can determine its significance and relevance. If you read the data before the instructions, you are likely to waste your time because you will have to reread the facts once you find out what you are to do with them. Also, more importantly, you are likely to begin to anticipate what the problem is about, which will often cause you to do things other than what is requested in the question.

# HOW TO APPROACH A MULTIPLE CHOICE EXAMINATION

1.  Work questions in the order in which they appear on the exam. If a question looks too long or difficult and you choose to skip over it, put a big question mark in the margin to remind yourself to return to that question after others are completed. Also put a mark in the margin for any question meriting additional review at the end of the exam period.

2.  Do not look at the answer choices until you have thoroughly processed the question stem (see 3 and 4 below). The wrong answers are called "distracters". The manner in which these "distractors" are developed causes them to likely mislead you or cause you to misinterpret the question if you read them too early in the process.

3.  Read each question very carefully. Start with the requirement or essence of the question first (this is usually the last sentence or last phrase of the stem of the question) so that you immediately focus on the question's intent. Now as you read through the rest of the stem and encounter data, you can tell which data are relevant. Underline keywords and important facts. Be especially careful to note exception words such as **not**. Prepare intermediary solutions as you read the question. Identify pertinent information with notations in the margin of the exam. If a set of data is the basis for two or more questions, read the requirements of each of the questions **before** reading the data and before beginning to work on the first question (sometimes the questions can be worked simultaneously or you may find it easier to work them out of order).

4.  Anticipate the answer before looking at the alternative solutions. Recall the applicable definition, concept, principle, rule, model, or format. If the question deals with a computation, perform the computation. Use abbreviations to descibe each component of your computation; this will greatly aid you in following your work and staying on target with the question.

5.  Read the answers and select the best answer choice. For computational questions, if the answer you have computed is not among the choices, check your math and the logic of your solution.

6.  When you have completed all questions, review each question again to verify your choices. Reread the question requirement, scan the data, look at your selected answer, scan your work, and determine the reasonableness of your choice.

# CHAPTER 15

# STOCKHOLDERS' EQUITY

## OVERVIEW

A major source of assets of an entity is owners' equity. Owners' equity of a corporation is called **stockholders' equity** or **shareholders' equity** because the owners of the business hold shares of stock as evidence of their ownership claims. Stockholders' equity typically has two major classifications for reporting purposes: **contributed capital (paid-in capital)** and **retained earnings**. Contributed capital includes the subclassifications of **capital stock** and **additional paid-in capital**.

This chapter discusses the issuance of stock and the reacquisition of shares. When shares are reacquired and held in the treasury, two alternative generally accepted accounting methods are available for use: the cost method and the par value method. The cost method is the more popular method.

The term **earnings** refers to net income for a period. The term **retained earnings** refers to accumulated earnings.  That is, retained earnings is the total of all amounts reported as net income since the inception of the corporation less the sum of any amounts reported as net losses and dividends declared since the inception of the corporation.  Thus, distributions of corporate profits to stockholders reduce retained earnings.  A corporation may distribute cash, noncash assets, or additional shares of the corporation's own stock to its owners in the form of dividends.  A distribution of assets may represent a distribution of income or a return of invested capital.  A distribution of a corporation's own stock results in capitalizing retained earnings.  Corporate distributions are also discussed in this chapter.

## SUMMARY OF LEARNING OBJECTIVES

1.     **Discuss the characteristics of the corporate form of organization.** Among the specific characteristics of the corporate form that affect accounting are: (1) influence of state corporate law; (2) use of the capital stock or share system; and (3) development of a variety of ownership interests. In the absence of restrictive provisions, each share of stock carries the right to share proportionately in (1) profits and losses; (2) management (the right to vote for directors); (3) corporate assets upon liquidation; (4) any new issues of stock of the same class (called the preemptive right).

2.     **Identify the key components of stockholders' equity.** Stockholders' or owners' equity is classified into two categories: contributed capital and earned capital. **Contributed capital (paid-in capital)** describes the total amount paid in on capital stock. Put another way, it is the amount that stockholders advance to the corporation for use in the business. Contributed capital includes items such as the par value of all outstanding capital stock and premiums less any discounts on issuance. **Earned capital (retained earnings)** is the capital that develops if the business operates profitably; it consists of all undistributed income that remains invested in the company.

3.     **Explain the accounting procedures for issuing shares of stock.** The accounting considerations involved in the issuance of different types of stock are: (1) **Par value stock:** Accounts required to be kept are (a) preferred stock or common stock; (b) paid-in capital in

excess of par or additional paid-in capital; and, (c) discount on stock. (2) **No-par stock:** No-par stock with a stated value requires the same accounts to be kept as a par value stock. No-par stock with no stated value requires only a capital stock account (preferred stock or common stock). (3) **Stock issued in combination with other securities (lump sum sales):** The two methods of allocation available are (a) the proportional method; and, (b) the incremental method. (4) **Stock issued in noncash transactions:** When stock is issued for services or property other than cash, the property or services should be recorded at either the fair market value of the stock issued or the fair market value of the noncash consideration received, whichever is more clearly determinable.

4.    **Explain the accounting for treasury stock.** The cost method is generally used in accounting for treasury stock. This method derives its name from the fact that the Treasury Stock account is maintained at the cost of the shares purchased. Under the cost method, a company debits the Treasury Stock account for the cost of the shares acquired and credits it for this same cost upon reissuance. The price received for the stock when originally issued does **not** affect the entries to record the acquisition and reissuance of the treasury stock.

5.    **Explain the accounting for and reporting of preferred stock.** Preferred stock is a special class of shares that possesses certain preferences or features not possessed by the common stock. The features that are most often associated with preferred stock issues are: (1) preference as to dividends, (2) preference as to assets in the event of liquidation, (3) convertible into common stock, (4) callable at the option of the corporation, and (5) nonvoting.  At issuance, the accounting for preferred stock is similar to that for common stock. When convertible preferred stock is converted into common stock, a company uses the book value method. It debits Preferred Stock along with any related additional paid-in capital account, and credits Common Stock and an additional paid-in capital account (if an excess exists).

6.    **Describe the policies used in distributing dividends.** The state incorporation laws normally provide information concerning the legal restrictions related to the payment of dividends. Corporations rarely pay dividends in an amount equal to the legal limit. This is due, in part, to the fact that assets represented by undistributed earnings are used to finance future operations of the business. If a company is considering declaring a dividend, it must ask two preliminary questions: (1) Is the condition of the corporation such that the dividend is **legally permissible**? (2) Is the condition of the corporation such that a dividend is **economically sound**?

7.    **Identify the various forms of dividend distributions.** Dividends are of the following types: (1) cash dividends, (2) property dividends (3) liquidating dividends (dividends based on capital other than retained earnings), (4) stock dividends (the issuance by a corporation of its own stock to its stockholders on a pro rata basis, but without receiving consideration).

8.    **Explain the accounting for small and large stock dividends, and for stock splits.** Generally accepted accounting principles require that the accounting for small stock dividends (less than 20 or 25%) be based on the fair market value of the stock issued. When declaring a small stock dividend, a company debits Retained Earnings for the fair market value of the stock to be distributed. The entry includes a credit to Common Stock Dividend Distributable for the par value times the number of dividend shares, with any excess credited to Paid-in Capital in Excess of Par. Between the declaration date and the date of issuance, common stock dividend distributable is reported as a capital stock item in the stockholders' equity section of the balance sheet. If the number of shares to be issued in the dividend exceeds 20 or 25% of the shares outstanding (large stock dividend), Retained Earnings is debited only for the par value of the dividend shares, and no additional paid-in capital is recorded.

A stock dividend is a capitalization of retained earnings that results in a reduction in retained earnings and a corresponding increase in certain contributed capital accounts. The par value per share and total stockholders' equity remain unchanged with a stock dividend. All stockholders retain their same proportionate share of ownership in the corporation. A stock split results in an increase or decrease in the number of shares outstanding, with a corresponding proportional decrease or increase in the par or stated value per share. No accounting entry is required for a stock split. Similar to a stock dividend, the dollar amount of total stockholders' equity remains unchanged. A stock split is usually intended to improve the marketability of the shares by causing a reduction in the market price of the stock being split.

9. **Indicate how to present and analyze stockholders' equity.** The stockholders' equity section of a balance sheet includes capital stock, additional paid-in capital, and retained earnings. A company may also present additional items such as treasury stock and accumulated other comprehensive income. Companies often provide a statement of stockholders' equity. Common ratios that use stockholders equity amounts include: rate of return on common stock equity, payout ratio, and book value per share.

*10. **Explain the different types of preferred stock dividends and their effect on book value per share.** The dividend preferences of preferred stock affect the dividends paid to stockholders Preferred stock can be (1) cumulative or noncumulative, and (2) fully participating, partially participating, or nonparticipating. If preferred dividends are in arrears, if the preferred stock is participating, or if preferred stock has a redemption or liquidation value higher than its carrying amount, retained earnings must be allocated between preferred and common stockholders in computing book value per share.

*This material is covered in Appendix 15A in the text.

## TIPS ON CHAPTER TOPICS

**TIP:** **Stockholders' equity** is often referred to as **capital**. In accounting for stockholders' equity, the emphasis is on the source of capital. **Retained earnings** is sometimes called **earned capital** because it is the portion of stockholders' equity which has been generated by the entity's operations. **Paid-in capital** is often called **contributed capital** or **invested capital** because it arises from owner contributions. Contributed capital includes capital stock accounts and additional paid-in capital accounts.

**TIP:** **Paid-in capital** is often called **contributed capital**. **Additional paid-in capital** is often called **additional contributed capital** or **paid-in capital in excess of par**. Although **capital surplus** is a term sometimes used for additional paid-in capital, it is not recommended terminology.

**TIP:** Make sure you understand the components of **total paid-in capital**, which include the capital stock accounts **plus** additional paid-in capital accounts. **Capital stock** accounts include Common Stock, Preferred Stock, and Stock Dividends Distributable.

**TIP:** Additional paid-in capital can arise from many situations which include the following: the issuance of capital stock at a price above par, some treasury stock transactions, the retirement of stock, the declaration of an ordinary (small) stock dividend, and the conversion of bonds to stock.

**TIP:** **Premium** on capital stock is defined as an excess of issuance price over par for newly issued stock. In recording the issuance, this excess is often credited to an account called Premium on Capital Stock or Paid-in Capital in Excess of Par. Regardless of the account title, the premium amount is usually reported on the balance sheet by the caption Additional Paid-in Capital.

**TIP:** As you progress through this chapter, pay particular attention to the effect of the various transactions on total paid-in capital, retained earnings, and total stockholders' equity.

**TIP:** There is a tremendous amount of terminology relating to capital stock. You should have a clear understanding of all of the terms mentioned in this chapter before going on to subsequent chapters.

**TIP:** **Stockholders** are often called **shareholders.**

**TIP:** The **market value** of a share of stock at a given point in time is the value at which the stock can be bought or sold.

**TIP:** **Dividends in arrears** are **not** to be reported as a liability. Dividends become a liability when they are declared. By definition, dividends in arrears are dividends on cumulative preferred stock which have been passed (not declared). Dividends in arrears should be disclosed, however, in the notes to the financial statements.

**TIP:** A corporation acquires resources (assets) from new owners by issuing stock; the issuance is recorded on the company's books by an increase in assets and an increase in owners' equity. When that initial owner later sells his (her) stock through the stock market, there is **no** journal entry to be made on the corporation's books; only the stockholders' name is changed in the corporation's records. The assets, liabilities, and owners' equity of the corporation are **not** affected by the purchase (or sale) of stock by investors in the stock market.

**TIP:** A preferred stock's preference as to dividends is usually expressed as a percentage of the par or stated value; sometimes, the preference is expressed in terms of dollars.

**TIP:** Retained earnings represents a source of corporate assets. The balance of the Retained Earnings account at any point in time reflects the total unspecified assets which have been obtained through profitable operations of the reporting entity. The balance of the Retained Earnings account has **no** direct relationship to the amount of cash held by the entity; a corporation can have a large balance in the Cash account and a small balance in Retained Earnings or a small balance in Cash and a large balance in Retained Earnings.

**TIP:** Dividends are **not** an expense; they do not meet the definition of expense. Dividends are a distribution of income, not a determinant of income. In recording the declaration of any dividend (except for a liquidating dividend), the accountant may use a temporary account called Dividends Declared, rather than debiting the Retained Earnings account directly. At the end of the period, in the closing process, the balance of the Dividends Declared account is closed directly to the Retained Earnings account.

## EXERCISE 15-1

**Purpose:**     (L.O. 3) This exercise will highlight the relationship between authorized, issued, outstanding, and subscribed shares.

The following data are available regarding the common stock of the Daffy Corporation at December 31, 2010:

| | |
|---|---:|
| Authorized shares | 200,000 |
| Unissued shares | 60,000 |
| Treasury shares | 12,000 |

## Instructions

Compute the number of outstanding shares.

## Solution to Exercise 15-1

| | |
|---|---:|
| Authorized shares | 200,000 |
| Unissued shares | (60,000) |
| Issued shares | 140,000 |
| Treasury shares | (12,000) |
| Outstanding shares | 128,000 |

**Approach and Explanation:** Write down the formula for determining the number of outstanding shares:

$$\text{Issued Shares - Treasury Shares = Outstanding Shares}$$

Fill in the data given. Authorized shares are either issued or unissued. Issued shares are either outstanding shares or treasury shares. The number issued can readily be computed in this situation. Treasury shares are issued shares but are not outstanding (in the hands of shareholders).

## CASE 15-1

**Purpose:**    (L.O. 4) This case will review the proper accounting procedures for the issuance of no par stock.

Problems may be encountered in accounting for transactions involving the stockholders' equity section of the balance sheet.

**Instructions**
(a)    Describe how to account for the issuance for cash of common stock with no par value at a price in excess of the stated value of the common stock.
(b)    Describe how to account for the costs of the issuance of stock.

(AICPA Adapted)

## Solution to Case 15-1

(a)    The issuance for cash of common stock with no par value at a price in excess of the stated value of the common stock is accounted for as follows:

- Cash is debited for the proceeds from the issuance of the common stock.

- Common Stock is credited for the stated value of the common stock.

- An additional paid-in capital account is credited for the excess of the proceeds from the issuance of the common stock over its stated value.

**TIP:**    A no-par stock with a stated value is accounted for in a manner similar to stock with a par value; that is, the stated value is recorded in the capital stock account and an excess of the issuance price over stated value is recorded in an additional paid-in capital account. The entire proceeds from the issuance of a no-par stock with no stated value is recorded in the capital stock account.

(b)    The costs of issuing  stock are accounted for as follows:

- Direct costs incurred to sell stock such as underwriting costs and commissions, accountants' fees, attorneys' fees, filing fees, printing costs, taxes, and costs to advertise the issue should be reported as a reduction of the amounts paid in. Issue costs are therefore charged (debited) to Paid-in Capital in Excess of Par (additional paid-in capital) because they are unrelated to corporate operations. In effect, issue costs are a cost of financing and should be viewed as a reduction of the proceeds received from the sale of the stock.

- Management salaries and other indirect costs related to the issuance of stock should be expensed as incurred because it is difficult to establish a relationship between these costs and the proceeds received upon sale. In addition, a corporation will annually incur costs for maintaining the stockholders' records and handling ownership transfers. These recurring costs, primarily registrar and transfer agent's fees, are normally charged to expense in the period in which they are incurred.

# EXERCISE 15-2

**Purpose:**    (L.O. 4) This exercise will illustrate how to record selected transactions related to the issuance of capital stock.

On February 1, 2010, Bimini Bay Corporation received authorization to issue 400,000 shares of $10 par value common stock and 100,000 shares of $50 par value preferred stock. The following transactions occurred during 2010:

Feb. 24    Issued 100,000 shares of common stock for cash at a price of $18 per share.

Feb. 28    Issued 50,000 shares of common stock in exchange for a group of modular warehouses.

Mar. 5    Sold 20,000 shares of Bimini Bay preferred stock at $51 each.

Mar. 23    Sold a package of shares for $1,340,000. The package consisted of 20,000 shares of Bimini Bay common stock and 20,000 shares of Bimini Bay preferred stock. The market value of the preferred was $51 per share, and the market value of the common was $18 per share at this date.

Nov. 4    Issued 20,000 shares of common stock at $24 per share.

Nov. 14    Sold a package of shares for $1,510,000. The package consisted of 20,000 shares of Bimini Bay common stock and 20,000 shares of Bimini Bay preferred stock. The market value of the common stock was $24 at this date; however, no recent quote on the preferred stock could be found.

## Instructions
Prepare the journal entries to record the transactions listed above.

## Solution to Exercise 15-2

### February 24

| | | |
|---|---|---|
| Cash (100,000 x $18) | 1,800,000 | |
| Common Stock (100,000 x $10) | | 1,000,000 |
| Paid-in Capital in Excess of Par—Common | | |
| (100,000 x $8) | | 800,000 |

### February 28

| | | |
|---|---|---|
| Warehouses (50,000 x $18) | 900,000 | |
| Common Stock (50,000 x $10) | | 500,000 |
| Paid-in Capital in Excess of Par—Common | | |
| (50,000 x $8) | | 400,000 |

**March 5**

| | | |
|---|---:|---:|
| Cash (20,000 x $51) | 1,020,000 | |
|     Preferred Stock (20,000 x $50) | | 1,000,000 |
|     Paid-in Capital in Excess of Par—Preferred | | |
|       (20,000 x $1) | | 20,000 |

**March 23**

| | | |
|---|---:|---:|
| Cash. . . . . | 1,340,000 | |
| Discount on Preferred Stock ($1,000,000 - $990,434) | 9,566 | |
|     Preferred Stock (20,000 x $50) | | 1,000,000 |
|     Common Stock (20,000 x $10) | | 200,000 |
|     Paid-in Capital in Excess of Par—Common | | |
|       ($349,566 - $200,000) | | 149,566 |

**Computations:**

| | | | | |
|---|---|---|---:|---|
| 20,000 x $18 | = | $ | 360,000 | fair value of common |
| 20,000 x $51 | = | | 1,020,000 | fair value of preferred |
| | | $ | 1,380,000 | total fair value |

$$\frac{\$360,000}{\$1,380,000} \text{ x } \$1,340,000 = \underline{\$349,566} \text{ allocated to common}$$

$$\frac{\$1,020,000}{\$1,380,000} \text{ x } \$1,340,000 = \underline{\$990,434} \text{ allocated to preferred}$$

**November 4**

| | | |
|---|---:|---:|
| Cash (20,000 x $24) | 480,000 | |
|     Common Stock (20,000 x $10) | | 200,000 |
|     Paid-in Capital in Excess of Par—Common | | |
|       (20,000 x $14) | | 280,000 |

**November 14**

| | | |
|---|---:|---:|
| Cash | 1,510,000 | |
|     Preferred Stock (20,000 x $50) | | 1,000,000 |
|     Paid-in Capital in Excess of Par—Preferred | | |
|       ($1,030,000* - $1,000,000) | | 30,000 |
|     Common Stock (20,000 x $10) | | 200,000 |
|     Paid-in Capital in Excess of Par—Common | | |
|       (20,000 x $14) | | 280,000 |

*20,000 x $24 = $480,000 market value of common
  $1,510,000 - $480,000 = $1,030,000 allocated to preferred

**Explanation:**

Feb. 24    The **issuance of stock in exchange for cash** is recorded by crediting stockholder equity accounts for the amount of the cash consideration received ($1,800,000). The par value ($10) per share is entered into the related capital stock account, and the excess of the issuance price over par value per share ($8) is recorded in the related additional paid-in capital account. When more than one class of stock is authorized, any additional paid-in capital amounts are properly identified to indicate the related class of stock.

Feb. 28    The **issuance of stock in exchange for noncash assets** requires an application of the historical cost principle. The asset and the stock are to be recorded at the fair value of the consideration given (the stock) or the fair value of the consideration received (warehouses), whichever is the more clearly determinable. Because some shares of common were issued only four days earlier at $18 per share, the February 24 transaction provides good evidence of the fair value (cash equivalent value) of the stock issued on February 28. No mention of the fair value of the warehouses is made.

Mar. 5    In recording the **issuance of preferred shares for cash**, the par value of the preferred shares issued is placed in a capital stock account for that class of stock. The amount received in excess of par is an element of additional paid-in capital; the account title clearly indicates the related class of stock. The account title "Premium on ... Stock" is sometimes used to record the excess of issuance price over par.

Mar. 23    When **shares of two classes of stock are sold for one lump sum** and the fair value of each class of security is known, the lump sum received is allocated between the two classes of securities on a proportional basis; that is, based on the relative fair values of the securities involved. Thus, a ratio is developed for each security, and that ratio is equal to the total fair value of the particular shares in question divided by the total fair value of all of the shares in the transaction. Therefore, 26.087% ($360,000 ÷ $1,380,000) of the proceeds are allocated to stockholder equity accounts attributable to common stock, and 73.913% ($1,020,000 ÷ $1,380,000) of the proceeds are allocated to the issuance price of the preferred stock. Because the proceeds attributable to the preferred stock ($990,434) are less than the par value of the preferred shares being sold ($50 x 20,000 shares), the preferred shares are being issued at a total discount of $9,566. The Discount on Preferred Stock account is a negative component of additional paid-in capital.

Nov. 4    The **issuance of stock for cash** increases assets and total stockholders' equity by the issuance proceeds. The par value of the issued shares is recorded in a capital stock account, regardless of the issuance price. An additional paid-in capital account is debited or credited (whichever is appropriate) for the difference between the total proceeds and the total par value of the shares.

Nov. 14    In a situation where **more than one class of securities are issued in a lump sum issuance**, and the market value of all classes of securities is **not** determinable, the incremental method may be used. The market value of the securities is used as a basis for those classes that are known (market value for common stock, in this case) and the remainder of the lump sum is allocated to the class for which the market value is **not** known (preferred stock, in this case).

## ILLUSTRATION 15-1
## COST METHOD OF ACCOUNTING FOR TREASURY STOCK (L.O. 4)

**When treasury stock is purchased:**
1.   Cash is credited for the cost of the treasury shares acquired.
2.   Treasury Stock is debited for the cost of the treasury shares acquired.

**When treasury stock is sold:**
1.   Cash is debited for the selling price of the treasury shares sold.
2.   Treasury Stock is credited for the cost of the treasury shares sold.
3.   The selling (reissuance) price of the treasury shares is compared with the cost of those shares:
a.   An excess of selling price over cost is credited to Paid-in Capital from Treasury Stock.
b.   An excess of cost over selling price is debited to any additional paid-in capital account related to previous treasury stock transactions or retirements of stock in the same class. When the balances in Paid-in Capital from Treasury Stock and Paid-in Capital from Retirements are exhausted, Retained Earnings is debited for the remainder.

---

**TIP:**   Memorize the definition of treasury stock: **Treasury stock** is a corporation's own stock that has been issued, fully paid, and subsequently reacquired, but not cancelled. Thus, treasury shares are issued shares but are not outstanding shares. Treasury stock is **not** an asset; rather it is a contraction of owners' equity.

**TIP:**   Regardless of the method used to account for treasury stock, the **purchase** of treasury stock will cause owners' equity to **decrease** by the cost of the shares acquired; the **sale** of treasury stock will cause owners' equity to **increase** by the selling price of the shares sold. Although the net impact is the same under both methods, the choice of method will affect the individual stockholders' equity accounts involved in recording the transaction.

**TIP:**   When the **cost method** is used to account for treasury stock, the Treasury Stock account is classified contra to the sum of all of the other stockholders' equity accounts, and its balance is the cost of the treasury shares held. When the **par value method** is used to account for treasury stock transactions, the Treasury Stock account is classified contra to the related capital stock account (such as Common Stock), and its balance is the par value of the treasury shares held.

**TIP:**   The par value method of accounting for treasury stock views treasury stock as if it were temporarily retired and records the acquisition the same way a retirement is recorded except that the par value of the stock is charged to Treasury Stock rather than to the capital stock account used in recording the original issuance.

**ILLUSTRATION 15-2**
**JOURNAL ENTRIES FOR RECORDING**
**TREASURY STOCK TRANSACTIONS USING THE COST METHOD (L.O. 4)**

Assume that the following transactions occur in chronological order and that there are no prior balances in any additional paid-in capital accounts.

**1.    1,000 shares of $10 par stock are sold for $13 per share.**

| | | |
|---|---|---|
| Cash . . . . ............................................................................... 13,000 | | |
| Common Stock................................................................ | | 10,000 |
| Paid-in Capital in Excess of Par....................................... | | 3,000 |

**2.    100 treasury shares are acquired for $11 each.**

| | | |
|---|---|---|
| Treasury Stock................................................................... | 1,100 | |
| Cash ............................................................................ | 1,100 | |

**3.    10 treasury shares are sold at $14 each.**

| | | |
|---|---|---|
| Cash      ................................................................... 140 | | |
| Treasury Stock.............................................................. | | 110 |
| Paid-in Capital from Treasury Stock ............................... | | 30 |

**4.    10 treasury shares are sold at $6 each.**

| | | |
|---|---|---|
| Cash      ...................................................................... 60 | | |
| Paid-in Capital from Treasury Stock ......................................... | 30 | |
| Retained Earnings ................................................................. | 20 | |
| Treasury Stock................................................................ | | 110 |

**5.    All 80 remaining treasury shares are retired.**

| | | |
|---|---|---|
| Common Stock ........................................................................ | 800 | |
| Paid-in Capital in Excess of Par............................................... | 240 | |
| Treasury Stock................................................................ | | 880 |
| Paid-in Capital from Retirement of Common<br>    Stock .......................................................................... | | 160 |

**TIP:** The accounts and amounts used to record the original issuance of shares are used to record the retirement of the same shares.

**TIP:** When the **cost method** is used to account for treasury stock transactions, a "gain on the sale of treasury stock" is an expression used to indicate that treasury stock was sold for a price in excess of the treasury stock's cost; a "loss on the sale of treasury stock" refers to treasury stock which is sold for a price that is less than the cost of the treasury shares. For example, transaction #3 above results in a "gain" of $3 ($14 - $11) per share and transaction #4 results in a "loss" of $5 ($11 - $6) per share.

## ILLUSTRATION 15-2 (Continued)

**TIP:** When a corporation engages in treasury stock transactions, a gain or loss is **never** reported on the income statement because a corporation cannot have an accounting gain or loss when dealing with the owners of the business in their capacity of being owners of the business. The purchase and sale of treasury stock are capital transactions; there is no element of income in a capital transaction.

**TIP:** Treasury stock transactions can sometimes **reduce** retained earnings but can **never increase** retained earnings.

**TIP:** Regardless of the method used to account for treasury stock, most state corporate laws require that retained earnings be restricted in the amount of the cost of treasury stock acquired. Restricted retained earnings are unavailable for dividend declaration.

**TIP:** Most companies use the cost method to account for treasury stock transactions, rather than the par value method.

**TIP:** When reporting treasury stock on the balance sheet using the cost method, the caption "Treasury stock" is shown along with the amount of the cost of the treasury shares being deducted from the subtotal of paid-in capital plus retained earnings to arrive at total stockholders' equity. When reporting treasury stock on the balance sheet using the par value method, the caption "Treasury stock" is shown along with the par amount of the treasury shares being deducted from the Capital Stock account. Thus, the Treasury Stock account is referred to as a contra stockholders' equity account using the cost method; with the par value method, the Treasury Stock account is classified as a contra capital stock account (which may be more broadly referred to as a contra stockholders' equity account).

## EXERCISE 15-3

**Purpose:** (L.O. 4, 9) This exercise will illustrate how the components of stockholders' equity should be reported in the balance sheet.

Bobbit Corporation's charter authorizes 200,000 shares of $20 par value common stock, and 50,000 shares of 6% cumulative and nonparticipating preferred stock, par value $100 per share.

The corporation engaged in the following stock transactions between the date of incorporation and December 31, 2010:
(1) Issued 40,000 shares of common stock for $1,920,000.
(2) Issued 10,000 shares of preferred stock in exchange for machinery valued at $1,120,000.
(3) Purchased 1,000 shares of common stock at $46 per share for the treasury. The cost method was used to record the transaction.
(4) Sold 500 shares of treasury stock for $51 per share.

At December 31, 2010, Bobbit's retained earnings balance was $2,200,000. State law requires that the amount of retained earnings available for dividends be restricted by an amount equal to the cost of treasury shares held.

## Instructions
Prepare the stockholders' equity section of the balance sheet in good form.

## Solution to Exercise 15-3

**Bobbit Corporation**
**PARTIAL BALANCE SHEET**
**December 31, 2010**

Stockholders' equity
Preferred stock, $100 par; 6% cumulative and
   nonparticipating; 50,000 shares authorized;
   10,000 shares issued and outstanding                                   $1,000,000
Common stock, $20 par; 200,000 shares authorized,
   40,000 shares issued, 39,500 shares outstanding                          800,000
Additional paid-in capital:
   From preferred stock                         $     120,000
   From common stock                                1,120,000
   From treasury stock                                  2,500     1,242,500
    Total paid-in capital                                        3,042,500
Retained earnings (restricted in the amount of
   $23,000 cost of treasury stock held)                          2,200,000
    Total paid-in capital and retained earnings                  5,242,500
Less:  Cost of 500 treasury common shares                               23,000
    Total stockholders' equity                                 $ 5,219,500

**Approach:** Reconstruct the journal entries for the transactions and post those entries to T-accounts. Use the resulting balances in the accounts to prepare the stockholders' equity section of the balance sheet at December 31, 2010.

**Explanation:**

(1)  Cash .................................................................... 1,920,000
    Common Stock (40,000 x $20) ..................................... 800,000
    Paid-in Capital in Excess of Par—Common
     ($1,920,000 - $800,000)............................................ 1,120,000

(2)  Machinery................................................................ 1,120,000
    Preferred Stock (10,000 x $100) ................................... 1,000,000
    Paid-in Capital in Excess of Par—Preferred
     ($1,120,000 - $1,000,000)......................................... 120,000

(3)  Treasury Stock—Common (1,000 x $46)......................... 46,000
    Cash ................................................................... 46,000

(4)  Cash (500 x $51)..................................................  25,500
     Treasury Stock—Common (500 x $46)...........................          23,000
     Paid-in Capital from Treasury Stock
        ($25,500 - $23,000)........................................           2,500

A restriction on retained earnings can be reported by parenthetical note in the retained earnings caption on the balance sheet or by a note to the financial statements. A restriction on retained earnings does **not** affect the total balance of retained earnings; it merely makes a portion of retained earnings unavailable to serve as the basis of a dividend declaration.

| Preferred Stock | | Common Stock | |
|---|---|---|---|
| | (2) 1,000,000 | | (1)   800,000 |

| Paid-in Capital in Excess of Par--Preferred | | Paid-in Capital in Excess of Par--Common | |
|---|---|---|---|
| | (2)   120,000 | | (1)   1,120,000 |

| Treasury Stock--Common | | Paid-in Capital from Treasury Stock | |
|---|---|---|---|
| (4)  46,000 | (5)    23,000 | | (5)      2,500 |
| Bal. 23,000 | | | |

---

**TIP:** The **par value** of a stock is an arbitrary value assigned to a share of stock at the time of incorporation and is printed on the stock certificate. Par value usually has **no** direct relationship to the stock's issuance price or to its market value at any date subsequent to the issuance date.    The **par value** of a stock has legal significance because it establishes the amount of **legal capital**, which is an amount of owners' equity that must be maintained by the corporation for the protection of creditors.

**TIP:** When a corporation issues more than one class of capital stock, each additional paid-in capital account should specify the class of stock to which it relates. Although a separate account may be maintained in the general ledger for each source of additional paid-in capital, the balances of all additional paid-in capital accounts are typically summed and reported by a single amount on the balance sheet by the caption Additional Paid-in Capital.

**TIP:** When stock is issued in a noncash exchange, the historical cost principle is used to determine the issuance price. Thus, the exchange price is the fair value (cash equivalent) of the consideration given or the fair value of the consideration received, whichever is the more objectively determinable.

# CASE 15-2

**Purpose:**     (L.O. 2, 3) This case examines the major classifications within the stockholders' equity section of the balance sheet.

Stockholders' equity is an important element of a corporation's balance sheet.

## Instructions

Identify and discuss the general categories of stockholders' equity (capital) for a corporation. Enumerate specific sources included in each general category.     (AICPA Adapted)

## Solution to Case 15-2

The general categories of a corporation's stockholders' equity are:
* Paid-in capital or contributed capital (capital stock **plus** additional paid-in capital).
* Retained earnings.
* Accumulated Other Comprehensive Income

Contributed capital represents the amounts paid in for all classes of shares of stock and the amounts capitalized by order of the corporation's board of directors. Included in contributed capital is legal capital, which is usually the aggregate par value or stated value of the shares issued. Legal capital is usually not subject to withdrawal; it is intended to protect corporate creditors. Contributed capital also includes other amounts in addition to the legal capital. These amounts are generally referred to as additional paid-in capital and include the following:

* Premiums on capital stock issued (excess of issuance price over par or stated value).
* Excess of proceeds from reissuing treasury stock over its cost when using the cost method of accounting for treasury stock.
* Assessments on stockholders.
* Conversion of convertible bonds or preferred stock to common stock. (See Chapter 16).
* Declaration of small (ordinary) stock dividend.
* Reacquisition and retirement of outstanding shares at an amount below their original issuance price.

> **TIP:**   Additional paid-in capital is a classification of accounts (like current assets is another classification). Therefore, there is no one account titled "additional paid-in capital"; rather, there are numerous individual accounts within that classification (such as Paid-in Capital in Excess of Par (or Premium on Common Stock), Paid-in Capital in Excess of Stated Value, and Paid-in Capital from Treasury Stock).

Retained earnings are the accumulated net earnings of a corporation in excess of any net losses from operations and dividends (cash or stock). Total retained earnings should also include prior-period adjustments as direct increases or decreases and may include certain restrictions on retained earnings, making a portion of the balance unavailable to serve as a basis for dividends. These restrictions may arise as a result of a restriction in a bond indenture or other formal agreement or they may be created at the discretion of the board of directors.

Accumulated Other Comprehensive Income reflects the sum of items reported to date as Other Comprehensive Income on the income statement.

Items reflected as credits (increases) in this sum include:
(1)    unrealized holding gains on available-for-sale securities held as an investment.
(2)    accumulated foreign currency translation gain adjustments.

Items reflected as debits (decreases) in this sum include:
(1)    unrealized holding losses on available-for-sale securities held as an investment.
(2)    accumulated foreign currency translation loss adjustments.
(3)    excess of additional pension liability over unrecognized prior service cost.
(4)    guarantees of employee stock option plan (ESOP) debt.
(5)    unearned or deferred compensation related to employee stock award plans.
(6)    amounts owed to a company by employees for loans to buy company stock.

## EXERCISE 15-4

**Purpose:**    (L.O. 6, 10) This exercise will illustrate the use of the cost method of accounting for treasury stock transactions under a variety of price relationships.

LaToya Corporation reported the following stockholder equity items at December 31, 2009:

| | |
|---|---:|
| Common Stock, $10 par | $ 350,000 |
| Paid-in Capital in Excess of Par | 70,000 |
| Retained Earnings | 710,000 |
| Total Stockholders' Equity | $ 1,130,000 |

During 2010, LaToya had the following treasury stock transactions:
1.    Purchased 1,000 shares at $15 per share.
2.    Purchased 1,000 shares at $13 per share.
3.    Sold 1,000 shares at $11 per share.
4.    Sold 1,000 shares at $14 per share.
5.    Purchased and immediately retired 1,000 shares at $16 per share.

### Instructions
Prepare the journal entries for the treasury stock transactions listed above assuming the cost method is used. Apply a FIFO approach in determining the cost of treasury shares sold.

### Solution to Exercise 15-4
**Cost Method**

| | | | |
|---|---|---:|---:|
| 1. | Treasury Stock (1,000 x $15)........................................ | 15,000 | |
| | Cash .................................................................. | | 15,000 |
| | | | |
| 2. | Treasury Stock (1,000 x $13)........................................ | 13,000 | |
| | Cash .................................................................. | | 13,000 |
| | | | |
| 3. | Cash (1,000 x $11)..................................................... | 11,000 | |
| | Retained Earnings...................................................... | 4,000 | |
| | Treasury Stock (1,000 x $15)................................ | | 15,000 |

| | | | |
|---|---|---|---:|
| 4. | Cash (1,000 x $14)................................................ | 14,000 | |
| | Treasury Stock (1,000 x $13)............................... | | 13,000 |
| | Paid-in Capital from Treasury Stock...................... | | 1,000 |
| | | | |
| 5. | Common Stock (1,000 x $10) ................................ | 10,000 | |
| | Paid-in Capital in Excess of Par (1,000 x $2)................. | 2,000* | |
| | Paid-in Capital from Treasury Stock............................. | 1,000 | |
| | Retained Earnings....................................................... | 3,000 | |
| | Cash (1,000 x $16)............................................ | | 16,000 |

> *$350,000 Common Stock balance ÷ $10 par = 35,000 shares issued
> $70,000 PIC in Excess of Par balance ÷ 35,000 shares = $2 original
> issuance premium per share

**Approach and Explanation:** Follow the guidelines listed in **Illustration 15-1** and the examples in **Illustration 15-2.** An explanation for each entry above is as follows:

1.  Treasury Stock is debited for the cost of the treasury shares acquired.

2.  Treasury Stock is debited for the cost of the treasury shares acquired.

3.  Cash is debited for the selling price of the treasury shares sold. Treasury Stock is credited for the cost of the treasury shares sold. The excess of the cost over the selling price of the treasury shares is to be charged to Paid-in Capital from Treasury Stock or Paid-in Capital from Retirements to the extent that these accounts have balances that came from previous transactions involving stock of the same class. In this scenario, there is no balance in either of these accounts so the entire excess is charged to Retained Earnings.

4.  Cash is debited for the selling price of the treasury shares sold. Treasury Stock is credited for the cost of the treasury shares sold. The excess of the selling price over the cost of the treasury shares is to be credited to Paid-in Capital from Treasury Stock.

5.  A retirement of stock is to be handled in a manner similar to the par value method of handling the purchase of treasury stock except that the capital stock account will be debited rather than Treasury Stock. Thus, the amounts recorded for the original issuance of the stock are removed from the accounts (debit Common Stock for $10 per share and debit Paid-in Capital in Excess of Par for $2 per share). The excess of the retirement price ($16 per share) over the original issuance price ($12 per share) is charged to additional paid-in capital arising from previous reissuances or retirements of treasury stock of the same class before reducing Retained Earnings. Because Paid-in Capital from Treasury Stock ($1,000) is insufficient to absorb the $4,000 excess in this situation, the remainder ($3,000) is charged to Retained Earnings.

## ILLUSTRATION 15-3
## DETERMINING HOW TO RECORD A DISTRIBUTION OF STOCK (L.O. 7, 8)

When a corporation distributes additional shares of its own stock to its existing stockholders for no consideration, the accountant must record the distribution as one of the following, whichever is appropriate: (1) a small stock dividend, (2) a large stock dividend, or (3) a stock split. The following flowchart will provide guidance in determining the proper treatment.

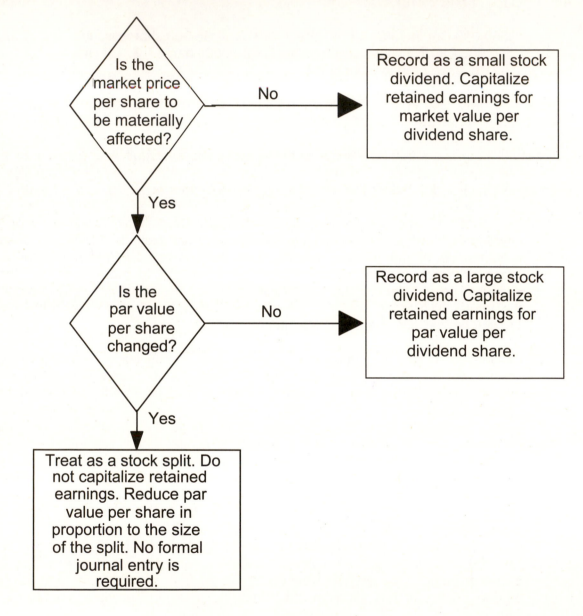

# ILLUSTRATION 15-4
# JOURNAL ENTRIES FOR RECORDING DIVIDENDS AND SPLITS (L.O. 7, 8)

### Cash Dividend

| | | | |
|---|---|---|---|
| **Data** | The board of directors declares a cash dividend of $100,000. | | |
| **Date of Declaration** | Retained Earnings (or Cash Dividends Declared)....... <br>     Dividends Payable............................................. | 100,000 | 100,000 |
| **Date of Payment** | Dividends Payable...................................................... <br>     Cash ................................................................. | 100,000 | 100,000 |

> **TIP:** There are three dates associated with the declaration of any dividend: (1) the declaration date, (2) the date of record, and (3) the date of payment (or distribution). A journal entry is required at the date of declaration and at the date of payment. There is no journal entry at the date of record.

> **TIP:** The declaration of a cash dividend reduces working capital; the payment of a previously declared (and unrecorded) cash dividend has no effect on working capital. Unless otherwise indicated, Dividends Payable will require a cash payment to settle the obligation.

### Property Dividend

| | | | |
|---|---|---|---|
| **Data** | Dave Jones Corporation declares a property dividend on March 1 to be distributed to stockholders on April 15. The property is an investment in shares of Bonnie Corporation and has a carrying value of $11,000. The market value of the Bonnie shares is $14,000 on March 1 and $14,900 on April 15. | | |
| **Date of Declaration** | Investments in Securities............................................ <br>     Gain on Appreciation of Securities ..................... | 3,000 | 3,000 |
| | Retained Earnings (or Property <br>    Dividends Declared)............................................... <br>     Property Dividends Payable ....................................... | 14,000 | 14,000 |
| **Date of Payment** | Property Dividends Payable ....................................... <br>     Investments in Securities................................... | 14,000 | 14,000 |

> **TIP:** Any change in the fair value of the property between the date of declaration and the date of payment of the dividend is ignored.

> **TIP:** A property dividend (dividend payable in assets of the corporation other than cash) is an example of a nonreciprocal transfer of nonmonetary assets. A nonreciprocal transfer is a transaction in which value is going only in one direction (one party gives but does not receive value; the other party receives but does not give value). This differs from an exchange transaction in which each of two parties both gives and receives value. Generally accepted accounting principles requires that a nonreciprocal transfer of nonmonetary assets be recorded at the fair value of the assets transferred. Thus, any difference between the transferred asset's fair value and its carrying amount is to be recognized as a gain or a loss.

## ILLUSTRATION 15-4 (Continued)

### Liquidating Dividend

**Data**          Harker Corporation declares a liquidating dividend of $4,000.

| | | | |
|---|---|---|---|
| **Date of** | Additional Paid-in Capital*............................................ | 4,000 | |
| **Declaration** | Dividends Payable.............................................. | | 4,000 |

*One of a number of additional paid-in capital accounts may be used, depend-
ing on the relevant state law, such as Paid-in Capital in Excess of Par or
Paid-in Capital from Treasury Stock.

| | | | |
|---|---|---|---|
| **Date of** | Dividends Payable................................................... | 4,000 | |
| **Payment** | Cash ................................................................ | | 4,000 |

> **TIP:** A **liquidating dividend** is a distribution to stockholders from invested capital. Thus, a liquidating dividend results in a reduction of paid-in capital (usually additional paid-in capital) and does not affect retained earnings. A stockholder's investment in the corporation is reduced, but maybe not eliminated, by this type of dividend. If a dividend is only **partially liquidating**, both paid-in capital and retained earnings are reduced.

### Small Stock Dividend

**Data**          D & E Henry Corporation has 100,000 shares of $10 par common stock outstanding on March 1, 2010. On March 2, the board of directors declares a 10% stock dividend distributable on April 4 to stockholders of record on March 16. The market price per share of common is $24 on March 2, $23 on March 16, and $25 on April 4.

| | | | |
|---|---|---|---|
| **Date of** | Retained Earnings (or Stock Dividend Declared)........ | 240,000 | |
| **Declaration** | Common Stock Dividend Distributable............... | | 100,000 |
| | Paid-in Capital in Excess of Par ................................. | | 140,000 |

        (10% x 100,000 = 10,000 shares)
        (10,000 shares x $24 = $240,000)
        (10,000 shares x $10 par = $100,000)
        ($240,000 - $100,000 = $140,000)

| | | | |
|---|---|---|---|
| **Date of** | Common Stock Dividend Distributable........................ | 100,000 | |
| **Distribution** | Common Stock .................................................. | | 100,000 |

> **TIP:** If a balance sheet is prepared between the date of declaration and the date of distribution, the Common Stock Distributable account is classified in the Paid-in Capital section of stockholders' equity.

> **TIP:** Although a stock dividend results in a reduction in retained earnings, it also causes an increase in paid-in capital by the same amount. There is **no change in total stockholders' equity** when a stock dividend is declared or distributed.

## ILLUSTRATION 15-4 (Continued)

---

**TIP:** The term **capitalization of retained earnings** refers to the process of transferring an amount from retained earnings to paid-in capital. Stock dividends result in the capitalization of retained earnings. Thus, stock dividends are declared as a means of informing stockholders that assets arising from past income will be retained in the business rather than distributed as dividends to the stockholders.

**TIP:** The amount of retained earnings to be capitalized for a stock dividend depends on whether or not the issuance of the dividend shares is expected to have a material effect on the market price per share of stock. If a material effect is **not** expected, the market price at the date of declaration is used; if a material effect is expected, the par value is used. Generally, when the number of shares in the dividend are equal to 20% or less of the number of shares currently outstanding, the dividend is called a **small or ordinary stock dividend**, and no material effect on market price per share is expected. When the number of shares in the dividend are equal to 25% or more of the number of shares currently outstanding, the dividend is called a **large stock dividend** or a **stock split-up effected in the form of a dividend**, and a material effect will likely occur.

**TIP:** The account title, Stock Dividend Payable, is a poor title for Stock Dividend Distributable. The word "payable" implies it is a liability; however, it is not a liability because there is no associated debt that must later be paid by the use of cash or other assets or services. Stock Dividend Distributable is a capital stock account and, there fore, is to be reported as an element of paid-in capital. This account only has a balance for the short period of time between the date of declaration and the date of distribution of the dividend.

---

### Large Stock Dividend

**Data**   JJH Corporation has 100,000 shares of $10 par common stock outstanding on March 1, 2010. On March 2, the board of directors declares a 40% stock split-up effected in the form of a dividend. The par value per share is unchanged. The dividend shares are to be distributed on April 3 to stockholders of record on March 15. The market price per share of common stock is $24 on March 2, $15 on March 15, and $16 on April 3.

**Date of Declaration**

| | | |
|---|---|---|
| Retained Earnings (or Stock Dividend Declared)........ | 400,000 | |
|    Common Stock Dividend Distributable .............. | | 400,000 |
|   (40% x 100,000 = 40,000 shares) | | |
|   (40,000 x $10 par = $400,000) | | |

**Date of Record**   No entry.

**Date of Distribution**

| | | |
|---|---|---|
| Common Stock Dividend Distributable........................ | 400,000 | |
|    Common Stock ................................................. | | 400,000 |

## ILLUSTRATION 15-4 (Continued)

### Stock Split

**Data**  Howell Cove Corporation has 100,000 shares of $10.00 par common stock outstanding on March 1, 2010. On March 2, the board of directors declares a 4-for-1 stock split. The par value per share is to be reduced to $2.50. The split is to be effective April 2 for shareholders of record on March 13.

**Date of Declaration**  No entry.

**Date of Record**  No entry.

**Date of Distribution**  No entry. Par value per share is reduced from $10.00 to $2.50. The number of shares outstanding is increased proportionally from 100,000 to 400,000. The balance of Common Stock remains at $1,000,000 (400,000 x $2.50).

**TIP:**  A stock split does not involve any transfer of retained earnings to paid-in capital; rather, the par value per share is changed in proportion to the multiple of issued shares.

## Instructions

For each transaction listed across the top of the following matrix, indicate the effect on each of the items listed down the left side of the matrix. Use "INC" to indicate an increase, "DEC" to indicate a decrease, and "NE" for no effect.

## TRANSACTION

| ITEM | Declaration of a cash dividend | Payment of a previously recorded cash dividend | Declaration & payment of a property dividend | Declaration & payment of a liquidating dividend | Declaration & distribution of a small stock dividend | Declaration & distribution of a large stock dividend | Stock Split |
|---|---|---|---|---|---|---|---|
| Working capital | | | | | | | |
| Assets | | | | | | | |
| Total capital stock | | | | | | | |
| Total additional paid-in capital | | | | | | | |
| Retained earnings | | | | | | | |
| Total stock-holders' equity | | | | | | | |
| Par value per share | | | | | | | |
| Total number of shares outstanding | | | | | | | |

# Solution to Exercise 15-5

## TRANSACTION

| ITEM | Declaration of a cash dividend | Payment of a previously recorded cash dividend | Declaration & payment of a property dividend | Declaration & payment of a liquidating dividend | Declaration & distribution of a small stock dividend | Declaration & distribution of a large stock dividend | Stock Split |
|---|---|---|---|---|---|---|---|
| Working capital | DEC | NE | DEC | DEC | NE | NE | NE |
| Assets | NE | DEC | DEC | DEC | NE | NE | NE |
| Total capital stock | NE | NE | NE | NE | INC | INC | NE |
| Total additional paid-in capital | NE | NE | NE | DEC | INC | NE | NE |
| Retained earnings | DEC | NE | DEC | NE | DEC | DEC | NE |
| Total stockholders' equity | DEC | NE | DEC | DEC | NE | NE | NE |
| Par value per share | NE | NE | NE | NE | NE | NE | DEC |
| Total number of shares outstanding | NE | NE | NE | NE | INC | INC | INC |

**Approach:** Write down the journal entry(ies) associated with each situation. (Refer **to Illustration 15-4** to check your entries.) Take the account in each entry and examine their individual effects on each of the items listed.

# EXERCISE 15-6

**Purpose:** (L.O. 9) This exercise will illustrate the preparation of a statement of stockholders' equity and the related stockholders' equity section of the balance sheet.

On January 1, 2010, Huseman Corporation had the following stockholders' equity balances:

| | |
|---|---|
| Common Stock ($1 stated value, 800,000 shares authorized) | $ 300,000 |
| Paid-in Capital in Excess of Stated Value | 710,000 |
| Retained Earnings | 390,000 |
| Accumulated Other Comprehensive Income | 30,000 |
| Treasury Stock (3,000 shares)(cost method) | 6,000 |

During 2010, the following occurred:
- Issued 50,000 shares of common stock at $3 per share.
- Declared a $70,000 cash dividend.
- Purchased 1,000 shares of treasury stock at $2 per share.
- Declared and distributed a 5% stock dividend when the market value was $3 per share.
- Earned net income for the year of $200,000
- Reported an unrealized holding loss on available-for-sale securities, net of tax, $8,000.

## Instructions
(a)   Prepare a statement of stockholders' equity for the year ending December 31, 2010.
(b)   Prepare the stockholders' equity section of the balance sheet as of December 31, 2010.

## Solution to Exercise 15-6
(a)

### Huseman Corporation
### STATEMENT OF STOCKHOLDERS' EQUITY
### For the Year Ended December 31, 2010

| | Total | Comprehensive Income | Retained Earnings | Accumulated Other Comprehensive Income | Common Stock ($1 Stated Value) | Paid-in Capital in Excess of Stated Value | Treasury Stock |
|---|---|---|---|---|---|---|---|
| Balance January 1 | $1,424,000 | | $390,000 | $30,000 | $300,000 | $710,000 | $(6,000) |
| Issued 50,000 shares of common stock at $3 | 150,000 | | | | 50,000 | 100,000 | |
| Declared a $70,000 cash dividend | (70,000) | | (70,000) | | | | |
| Purchased 1,000 shares for treasury at $2 | (2,000) | | | | | | (2,000) |
| Declared & distributed a 5% stock dividend | | | (51,900) | | 17,300 | 34,600 | |
| Net income for year | 200,000 | $200,000 | 200,000 | | | | |
| Other Comprehensive Income | (8,000) | (8,000) | | (8,000) | | | |
| Balance, December 31 | $1,694,000 | $192,000 | $468,100 | $22,000 | $367,300 | $844,600 | $(8,000) |

**TIP:**   Notice how the columns on this statement foot (add down) and crossfoot (add across). Also notice that in the cross footing process, to avoid double counting,

> we ignore the amounts in the Comprehensive Income column because those amounts are already included in the Accumulated Other Comprehensive Income column or in the Retained Earnings column.

**Explanation:** A corporation is to disclose **all** changes that took place in **all** stockholder equity items during the reporting period. A convenient and effective way of meeting that requirement is to present a **statement of stockholders' equity** (sometimes called a stockholders' equity statement). When this statement is presented, it replaces the statement of retained earnings because it contains all the information that a statement of retained earnings would contain plus data regarding changes in other components of stockholders' equity.

The computations for the 5% stock dividend are as follows:
350,000 shares issued - 4,000 treasury shares = 346,000 shares outstanding.
346,000 shares outstanding x 5% = 17,300 dividend shares.
17,300 shares x $3 market value = $51,900 decrease in Retained Earnings.
17,300 shares x $1 stated value = $17,300 increase in Common Stock.
17,300 shares x ($3 - $1) = $34,600 increase in additional paid-in capital.

> **TIP:** Refer to **Illustration 4-4** of this *Problem Solving Survival Guide* for a more comprehensive discussion of the reporting of other comprehensive income for a period of time and the resulting accumulated other comprehensive income amount. When a company has reported components of other comprehensive income, an item called Accumulated Other Comprehensive Income (or Loss) is to be reported as a separate component of stockholders' equity. It may be a positive or negative element of stockholders' equity.

(b)

**Huseman Corporation**
**BALANCE SHEET (Partial)**
**As of December 31, 2010**

| | |
|---|---:|
| Stockholders' Equity | |
| Paid-in capital | |
| Common stock ($1 stated value, 800,000 shares authorized, 367,300 shares issued, 363,300 shares outstanding | $ 367,300 |
| Paid-in capital in excess of stated value | 844,600 |
| Total paid-in capital | 1,211,900 |
| Retained earnings | 468,100 |
| Total paid-in capital and retained earnings | 1,680,000 |
| Accumulated other comprehensive income | 22,000 |
| Treasury stock, 4,000 shares, at cost | (8,000) |
| Total stockholders' equity | $1,694,000 |

# ILLUSTRATION 15-5
# RATIOS FOR ANALYSIS OF STOCKHOLDERS' EQUITY (L.O. 9)

The following three ratios use stockholders' equity amounts to evaluate a company's profitability and long-term solvency.

1.  **Rate of return on common stock equity.** This widely used ratio measures profitability from the common stockholders' viewpoint. This ratio shows how many dollars of net income were earned for each dollar invested by the owners. The ratio is computed as follows:

$$\text{Rate of return on common stock equity} = \frac{\text{Net income - preferred dividends}}{\text{Average common stockholders' equity}^a}$$

[a]The par value of preferred stock is deducted from total stockholders' equity to arrive at the amount of common stock equity used in this ratio.

> **TIP:** When the rate of return on common stock equity is greater than the rate of return on total assets, the company is said to be "trading on the equity at a gain" or "favorably trading on the equity." **"Trading on the equity"** describes the practice of using borrowed money at fixed interest rates or issuing preferred stock with constant dividend rates in hopes of using the assets obtained (by use of the money from the borrowing or issuance of preferred stock) in such a way that the rate of return on the assets exceeds the rate of interest or dividends. If this can be done, the capital obtained from bondholders or preferred stockholders earns enough to pay interest or dividends and to leave a margin for the common stockholders. When this condition exists, trading on the equity is profitable. However, if the cost of debt exceeds the return on total assets, the return on common stockholders' equity will be less than the return on total assets; hence, the entity will be **unfavorably trading on the equity.**

2.  **Payout ratio.** The payout ratio is the relationship of cash dividends to net income; it is a measure of profitability. The ratio is computed for common stockholders as follows:

$$\text{Payout ratio} = \frac{\text{Cash dividends}}{\text{Net income less preferred dividends}}$$

> **TIP:** Some investors look for a stock that has a payout ratio sufficiently high to provide a good yield on the stock; other investors view the potential appreciation in the market value of the stock as more important than the prospect of high dividends.

> **TIP:** Another closely watched ratio is the **dividend yield** which is computed by dividing the cash dividend per share by the market price of the stock. This ratio affords investors of some idea of the rate of return that will be received in cash dividends from their investment.

3.   **Book value per share.** The book value or **equity value per share** of stock is a much-used basis for evaluating the net worth of a corporation. Book value per share of stock is the amount each share would receive **if** the company were liquidated on the basis of amounts reported on the balance sheet. The ratio loses much of its relevance if the valuations on the balance sheet do not approximate fair market value of the assets. Assuming no preferred stock is outstanding, the ratio is as follows:

$$\text{Book value per share} = \frac{\text{Common stockholders' equity}}{\text{Outstanding shares}}$$

**TIP:**   Refer to **Exercise 15-9** for an example of how to handle the computation of book value per share when both preferred stock and common stock are outstanding.

## EXERCISE 15-7

**Purpose:**   (L.O. 9) This exercise will give you an example of how to compute the return on common stock equity.

|  | Dec. 31 2009 | Dec. 31 2010 |
|---|---|---|
| Preferred stock, 8%, par $100, noncumulative | $250,000 | $250,000 |
| Common stock | 600,000 | 800,000 |
| Retained earnings | 150,000 | 370,000 |
| Dividends paid on preferred stock for the year | 20,000 | 20,000 |
| Net income for the year | 120,000 | 240,000 |

## Instructions

Compute Bradley's return on common stockholders' equity (rounded to the nearest percentage) for 2010.

## Solution to Exercise 15-7

$$\text{Return on common stockholders' equity} = \frac{\text{Net income} - \text{Preferred dividends}}{\text{Average common stockholders' equity}}$$

$$\frac{\$240,000 - \$20,000}{1/2\ (\$750,000^1 + \$1,170,000^2)} = \frac{\$220,000}{\$960,000} = \underline{23\%}$$

[1]Beginning total stockholders' equity ($250,000 + $600,000 + $150,000) - par value of preferred stock ($250,000) = $750,000 beginning common stockholders' equity.

[2]Ending total stockholders' equity ($250,000 + $800,000 + $370,000) - par value of preferred stock ($250,000) = $1,170,000 ending common stockholders' equity.

**Explanation:** A widely used ratio that measures profitability from the common stockholders' viewpoint is **return on common stockholders' equity.** This ratio shows how many dollars of net income were earned for each dollar invested by the owners. It is computed by dividing net income applicable to common stockholders (net income - preferred dividends) by average common stockholders' equity.

## ILLUSTRATION 15-6
## STEPS IN ALLOCATING DIVIDENDS TO
## PREFERRED AND COMMON STOCKHOLDERS (L.O. 10)

### Step 1: Assign arrearage to preferred, if any.
If there are any dividends in arrears, the amount of arrearage is first allocated to the preferred stockholders. The remaining amount of dividends to be allocated is computed. (If the amount declared is not enough to cover the arrearage, all dividends declared go to preferred holders, the remaining arrearage is computed for disclosure, and the rest of the steps are not performed.)

### Step 2: Assign current period preference to preferred.
The amount of the preferred stockholders' current year preference is computed and that amount is allocated to the preferred stockholders. The remaining amount of dividends to be allocated is computed. (If the dividends declared are not enough to cover the preferred's current year preference, all of the dividends declared are allocated to the preferred stock-holders, the remaining arrearage is computed for disclosure, and the rest of the steps are not performed.)

### Step 3: Assign common an equal percentage dividend.
An amount of dividends to common stockholders to "match" the "percentage-on-par" dividend given to preferred (for current year preference only) is computed. If the remaining amount of dividends is sufficient to cover this "matching process," the amount of "matching" is allocated to common and the remaining amount of dividends is the amount in which both preferred and common will "participate." (If the amount declared is not enough to "match" the preferred, whatever is available after the preferred get their portion as calculated in steps "1" and "2" is allocated to common.)

### Step 4: Assign the participation amount to preferred and common.
If the preferred stock is nonparticipating, any remaining dividends are assigned to the common stockholders. If the preferred stock is participating, the amount of dividends available for "participation" is allocated between preferred and common based on an "equal percentage on par basis." That percentage is determined by dividing the amount of dividends available for participation by the sum of the aggregate par value of the preferred and the aggregate par value of the common.

### Step 5: Total the amounts allocated and compute per share amounts.
The amounts from the previous steps are added for each class. The total amount allocated to preferred stockholders and to common stockholders is often expressed on a per share basis. To calculate the amount per share, divide the total dividends allocated to the class by the number of outstanding shares in that class.

## *EXERCISE 15-8

**Purpose:**    (L.O. 10) This exercise will illustrate the allocation of dividends when a corporation has both preferred stock and common stock outstanding.

Charlie B. Daly Corporation has the following stock outstanding without any changes for years 2009, 2010, and 2011.

| | |
|---|---|
| 50,000 shares of $10 par, 4% preferred | $   500,000 |
| 200,000 shares of $5 par common | 1,000,000 |
| | $ 1,500,000 |

Dividends are declared as follows:

| | |
|---|---|
| 2009 | $15,000 |
| 2010 | $50,000 |
| 2011 | $72,000 |

## Instructions

Compute the amount of dividends (total and per share) to be allocated to the preferred stockholders and the common stockholders for each of the three years under each of the **independent** assumptions below:
(a)    The preferred stock is noncumulative and nonparticipating.
(b)    The preferred stock is cumulative and nonparticipating.
(c)    The preferred stock is cumulative and participating.

## Solution to Exercise 15-8

**Approach:** Compute the preferred's current year preference (50,000 shares x $10 par x 4% = $20,000) and the amount to "match" the common holders (200,000 shares x $5 par x 4% = $40,000). Then use the steps listed in **Illustration 15-6** to solve.

(a)

|  |  | Preferred | Common | Total |
|---|---|---|---|---|
| **2009:** | Total to distribute |  |  | $15,000 |
|  | Step 1: |  |  |  |
|  | Step 2: Less than preference | $15,000 |  | $15,000 |
|  | Step 3: |  |  |  |
|  | Step 4: |  |  |  |
|  | Step 5: | $15,000 | $ -0- | $15,000 |
|  | ÷ by | 50,000 | 200,000 |  |
|  | = | $ .30 | $ .00 |  |
| **2010:** | Total to distribute |  |  | $50,000 |
|  | Step 1: |  |  |  |
|  | Step 2: 4% x $500,000 | $20,000 |  | $20,000 |
|  | Step 3: Remainder |  | $30,000 | 30,000 |
|  | Step 4: |  |  |  |
|  | Step 5: | $20,000 | $30,000 | $50,000 |
|  | ÷ by | 50,000 | 200,000 |  |
|  | = | $ .40 | $ .15 |  |
| **2011:** | Total to distribute |  |  | $72,000 |
|  | Step 1: |  |  |  |
|  | Step 2: 4% x $500,000 | $20,000 |  | $20,000 |
|  | Step 3: 4% x $1,000,000 |  | $40,000 | 40,000 |
|  | Step 4: Remainder |  | 12,000 | 12,000 |
|  | Step 5: | $20,000 | $52,000 | $72,000 |
|  | ÷ by | 50,000 | 200,000 |  |
|  | = | $ .40 | $ .26 |  |

(b)

|  |  | Preferred | Common | Total |
|---|---|---|---|---|
| **2009:** | Total to distribute |  |  | $15,000 |
|  | Step 1: |  |  |  |
|  | Step 2: Less than preference | $15,000 |  | $15,000 |
|  | Step 3: |  |  |  |
|  | Step 4: |  |  |  |
|  | Step 5: | $15,000 | $ -0- | $15,000 |
|  | ÷ by | 50,000 | 200,000 |  |
|  | = | $ .30 | $ .00 |  |
| **2010:** | Total to distribute |  |  | $50,000 |
|  | Step 1: $20,000 - $15,000 | $ 5,000 |  | $ 5,000 |
|  | Step 2: 4% x $500,000 | 20,000 |  | 20,000 |
|  | Step 3: Remainder |  | $25,000 | 25,000 |
|  | Step 4: |  |  |  |
|  | Step 5: | $25,000 | $25,000 | $50,000 |
|  | ÷ by | 50,000 | 200,000 |  |
|  | = | $ .50 | $ .125 |  |

|  |  | Prefered | Common | Total |
|---|---|---|---|---|
| **2011** | Total to distribute | | | $72,000 |
| | Step 1: | | | |
| | Step 2: 4% x $500,000 | $20,000 | | $20,000 |
| | Step 3: 4% x $1,000,000 | | $40,000 | 40,000 |
| | Step 4: Remainder | | 12,000 | 12,000 |
| | Step 5: | $20,000 | $52,000 | $72,000 |
| | ÷ by | 50,000 | 200,000 | |
| | = | $ 40 | $ 26 | |

(c)

|  |  | Preferred | Common | Total |
|---|---|---|---|---|
| **2009:** | Total to distribute | | | $15,000 |
| | Step 1: | | | |
| | Step 2: Less than preference | $15,000 | | $15,000 |
| | Step 3: | | | |
| | Step 4: | | | |
| | Step 5: | $15,000 | $ -0- | $15,000 |
| | ÷ by | 50,000 | 200,000 | |
| | = | $ .30 | $ .00 | |
| **2010:** | Total to distribute | | | $50,000 |
| | Step 1: $20,000 - $15,000 | $ 5,000 | | $ 5,000 |
| | Step 2: 4% x $500,000 | 20,000 | | 20,000 |
| | Step 3: Remainder | | $25,000 | 25,000 |
| | Step 4: | | | |
| | Step 5: | $25,000 | $25,000 | $50,000 |
| | ÷ by | 50,000 | 200,000 | |
| | = | $ .50 | $ .125 | |

> **TIP:** Notice that in performing step 3, the remaining dividends ($25,000) are not sufficient in amount to allocate a "matching" dividend to the common stockholders (4% x $1,000,000 > $25,000).

|  |  | Preferred | Common | Total |
|---|---|---|---|---|
| **2011:** | Total to distribute | | | $72,000 |
| | Step 1: | | | |
| | | $20,000 | | $20,000 |
| | Step 2: 4% x $500,000 | | $40,000 | 40,000 |
| | Step 3: 4% x $1,000,000 | 4,000 | 8,000 | 12,000 |
| | Step 4: To participate at .8%* | $24,000 | $48,000 | $72,000 |
| | Step 5: | | | |
| | ÷ by | 50,000 | 200,000 | |
| | = | $ .48 | $ .24 | |

*Amount to participate $\dfrac{\$12,000}{\$1,500,000}$ = .008 or .8%

Total par

.008 x $500,000 = $4,000 allocated to preferred
.008 x $1,000,000 = $8,0000 allocated to common

---

| | |
|---|---|
| **TIP:** | Notice that in 2011 under assumption (c) that the common stockholders receive a total dividend that is equal—percentage wise on par—to the dividend received by the preferred stockholders ($.48 ÷ $10 = 4.8%; $.24 ÷ $5 = 4.8%). This happens when the three following conditions are met: |

(1)     The preferred stock is fully participating.
(2)     There are enough dividends declared to reach the point where both classes
        "participate."
(3)     There are no dividends in arrears.

## *EXERCISE 15-9

**Purpose:**     (L.O. 10)  This exercise will illustrate the computation of book value per share when more than one class of stock is outstanding.

The stockholders' equity section of a recent balance sheet is presented below:

**AL GORE CORPORATION**
**Partial Balance Sheet**
**December 31, 2010**

Stockholders' equity
    Paid-in capital
        Capital stock
            6% preferred stock, $100 par value, cumulative call price
                $105, 50,000 shares authorized, 10,000 shares

| | | |
|---|---|---:|
| issued and outstanding | | $1,000,000 |
| Common stock, $20 par, 200,000 shares authorized | | |
| 41,500 shares issued, 40,000 shares outstanding | | 830,000 |
| Total capital stock | | 1,830,000 |
| Additional paid-in capital | | |
| In excess of par value—preferred stock | $  120,000 | |
| In excess of par value—common stock | 1,165,000 | |
| From treasury stock—common | 2,500 | |
| Total additional paid-in capital | | 1,287,500 |
| Total paid-in capital | | 3,117,500 |
| Retained earnings | | 2,200,000 |
| Total paid-in capital and retained earnings | | 5,317,500 |
| Less: Treasury stock—common (1,500 shares) | | 69,000 |
| Total stockholders' equity | | $5,248,500 |

**Instructions**
Assuming the preferred stockholders have annually received dividends equal to their current year preference in all prior years except 2009 and 2010:
(a)  Determine the book value per share of preferred stock.
(b)  Determine the book value per share of common stock.

## Solution to Exercise 15-9

(a) The book value per share of preferred stock is $117 which is computed as follows:

| | |
|---|---|
| Call price per preferred share | $105 |
| Dividends in arrears per preferred share | |
| ($100 par x 6% preference per year x 2 years) | 12 |
| Book value per preferred share | $117 |

(b)

| | | |
|---|---|---|
| Total stockholders' equity | | $5,248,500 |
| Less: Total preferred stock equity: | | |
| Call price ($105 x 10,000 shares) | $1,050,000 | |
| Dividends in arrears ($100 X 6% X 2 X 10,000 shares) | 120,000 | 1,170,000 |
| Common stock equity | | $4,078,500 |
| | | |
| Shares of common stock outstanding | | 40,000 |
| | | |
| Book value per share of common stock ($4,078,500 ÷ 40,000) | | $101.9625 |

> **TIP:** Notice that **none** of the paid-in capital in excess of par value arising from the issuance of preferred stock at a price above par ($120,000) is directly allocated to preferred stock in the book value per share of preferred stock computation.
>
> **TIP:** If only one class of stock is outstanding, the book value of common is computed simply by dividing total stockholders' equity by the total number of shares outstanding.

**Approach:** To compute the book value per share of common stock when there is preferred stock also outstanding, use the following steps:

**Step 1:** **Compute the total book value of preferred stock** by multiplying the book value per share of preferred stock by the number of preferred shares outstanding. The book value per share of preferred is one of the following (listed) in order of preference):
    a. Liquidation value of preferred plus dividends in arrears.
    b. Call or redemption price of preferred plus dividends in arrears.
    c. Par value of preferred plus dividends in arrears.

**Step 2:** **Compute the total book value of common stock** by deducting the total book value of preferred stock from total stockholders' equity.

**Step 3:** **Compute the book value per share of common stock** by dividing the total book value of common stock by the number of common stock shares outstanding.

## ANALYSIS OF MULTIPLE-CHOICE TYPE QUESTIONS

**QUESTION**

1.   (L.O. 5) Which of the following rights does a preferred stockholder normally possess?
    a.    right to vote
    b.    right to receive a dividend before a common shareholder
    c.    preemptive right
    d.    right to participate in management

**Explanation:** A preferred stockholder usually has a preference over common stockholders as to dividends and as to distribution of assets upon liquidation. A preferred stockholder normally has to forego other rights because of the preference described above. The rights the preferred stockholder normally forgoes are the right to participate in management (right to vote on operational and financial decisions) and the preemptive right. A common stockholder normally has the right to vote and the preemptive right (right to maintain the same percentage ownership when additional shares of common stock are issued). (Solution = b.)

**QUESTION**

2.   (L.O. 3) The Tom Powell Corporation has 10,000 shares of $10 par common stock authorized. The following transactions took place during 2010, the first year of the corporation's existence:
    •    Sold 1,000 shares of common stock for $18 per share.
    •    Issued 1,000 shares of common stock in exchange for a patent valued at $20,000.
    •    Reported net income of $7,000.
    At the end of Tom Powell's first year, total paid-in capital amounted to:
    a.    $8,000.
    b.    $18,000.
    c.    $20,000.
    d.    $28,000.
    e.    none of the above.

**Approach and Explanation:** (1) Write down the components of paid-in capital: (a) balances of capital stock accounts, and (b) balances of additional paid-in capital accounts. (2) Reconstruct the journal entries for the transactions listed and post those entries to T-accounts. (3) Compute the balances of the relevant accounts. (4) Sum the relevant account balances.

Cash .................................................................................................. 18,000
    Common Stock.......................................................................................    10,000
    Paid-in Capital in Excess of Par ...................................................    8,000

Patent        20,000
    Common Stock.......................................................................................    10,000
    Paid-in Capital in Excess of Par ...................................................    10,000

Income Summary ...............................................................................    7,000
    Retained Earnings ...............................................................................    7,000

| Common Stock | | | Paid-in Capital in Excess of Par | | |
|---|---|---|---|---|---|
| | | 10,000 | | | 8,000 |
| | | 10,000 | | | 10,000 |
| | Bal. | 20,000 | | Bal. | 18,000 |

Common stock                              $ 20,000
Additional paid-in capital                      18,000
Total paid-in capital                        $ 38,000        (Solution = e.)

**QUESTION**

3.  (L.O. 3) Which of the following represents the total number of shares that a corporation may issue under the terms of its charter?

a.  authorized shares
b.  issued shares
c.  unissued shares
d.  outstanding shares
e.  treasury shares

**Approach and Explanation:** Explain the meaning of each of the terms used as answer selections. Choose the one that matches the stem of the question. Issued shares (ones the corporation has issued to date) **plus** unissued shares (shares that have not been issued yet but may be issued in the future in accordance with the terms of the charter) **equals** total authorized (approved) shares. Outstanding shares are the issued shares which are now in the hands of the public. Treasury shares are issued shares which are not outstanding at the present time. (Solution = a.)

**QUESTION**

4.  (L.O. 3) If common stock with a par value is issued by a closely-held corporation for noncash assets, the amount to be recorded as paid-in capital related to this transaction is determined by the:

a.  fair market value of the noncash assets received.
b.  par value of the stock issued.
c.  legal value of the stock issued.
d.  book value of the noncash assets on the seller's books.

**Approach and Explanation:** Recall that any time assets are acquired, the historical cost principle is applied; that is, the assets are to be recorded at historical cost. Cost is measured by the fair market value (cash equivalent value) of the consideration given or the fair market value of the consideration received, whichever is the more objectively determinable. Assuming equipment with a fair value of $70,000 is received in exchange for stock of a closely-held corporation with a par value of $20,000, the journal entry to record the transaction would be as follows:

Equipment ..................................................................................70,000
    Common Stock.........................................................................          20,000
    Paid-in Capital in Excess of Par Value ...................................          50,000

Notice that two paid-in capital accounts (one capital stock account and one additional paid-in capital account) are affected. The increase in total paid-in capital is $70,000. (Solution = a.)

**QUESTION**

5.  (L.O. 4) Treasury shares are:

a.  shares held as an investment by the treasurer of the corporation.
b.  shares held as an investment of the corporation.
c.  issued and outstanding shares.
d.  unissued shares.
e.  issued but not outstanding shares.

**Approach and Explanation:** Write down the definition of treasury stock. Treasury stock is a corporation's own stock that has been issued, fully paid for, and reacquired by the corporation but **not** retired (cancelled). Treasury shares are shares that have been issued previously (so are not unissued) but are not outstanding now, as they have been subsequently reacquired by the company. Treasury shares refer to a company's own shares so they cannot be an investment. A company cannot own itself. The acquisition of treasury stock represents a contraction of capital (owners' equity) rather than the acquisition of an asset. (Solution = e.)

| **TIP:** | If and when treasury shares are formally retired, they revert back to an unissued status. |
|---|---|

**QUESTION**

6.    (L.O. 4) Assume the cost method is used to account for treasury stock. A "gain" on the sale of treasury stock should be classified as an:

a.    extraordinary item on the income statement.
b.    element of other income on the income statement.
c.    increase in additional paid-in capital.
d.    increase in retained earnings.

**Explanation:** When the cost method is used, a "gain" on the sale of treasury stock refers to the disposition of treasury stock at a price in excess of cost. This excess is recorded as a credit to Paid-in Capital from Treasury Stock. Selections "a" and "b" are incorrect because treasury stock transactions are capital transactions and capital transactions do not give rise to components of income determination. Answer selection "d" is incorrect because, regardless of the method used, treasury stock transactions can sometimes reduce retained earnings but may **never** increase retained earnings. (Solution = c.)

**QUESTION**

7.    (L.O. 3, 4) Wheeler Corporation started business in 2000 by issuing 100,000 shares of $10 par common stock for $24 each. In 2006, 10,000 of these shares were purchased for $35 per share by Wheeler Corporation and held as treasury stock. (The cost method is used to account for treasury stock.) On April 15, 2010, these 10,000 shares were exchanged for a piece of land adjacent to some property currently owned by Wheeler. The property had an assessed value of $270,000 on the rolls of the county's property tax assessor. Wheeler's stock is actively traded and had a market price of $40 on April 15, 2010. The amount of paid-in capital from treasury stock transactions resulting from the above events would be:

a.    $50,000.
b.    $130,000.
c.    $160,000.
d.    $300,000.

**Approach and Explanation:** Prepare and analyze journal entries to record the purchase and "sale" of the treasury shares.

| | | |
|---|---|---|
| Treasury Stock ............................................................................ | 350,000 | |
| Cash .................................................................................... | | 350,000 |
| (Purchase of 10,000 shares for treasury at $35 each) | | |
| | | |
| Land ............................................................................................... | 400,000 | |
| Treasury Stock.............................................................. | | 350,000 |
| Paid-in Capital from Treasury Stock ...................................... | | 50,000 |

The issuance (and reissuance) of stock is always recorded at the fair value of the consideration given (the stock) or the fair value of the consideration received (the land), whichever is the more objectively determinable. The stock is actively traded in this case so the $40 current market price of a share of stock (the consideration given) is more objectively determinable than the fair value of the land received in exchange. Using the $400,000 ($40 x 10,000 shares) as the "selling price" of the treasury stock, that exceeds the cost of the treasury shares ($35 x 10,000 shares = $350,000) by $50,000. Hence, the paid-in capital from treasury stock transactions is $50,000 from the data given. (Solution = a.)

**QUESTION**

8.    (L.O. 4) Refer to **Question 7** above. What effect did the exchange of treasury stock for land on April 15, 2010 have on total stockholders' equity?

a.    Increase of $50,000.
b.    Increase of $60,000.
c.    Increase of $300,000.
d.    Increase of $400,000.

**Approach and Explanation:** Analyze the journal entry to record the exchange of treasury stock for land. That entry is shown in the **Explanation for Question 7** above. The credit to Treasury Stock for $350,000 increases stockholders' equity by $350,000 because of the reduction of the contra equity account Treasury Stock. The credit to Paid-in Capital from Treasury Stock increases additional paid-in capital by $50,000 and thus increases total paid-in capital. Thus, assets increase by $400,000 and stockholders' equity increases by $400,000 which is the selling price of the treasury shares. The purchase of treasury stock typically decreases assets and stockholders' equity by the cost of the treasury shares, and the sale of treasury stock typically increases assets and shareholders' equity by the selling price of the treasury shares. (Solution = e.)

**QUESTION**
9. (L.O. 5) Preferred stock which can be returned to the corporation and exchanged for common stock at the option of the shareholder is referred to as:
a. cumulative preferred stock.
b. convertible preferred stock.
c. participating preferred stock.
d. callable preferred stock.

**Approach and Explanation:** Holders of **convertible preferred stock** may, at their option, exchange their preferred shares for common stock at a predetermined ratio. Holders of **cumulative preferred stock** are entitled to receive dividends in arrears before any dividends can be paid to common stockholders; dividends in arrears refers to a passed dividend. Thus, dividends not paid in any year on cumulative preferred must be made up in a later year before any profits can be distributed to common stockholders. Holders of **participating preferred stock** share ratably with common stockholders in any dividend distributions beyond the preferred stock's annual preference. With **callable preferred stock**, the issuing corporation can call or redeem at its option the outstanding preferred shares at specified future dates and at stipulated prices. (Solution = b.)

**QUESTION**
10. (L.O. 5) According to a proposed accounting standard, redeemable preferred stock should be:
a. included with common stock.
b. included with nonredeemable preferred stock.
c. excluded from the stockholders' equity heading.
d. included as a contra item in stockholders' equity.

**Approach and Explanation: Redeemable preferred stock** is preferred stock that has a mandatory redemption date or a redemption feature that is outside the control of the issuer. In these cases, the company has given to the holder a right to receive future cash flows of the company, and many believe this obligation should be reported as debt rather than equity. Under current accounting standards, most companies report redeemable preferred stock between debt and equity classifications. Under a proposed accounting standard, companies will be required by the FASB to report redeemable preferred stock as debt. (Solution = c.)

**QUESTION**
11. (L.O. 7) The date that determines who is to be considered a stockholder for the purpose of receiving a dividend is the:
a. declaration date.
b. record date.
c. payment date.
d. distribution date.

**Explanation:** The date the board of directors formally declares (authorizes) a dividend and announces it to stockholders is called the **declaration date.** The **record date** marks the time when ownership of the outstanding shares is determined for dividend purposes from the stockholders' records maintained by the corporation. On the **payment date,** the dividend checks are mailed to the stockholders. (Solution = b.)

## QUESTION

12.    (L.O. 7) The declaration and payment of cash dividends by a corporation will result in a(an):
a.     increase in Cash and an increase in Retained Earnings.
b.     increase in Cash and a decrease in Retained Earnings.
c.     decrease in Cash and an increase in Retained Earnings.
d.     decrease in Cash and a decrease in Retained Earnings.

**Approach and Explanation:** Prepare the journal entries required to record the declaration and payment of a cash dividend. Separately analyze each debit and credit to determine the effect on the balance of Cash and on the Retained Earnings account. Assuming cash dividends of $10,000 are declared, the entries and analysis are as follows:

**At the date of declaration:**                                                **Effect**
Retained Earnings                10,000                     Decrease in Retained Earnings
    Dividends Payable                        10,000         Increase in current liabilities

**At the date of payment:**                                                    **Effect**
Dividends Payable                10,000                     Decrease in current liabilities
    Cash                                          10,000         Decrease in Cash

The net effect of the declaration and payment of a cash dividend is to reduce retained earnings (and, thus, total stockholders' equity) and Cash (and, thus, total assets). (Solution = d.)

## QUESTION

13.    (L.O. 7) Barney's Corporation has an investment in 1,000 shares of Phil Jones Corporation common stock with a cost of $29,000. These shares are used in a property dividend to stockholders of Barney's. The property dividend is declared on March 23 and scheduled to be distributed on April 30 to stockholders of record on April 15. The market value per share of Phil Jones stock is $42 on March 23, $44 on April 15, and $45 on April 30. The net effect of this property dividend on retained earnings is a reduction of:
a.     $29,000.
b.     $42,000.
c.     $44,000.
d.     $45,000.

**Approach and Explanation:** Write down the journal entries involved in accounting for this dividend. Examine each account in the entries for its effect on retained earnings. Summarize the results. The entries and their effects on retained earnings (RE) would be as follows:

|  |  |  | **Effect on RE** |  |
|---|---|---|---|---|
| 3/23 | Investments in Securities..................................................... | 13,000 | -0- | |
| | Gain on Appreciation of Securities ................................... | 13,000 | ↑ | $13,000 |
| | [($42 x 1,000) - $29,000 = $13,000] | | | |
| | Retained Earnings............................................................ | 42,000 | ↓ | 42,000 |
| | Property Dividends Payable ............................................. | 42,000 | -0- | |
| 4/30 | Property Dividends Payable ............................................. | 42,000 | -0- | |
| | Investments in Securities.................................................. | 42,000 | -0- | |
| | Net effect on retained earnings = | | ↓ | $29,000 |

(Solution = a.)

**TIP:**    Although a property dividend gets recorded at the **fair value** of the asset to be distributed, retained earnings is decreased by the **carrying value** of the asset due to the recognition of the increase or decrease in the fair value of the asset (this increase or decrease goes through net income, which is closed into retained earnings).

**QUESTION**
14.   (L.O. 7) The net effect of the declaration and payment of a liquidating dividend is a decrease in:
a.       retained earnings and a decrease in total assets.
b.       total paid-in capital and a decrease in total assets.
c.       total paid-in capital and an increase in retained earnings.
d.       total stockholders' equity and an increase in liabilities.

**Explanation:** A dividend based on paid-in capital (rather than retained earnings) is termed a **liquidating dividend**, because the amount originally paid in by stockholders is being reduced or "liquidated." (Solution = b.)

**QUESTION**
15.   (L.O. 8) What effect does the declaration and distribution of a 30% stock split-up effected in the form of a dividend have on the following?

|     | Retained Earnings | Total Paid-in Capital | Total Stockholders' Equity |
| --- | --- | --- | --- |
| a.  | Decrease | Increase | No Effect |
| b.  | Decrease | No Effect | No Effect |
| c.  | Decrease | No Effect | Decrease |
| d.  | No Effect | No Effect | No Effect |

**Approach and Explanation:** Write down the journal entries for the declaration and distribution of a large stock dividend. Analyze the accounts in each entry separately to determine the impact on the three items requested.

The journal entry to record the declaration will reduce retained earnings and increase stock dividend distributable (a component of total capital stock and, therefore, a component of total paid-in capital) by the par value multiplied by the number of shares to be distributed in the dividend. That entry will **decrease retained earnings** and **increase total paid-in capital** by identical amounts, and thus have **no effect on total stockholders' equity**. The entry to record the distribution will reduce the dividend distributable balance (one capital stock account) and increase the common stock account (another capital stock account). Thus, the distribution entry will have **no effect** on any total within the major classifications of stockholders' equity. (Solution = a.)

**QUESTION**
16.   (L.O. 3, 8) A 300% stock dividend will have the same impact on the number of shares outstanding as a:
a.       2-for-1 stock split.
b.       3-for-1 stock split.
c.       4-for-1 stock split.
d.       5-for-1 stock split.

**Approach and Explanation:** Set up an example with numbers. For instance, assume we begin with 10,000 shares outstanding. A 300% stock dividend (or stock split-up effected in the form of a dividend) will mean 30,000 new shares will be distributed and there will then be 40,000 total shares outstanding. A 2-for-1 split will cause 10,000 shares to be replaced by 20,000. A 3-for-1 split will result in 30,000 total shares. A 4-for-1 split will cause the 10,000 shares to be replaced by 40,000 shares. The example proves that a 300% stock dividend (shares are increased **by** 300%) has the same effect on the number of shares outstanding as does a 4-for-1 split (each share is replaced with four shares). (Solution = c.)

**QUESTION**

17.   (L.O. 8) Pat Trim Corporation declared a stock dividend of 10,000 shares when the par value was $1 per share, the market value was $5 per share, and the number of shares outstanding was 200,000. How does the entry to record this transaction affect retained earnings?

a.   No effect
b.   $10,000 decrease
c.   $40,000 decrease
d.   $50,000 decrease

**Approach and Explanation:** Analyze the data to determine the size of the stock dividend. Prepare the journal entry to record the declaration of the stock dividend and analyze the entry's effect on retained earnings. Comparing the 10,000 dividend shares to the 200,000 outstanding shares prior to the dividend yields a 5% relationship; thus, the stock dividend is an ordinary (small) stock dividend. An ordinary stock dividend is recorded by transferring retained earnings equal to the market value of the dividend shares to paid-in capital. Therefore, 10,000 shares multiplied by $5 means retained earnings is to be charged for $50,000. (Solution = d.)

**QUESTION**

18.   (L.O. 8) A 4-for-1 stock split will cause a decrease in:
   a.   total assets.
   b.   total stockholders' equity.
   c.   retained earnings.
   d.   the par value per share.

**Explanation:** A stock split involves the issuance of additional shares of stock to existing stockholders according to the number of shares presently owned. A stock split does **not** result in the capitalization of any retained earnings; rather, the par value per share is reduced in proportion to the increase in shares. Thus, in a 2-for-1 split, the number of shares are doubled and the par value per share is cut in half. Whereas with a 4-for-1 stock split, the number of total shares is four times what the number was before the split and the par value per share after the split is 1/4 of the par value per share before the split. Assets are not affected. (Solution = d.)

**QUESTION**

19.   (L.O. 2, 9) The balance of the Retained Earnings account represents:
a.   cash set aside for specific purposes.
b.   the earnings for the most recent accounting period.
c.   the balance of unrestricted cash on hand.
d.   the total of all amounts reported as net income since the inception of the corporation minus the sum of any amounts reported as net loss and dividends declared since the inception of the corporation.

**Approach and Explanation:** Define retained earnings and select the answer that most closely matches that definition. Retained earnings is net income retained in a corporation. Retained earnings is often referred to as earnings retained for use in the business. Thus, net income (earnings for a period) increases the balance of retained earnings. Distributions of earnings to stockholders (owners) are called dividends; they reduce the balance of retained earnings. (Solution = d.)

**QUESTION**

20.   (L.O. 9) Assume common stock is the only class of stock outstanding in the B-Bar-B Corporation. Total stockholders' equity divided by the number of common stock shares outstanding is called:
a.   book value per share.
b.   par value per share.
c.   stated value per share.
d.   market value per share.

**Approach and Explanation:** Briefly define each of the answer selections. **Book value** per common stock share represents the equity a common stockholder has in the net assets of the corporation. When only one class of stock is outstanding, book value per share is determined by dividing total stockholders' equity by the number of shares outstanding. **Par value** is an arbitrary value which does not have much significance except in establishing legal capital and in determining the amount to appear in the Common Stock account for each share issued. **Stated value** refers to an arbitrary value that may be placed on a stock by the board of directors. Stated value has about the same significance as par value. **Market value** refers to the price for which a stock is currently being bought and sold in the open market. (Solution = a.)

## QUESTION

21.   (L.O. 9) A corporation has two classes of stock outstanding. The return on common stock equity is computed by dividing net income:

a.   minus preferred dividends by the number of common stock shares outstanding at the balance sheet date.

b.   plus interest expense by the average amount of total assets.

c.   by the number of common stock shares outstanding at the balance sheet date.

d.   minus preferred dividends by the average amount of common stockholders' equity during the period.

**Explanation:** The return on common stock equity is computed by dividing the amount of earnings applicable to the common stockholders' interest in the company by the average amount of common stockholders' equity during the period. The amount of earnings applicable to the common stockholders is the amount of net income for the period less the dividends declared on preferred stock during the period. (Solution = d.)

# CHAPTER 16

# DILUTIVE SECURITIES AND EARNINGS PER SHARE

## OVERVIEW

During the past four to five decades, many corporations have engaged in heavy merger activity. These business combinations have utilized an increasing amount of dilutive securities such as convertible bonds, convertible preferred stocks, and stock warrants. The accounting procedures for each of these are discussed in this chapter.

Executives of corporations are usually given some type of stock-based compensation. The type of plan used can materially affect the corporation's financial statements. Accounting procedures for employee stock options and other stock-based compensation plans such as restricted-stock plans are discussed in this chapter.

Earnings per share (EPS) is typically the most widely quoted financial ratio. The computation of earnings per share is complicated by situations where dilutive securities, as well as common stock, are outstanding. EPS computations are also discussed in this chapter.

## SUMMARY OF LEARNING OBJECTIVES

1. **Describe the accounting for the issuance, conversion, and retirement of convertible debt securities.** The method for recording convertible bonds at the date of issuance follows that used to record straight (nonconvertible) debt issues. Companies amortize any discount or premium that results from the issuance of convertible bonds, assuming the bonds will be outstanding to maturity. If bonds are converted into other securities, the principal accounting problem is to determine the amount at which to record the securities exchanged for the bonds. The book value method is used in practice and is considered GAAP. The retirement of convertible debt is considered a debt retirement, and the difference between the carrying amount of the retired convertible debt and the cash paid should result in a gain or loss.

2. **Explain the accounting for convertible preferred stock.** When convertible preferred stock is converted, a company uses the book value method. It debits Preferred Stock and any related Paid-in Capital in Excess of Par, and credits Common Stock and Paid-in Capital in Excess of Par (if any excess exists).

3. **Contrast the accounting for stock rights issued to existing shareholders and stock warrants issued with other securities.** *Stock warrants:* Companies should allocate the proceeds from the sale of debt securities with detachable stock warrants between the two securities. Warrants that are detachable can be traded separately from the debt, and, therefore companies can determine their market value. Two methods of allocation are available: the proportional method and the incremental method. Nondetachable warrants do not require an allocation of the proceeds between the debt securities and the warrants; companies record the entire proceeds as debt. *Stock rights:* No entry is required when a company issues rights (warrants) to existing stockholders. The company needs only to make a memorandum entry to

indicate the number of rights issued to existing stockholders and to ensure that the company has additional unissued stock registered for issuance in case the stockholders exercise the rights.

4. **Describe the accounting for stock compensation plans under generally accepted accounting principles.** Companies must use the fair-value approach to account for stock-based compensation. Under this approach, a company computes total compensation expense based on the fair value of the options (that are expected to vest) on the grant date. Companies recognize compensation expense in the periods in which the employee performs the services. Restricted-stock plans follow the same general accounting principles as those for stock options. Companies estimate total compensation cost at the grant date based on the fair value of the restricted stock; they expense that cost over the service period. If vesting does not occur, companies reverse the compensation expense.

5. **Discuss the controversy involving stock compensation plans.** When first proposed, there was considerable opposition to the recognition provisions contained in the fair-value approach, because that approach could result in substantial compensation expense that was not previously recognized. Corporate America, particularly the high technology sector, vocally opposed the proposed standard. They believed that the standard would place them at a competitive disadvantage with larger companies that can withstand higher compensation charges. Offsetting such opposition is the need for greater transparency in financial reporting, on which our capital markets depend.

6. **Compute earnings per share in a simple capital structure.** When a company has both common and preferred stock outstanding, it subtracts the current year preferred stock dividend from net income to arrive at income available to common stockholders. The formula for computing earnings per share is net income less preferred stock dividends, divided by the weighted average of shares of common stock outstanding.

7. **Compute earnings per share in a complex capital structure.** A complex capital structure requires a dual presentation of earnings per share, each with equal prominence on the face of the income statement. These two presentations are referred to as basic earnings per share and diluted earnings per share. Basic earnings per share relies on the number of weighted average common shares outstanding (i.e., equivalent to EPS for a simple capital structure). Diluted earnings per share indicates the dilution of earnings per share that would have occurred if all potential issuances of common stock that would have reduced earnings per share had taken place. Companies with complex capital structures should exclude antidilutive securities when computing earnings per share.

*8. **Explain the accounting for stock-appreciation rights.** The accounting for stock-appreciation rights depend on whether the rights are classified as equity- or liability-based. If equity-based, the accounting is similar to that used for stock options. If liability-based, companies re-measure compensation expense each period and allocate it over the service period using the percentage approach.

　　　　*This material is covered in Appendix 16A in the text.

**9. **Compute earnings per share in a complex situation.** For diluted EPS, make the following computations: (1) For each potentially dilutive security, determine the per share effect assuming exercise/conversion. (2) Rank the results from most dilutive to least dilutive. (3) Recalculate EPS starting with the most dilutive, and continue adding securities until EPS does not change or increases (from an antidilutive security). The antidilutive security is then omitted from the EPS calculation.

　　　　**This material is covered in Appendix 16B in the text.

## TIPS ON CHAPTER TOPICS

**TIP:**  When accounting for convertible bonds and bonds issued with detachable warrants, follow the basic recording rules for bonds discussed in **Chapter 14** (see your *Problem Solving Survival Guide*). These include:

1.  Record the par (face) amount of the bonds issued in the Bonds Payable account.

2.  Record an excess of issuance price over par for the bonds in the Premium on Bonds Payable account; record an excess of par over issuance price in the Discount on Bonds Payable account.

3.  Record debt issuance costs in an asset account to be amortized over the life of the bonds.

4.  Remove all related amounts from the accounts when the debt is extinguished. The net carrying amount of the debt is eliminated from the accounts when the debt is settled.

**TIP:**  An options market exists that works similarly to the stock market. For example, an investor may purchase a share of Apple stock for $100 per share or he may purchase an option to buy Apple stock. Assume the option allows the holder to buy Apple stock for $110 anytime within the next six months. This type of option is created by the marketplace, not by Apple Corporation. Therefore, the Apple Corporation is not involved with accounting for this type of security. In this chapter, the only type of options addressed are employee stock options which are granted by the related corporation.

**TIP:**  A **dilutive security** is a security which would reduce earnings per share (EPS) if it became common stock. An **antidilutive security** is one which would result in an increase in the amount reported as EPS or a decrease in the amount reported as a net loss per share.

**TIP:**  In computing diluted EPS, any antidilutive security is to be excluded. This means that a convertible bond will be assumed to be converted to common stock for the purposes of computing diluted EPS **if** the effect of that assumption is dilutive. The convertible bond will **not** be assumed to be converted in computing EPS **if** the effect of that assumption is antidilutive.

**TIP:**  Assume a corporation has no discontinued operations, no extraordinary item, and no cumulative effect of a change in accounting principle. If the corporation has a **loss per share** result from the basic EPS formula, any and **all assumptions will be antidilutive**; therefore, a single EPS presentation will be made. A loss per share can result in the basic formula for the following conditions:

1.  Corporation has a net loss on its income statement for the period.

2.  Corporation has net income for the period but the amount of preferred dividends for the period exceeds the amount of net income.

3.  Corporation has a net loss and preferred stock dividends (this situation results in a large negative numerator for the EPS ratio).

## EXERCISE 16-1

**Purpose:**     (L.O. 1) This exercise will illustrate how to record the issuance of convertible debt and its subsequent conversion to common stock.

Oviedo Oatmeal Corporation has 300,000 shares of its $10 par value common stock outstanding with a market price of $52 per share on January 1, 2010 when it issues convertible bonds. The debt issue is comprised of 1,000 bonds at $1,000 par with a 20-year term and a 10% stated interest rate. Each bond is sold at 101 and is convertible into 20 shares of common stock. Oviedo Oatmeal incurs costs of $80,000 related to the issue. The straight-line method is to be used to amortize any related premium or discount. An underwriter advises the issuer that the bonds would likely have sold for 99 without the conversion feature.

## Instructions
(a)     Record the issuance of the convertible bonds on January 1, 2010.
(b)     Explain why a portion of the issuance proceeds is or is not allocated to the conversion feature.
(c)     Record the conversion of 50% of the bonds on January 1, 2012, using the book value method.
(d)     Record the additional entry required on January 1, 2012 if 500 additional shares of common stock are issued by Oviedo Oatmeal as an inducement for conversion in either part (c) or part (d) above.
(e)     Record the additional entry required on January 1, 2012 if costs of $21,000 are incurred in administering (but not inducing) the conversion that takes place in part (c) above.

## Solution to Exercise 16-1

(a)     Cash.............................................................................. 930,000
Unamortized Bond Issue Costs .......................................... 80,000
    Bonds Payable ........................................................... 1,000,000
    Premium on Bonds Payable....................................... 10,000
      ($1,000 x 1,000 = $1,000,000 par)
      ($1,000,000 x 101% = $1,010,000 issuance price)
      ($1,010,000 - $80,000 = $930,000 net proceeds)
      ($1,010,000 - $1,000,000 = $10,000 premium)

> **TIP:** No portion of the proceeds from the issuance of convertible debt should be allocated to the conversion feature; therefore, **none** of the proceeds should be recorded as paid-in capital. Thus, convertible bonds do not affect paid-in capital until they are converted to stock.
>
> **TIP:** Bonds issued with nondetachable stock warrants are similar to convertible bonds and are accounted for in the same manner; all of the proceeds are recorded in liability accounts.

(b)     No portion of the proceeds from the issuance of convertible debt is allocated to the conversion feature for accounting purposes because the FASB indicates that the conversion option is inseparable from the debt security.

(c)     Bonds Payable (50% x $1,000,000).......................................... 500,000
Premium on Bonds Payable (50% x $10,000 x 18/20) ......................... 4,500
     Unamortized Bond Issue Costs ............................................... 36,000
      (50% x $80,000 x 18/20)
     Common Stock................................................................. 100,000
      (50% x 1,000 bonds x 20 shares x $10 par)
     Paid-in Capital in Excess of Par (Difference) ............................ 368,500*

| | |
|---|---:|
| *Par value of bonds converted (50% x 1,000 x $1,000) | $ 500,000 |
|   Related unamortized premium (50% x $10,000 x 18/20) | 4,500 |
|   Book value of bonds converted | 504,500 |
|       Unamortized bond issue costs (50% x $80,000 x 18/20) | (36,000) |
|   Net book value of bonds converted | 468,500 |
|   Par value of stock issued (50% x 1,000 bonds x | |
|     20 shares x $10 par) | (100,000) |
|   Additional paid-in capital recorded | $ 368,500 |

**Explanation:** The net book value of bonds payable is removed from the accounts and that net amount is recorded in appropriate stockholder equity accounts. No gain or loss is recorded.

> **TIP:**  The **book value method** of recording the conversion of bonds payable to common stock simply removes the net book value of the bonds from debt accounts and records that amount in appropriate stockholder equity accounts. **No gain or loss is recorded** when the book value method is used.
>
> **TIP:**  Recall from **Chapter 14** that **book value** is synonymous with **carrying value** and **carrying amount**.

(d)     Debt Conversion Expense (500 x $52) ........................................ 26,000
     Common Stock (500 x $10) ..................................................... 5,000
     Paid-in Capital in Excess of Par [500 x ($52 - $10)]..................... 21,000

**Explanation:** When an additional payment is needed to make bondholders convert, the payment is for a service (bondholders converting at a given time) and should be reported as an expense. The additional payment is called a **sweetener** to induce conversion; it should be recognized as an expense of the current period at an amount equal to the fair value of the additional securities or other consideration given.

(e)     Paid-in Capital in Excess of Par............................................... 21,000
     Cash........................................................................... 21,000

**Explanation:** If the administrative costs of conversion are viewed to be costs of issuing the stock, treatment similar to any other stock issuance costs is used, which will mean a charge to additional paid-in capital in this case. When a corporation is in the process of initial formation, stock issuance costs are charged to additional paid-in capital (as is shown in this solution). If the costs are viewed as connected with an inducement to convert, they should be expensed in the current period.

## EXERCISE 16-2

**Purpose:**   (L.O. 2) This exercise will illustrate how to account for convertible preferred stock.

Roy Rogers Corporation has 1,000 shares of $50 par 6% convertible preferred stock outstanding at December 31, 2010. Each share was issued in a prior year at $54. The preferred stock is convertible into $10 par common stock.

### Instructions
(a)   Record the conversion of 100 shares of preferred stock if one share of preferred is convertible into four shares of common.
(b)   Record the conversion of 100 shares of preferred if the conversion ratio is 6:1.

### Solution to Exercise 16-2

| | | |
|---|---:|---:|
| (a)   Convertible Preferred Stock (100 x $50)..................................... | 5,000 | |
| Paid-in Capital in Excess of Par—Preferred (100 x $4)......................... | 400 | |
|    Common Stock (100 x 4 x $10)................................................... | | 4,000 |
|    Paid-in Capital in Excess of Par—Common.............................. | | 1,400 |
|       [100 x ($54 - $40)] | | |
| | | |
| (b)   Convertible Preferred Stock (100 x $50)..................................... | 5,000 | |
| Paid-in Capital in Excess of Par—Preferred (100 x $4)......................... | 400 | |
| Retained Earnings [100 x 6 x $10 - (100 x $54)] .................................. | 600 | |
|    Common Stock (100 x 6 x $10)................................................. | | 6,000 |

**Approach:** Use the following guidelines to record the conversion of preferred stock to common stock:
1.   No gain or loss is recorded. This is a capital transaction. A corporation cannot record an accounting gain or loss when dealing with its stockholders in their capacity of being owners of the business.
2.   The amount originally recorded (at issuance) in the Convertible Preferred Stock account and a related additional paid-in capital account is removed from those accounts and recorded in the Common Stock account and a related additional paid-in capital account. As usual, the par amount goes in the Common Stock account and any excess goes in an additional paid-in capital account.
3.   If the par value of the common stock exceeds the recorded value of the preferred, the difference is charged to retained earnings (or some states allow for a charge to additional paid-in capital from other sources).

# EXERCISE 16-3

**Purpose:**   (L.O. 3) This exercise will review the accounting procedures for the issuance of debt securities with detachable warrants.

A new issue of 1,000 bonds was sold at 102.5 on January 1, 2010. Each bond had a face amount of $1,000 and one detachable warrant attached. One warrant allowed the holder to purchase 10 shares of $10 par common stock at $43 per share. The market value of the common stock at January 1, 2010 was $46. Shortly after issuance of the bonds and warrants, quotes were 98.5 for a bond ex-warrant and $48 for a common stock warrant. A few months later, 800 warrants were exercised. Two years later, the remaining 200 warrants expired.

## Instructions

(a)    Record the issuance of the 1,000 bonds with detachable warrants.
(b)    Record the exercise of 800 warrants.
(c)    Record the expiration of 200 warrants.
(d)    Indicate the effect of each of the entries [(a), (b), and (c)] above on (1) assets, (2) total paid-in capital, and (3) number of common stock shares outstanding. State the direction and amount of each effect.
(e)    Explain how the journal entry for part (a) would differ if the market value of a bond ex-warrant was unknown.

## Solution to Exercise 16-3

(a)    Cash (1,000 x $1,000 x 102.5%)............................................ 1,025,000
Discount on Bonds Payable........................................................... 22,628[b]
    Bonds Payable (1,000 x $1,000).......................................... 1,000,000
    Paid-in Capital—Stock Warrants.......................................... 47,628[a]

$$a\frac{\$48{,}000}{\$48{,}000\ +\ \$985{,}000}\ \text{x}\ \$1{,}025{,}000 = \$47{,}628\ \text{amount to allocate to warrants}$$

[b]$1,025,000 total proceeds - $47,628 allocated to the warrants
        = $977,372 allocated to the bonds.
  $1,000,000 face amount of bonds - $977,372 carrying value of bonds
        = $22,628 to record for discount on bonds payable.

**Explanation:** The proportional method is used; thus, the proceeds are allocated to the two securities based on their relative market values. The amount to be allocated to the warrants is determined by the formula:

$$\frac{\text{MV Warrants}}{\text{MV Warrants}\ +\ \text{MV Bonds Ex - Warrants}}\ \text{x}\ \frac{\text{Total}}{\text{Proceeds}} = \frac{\text{Paid - in Capital}}{\text{To Record}}$$

The formula above computes the amount of proceeds to be allocated to the warrant. The remaining proceeds are recorded in bond accounts (the par value of the bonds always goes in the Bonds Payable account). The $22,628 excess of the bonds' par value over the proceeds allocated to the bonds [$1,000,000 - ($1,025,000 - $47,628) = $22,628] represents a discount on the bonds.

> **TIP:**   The amount of proceeds to be allocated to the bonds can be independently verified by using the formula above and substituting the "Market Value of the Bonds Ex-Warrants" in the numerator of the fraction. The result will then be the amount of "Debt to Record."
>
> **TIP:**   By use of the formula above, the proceeds from the issuance of **bonds with detachable stock warrants** are allocated between the bonds and the stock warrants based on the relative market values of the two securities. This is referred to as the **proportional method** and is the preferred method. If the market value of the bonds ex-warrants is not known or not determinable, the warrants are recorded at their market value and the remaining proceeds are allocated to the debt. This latter approach is called the **incremental method**.
>
> **TIP:**   Recall from your study of bonds payable that a bond's price is quoted in terms of a percentage of its par value. Carefully compute the bond's price before proceeding with the formula in this exercise. A very common error would be to use $98.50 for the price of one bond in this situation rather than the **correct** price of $985.00 (98.5% of $1,000 par = $985.00).
>
> **TIP:**   Warrant prices are quoted like stock prices—in terms of dollars. The price of a bond ex-warrants refers to the price of a bond without warrants.
>
> **TIP:**   When using the proportional method, the amount determined for allocation to the warrants should be close (but usually **not** equal) to the market value of the warrants. In part (a) of this problem, $47,628 is close to $48,000 (1,000 x $48); therefore, the amount determined by the formula is reasonable.

| | | | |
|---|---|---:|---:|
| (b) | Cash (800 x 10 x $43)..................................................... | 344,000 | |
| | Paid-in Capital—Stock Warrants (800/1,000 x $47,628) ...................... | 38,102 | |
| | Common Stock (800 x 10 x $10)................................................ | | 80,000 |
| | Paid-in Capital in Excess of Par................................................ | | 302,102* |

| | |
|---|---:|
| *Cash proceeds from exercise (800 warrants x 10 shares each x $43 exercise price) | $ 344,000 |
| Amount recorded on the books for the warrants exercised (800 warrants exercised out of 1,000 outstanding = 80%; 80% x $47,628) | 38,102 |
| Total consideration received for stock issued | 382,102 |
| Par value of stock issued (800 x 10 x $10) | (80,000) |
| Excess of consideration received over par for stock issued upon exercise of warrants | $ 302,102 |

> **TIP:**   The number of shares of stock obtainable upon the exercise of one warrant does **not** effect the computations and recording in part (a) [issuance date of bonds plus warrants] but it **does** effect the computations in part (b) [exercise date of the warrants].

| | | |
|---|---|---:|
| (c) | Paid-in Capital—Stock Warrants ($47,628 - $38,102) .............. | 9,526 |

Paid-in Capital from Expired Stock Warrants............................. 9,526

(d)     Effect on:

| | (1) Assets | (2) Total Paid-in Capital | (3) Number of Common Shares Outstanding |
|---|---|---|---|
| (a) | Increase $1,025,000 | Increase $47,628 | No effect |
| (b) | Increase $344,000 | Increase $344,000 | Increase 8,000 |
| (c) | No effect | No effect | No effect |

(e)     The incremental method would be used. Thus, the market value of the warrants would be used to record the warrants and the remaining proceeds would be recorded in debt accounts. The entry would be as follows:

| | | |
|---|---|---|
| Cash (1,000 x $1,000 x 102.5%) ....................................................... | 1,025,000 | |
| Discount on Bonds Payable.............................................................. | 23,000 | |
| Bonds Payable (1,000 x $1,000)............................................. | | 1,000,000 |
| Paid-in Capital—Stock Warrants (1,000 x $48)...................... | | 48,000 |

# EXERCISE 16-4

**Purpose:**    (L.O. 3) This exercise reviews the accounting rules for the issuance of stock rights to existing stockholders.

Hot Videos Corporation wished to raise additional capital. One right was distributed for each of the 100,000 shares of stock outstanding. Four rights and $30 cash were required to purchase one new share of $10 par value common stock. Ninety percent (90%) of the rights were exercised and the rest expired three weeks after their issuance. The market value of the stock was $32 per share at the date the rights were distributed and $35 per share at the date the rights were exercised.

## Instructions
(a)     Explain the most likely reason for the distribution of the stock rights to existing stockholders. Why are these rights good for a very limited time period?
(b)     Record the issuance of the rights.
(c)     Record the exercise of the rights.
(d)     Record the expiration of the rights.

## Solution to Exercise 16-4

(a) The existing stockholders likely have the preemptive right (privilege to purchase newly issued shares in proportion to their holdings before the new issuance); thus, they must have the first opportunity to acquire new shares. The distribution of the rights (warrants) is a way to administer that opportunity. The rights have a short life because the corporation is anxious to sell the new shares to somebody; if the existing stockholders do not wish to buy them, they are offered to the general public.

(b) Only make a memorandum entry at the grant (issuance) date. The corporation has received no consideration; no exchange has taken place; there are no proceeds to allocate.

(c) 

| | | |
|---|---:|---:|
| Cash | 675,000* | |
| Common Stock (22,500 x $10) | | 225,000 |
| Paid-in Capital in Excess of Par | | 450,000 |
| ($675,000 - $225,000) | | |

*100,000 x 90% = 90,000 rights exercised
90,000 rights ÷ 4 = 22,500 common stock shares issued
22,500 shares x $30 = $675,000 proceeds

> **TIP:** When the rights are exercised, the issuance of the stock is recorded as any other stock issuance. At this date, assets and owners' equity are increased by the amount of the proceeds received.

(d) Only make a memorandum entry at the expiration date.

# ILLUSTRATION 16-1
# ACCOUNTING FOR STOCK COMPENSATION PLANS (L.O. 4)

The following guidelines pertain to accounting for a stock option, purchase, or award plan:

1.  The consideration that a corporation receives for stock issued through a stock option, purchase, or award plan consists of cash or other assets, if any, plus services received from the employee.

2.  Compensation for services should be measured by the **fair-value method.** Companies compute **total compensation expense** based on the fair value of the options on the date the employer grants the options (i.e. grant date) to employees. Only options that are expected to eventually vest are considered. Public companies estimate fair value by using an appropriate option pricing model. After this expense is computed, it is **not** adjusted up or down for changes in the stock price that occur subsequent to the grant date.

3.  Compensation cost should be recognized as an expense of one or more periods in which an employee performs services (often called **the service period**) by a debit to Compensation Expense and a credit to Paid-in Capital—Stock Options. The grant or award may specify the periods, or the periods may be inferred from the terms or from the past pattern of grants or awards. Unless otherwise specified, the service period is the vesting period—the time between the grant date and the vesting date. The vesting date is the date the employee's right to receive or retain shares of stock or cash under the award is no longer contingent upon the employee remaining in the service of the employer.

4.  If **employees fail to exercise** the stock options before their expiration date, the company does not adjust the compensation expense. An unexercised stock option does not nullify the need to record the costs of services received from executives and attributable to the stock option plan.

5.  If an **employee forfeits a stock option** because the employee fails to satisfy a service requirement (e.g., leaves employment), the company should adjust the estimate of compensation expense recorded in the current period (as a change in estimate). A company records this change in estimate by debiting Paid-in Capital—Stock Options and crediting Compensation Expense for the amount of cumulative compensation expense recorded to date for the departing employee's forfeited options. This entry thus decreases compensation expense in the period of forfeiture.

6.  The exercise of stock options is recorded by a debit to Cash for the amount of the exercise price, a debit to Paid-in Capital—Stock Options for the amount of compensation expense related to the options being exercised, a credit to Common Stock for the par value of the stock being given to the employee upon exercise of the options and a credit to Paid-in Capital in Excess of Par for the excess of the fair value of these options at the grant date (which is equal to the sum of the exercise price [amount of cash] and the compensation expense related to these options) over the par value of the stock given to the employee upon exercise of the options.

## EXERCISE 16-5

**Purpose:**    (L.O. 4) This exercise will illustrate the application of the fair-value method in accounting for a compensatory stock option plan.

Worldwise Corporation granted options for 10,000 shares of its $10 par value common stock to certain executives on January 1, 2010, when the stock was selling for $44 per share. The options stipulate a price of $44 per share for the stock and must be exercised between January 1, 2012 and December 31, 2014, at which time they expire. The options state that the service period is January 1, 2010 through December 31, 2011. An option pricing model determined that, at the date of grant, the estimated fair value of these options was $500,000.

### Instructions
(a)    Prepare the journal entries for the following (items 3 and 4 are independent assumptions):
(1)    To record the issuance of the options (grant of options) on January 1, 2010.
(2)    To record compensation expense. Date the entry(s). Assume all employees remain employed by the corporation.
(3)    To record the exercise of the options, assuming all of the options were exercised on the earliest possible date, January 1, 2012.
(4)    To record the expiration of the options, assuming all of the options were **not** exercised because the market price fell below the exercise price before January 1, 2012 and stayed below that level for the balance of the option period.
(b)    Describe the intrinsic value method of accounting for stock options that was used prior to a FASB Standard that now requires the fair-value method to be used.

### Solution to Exercise 16-5

(a)
(1)                        **January 1, 2010**
    No entry

(2)                        **December 31, 2010**
    Compensation Expense ................................................................ 250,000
        Paid-in Capital—Stock Options ...........................................        250,000

                           **December 31, 2011**
    Compensation Expense ................................................................ 250,000
        Paid-in Capital—Stock Options ...........................................        250,000

(3)                        **January 1, 2012**
    Cash        440,000
    Paid-in Capital—Stock Options ...................................................... 500,000
        Common Stock ...................................................................        100,000
        Paid-in Capital in Excess of Par ..........................................        840,000

                           **December 31, 2014**
(4)    Paid-in Capital—Stock Options ...................................................... 500,000
        Paid-in Capital from Expired Stock Options ........................        500,000

---

**TIP:**    Refer to **Illustration 16-1** for an explanation of the accounting procedures for stock option plans.

**TIP:**    The **option price** is often called the **exercise price**.

---

(b)    Prior to the issuance of SFAS 123(R) many companies used the intrinsic method. The intrinsic method computed compensation expense as the excess of the market price at the date of grant over the option price. (In the situation at hand, that amount would be zero.) The intrinsic method used the same time period of recognizing expense (service period) as does the fair-value method.

# EXERCISE 16-6

**Purpose:**    (L.O. 4) This exercise will illustrate the proper accounting for a restricted-stock compensation plan.

On January 1, 2010, Comustat Company issues 2,000 shares of restricted stock to its CFO. The stock has a fair value of $30 per share on January 1, 2010. The stock is for a service period of the next four years. Vesting occurs at the end of that four year period. The par value of the stock is $1 per share.

## Instructions
(a)    Prepare the journal entry to record the issuance of the restricted stock on January 1, 2010.
(b)    Explain the nature of the Unearned Compensation account and where its balance is to be reported on a balance sheet.
(c)    Prepare the journal entry at December 31, 2010 to record the related expense for 2010.
(d)    Assume the CFO leaves the company on July 3, 2012 (before any expense has been recorded for 2012). Company policy calls for the employee to forfeit his/her rights to the stock when the employee leaves the company before vesting occurs. Prepare the journal entry on July 3, 2012 to record the forfeiture.

# SOLUTION 16-6

(a)    Unearned Compensation (2,000 X $30)                            60,000
           Common Stock (2,000 X $1)                                                    2,000
           Paid-in Capital in Excess of Par (2,000 X $29)                           58,000

**Explanation:** The debit to Unearned Compensation (often called Deferred Compensation Expense) is for the total compensation expense to be recognized over the next four years (service period).

(b)    Unearned Compensation represents the cost of employee services yet to be performed. The balance of this account, is to be reported in the stockholders' equity section of the balance sheet. It is a contra-equity item, similar to treasury stock.

(c)    Compensation Expense                                                       15,000
           Unearned Compensation                                                             15,000

| (d) | Common Stock | 2,000 | |
| | Paid-in Capital in Excess of Par | 58,000 | |
| | Compensation Expense | | 30,000 |
| | Unearned Compensation | | 30,000 |

# ILLUSTRATION 16-2
# STEPS IN COMPUTING EARNINGS PER SHARE (EPS) (L.O. 6, 7, *9)

**Step 1:    Compute the weighted average number of common stock shares outstanding.**

A.    When common shares are issued for assets during the period, weight them according to the length of time in the period the stock is outstanding in relation to the total time in the period.

B.    When common shares are issued in connection with a stock split or stock dividend declared during the period, give retroactive treatment to these shares. Retroactive treatment here means to restate the shares outstanding before the split or stock dividend. Give retroactive treatment even if the stock dividend or split is declared after the end of the period (but before the financial statements are published). Also, restate EPS in financial statements for prior periods presented.

> **TIP:**    See **Illustration 16-3** for a short-cut method of computing the weighted-average number of common stock shares outstanding.

**Step 2:    Compute basic EPS (EPS before any assumptions or adjustments).**

Basic Formula:    $$\frac{\text{Net Income} - \text{Preferred Dividends}}{\text{Weighted-Average Number of Common Shares Outstanding}}$$

The numerator should be the income available to common stockholders which is net income minus preferred stock dividend requirements. Thus, in the numerator, deduct the preferred dividends actually declared. If the preferred stock is cumulative, deduct the preferred's current year preference as to dividends, even if no dividends were declared. Dividends in arrears for prior years have no effect on the current year's basic EPS calculation, they were used for EPS calculations in prior years.

> **TIP:**    Dividends declared and/or paid during the year on common stock have no effect on this computation.

> **TIP:**    If there is a net loss rather than a net income, the amount of the loss is increased by the preferred dividends.

## ILLUSTRATION 16-2 (Continued)

### Step 3:  Compute diluted earnings per share.

A.      The basic formula is adjusted as follows:

$$\frac{\text{Net Income - Preferred Dividends} \pm \text{Adjustments}}{\substack{\text{Weighted Average Number of Common Shares Outstanding} \ + \\ \text{Weighted Average Number of Potential Common Shares}}}$$

B.      Treatment of convertibles: Use the **if converted** method.

   1.    Assume the convertible is converted to common stock, if the effect of that assumption is dilutive.

   > **TIP:**   **Dilution (dilutive)** is a reduction in earnings per share. **Antidilution (antidilutive)** is an increase in earnings per share amounts or a decrease in loss per share amounts.
   >
   > **TIP:**   A quick test to determine if a convertible debt instrument is antidilutive is as follows: if the amount of interest net of taxes per common share obtainable upon conversion exceeds basic EPS, the effect is antidilutive.
   >
   > **TIP:**   A quick test to determine if a convertible preferred stock is antidilutive is as follows: if the amount of preferred dividends per common share obtainable on conversion exceeds basic EPS, the effect is antidilutive.

   2.    For a convertible preferred, add back the preferred dividends (that had been deducted in the basic formula) in the numerator and add an appropriate weighted average number of potential common shares (assumed to be outstanding) in the denominator of the diluted EPS formula.

   3.    For convertible debt, add back interest and deduct tax savings due to interest in the numerator and add an appropriate weighted average number of potential common shares in the denominator.

   > **TIP:**   In using the "if converted" method for a convertible bond, interest expense is added back in the numerator of the EPS formula and the related tax effect is deducted. In using the "if converted" method for a convertible preferred stock, preferred dividends are added back in the numerator (because they were deducted in the numerator of the basic formula); however, there is **no** related tax effect because preferred dividends are not a tax deductible item.

## ILLUSTRATION 16-2 (Continued)

4.    Assume the conversion takes place at the beginning of the period for which EPS is being calculated or at the date of the issuance of the convertible, whichever is later (more recent).

5.    If there is a scale of conversion rates, use the rate that is the most advantageous from the standpoint of the security holder.

C.    Treatment of options and warrants:

1.    Assume the options and warrants are exercised **if** the effect of that assumption is dilutive.

> **TIP:**    An option or warrant is dilutive if the average market price of the common stock during the period is greater than the exercise price of the option or warrant.

2.    Use the **treasury stock method**. Assume that the proceeds (from the exercise of the options or warrants) are used to purchase treasury stock at the **average market price** for the period. Thus, shares will be added to the EPS denominator because of the assumed exercise, and then a smaller number of shares will be deducted from the denominator because of the assumed purchase of treasury stock. Weight the resulting **net** number of common equivalent shares according to the time they are assumed to be outstanding.

3.    Assume the exercise occurs at the beginning of the period or at the date of the issuance of the options or warrants, whichever is the later.

D.    Treatment of contingent issuance agreements.

1.    Common stock contingently issuable with the only condition being the mere passage of time should be assumed to be outstanding for computing diluted EPS.

2.    Common stock contingently issuable upon condition of the attainment or maintenance of a level of earnings should be considered outstanding in computing diluted EPS **if** that level is currently being attained.

3.    Common stock contingently issuable upon condition of the attainment of a market price level should be considered outstanding shares **if** that level is met at the end of the current year.

**ILLUSTRATION 16-2** (Continued)

**TIP:** An entity with a **simple capital structure,** that is, one with only common stock outstanding, must report **basic-per-share** amounts for income from continuing operations and for net income on the face of the income statement. An entity with a **complex capital structure** (i.e., a structure with one or more potentially dilutive securities outstanding) must report **basic and diluted per share** amounts for income from continuing operations and for net income on the face of the income statement with equal prominence.

**TIP:** Securities such as options, warrants, convertible bonds, convertible preferred stock, or contingent stock agreements are referred to as "potential common stock" or "potentially dilutive securities."

**TIP:** The computation of diluted EPS should not assume conversion, exercise, or **contingent issuance** of securities that would have an **antidilutive** effect on earnings per share. Shares issued on actual conversion, exercise, or satisfaction of certain conditions for which the underlying potential common shares were antidilutive shall be included in the computation as outstanding common shares from the date of conversion, exercise, or satisfaction of those conditions, respectively. In determining whether potential common shares are dilutive or antidilutive, each issue or series of issues of potential common shares should be considered separately rather than in the aggregate.

**TIP:** When a company has a complex capital structure and a dual presentation of earnings per share, it must disclose a reconciliation of the numerators and denominators of the basic and diluted per share computations, including individual income and share amount effects of all securities that affect EPS.

**TIP:** Including potential common shares in the denominator of a diluted per-share computation for continuing operations always will result in an antidilutive per-share amount when an entity has a *loss* from continuing operations or a *loss* from continuing operations available to common stockholders (that is, after any preferred dividend reductions). Although including those potential common shares in the other diluted per-share computations may be dilutive to their comparable basic per-share amounts, no potential common shares should be included in the computation of any diluted per-share amount when a loss from continuing operations exists, even if the entity reports net income.

## ILLUSTRATION 16-2 (Continued)

**\*\*TIP:** Convertible securities may be dilutive on their own but antidilutive when included with other potential common shares in computing diluted EPS. To reflect maximum potential dilution, each issue or series of issues of potential common shares shall be considered in sequence from the most dilutive to the least dilutive. That is, dilutive potential common shares with the lowest "earnings per incremental share" shall be included in diluted EPS before those with a higher earnings per incremental share. (Options and warrants generally will be included first because use of the treasury stock method does not impact the numerator of the computation.)

**\*\*TIP:** An entity that reports a discontinued operation, an extraordinary item, or the cumulative effect of an accounting change in a period should use income from continuing operations (adjusted for preferred dividends) as the "control number" in determining whether those potential common shares are dilutive or antidilutive. That is, the same number of potential common shares used in computing the diluted per-share amount for income from continuing operations should be used in computing all other reported diluted per-share amounts even if those amounts will be antidilutive to their respective basic per-share amounts.

For example, assume that Corporation A has income from continuing operations of $2,400, a loss from discontinued operations of $(3,600), a net loss of $(1,200), and 1,000 common shares and 200 potential common shares outstanding. Corporation A's basic per-share amounts would be $2.40 for continuing operations, $(3.60) for the discontinued operations, and $(1.20) for the net loss. Corporation A would include the 200 potential common shares in the denominator of its diluted per-share computation for continuing operations because the resulting $2.00 per share is dilutive. (For illustrative purposes, assume no numerator impact of those 200 potential common shares.) Because income from continuing operations is the control number, Corporation A also must include those 200 potential common shares in the denominator for the other per-share amounts, even though the resulting per-share amounts [$(3.00) per share for the loss from discontinued operations and $(1.00) per share for the net loss] are antidilutive to their comparable basic per-share amounts; that is, the loss per-share amounts are less.

\*\*This material is covered in **Appendix 16B** in the text.

# ILLUSTRATION 16-3
# SHORT-CUT METHOD FOR COMPUTING WEIGHTED AVERAGE
# NUMBER OF COMMON STOCK SHARES OUTSTANDING* (L.O. 6)

**Step 1:** Begin with the number of common shares outstanding at the beginning of the period. Assume they were outstanding the entire year; multiply the number by 12/12 to get an equivalent amount. Enter the equivalent amount in the Weighted Average column.

**Step 2:** Take the first transaction that occurred during the year that changed the number of shares outstanding and properly adjust the balance in the Weighted Average column.

a. **If shares were issued for assets, weight the new shares** by multiplying them by a fraction. The numerator of the fraction is the number of months in the period the shares were outstanding; the denominator is the number of months in the year. Add this equivalent amount in the Weighted Average column; arrive at a new balance.

b. **If shares were issued in a stock dividend or a stock split, retroactively adjust for these shares** by taking an appropriate multiple of the existing balance in the Weighted Average column. Ignore the date of the stock dividend or split; the multiple is determined by the size of the stock dividend or split. Arrive at a new balance.

c. **If shares were acquired as treasury stock or retired by the corporation, weight** the shares for the time they were **not** outstanding and deduct this equivalent amount from the existing balance. Arrive at a new balance.

**Step 3:** Take each of the other transactions that occurred during the year that changed the number of common shares outstanding and properly adjust the balance in the Weighted Average column as shown in Step 2 above. Handle each transaction in order of date.

## EXAMPLE:
**Data:**

| | | |
|---|---|---|
| January 1, 2010 | 100,000 shares were outstanding. | |
| April 1, 2010 | Issued 40,000 shares for cash. | |
| June 1, 2010 | Declared a 40% stock dividend. | |
| October 1, 2010 | Declared a 2-for-1 split. | |
| December 1, 2010 | Issued 60,000 shares for cash. | |

*The reporting period is assumed to be one year.

## ILLUSTRATION 16-3 (Continued)

**Computation:**

| Date | | Weighted Average |
|------|---|---|
| 1/1/10 | 100,000 x 12/12 = | 100,000 |
| 4/1/10 | 40,000 x 9/12 = | 30,000 |
| | New balance | 130,000 |
| 6/1/10 | 40% stock dividend | x 140%** |
| | New balance | 182,000 |
| 10/1/10 | 2-for-1 split | x 2*** |
| | New balance | 364,000 |
| 12/1/10 | 60,000 x 1/12 | 5,000 |
| | New balance | 369,000 |

**The appropriate multiple for a stock dividend is 100% plus the percentage used in the dividend. Thus, 100% + 40% dividend = 140% as the multiplier.

***The appropriate multiple for a stock split is the size of the split. Thus, for a 2-for-1 split, multiply by 2.

**TIP:** Notice how the computation for the weighted-average number of common stock shares outstanding for the period differs from the computation for the actual number of common stock shares outstanding at the end of the period. The number of common stock shares actually outstanding at December 31, 2010 can be computed as follows:

| Date | | Actual Shares |
|------|---|---|
| 1/1/10 | Balance | 100,000 |
| 4/110 | Issued for assets | 40,000 |
| | New balance | 140,000 |
| 6/1/10 | 40% stock dividend | 56,000 |
| | New balance | 196,000 |
| 10/1/10 | 2:1 split | 196,000 |
| | New balance | 392,000 |
| 12/1/10 | Issued for assets | 60,000 |
| | New balance | 452,000 |

**TIP:** Assume that in addition to the transactions listed above, a 10% stock dividend was declared on January 7, 2011, before the financial statements for 2010 were issued. The weighted average number of common stock shares outstanding for purposes of computing EPS for 2010 would be 405,900 (369,000 x 110% = 405,900) and the actual number of common stock shares outstanding to be reported on the balance sheet at December 31, 2010 would be 452,000.

## EXERCISE 16-7

**Purpose:**    (L.O. 6) This exercise will apply the guidelines for computing the weighted average number of common stock shares outstanding.

When the number of common stock shares varies during the year, the weighted average number of common stock shares outstanding must be calculated before the EPS can be computed.

Listed below are the details regarding common stock shares outstanding for four different companies:

1.    Michael Jackson Corporation had 100,000 shares of common stock outstanding on January 1, 2010. On March 1, 2010, 6,000 shares of common stock were issued for cash.

2.    Jimmy Buffet Corporation had 100,000 shares of common stock outstanding on January 1, 2010. On March 1, 6,000 shares of common stock were issued for cash. On July 1, a 4-for-1 split was declared.

3.    Emmy Lou Harris Corporation had 100,000 shares of common stock outstanding on January 1, 2010. On March 1, 2010, 6,000 shares of common stock were reacquired by the corporation.

4.    Elton John Corporation had 100,000 shares of common stock outstanding on January 1, 2010. On March 1, 2010, 6,000 shares of common stock were issued for cash. On June 1, 2010, a 10% stock dividend was declared. On December 1, 2010, 12,000 shares of common stock were issued for cash.

### Instructions
(a)    Compute the weighted average number of common stock shares outstanding for 2010 (to be used to compute EPS) for **each** of the **independent** situations above.
(b)    Compute the number of common stock shares outstanding to be reported on the balance sheet at December 31, 2010 for Elton John Corporation (situation 4).

### Solution to Exercise 16-7

(a)    **Approach and Explanation:** Use the short-cut method explained in **Illustration 16-3**.

| | Date | | Weighted Average |
|---|---|---|---|
| 1. | 1/1/10 | 100,000 x 12/12 = | 100,000 |
| | 3/1/10 | 6,000 x 10/12 = | 5,000 |
| | | New balance | 105,000 |

> **TIP:** The weighted average calculation for common stock shares uses the same concept that is applied in computing equivalent units of production for a manufacturing firm. In the situation above, the computation indicates that having 6,000 shares outstanding for ten months of the year is equivalent to having 5,000 shares outstanding for twelve months. The weighted average number of shares outstanding is sometimes referred to as equivalent shares.

|    | Date | | **Weighted Average** |
|----|------|---|------|
| 2. | 1/1/10 | 100,000 x 12/12 = | 100,000 |
|    | 3/1/10 | 6,000 x 10/12 = | 5,000 |
|    |        | New balance | 105,000 |
|    | 7/1/10 | 4-for-1 split | x    4 |
|    |        | New balance | 420,000 |
|    |        | | |
| 3. | 1/1/10 | 100,000 x 12/12 = | 100,000 |
|    | 3/1/10 | (6,000) x 10/12 = | (5,000) |
|    |        | New balance | 95,000 |
|    |        | | |
| 4. | 1/1/10 | 100,000 x 12/12 = | 100,000 |
|    | 3/1/10 | 6,000 x 10/12 = | 5,000 |
|    |        | New balance | 105,000 |
|    | 6/1/10 | 10% stock dividend | x  110% |
|    |        | New balance | 115,500 |
|    | 12/1/10 | 12,000 x 1/12 = | 1,000 |
|    |        | New balance | 116,500 |

> **TIP:** If you want, you can prove the answer of 116,500 by a more complex procedure as follows:
>
> | Dates Outstanding | Actual Shares[a] | Restatement | Fraction | Weighted Shares |
> |---|---|---|---|---|
> | 1/1/10 to 2/28/10 | 100,000 | 1.1 | 2/12 | 18,333 |
> | 3/1/10 to 5/31/10 | 106,000 | 1.1 | 3/12 | 29,150 |
> | 6/1/10 to 11/30/10 | 116,600 | | 6/12 | 58,300 |
> | 12/1/10 to 12/31/10 | 128,600 | | 1/12 | 10,717 |
> | | | | | 116,500 |
>
> [a]See solution to part (b) for computations.

A stock dividend or a stock split requires retroactive restatement of shares for the computation of EPS. A 10% stock dividend causes a 10% increase in the number of shares outstanding. Therefore, to restate the number of shares outstanding at a certain date in the past as to give retroactive effect to a subsequently declared 10% stock dividend, the old number of shares is multiplied by 110% (which is 1.1 in decimal form).

> **TIP:** When shares are issued for assets, they are weighted for the number of months they are outstanding in relation to the number of months in the period for which EPS is being computed. When shares are issued in a stock dividend or a stock split, they are **not** weighted; rather, retroactive adjustment is made for these additional shares in the weighted average shares calculation. The reason for the difference in treatment is that when assets are received, the entity has more resources and, therefore, an opportunity to increase the net income figure by earning a rate of return on those new assets for the months the new resources are available. When shares are issued in connection with a stock dividend or stock split, there are no new resources and, therefore, no changes in net income. In order for EPS figures for successive periods for a company to be meaningful, they must all be based on the rearranged capital structure; therefore, stock dividends and stock splits must be handled retroactively. This **retroactive treatment** causes adjustment to the weighted average shares computation for EPS **for all periods presented**. Therefore, when the financial statements for a prior period are republished in comparative statements, the EPS amounts for the prior period are to be restated for all stock dividends and stock splits occurring subsequent to the prior period. Thus, a stock dividend declared in 2010 calls for retroactive restatement of the 2009 EPS figure when the 2009 income statement is republished in 2010 for comparative purposes.

(b)

| Date | | Actual Shares |
|------|---|---------------|
| 1/1/10 | Balance | 100,000 |
| 3/1/10 | Issued for assets | 6,000 |
| | New balance | 106,000 |
| 6/1/10 | 10% stock dividend | 10,600 |
| | New balance | 116,600 |
| 12/1/10 | Issued for assets | 12,000 |
| | New balance | 128,600 |

## EXERCISE 16-8

**Purpose:**    (L.O. 7) This exercise will illustrate the application of the treasury stock method.

Jeremy Sherr Corporation had 200,000 shares of common stock outstanding during 2010. On January 1, 2010 40,000 stock options were granted. Each option entitles the holder to purchase one share of common stock at $40. The options become exercisable in 2012. Net income for 2010 was $400,000. The average market price of stock during 2010 was $50; the closing market price was $54.

## Instructions
(a)    Compute the amount(s) that Jeremy Sherr Corporation should report for earnings per share for 2010.
(b)    Explain how your answer(s) to Part (a) would change if the options were issued on April 1, 2010 rather than January 1, 2010.

## Solution to Exercise 16-8

(a)    **Explanation and Approach:** Follow the steps for computing EPS as outlined in **Illustration 16-2**.

Step 1:        **Compute the weighted average number of common stock shares outstanding.**
There were no changes in the 200,000 shares of common stock outstanding during 2010. Therefore, the weighted average is 200,000 shares.

Step 2:        **Compute basic EPS before any assumptions** (basic formula without adjustment).

$$\frac{\$400,000 \; - \; \$0}{200,000} = \underline{\$2.00}$$

Step 3:        **Compute diluted earnings per share.**
- Use the treasury stock method for the options.
- Use the quick test to determine if these options are dilutive. Compare the option price and the current market price. The option price ($40) is less than the average market price ($50), so the options will have a dilutive effect on EPS.
- Adjust the basic formula:

$$\frac{\$400,000 \; - \; \$0}{200,000 \; + \; 40,000^{\,a} \; - \; 32,000^{\,b}} = \underline{\$1.92}$$

[a]Number of shares to be issued upon exercise of options.
[b]Number of shares that could be purchased for the treasury at $50 (average market price for the period) per share from the proceeds of the exercise of the options:
    40,000 x $40 = $1,600,000 proceeds
    $1,600,000 ÷ $50 = 32,000 assumed treasury shares

TIP:    Notice the incremental number of shares calculated by use of the treasury stock method is 8,000 in this example (40,000 - 32,000). If the average market price was less than the option price, the number of assumed treasury shares would exceed the number of shares assumed issued upon exercise of the options, and the result would be to decrease the denominator from the figure used in the basic formula. That decrease in the denominator would have an antidilutive effect on EPS; therefore, the exercise of the options would **not** be assumed in that circumstance. **Never make assumptions in computing diluted EPS that are antidilutive.**

TIP:    Notice why the treasury stock method is so named; the proceeds from the assumed exercise of stock options are assumed to be used for the purchase of treasury stock.

Jeremy Sherr Corporation should report a dual presentation for 2010 as follows:

$2.00 basic earnings per share, and
$1.92 diluted earnings per share

(b)    The exercise of the options would be assumed to have taken place on April 1 rather than at the beginning of the year. Therefore, the assumed shares in the denominator would have to be weighted as follows:

$$9/12 \ (40,000 - 32,000) = 6,000$$

Therefore, the computation for diluted EPS would then be:

$$\frac{\$400,000}{200,000 \ + \ 6,000} = \underline{\$1.94} \text{ diluted EPS.}$$

# *EXERCISE 16-9

**Purpose:**    (L.O. 7, 9) This exercise will illustrate the proper treatment of convertible securities in the EPS computations. It will also demonstrate how to test for dilution when more than one potentially dilutive security exists.

The following data pertain to the Star Trek Corporation at December 31, 2010:

| | |
|---|---|
| Net income for the year | $1,600,000 |
| 6% convertible bonds issued at par in a prior year, convertible | |
| into 200,000 shares of common stock | $3,000,000 |
| 8% convertible, cumulative, preferred stock, $100 par, issued in a | |
| prior year (each share is convertible into 6 shares of common) | $2,000,000 |
| Common stock, $10 par, issued in prior years | $6,000,000 |
| Additional paid-in capital | $3,400,000 |
| Retained earnings | $5,200,000 |
| Tax rate for 2010 | 40% |

There were no changes during 2010 in the number of common stock shares, preferred stock shares, or convertible bonds outstanding. There is no treasury stock held.

# Instructions
(a)    Compute the basic earnings per share for 2010.
(b)    Compute the diluted earnings per share for 2010.
(c)    Explain whether a dual presentation should be presented for EPS for 2010.

## Solution to Exercise 16-9

(a)   $2.40 (See Step 2 below.)

(b)   $1.86 (See Step 3 below.)

(c)   Yes, a dual presentation must be reported in 2010 because the corporation has some dilutive securities outstanding.

> **TIP:**   Whenever a situation involves the EPS computation(s), follow the steps (in order) listed in **Illustration 16-2**. By using this organized approach to these situations, you are less likely to overlook guidelines that may affect your solution.

**Approach and Explanation:**
**Step 1:**   **Compute the weighted average number of common stock shares outstanding.**
There were no changes in the number of common shares outstanding during 2010. There are no treasury shares; thus, the number of shares outstanding is equal to the number of shares issued. The number of common shares issued can be computed by:

$$\$6,000,000 \div \$10 \text{ par} = 600,000 \text{ shares}$$

**Step 2:**   **Compute basic EPS (before any assumptions).**

$$\frac{\$1,600,000 \ - \ \$160,000^a}{600,000} = \underline{\$2.40}$$

[a]8% x $2,000,000 par = $160,000 preferred dividends.

> **TIP:**   Recall that with cumulative preferred stock, the preferred's current year preference as to dividends is deducted in the basic EPS formula, whether or not the dividends were declared.

**Step 3:**   **Compute diluted earnings per share.**

$$\frac{\$1,600,000 \ - \ \$160,000 \ + \ \$180,000^a \ - \ \$72,000^b \ + \ \$160,000}{600,000 \ + \ 200,000 \ + \ 6(20,000)^c} = \underline{\$1.86}$$

[a]6% x $3,000,000 par = $180,000 interest expense.
[b]$180,000 interest x 40% tax rate = $72,000 tax effect of interest.
[c]$2,000,000 par ÷ $100 per share = 20,000 shares of preferred issued.

> **TIP:**   Notice why the "if converted method" is so named; the earnings per share computation assumes conversion of the convertible securities.

When there is more than one potentially dilutive security outstanding, the steps for computing diluted earnings per share are as follows:

1. Determine, for each dilutive security, the per share effect assuming exercise/conversion.
2. Rank the results from Step 1 from smallest to largest earnings effect per share; that is, rank the results from most dilutive to least dilutive.
3. Beginning with the earnings per share based upon the weighted average of common shares outstanding ($2.40 in this problem), recalculate earnings per share by adding the smallest per share effects from Step 2. If the results from this recalculation are less than $2.40, proceed to the next smallest per share effect and recalculate earnings per share. This process is continued so long as each recalculated earnings per share is smaller than the previous amount. The process will end either because there are no more securities to test or a particular security maintains or increases earnings per share (is antidilutive).

> **TIP:** This means that dilutive potential common stock with the lowest "earnings per incremental share" will be included in diluted EPS before those with a higher "earnings per incremental share."

The 3 steps are now applied to the Star Trek Corporation. The Star Trek Corporation has two securities (6% and 8% convertible bonds) that could reduce EPS.

The first step in the computation of diluted earnings per share is to determine a per share effect for each potentially dilutive security.

## Step 1: Determine the per share effect of each dilutive security.
**Convertible bonds:**

| | |
|---|---:|
| Interest expense for year (6% x $3,000,000) | $180,000 |
| Income tax reduction due to interest (40% x $180,000) | 72,000 |
| Interest expense avoided (net of tax) | $108,000 |
| | |
| Number of additional common shares issued assuming conversion of bonds | 200,000 |

Per share effect:

$$\frac{\text{Incremental Numerator Effect:}}{\text{Incremental Denominator Effect:}} \quad \frac{\$108,000}{200,000 \text{ shares}} = \$.54$$

**Convertible preferred stock:**

| | |
|---|---:|
| Dividend requirement on cumulative preferred (20,000 shares X 8% X $100) | $160,000 |
| Income tax effect (dividends are not a tax deduction) | none |
| Dividend requirement avoided | $160,000 |
| | |
| Number of additional common shares issued assuming conversion of preferred (6 x 20,000 shares) | 120,000 |

Per share effect:

| | | | |
|---|---|---|---|
| Incremental Numerator Effect: | $160,000 | = | $1.33 |
| Incremental Denominator Effect: | 120,000 shares | | |

### Step 2:  Rank the results from Step 1.

The ranking of the two potentially dilutive securities is as follows (lowest earnings per incremental share to the largest):

| | Effect Per Share |
|---|---|
| 1.  6% convertible bonds | $.54 |
| 2.  8% convertible preferred | 1.33 |

### Step 3:  Determine diluted earnings per share.

The next step is to determine earnings per share giving effect to the ranking above. Starting with the earnings per share of $2.40 computed previously, add the incremental effects of the options to the original calculation, as follows:

#### 6% Convertible Bonds

| | |
|---|---|
| Numerator from previous calculation | $1,440,000 |
| Add: Interest expense avoided (net of tax) | 108,000 |
| Total | $1,548,000 |
| | |
| Denominator from previous calculation (shares) | 600,000 |
| Add: Number of common shares assumed issued upon assumed conversion of bonds | 200,000 |
| Total | 800,000 |
| | |
| Recomputed earnings per share ($1,548,000 ÷ 800,000 shares) | $1.94 |

Since the recomputed earnings per share is reduced (from $2.40 to $1.94), the effect of the 6% bonds is dilutive.

Next, earnings per share is recomputed assuming the conversion of the 8% preferred stock. This is shown below:

#### 8% Convertible Preferred

| | |
|---|---|
| Numerator from previous calculation | $1,548,000 |
| Add: Dividend requirement avoided | 160,000 |
| Total | $1,708,000 |
| | |
| Denominator from previous calculation (shares) | 800,000 |
| Add: Number of common shares assumed issued upon conversion of preferred stock | 120,000 |
| Total | 920,000 |
| | |
| Recomputed earnings per share ($1,708,000 ÷ 920,000 shares) | $1.86 |

Since the recomputed earnings per share is reduced, the effect of the 8% convertible preferred is dilutive. Diluted earnings per share is $1.86.

# ILLUSTRATION 16-4
# ACCOUNTING FOR STOCK- APPRECIATION RIGHTS (L.O. 8)

The use of stock-appreciation rights is a stock-based compensation plan whereby the company gives an executive the right to receive compensation equal to share appreciation. Share appreciation is the excess of the market price of the stock at the date of exercise over a pre-established price. The company may pay the share appreciation in cash, shares, or a combination of both. The company simply awards the executive cash or stock having a market value equivalent to the appreciation   over a period of time. The accounting for stock appreciation rights depends on whether the company classifies the rights as equity or as a liability.

a. **SARs-Share-Based Equity-Awards.**
In an equity SAR, the holder receives (upon exercise) the shares with a market value in an amount equal to the share price appreciation (the difference between the market price and the pre-established price). At the date of grant, the company determines a fair value for the SAR and then allocates this amount to compensation expense over the service period of the employees, similar to the accounting for stock options granted.

b. **SARS-Share- Based Liability Awards.**
In a liability SAR, the holder receives a cash payment (rather than shares) equal to the amount of share price appreciation. The company's compensation expense therefore changes as the value of the liability changes.

The following procedures are followed:

1. Measure the fair value of the award at the grant date and accrue compensation over the service period. Debit Compensation Expense and credit Liability Under Stock Appreciation Plan.
2. Remeasure the fair value each reporting period, until the award is settled, and adjust the compensation cost each period for changes in fair value pro-rated for the portion of the service period completed. (In a period that the value of the stock declines, a negative expense may be recorded as a debit to Liability Under Stock Appreciation Plan and a credit to Compensation Expense.)
3. Once the service period is completed, determine compensation expense each subsequent period by reporting the full change in market price as an adjustment to compensation expense.
4. The payout to the employee removes the liability and an entry is made to debit Liability Under Stock Appreciation Plan and to credit Cash.


# ANALYSIS OF MULTIPLE-CHOICE TYPE QUESTIONS

**QUESTION**
1. (L.O. 1) For the purpose of inducing conversion, a corporation with convertible bonds increases the number of common shares into which this debt may be converted. Upon conversion, the fair value of the additional shares given should be reported as:
a.    an expense of the current period.
b.    an extraordinary item.
c.    a direct reduction of owners' equity.
d.    a deferred expense.

**Explanation:** When an issuer offers some form of additional consideration (cash, other assets, or common stock), called "sweetener," to induce conversion of convertible debt, *SFAS No. 84* requires that the sweetener be recognized as an expense equal to the fair value of the additional securities or other consideration given. (Solution = a.)

**QUESTION**

2.   (L.O. 1) The Goodings Corporation issued 1,000 8% convertible bonds with a face value of $1,000 each at a price of 102. An underwriter advised the corporation that without the conversion feature, the bonds could not have been issued at a price above 99. At the date of issuance, the amount to be recorded as paid-in capital attributable to the conversion feature is:

a.   $0.
b.   $10,000.
c.   $20,000.
d.   $30,000.

**Approach and Explanation:** State the rule related to accounting for the issuance of convertible bonds. All proceeds received from the issuance of convertible debt are to be recorded in liability accounts; none of the proceeds is to be allocated to the conversion feature under current generally accepted accounting principles. The journal entry to record the issuance of these bonds is no different than the recording of bonds without the conversion feature. That entry would be as follows for the bonds in question:

| | | |
|---|---:|---:|
| Cash | 1,020,000 | |
| Bonds Payable | | 1,000,000 |
| Premium on Bonds Payable | | 20,000 |

(Solution = a.)

**QUESTION**

3.   (L.O. 1) A corporation issued convertible bonds with a face value of $800,000 at a discount. At a date when the unamortized discount was $50,000, the bonds were converted to stock having a par value of $200,000 and a market value of $870,000. Using the book value method, the amount of gain/loss to record on the conversion is:

a.   $0.
b.   $70,000.
c.   $120,000.
d.   $670,000.

**Approach and Explanation:**  Reconstruct the journal entry to record the conversion. The book value of bonds is removed from the accounts and that book value amount is recorded in appropriate stockholders' equity accounts. There is **never** a gain or loss recognized when the book value method is used to record the conversion of bonds to stock. The journal entry is as follows:

| | | |
|---|---:|---:|
| Bonds Payable | 800,000 | |
| Discount on Bonds Payable | | 50,000 |
| Common Stock | | 200,000 |
| Paid-in Capital in Excess of Par | | 550,000 |

Support for the book value method is based on the argument that an agreement was  established at the date of the issuance either to pay a stated amount of cash at maturity or to issue a stated number of shares of equity securities. Therefore, when the debt is converted to equity in accordance with the preexisting contract terms, no gain or loss should be recognized upon conversion.
        (Solution = a.)

**QUESTION**

4.   (L.O. 3) A corporation issues bonds with detachable warrants. The amount to be recorded as paid-in capital is preferably:

a.   zero.
b.   calculated by the excess of the proceeds over the face amount of the bonds.
c.   equal to the market value of the warrants.

d.        based on the relative market values of the two securities involved.

**Explanation:** When both the market value of a warrant and the market value of a bond ex-warrant are known, the proportional method is to be employed; hence, the proceeds are allocated to the warrant (paid-in capital) and the debt instrument (liabilities), based on the relative market values of the warrants and bonds. The incremental method (answer section "c") would be appropriate in this case if the market value of the bonds ex-warrants is not known. Answer section "a" (zero) is appropriate only if the warrants are nondetachable (another type of convertible debt instrument). (Solution = d.)

**QUESTION**
5.    (L.O. 3) The distribution of stock rights to existing common stockholders will increase paid-in capital at the:

|     | Date of<br>Issuance of<br>the Rights | Date of<br>Exercise of<br>the Rights |
|-----|-----------------|-----------------|
| a.  | Yes | Yes |
| b.  | Yes | No  |
| c.  | No  | Yes |
| d.  | No  | No  |

**Approach and Explanation:** Quickly reconstruct and review the journal entries involved in accounting for stock rights. Analyze the effect of each entry on paid-in capital. At the date of issuance of the rights, there is no debit and credit entry; thus, no effect on paid-in capital. At the date of exercise, assets and paid-in capital increase by the exercise price multiplied by the number of related shares. (Solution = c.)

| TIP: | A **stock right** is defined as a privilege extended by a corporation to acquire additional shares of its capital stock. A **stock warrant** is defined as the physical evidence of stock rights. The warrant specifies the number of rights conveyed, the number of shares to which the rightholder is entitled, the exercise price, and the exercise period. Although the terms "stock right" and "stock warrant" have distinct meanings, they are often used interchangeably; thus, "to record the issuance of stock rights" means the same thing as "to record the issuance of stock warrants." |
|------|------|

**QUESTION**
6.    (L.O. 4) Stock options allowing selected executives to acquire 10,000 shares of $1 par common stock are granted on January 1, 2010. The market price at January 1, 2010 is $22. The option price is $10. The options are for services to be performed over four years from the date of grant. The options become exercisable on January 1, 2012 and expire on December 31, 2014. An option pricing model estimates the fair value of each option to be $30. The amount of compensation cost related to these options to be charged to expense for 2010 (using the fair value method) is:

a.    $60,000.
b.    $75,000.
c.    $120,000.
d.    $150,000.
e.    $0.

**Explanation:** The fair value of the options = $30 X 10,000 = $300,000. The fair value of the options is the measure of compensation cost to be recognized as expense over the service period (which is stated to be four years). $300,000 ÷ 4 years = $75,000 per year. (Solution = b.)

**QUESTION**

7. (L.O. 4) Stock options allowing selected executives to acquire 10,000 shares of $1 par common stock are granted on January 1, 2010. The market price at January 1, 2010 is $22. The option price is $10. The options become exercisable on January 1, 2012 and expire on December 31, 2014. The option pricing model estimates the fair value of each option to be $30. The amount of compensation cost related to these options to be charged to expense for 2010 if the intrinsic value method is used is:

a. $0.
b. $24,000.
c. $30,000.
d. $60,000.
e. $120,000.

**Approach and Explanation:** (1) Compute the total compensation cost. It is the excess of the market price over the option price at the grant date. Therefore, ($22 - $10) X 10,000 shares = $120,000 total compensation cost. (2) Determine the service period—span of time over which the employees are to provide services in exchange for the options. Unless otherwise specified, the service period is the vesting period—the time between the grant date and the vesting date. In this case, that is years 2010 and 2011. (3) Divide total compensation cost ($120,000) by the service period (2 years) to arrive at $60,000 per year. Note: The intrinsic value method is **no** longer acceptable to be used for reporting purposes. (Solution = d.)

**QUESTION**

8. (L.O. 4) On January 1, 2010 Stuart Chandler, Inc. granted stock options to officers and key employees for the purchase of 100,000 shares of the company's $1 par common stock at $20 per share as additional compensation for services to be rendered over the next two years. The options are exercisable during a four-year period beginning January 1, 2012 by grantees still employed by Stuart Chandler. The market price of Stuart Chandler's common stock was $26 per share at the date of grant. An option pricing model estimates the fair value of each option to be $32. Assuming the fair-value method is used, the journal entry to record the compensation expense related to these options for 2010 would include a credit to the Paid-in Capital—Stock Options account for:

a. $50,000.
b. $300,000.
c. $600,000.
d. $1,600,000.
e. $3,200,000.

**Approach and Explanation:** Reconstruct the journal entry to record the compensation expense for 2010. It would be as follows:

Compensation Expense          1,600,000
        Paid-in Capital—Stock Options ..........................................................          1,600,000

The total compensation cost is determined by the fair value of an option ($32) multiplied by the number of options granted (100,000 options). The total compensation cost is allocated to the periods included in the service period (two years). $3,200,000 ÷ 2 = $1,600,000. (Solution = d.)

**QUESTION**

9. (L.O. 6) Peter Wong Corporation had net income reported for 2010 of $880,000. During 2010 dividends of $120,000 were declared on preferred stock and $200,000 were declared on common stock. There were no changes in the 200,000 shares of common stock or the 40,000 shares of preferred stock outstanding during 2010. There were no potentially dilutive securities outstanding. The earnings per share to be reported for 2010 is:

a. $4.40.
b. $3.80.
c. $3.67.

d.    $2.80.
e.    none of the above.

**Approach and Explanation:** Write down the basic EPS formula. Solve using the data in this question.

$$\frac{\text{Net Income} \quad - \quad \text{Preferred Stock Dividends}}{\text{Weighted Average Number of Common Shares Outstanding}}$$

$$\frac{\$880,000 \ - \ \$120,000}{200,000} = \underline{\$3.80}$$

(Solution = b.)

**QUESTION**
10.(L.O. 6) The following data pertain to the Colby Corporation:

|  |  |  |
|---|---|---|
| January 1, 2010 | Shares outstanding | 500,000 |
| April 1, 2010 | Shares issued | 80,000 |
| July 1, 2010 | Treasury shares purchased | 30,000 |
| October 1, 2010 | Shares issued in a 100% stock dividend | 550,000 |

The number of shares to be used in computing earnings per common share for 2010 is:
a.    682,500.
b.    1,090,000.
c.    1,095,000.
d.    1,100,000.
e.    1,130,000.

**Approach and Explanation:**  Follow the steps listed in **Illustration 16-3** to compute the weighted average number of common stock shares outstanding for 2010.

| Date |  | Weighted Average |
|---|---|---|
| 1/1/10 | 500,000 X 12/12 = | 500,000 |
| 4/1/10 | 80,000 X 9/12 = | 60,000 |
|  | New balance | 560,000 |
| 7/1/10 | 30,000 X 6/12 = | (15,000) |
|  | New balance | 545,000 |
| 10/1/10 | 100% stock dividend | X    200%* |
|  | New balance | 1,090,000 |

*The appropriate multiple for a stock dividend is 100% plus the percentage used in the dividend. Thus, 100% + 100% dividend = 200% as the multiplier.  (Solution = b.)

**QUESTION**
11.    (L.O. 6) Refer to **Question 10** above. The number of shares actually outstanding at the end of 2010 is:
a.    550,000.
b.    1,100,000.
c.    1,130,000.
d.    1,160,000.

**Explanation:**

| Date |  | Weighted Average |
|---|---|---|
| 1/1/10 | Balance | 500,000 |
| 4/1/10 | Issued for assets | 80,000 |
|  | New balance | 580,000 |
| 7/1/10 | Acquired for treasury | (30,000) |
|  | New balance | 550,000 |
| 10/1/10 | 100% stock dividend | 550,000 |

New balance                                                  1,100,000
                                                      (Solution = b.)

**QUESTION**
12. (L.O. 6) At December 31, 2009 Opal Company had 200,000 shares of common stock and 5,000 shares of 8%, $100 par value cumulative preferred stock outstanding. No dividends were declared on either the preferred or common stock in 2009 or 2010 On February 10, 2011, prior to the issuance of its financial statements for the year ended December 31, 2010, Opal declared a 100% stock split on its common stock. Net income for 2010 was $480,000. In its 2010 financial statements, Opal's 2010 earnings per common share should be:

a.  $2.40.
b.  $2.20.
c.  $2.00.
d.  $1.20.
e.  $1.10.
f.  $1.00.

**Explanation:**   $\dfrac{\$480,000 - 5,000(8\% \times \$100)}{200,000 \times 2} = \underline{\$1.10}$

Dividends on **cumulative** preferred stock are deducted in the numerator, whether declared or not. However, only the current year's preference is used; dividends in arrears for prior years do not affect the EPS computation. Stock dividends and stock splits are given retroactive treatment for all periods presented, even if they occur after the end of the current year, but before the financial statements are issued. (Solution = e.)

**QUESTION**
13. (L.O. 6, 7) Tempo, Inc. had 200,000 shares of common stock issued and outstanding at December 31, 2009. On July 1, 2010 an additional 200,000 shares were issued for cash. Tempo also had stock options outstanding at the beginning and end of 2010 which allow the holders to purchase 60,000 shares of common stock at $20 per share. The average market price of Tempo's common stock was $15 during 2010. The market price of Tempo's common stock was $25 at December 31, 2010. What is the number of shares that should be used in computing diluted earnings per share for the year ended December 31, 2010?

a.  400,000
b.  300,000
c.  360,000
d.  415,000
e.  320,000
f.  280,000

**Approach and Explanation:** Use the treasury stock method to compute the number of shares to be used in determining diluted EPS. **However**, only make assumptions about the exercise of stock options when those assumptions are **not** antidilutive. A quick test to determine whether these options are dilutive or antidilutive is to compare the average market price ($15) with the option price ($20). The market price is **not** higher; therefore, the assumed exercise of stock options in applying the treasury stock method when computing EPS will have an antidilutive effect. Therefore, no assumptions should be made. Only the weighted average actual outstanding shares should be used in computing EPS in this situation.

| | | | |
|---|---|---|---|
| Jan. 1 Shares outstanding: 200,000 x 12/12 | = | 200,000 | |
| July 1 Issued for assets: 200,000 x 6/12 | = | 100,000 | |
| Weighted average shares outstanding | = | 300,000 | (Solution = b.) |

**TIP:** You could calculate EPS using the basic formula and calculate diluted EPS assuming the exercise of the options and application of the treasury stock method. Because this would entail an assumption of $1,200,000 proceeds being used to buy back stock at $15 (average market price) per share, this would result in making adjustments to the denominator as follows:

> - Add 60,000 shares because of assumed exercise of options.
> - Deduct 80,000 shares because of assumed purchase of treasury stock with $1,200,000 proceeds from assumed exercise of options.
>
> The net result of these assumptions is a **decrease** in the number of shares used to calculate diluted EPS, which indicates an antidilutive effect on EPS. Thus, these assumptions should **not** be made in the scenario described in this question.

## QUESTION

14. (L.O. 6, 7) Refer to the facts of **Question 13** above. If the average market price of Tempo's common stock was $25 rather than $15 during 2010, what is the number of shares that should be used in computing diluted earnings per share for the year ended December 31, 2010?
    a. 330,000
    b. 448,000
    c. 412,000
    d. 320,000
    e. 348,000
    f. 312,000

**Approach and Explanation:** Use the treasury stock method to compute the number of shares to be used in determining diluted EPS. The weighted average number of shares actually outstanding is 300,000 (see Explanation to **Question 13** above for this computation). The average market price of the common stock ($25) should be used in determining the number of assumed treasury stock shares in computing diluted EPS. The average market price ($25) of Tempo's common stock exceeds the option price ($20); thus the effect of assuming the exercise of the options and purchase of treasury stock with the assumed proceeds is dilutive. Thus, the computation of the number of shares used in computing diluted EPS is as follows:

| | |
|---|---:|
| Weighted average actual shares outstanding | 300,000 |
| Shares assumed issued upon exercise of options | 60,000 |
| Assumed shares purchased for the treasury ($1,200,000 ÷ $25) | (48,000) |
| Shares used for denominator of diluted EPS | 312,000 |

(Solution = f.)

> **TIP:** A comparison of 312,000 shares (determined by use of the treasury stock method) with the weighted average number of common stock shares actually outstanding (300,000) indicates a dilutive effect on EPS.

## QUESTION

15. (L.O. 7) A convertible bond issue should be included in the diluted earnings per share computation as if the bonds had been converted into common stock, if the effect of its inclusion is:

| | **Dilutive** | **Antidilutive** |
|---|---|---|
| a. | Yes | Yes |
| b. | Yes | No |
| c. | No | Yes |
| d. | No | No |

**Explanation:** A convertible security is a potentially dilutive security. All potentially dilutive securities should be included in the diluted EPS computation, if the effect of inclusion is dilutive. **No** antidilutive assumptions are to be made in computing diluted EPS. (Solution = b.)

# CHAPTER 17

# INVESTMENTS

## OVERVIEW

Oftentimes an entity has cash that is temporarily in excess of its immediate needs. That cash should be invested wisely so that it produces income while being a ready source of funds. Sometimes an entity invests in the stocks and bonds of other entities for long-term purposes. Accounting for both short-term (temporary) and long-term investments is discussed in this chapter.

## SUMMARY OF LEARNING OBJECTIVES

1. **Identify the three categories of debt securities and describe the accounting and reporting treatment for each category.** (1) **Held-to-maturity debt securities:** Carry and report at amortized cost. (2) **Trading debt securities:** Value for reporting purposes at fair value, with unrealized holding gains or losses included in net income. (3) **Available-for-sale debt securities**: Value for reporting purposes at fair value, with unrealized holding gains or losses reported as other comprehensive income and as a separate component of stockholders' equity.

2. **Understand the procedures for discount and premium amortization on bond investments.** Similar to bonds payable, companies should amortize discount or premium on bond investments using the effective-interest method. They apply the effective interest rate or yield to the beginning carrying value of the investment for each interest period in order to compute interest revenue.

3. **Identify the categories of equity securities and describe the accounting and reporting treatment for each category.** The degree to which one corporation (investor) acquires an interest in the common stock of another corporation (investee) generally determines the accounting treatment for the investment. Long-term investments by one corporation in the common stock of another can be classified according to the percentage of the voting stock of the investee held by the investor. Refer to **Illustration 18-3** for a summary of the accounting and reporting for equity securities by category.

4. **Explain the equity method of accounting and compare it to the fair value method for equity securities.** Under the equity method, the investor and the investee acknowledge a substantive economic relationship. The company originally records the investment at cost but subsequently adjusts the amount each period for changes in the net assets of the investee. That is, the investor's proportionate share of the earnings (losses) of the investee periodically increases (decreases) the investment's carrying amount. All dividends received by the investor from the investee decrease the investment's carrying value. Under the fair value method, a company reports the equity investment at fair value each reporting period irrespective of the investee's earnings or dividends paid to the investor. A company applies the equity method to investment holdings between 20% and 50% of ownership. It applies the fair value method to holdings below 20%.

5.   **Describe the accounting for the fair value option.** Companies have the option to report most financial instruments at fair value, with all gains and losses related to changes in fair value reported in the income statement. This option is applied on an instrument-by-instrument basis. The fair value option is generally available only at the time a company first purchases the financial asset or incurs a financial liability. If a company chooses to use the fair value option, it must "measure" this instrument at fair value until the company no longer has ownership.

6.   **Discuss the accounting for impairments of debt and equity investments.** Impairments of debt and equity securities are losses in value that are determined to be other than temporary, are based on a fair value test, and are charged to income.

7.   **Explain why companies report reclassification adjustments.** A company needs a reclassification adjustment when it reports realized gains or losses as part of net income but also shows the amounts as part of other comprehensive income in the current or in previous periods. Companies should report unrealized holding gains or losses related to available-for-sale securities in other comprehensive income and the aggregate balance as accumulated comprehensive income on the balance sheet.

8.   **Describe the accounting for transfers of investment securities between categories.** Transfers of securities between categories of investments are accounted for at fair value, with unrealized holding gains or losses treated in accordance with the nature of the transfer.

*9.  **Explain who uses derivatives and why.** Any company or individual that wants to ensure against different types of business risks often uses derivative contracts to achieve this objective. In general, these transactions involve some type of hedge. Speculators also use derivatives, attempting to find an enhanced return. Speculators are very important to the derivatives market because they keep the market liquid on a daily basis. Arbitrageurs attempt to exploit inefficiencies in various derivative contracts. A company primarily uses derivatives for purposes of hedging a company's exposure to fluctuations in interest rates, foreign currency exchange rates, and commodity prices.
        *This material is covered in Appendix 17A in the text.

*10.  **Understand the basic guidelines for accounting for derivatives.** Companies should recognize derivatives in the financial statements as assets and liabilities and report them at fair value. Companies should recognize gains and losses resulting from speculation immediately in income. They report gains and losses resulting from hedge transactions in different ways, depending upon the type of hedge.
        *This material is covered in Appendix 17A in the text.

*11.  **Describe the accounting for derivative financial instruments.** A company records derivative financial instruments at fair value and reports them in the balance sheet at fair value. Except for derivatives used in hedging, companies record realized and unrealized gains and losses on derivative financial instruments in income.
        *This material is covered in Appendix 17A in the text.

*12.  **Explain how to account for a fair value hedge.** A company records the derivative used in a qualifying fair value hedge at its fair value and reports it in the balance sheet, recording any gains and losses in income. In addition, the company also accounts for the item being hedged with the derivative at fair value. By adjusting the hedged item to fair value, with the gain or loss recorded in earnings, the accounting for the hedged item may deviate from GAAP in the absence of a hedge relationship. This special accounting is justified in order to report accurately the nature of the hedging relationship between the derivative hedging instruments and the hedged item. A company reports both in the balance sheet at fair value, reporting offsetting gains and losses in income in the same period.
        *This material is covered in Appendix 17A in the text.

*13.     **Explain how to account for a cash flow hedge.** Companies account for derivatives used in qualifying cash flow hedges at fair value on the balance sheet, but record gains or losses in equity as part of other comprehensive income. Companies accumulate these gains or losses and reclassify them in income when the hedged transaction's cash flows affect earnings. Accounting is according to GAAP for the hedged item.

         *This material is covered in Appendix 17A in the text.

*14.     **Identify the special reporting issues related to derivative financial instruments that cause unique accounting problems.** A company should separate a derivative that is embedded in a hybrid security from the host security and account for it using the accounting for derivatives. This separation process is referred to as bifurcation. Special hedge accounting is allowed only for hedging relationships that meet certain criteria. The main criteria are: (1) There is formal documentation of the hedging relationship, the entity's risk management objective, and the strategy for undertaking the hedge, and the company designates the derivative as either a cash flow or fair value hedge. (2) The company expects the hedging relationship to be highly effective in achieving offsetting changes in fair value or cash flows. (3) "Special" hedge accounting is necessary only when there is a mismatch of the accounting effects for the hedging instrument and the hedged item under GAAP.

         *This material is covered in Appendix 17A in the text.

**15.    **Describe the accounting for variable-interest entities.** Special variable-interest accounting is used in situations where control cannot be determined based on voting rights. A company is required to consolidate a variable-interest entity if it is the primary beneficiary of the variable-interest entity.

         **This material is covered in Appendix 17B in the text.

## TIPS ON CHAPTER TOPICS

**TIP:** The emphasis of this chapter is on accounting for investments in debt and equity securities. These investments may be classified under current assets or long-term investments. Also included in the long-term investment classification of a corporation's balance sheet are the following: (1) long-term receivables, (2) long-term investments in stocks and bonds and stock rights of other entities, (3) restricted funds, (4) cash surrender value of life insurance, and (5) land held for future plant site.

**TIP:** The cost of an investment includes its purchase price and all other costs necessary to acquire the investment. Thus, the cost of an investment in stock or bonds is likely to include broker commissions and incidental fees.

**TIP:** A significant portion of the details of this chapter pertain to the following points: Changes in the valuation account for investment securities classified as trading should be included in the determination of **net income** of the period in which they occur. The amount of increase or decrease in the valuation account for investment securities classified as available-for-sale should be reported as a component of **other comprehensive income**; the amount of accumulated changes in this valuation account should be included in the equity section of the balance sheet and shown separately there as part of Accumulated Other Comprehensive Income. (Selection of the fair value option will eliminate the need for a valuation account and changes of fair value will then be included in **net income** rather than other comprehensive income).

**TIP:** Premiums and discounts on investments in debt securities should be amortized. The **effective interest method** is the prescribed method; however, the **straight-line method** is often justifiably used based on the immaterial difference between its results and the effect of the preferable method. Other names for the **effective interest method** include **present value method**, **compound interest method**, **effective yield method**, **yield method**, **interest method**, and the **effective method**. The term **accumulation of bond investment discount** is another way of referring to amortization of discount on bonds held as an investment.

**TIP:** An investment in stocks or bonds of other companies may be classified as a current asset (if it is a short-term investment) or as a noncurrent asset (if it is a long-term investment). For an investment in available-for-sale securities to be classified as a **current asset**: (1) it should be readily marketable, and (2) there should be a lack of management intent to hold it for long-term purposes.

**TIP:** If the **effective interest method of amortization** is used to account for an investment in bonds, the following relationships will exist:
1. The interest rate is constant each period.
2. The interest revenue is an increasing amount each period if the bond is purchased as a discount (because a constant rate is applied to an increasing carrying amount each period).
3. The interest revenue is a decreasing amount each period if the bond is purchased at a premium (because a constant rate is applied to a decreasing carrying amount each period).
4. The amount of amortization increases each period because the difference between the effective interest revenue and the cash interest widens each period.

**TIP:** Review **Illustration 14-2** for formats for common computations involving bonds payable. Think about how those same formats can be used to apply to computations involving an investment in bonds; the major difference is that the investor has an asset (rather than a liability) and interest revenue (rather than interest expense). Also, the investor lacks unamortized debt issue costs and will have a gain (rather than a loss) if the redemption price is higher than the bond's carrying value.

**TIP:** Review **Illustration 14-3** for the graph to depict interest patterns for bonds. Notice how that graph can be used to solve questions relating to bonds held as an investment; simply change interest expense to interest revenue when using the graph from an investor's viewpoint.

**TIP:** When the accounting period ends on a date other than an interest date, the amortization schedule for a bond investment is unaffected by this fact. That is, the schedule is prepared and computations are made according to the bond interest periods, ignoring the details of the accounting period. The interest revenue amounts shown in the amortization schedule are then apportioned to the appropriate accounting period(s). As an example, if the interest revenue for the six months ending April 30, 2010 is $120,000, then $40,000 of that amount would go on the income statement for the 2009 calendar year and $80,000 of it should be reflected on the income statement for the 2010 calendar year.

**\*TIP:** In a general sense, **financial instruments** are defined as cash, an ownership interest in an entity, or a contractual right to receive or deliver cash or another financial instrument on potentially favorable or unfavorable terms. By this definition, traditional assets and liabilities such as accounts and notes receivable, accounts and notes payable, investment in debt and equity securities, and bonds payable are considered financial instruments. But the definition also includes many innovative and complex financial instruments such as futures, options, forwards, and swaps.

These innovative financial instruments are referred to as **derivative financial instruments** (or just simply "derivatives") because their value is derived from the value of some underlying asset, (i.e., stocks, bonds, or commodities) or is tied to a basic indicator (i.e., interest rates, Dow-Jones Industrial average). The following are some of the most common financial instruments.

| **Traditional** | **Derivatives** |
|---|---|
| Accounts receivable and payable | Interest-rate swaps and options |
| Corporate bonds and notes | Currency futures and options |
| Municipal bonds | Stock-index futures and options |
| Treasury bonds, bills, and notes | Caps, floors, and collars |
| Bank certificates of deposit | Commodity futures and options |
| Mortgages | Swaptions and leaps |
| Currencies | Collateralized mortgage obligations |

# ILLUSTRATION 17-1
# SUMMARY OF INVESTMENTS IN
# DEBT AND EQUITY SECURITIES (L.O. 1, 3, and 4)

Investments in the stocks of other companies are often referred to as investments in **equity securities** or stock investments. Investments in the bonds of other companies are often referred to as investments in **debt securities** or debt investments.

The major categories for investments in debt and equity securities and their reporting treatments are summarized below.

| Category | Balance Sheet | Income Statement |
|---|---|---|
| Trading (debt and equity securities) | Investments are shown at fair value. Current assets. | Interest and dividends are recognized as revenue. Unrealized holding gains and losses are included in income. Gains and losses from sale are included in income. |
| Available-for-Sale (debt and equity securities) | Investments are shown at fair value in current or long-term assets. Unrealized holding gains and losses are recognized in other comprehensive income and as a separate component of stockholders' equity. | Interest and dividends are recognized as revenue. Unrealized holding gains and losses are **not** included in net income; they are reported as other comprehensive income. Gains and losses from sale are included in net income. |
| Held-to-Maturity (debt securities) | Investments are shown at amortized cost (unrealized holding gains and losses are not recognized). Current or long-term assets. | Interest is recognized as revenue. Gains and losses from sale are included in income (it is rare to sell). |
| Equity method and/or Consolidation (equity securities) | Investments are carried at cost, are periodically adjusted by the investor's share of the investee's earnings or losses, and are decreased by all dividends received from the investee. Classified in long-term assets. | Revenue is recognized to the extent of the investee's earnings or losses reported subsequent to the date of investment (adjusted by amortization of the difference between cost and underlying book value). Gains and losses from sale are included in income. |

**TIP:** **Fair value** is the price that would be received to sell an asset or paid to transfer a liability in an orderly transaction between market participation at the measurement date. **Amortized cost** is the acquisition cost adjusted for the amortization of discount or premium, if appropriate.

**TIP:** Investments in debt securities and investments in equity securities that do **not** qualify for treatment by the equity method are categorized as follows:

**Trading securities:** Debt and equity securities held with the intention of selling them in a short period of time (generally less than a month); held to generate income on short-term price swings.

**Held-to-maturity securities:** Debt securities that the investor has the intent and ability to hold to maturity.

**Available-for-sale securities:** Debt and equity securities that are not classified as trading or held-to-maturity; securities that may be sold in the future.

## ILLUSTRATION 17-2
## USE OF A SECURITIES FAIR VALUE ADJUSTMENT ACCOUNT (L.O. 1, 3)

The only time an accountant records an entry affecting the Securities Fair Value Adjustment (Trading) account or the Securities Fair Value Adjustment (Available-for-Sale) account is in the adjusting process at the end of an accounting period. Thus, when securities are purchased and/or sold during the period, the accountant **ignores** the related valuation account and its contents. The balance of a valuation account should be adjusted as needed at the end of the period by performing the following three easy steps for the related portfolio (after recording permanent impairments for any individual securities):

**Step 1:**　　**Determine the total fair value:** Determine the aggregate fair value of the portfolio. This amount gets reported in the balance sheet.

**Step 2:**　　**Determine the desired balance in the related valuation account:** Compute the difference between the aggregate cost and the aggregate fair value of the portfolio at the balance sheet date.

**Step 3:**　　**Determine the amount of adjustment required:** Compare the result of Step 2 with the existing balance in the valuation account (which is the result of entries in previous periods, if any, and a reclassification adjustment, if any). The difference is the required adjustment (either increase or decrease in the valuation account).

| | |
|---|---|
| **TIP:** | Investments in debt and equity securities which are classified as trading or available-for-sale are initially recorded at cost, but they are to be reported at fair value at a balance sheet date. The writeup or writedown of such an investment will be accomplished by the use of a valuation account; thus, original cost information is preserved in the investment account. (If the fair value option is elected, the need for a valuation account is eliminated. This option is explained in **Illustration 17-5.**) |
| **TIP:** | When there is a price decline in a debt or equity security held as an investment, assume the decline is temporary unless otherwise indicated. |
| **TIP:** | If a decline in fair value is judged to be other than temporary for a security classified as available-for-sale or held-to-maturity, the cost basis of the individual security shall be written down to fair value as a new cost basis (thus, the investment account rather than the valuation account is credited). The amount of the writedown shall be accounted for as a realized loss and included in net income. The new cost basis is not changed for subsequent recoveries in fair value. Subsequent temporary changes in the fair value of an available-for-sale security are to be included in the separate component of equity. |
| **TIP:** | Temporary price declines and subsequent recoveries of market value affect net income **only if** they relate to trading securities (or if the fair value option is elected as explained in **Illustration 17-5.**) Permanent price declines (impairments) affect net income regardless of which classification the related securities are in. |

## ILLUSTRATION 17-2 (Continued)

**TIP:** The journal entry to record an increase in the fair value of securities held as an investment would be as follows:

Securities Fair Value Adjustment ............................................... xxx
          Unrealized Holding Gain or Loss.................................... xxx

The entry to adjust the valuation account for the trading securities classification is the same as the entry to adjust the valuation account for the available-for-sale classification; however, a change in the valuation account for the trading securities classification goes through earnings, whereas a change in the valuation account for the available-for-sale classification does **not** get reported in the net income figure; rather it is reported as a component of other comprehensive income which is transferred to a separate component of stockholders' equity called Accumulated Other Comprehensive Income.

**TIP:** For the available-for-sale classification, notice that the balance of the Securities Fair Value Adjustment account will **always** be equal in amount to the balance of the Unrealized Holding Gain or Loss—Equity account (because they are both real accounts and are always involved in an entry to adjust the portfolio to fair value). However, for the trading classification, the balance of the Securities Fair Value Adjustment account will **rarely** be equal in amount to the balance of the Unrealized Holding Gain or Loss—Income account for the current period (because the adjustment account is a real account and the other account is a nominal account).

**TIP:** **Market value** is usually used as a measure of **fair value** for investments in debt and equity securities.

**TIP:** The accounts, Gain on Sale of Securities, Loss of Sale of Securities, Unrealized Holding Gain or Loss—Income, and Loss on Impairment, are to be classified as "Other revenues, gains, expenses, and losses" on the multiple-step format for an income statement.

**TIP:** The balance of an investment account and its related valuation account are often combined and reported net on a balance sheet.

**TIP:** Significant net realized and net unrealized gains and losses that arise after the balance sheet date may be disclosed in the notes to the financial statements; they should **not** be reflected in the body of the statements.

**TIP:** If an investor purchases a security and later sells it for less than the security's cost, the investor has a **realized loss** (loss on sale of investment). If the market price of a security changes while an investor holds the security, changes in the market price (fair value) are referred to as **unrealized holding gains and losses.** Thus, if an investor purchased a security for $1,000 and the fair value is $700 at the balance sheet date, the investor has an unrealized holding loss of $300. If the security is one which is to be reported at fair value on the balance sheet, the writedown of the investment is accomplished by the use of a valuation account (Securities Fair Value Adjustment); thus, original cost information is preserved in the investment account.

## ILLUSTRATION 17-2 (Continued)

The journal entry to record the decline in the fair value of the investment if the security is classified as trading is as follows:

Unrealized Holding Gain or Loss—Income....................................        XX
       Securities Fair Value Adjustment (Trading)........................                XX

The effects of this entry on the basic accounting equation and on net income are as follows;

$$A = L + OE \quad NI$$
$$\downarrow \qquad \downarrow \quad \downarrow$$

The journal entry to record the decline in fair value if the security is classified as available-for-sale is as follows:

Unrealized Holding Gain or Loss—Equity .....................................        XX
       Securities Fair Value Adjustment (Available-for-Sale)..........                XX

The effects of this entry on the basic accounting equation and on net income are as follows:

$$A = L + OE \quad NI$$
$$\downarrow \qquad \downarrow \quad NE$$

A = Assets            L = Liabilities            OE = Owners' Equity
NI = Net Income      NE = No Effect

From the above, you can see that changes in the valuation account (Securities Fair Value Adjustment) for investment securities classified as trading are included in the determination of **net income** of the period in which they occur. The amount of increase or decrease in the valuation account for investment securities classified as available-for-sale shall be reported as a component of **other comprehensive income;** the amount of accumulated changes in this valuation account are included in the equity section of the balance sheet and shown separately there as part of Accumulated Other Comprehensive Income.

# ILLUSTRATION 17-3
# ACCOUNTING AND REPORTING FOR
# EQUITY SECURITIES BY CATEGORY (L.O. 3, 4)

The accounting and reporting for equity securities depends upon the level of influence and the type of security involved, as shown below:

| Category | Valuation | Unrealized Holding Gains or Losses | Other Income Effects |
|---|---|---|---|
| Holdings less than 20%[a] | | | |
| 1. Available-for-sale | Fair value | Recognized in other comprehensive income and as a separate component of stockholders' equity. | Dividends declared; gains and losses from sale. |
| 2. Trading | Fair value | Recognized in net income. | Dividends declared; gains and losses from sale. |
| Holdings between 20% and 50%[b] | Equity | Not recognized. | Proportionate share of investee's net income or net loss (adjusted for amortization of the difference between cost and the underlying book value); gains and losses from sale. |
| Holdings more than 50%[c] | Consolidation | Not recognized. | Not applicable. |

[a]Unless there is evidence to the contrary, the investor is assumed to have only a little or no influence over the investee.

[b]Unless there is evidence to the contrary, the investor is assumed to have significant influence over the investee.

[c]The investor has a controlling interest in the investee.

## EXERCISE 17-1

**Purpose:**     (L.O. 1) This exercise will quickly review the process of determining the required year-end entry to adjust the valuation account for an investment in debt securities classified as available-for-sale.

Nevercrash Airlines has a portfolio of marketable debt securities classified as available-for-sale securities, the first of which was acquired in 2009. The aggregate cost and fair value of the securities contained in that investment portfolio for five balance sheet dates are as follows:

| Date | Aggregate Cost | Aggregate Fair Value | Net Unrealized Gains (Losses) |
|------|---------------|---------------------|------------------------------|
| 12/31/09 | $ 142,000 | $ 138,000 | $    (4,000) |
| 12/31/10 | 159,000 | 143,000 | (16,000) |
| 12/31/11 | 172,000 | 163,000 | (9,000) |
| 12/31/12 | 190,000 | 203,000 | 13,000 |
| 12/31/13 | 190,000 | 184,000 | (6,000) |

### Instructions
At each balance sheet date, determine the following:
(a)     Reported value for the portfolio.
(b)     Desired balance in the related valuation account and indicate whether the desired balance is a debit or a credit.
(c)     Amount of adjustment required to the related valuation account and indicate whether the required adjustment to the related allowance account is a debit or credit.

### Solution to Exercise 17-1

| | (a) | | (b) | | (c) | |
|---|-----|----|-----|----|-----|----|
| 12/31/09 | $138,000 | FV | $ 4,000 | credit | $ 4,000 | credit |
| 12/31/10 | 143,000 | FV | 16,000 | credit | 12,000 | credit |
| 12/31/11 | 163,000 | FV | 9,000 | credit | 7,000 | debit |
| 12/31/12 | 203,000 | FV | 13,000 | debit | 22,000 | debit |
| 12/31/13 | 184,000 | FV | 6,000 | credit | 19,000 | credit |

**Explanation:** Investments in debt securities which are classified as available-for-sale are initially recorded at cost, but they are to be reported at fair value at a balance sheet date. The writeup or writedown of the investment is accomplished by the use of a valuation account. A debit balance in a valuation account is needed when fair value exceeds cost; a credit balance in the valuation account is needed when cost exceeds fair value. The desired balance in the valuation account is the amount by which aggregate cost differs from aggregate fair value at the particular balance sheet date. The balance of the valuation account is adjusted, as needed, at each balance sheet date.

> **TIP:**     Apply the steps in **Illustration 17-2** in solving this exercise.
>
> **TIP:**     The portfolio in this exercise may be classified as a current asset or a noncurrent asset. The responses in this exercise are not affected by whether it is a current or noncurrent classification.

# ILLUSTRATION 17-4
# RECLASSIFICATION ADJUSTMENTS FOR
# AVAILABLE-FOR-SALE SECURITIES (L.O. 7)

As indicated in **Chapter 4,** changes in unrealized holding gains and losses related to available-for-sale securities are reported as part of other comprehensive income. Companies have the option to display the components of other comprehensive income (1) in a combined statement of income and comprehensive income, (2) in a separate statement of comprehensive income that begins with net income, or (3) in a statement of stockholders' equity. Refer to **Illustration 4-4** for an example of these three alternative display options.

The reporting of changes in unrealized gains or losses in comprehensive income is straightforward unless securities are sold during the year. In this situation, double counting results when realized gains or losses are reported as part of net income but also are shown in other comprehensive income as unrealized holding gains or losses in the period in which they arose (in the current period or in previous periods). Adjustments are to be made to avoid this double counting. Those realized gains must be deducted (or realized losses must be added) through other comprehensive income of the period in which they are included in net income to avoid including them in comprehensive income twice. These adjustments are referred to as **reclassification adjustments.**

> **TIP:** Net income for a period is closed to Retained Earnings. The total of other comprehensive income for a period is transferred to a separate component of stockholders' equity on the balance sheet called Accumulated Other Comprehensive Income. If the reporting entity has had more than one type of transaction reported as other comprehensive income, it must disclose accumulated balances for each classification in that separate component of stockholders' equity; this disclosure can be made on the face of the balance sheet, in a statement of stockholders' equity, or in the notes that accompany the financial statements.

## EXERCISE 17-2

**Purpose:** (L.O. 3) This exercise will review the accounting for investments in available-for-sale equity securities.

At December 31, 2008, Ed & Kay Hastings Company had no investments. One equity security is purchased for $34,680 on November 15, 2009; commission costs on the purchase amount to $320. At December 31, 2009, a balance sheet date, the fair value of that security is $32,000. At December 31, 2010, the security is still held and the fair value is $40,000. The security is classified as available-for-sale in noncurrent assets. On January 15, 2011, the security is sold for a price of $42,800.

## Instructions

(a)    Prepare the journal entry for the purchase of the security on November 15, 2009.
(b)    Prepare the appropriate adjusting entry on December 31, 2009.
(c)    Describe what will appear on the 2009 financial statements with regard to this investment.
(d)    Prepare the appropriate adjusting entry on December 31, 2010.
(e)    Describe what will appear on the 2010 financial statements with regard to this investment.
(f)    Prepare the journal entry to record the sale of the investment on January 15, 2011.
(g)    Prepare the appropriate adjusting entry on December 31, 2011.
(h)    Describe what will appear on the 2011 financial statements with regard to this investment.

## Solution to Exercise 17-2

(a)                                **November 15, 2009**
Available-for-Sale Securities.......................................................................... 35,000
    Cash ($34,680 + $320) ...................................................................                35,000

(b)                                **December 31, 2009**
Unrealized Holding Gain or Loss—Equity....................................................... 3,000
    Securities Fair Value Adjustment (Available-for-Sale) ......................                3,000

(c)    The investment will be reported at a net amount of $32,000 ($35,000 - $3,000) in the long-term investment section of the balance sheet at December 31, 2009. The unrealized holding loss of $3,000 is reported as a component of other comprehensive income (loss) and as a separate item in the stockholders' equity section of the balance sheet at December 31, 2009. Because, in this case, that item has a debit balance, it appears as a reduction of stockholders' equity.  The purchase of an investment will appear as a $35,000 outflow of cash in the investing section of the statement of cash flows.

(d)                                **December 31, 2010**
Securities Fair Value Adjustment (Available-for-Sale) .................................... 8,000
    Unrealized Holding Gain or Loss—Equity...........................................                8,000

(e)   The investment will be reported at the fair value of $40,000 ($35,000 cost plus $5,000 excess of fair value over cost reflected in the Securities Fair Value Adjustment account) on the balance sheet at December 31, 2010. The increase in market price of $8,000 during the period is reported as a positive component of other comprehensive income during the period. The net unrealized holding gain of $5,000 appears as Other Accumulated Comprehensive Income — a separate credit item in the stockholders' equity section of the balance sheet at December 31, 2010 (thus, in this case, it increases the total stockholders' equity balance).

(f)                              **January 15, 2011**
Cash   ............................................................................................42,800
     Available-for-Sale Securities ................................................            35,000
     Gain on Sale of Securities ($42,800 - $35,000) .................................             7,800

(g)                              **December 31, 2011**
Unrealized Holding Gain or Loss—Equity......................................................            5,000
     Securities Fair Value Adjustment (Available-for-Sale) ........................            5,000

**Explanation:** There is no investment held at December 31, 2011 and no need for a valuation account; hence, its entire balance is eliminated. The adjusting entry also eliminates the $5,000 balance in the related stockholders' equity account. This $5,000 entry also contains the amount of the reclassification adjustment.
**(See Illustration 17-4).**

(h)   There will be no investment and no separate component of stockholders' equity related to unrealized holding gains or losses on the December 31, 2011 balance sheet. The income statement for 2011 will reflect a $7,800 realized gain on sale of securities ($42,800 net selling price - $35,000 cost) in the "other revenues and gains" section of a multiple-step income statement. There will be a $5,000 reclassification adjustment (see **Illustration 17-4**) shown as a deduction in other comprehensive income for 2011. The proceeds from the sale of an investment will appear as an inflow of cash in the investing section of the statement of cash flows.

**Approach:** Follow the steps listed in **Illustration 17-2**.

| | |
|---|---|
| **TIP:** | Some accountants would report the increase in market value during 2011 (selling price of $42,800 less fair value $40,000 at last balance sheet date = $2,800) as a component of other comprehensive income. If this is done, the reclassification adjustment described above must be increased by that same amount ($2,800) to $7,800. |
| **TIP:** | Notice the items that got reported on the combined statement of comprehensive income for the three-year period covered by the exercise. First, in the other comprehensive income section: |

($3,000) in 2009
8,000 in 2010
($5,000) in 2011

These amounts net to zero.
Second, in the other revenues and other gains section:

$7,800 in 2011

The net impact is a gain of $7,800 and this amount appears as a realized gain on the sale of an investment on the income statement for the year 2011.

## EXERCISE 17-3

**Purpose:**     (L.O. 1, 3) This exercise will review the accounting for an investment in trading securities.

On December 27, 2010, Dave Alexander Company purchased the following three securities for a trading portfolio:

| Security | Cost |
|----------|------|
| A | $ 12,000 |
| B | 20,000 |
| C | 30,000 |
| Total | $ 62,000 |

On December 31, 2010, the three securities were still held and the respective fair values were as follows:

| Security | Fair Value |
|----------|------------|
| A | $ 13,500 |
| B | 18,000 |
| C | 34,000 |
| Total | $ 65,500 |

The three securities were all sold on January 2, 2011 for the following amounts:

| Security | Sales Price |
|----------|-------------|
| A | $ 13,500 |
| B | 18,000 |
| C | 34,000 |
| Total | $ 65,500 |

No more trading securities were held or acquired.

## Instructions
(a)     Prepare all journal entries related to these securities.
(b)     Describe what will appear on the financial statements for 2010 with regard to these securities. Assume a calendar year reporting period.
(c)     Describe what will appear on the financial statements for 2011 with regard to these securities.

## Solution to Exercise 17-3

(a)                                  **December 27, 2010**

| | | |
|---|---|---|
| Trading Securities | 62,000 | |
|     Cash | | 62,000 |

**December 31, 2010**

| | | |
|---|---|---|
| Securities Fair Value Adjustment (Trading) | 3,500 | |
|     Unrealized Holding Gain or Loss—Income | | 3,500 |

**January 2, 2011**

| | | |
|---|---|---|
| Cash | 65,500 | |
|     Trading Securities | | 62,000 |
|     Gain on Sale of Securities | | 3,500 |

**December 31, 2011**

| | | |
|---|---|---|
| Unrealized Holding Gain or Loss—Income | 3,500 | |
|     Securities Fair Value Adjustment (Trading) | | 3,500 |

(b)    The securities will be reported at the fair value of $65,500 ($62,000 cost plus $3,500 excess of fair value over cost reflected in the securities fair value adjustment account) in the current asset section of the balance sheet at December 31, 2010. An unrealized holding gain of $3,500 will be reported in the "other revenues and gains" section of the income statement for the year ending December 31, 2010.

(c)    There are no securities reported on the balance sheet at December 31, 2011. The gain on sale of securities of $3,500 is reported in the "other revenues and gains" section of the income statement and the $3,500 unrealized holding loss is reported in the "other expenses and losses" section of the income statement for the year ending December 31, 2011.

> **TIP:**    Notice that the realized gain on sale of $3,500 during 2011 is offset by the unrealized loss of $3,500 (caused by the necessary adjustment of the valuation account). There was a net profit or gain of $3,500 from this investment and it was recognized during the period (2010) in which there was an increase in the fair value rather than in the period of sale.

# EXERCISE 17-4

**Purpose**:    (L.O. 1, 3)  This exercise will illustrate how to account for investments in trading and available-for-sale securities.

Accolades Cruise Company has two investment portfolios at the December 31, 2010 balance sheet date. The securities contained in these portfolios are all equity securities and were purchased during 2010, Accolades' first year of operations.  None of the investments are accounted for by the equity method.  No investments were sold during 2010.  Details are as follows:

**Trading Portfolio**

| | December 31, 2010 | | |
|---|---|---|---|
| | **Cost** | **Market** | **Difference** |
| Stock of ABC Co. | $100,000 | $ 80,000 | $(20,000) |
| Stock of DEF Co. | 70,000 | 92,000 | 22,000 |
| Stock of GHI Co. | 60,000 | 50,000 | (10,000) |
|     Total | $230,000 | $222,000 | $( 8,000) |

**Available-for-Sale Portfolio--Long-term**

**December 31, 2010**

|  | Cost | Market | Difference |
|---|---|---|---|
| Stock of JKL Co. | $140,000 | $153,000 | $13,000 |
| Stock of MNO Co. | 120,000 | 135,000 | 15,000 |
| Stock of PQR Co. | 150,000 | 121,000 | (29,000) |
| Stock of STU Co. | 160,000 | 136,000 | (24,000) |
| Total | $570,000 | $545,000 | $(25,000) |

**Instructions**

(a) Prepare the appropriate adjusting entry(s) at December 31, 2010.

(b) Explain how the data will be displayed on the balance sheet. Also, explain what will appear and where on the combined statement of comprehensive income for the year ending December 31, 2010. (Assume at the balance sheet date, Accolades has a balance of $400,000 in its Common Stock account, $600,000 in its Retained Earnings account, and $0 in Accumulated Comprehensive Income. Also, assume net income for 2010 is $92,000.)

(c) Assuming the stock of DEF Co. is sold for $94,000 on January 7, 2011 and the stock of STU Co. is sold for $141,000 on January 8, 2011, prepare the journal entries to record these sales and explain what will appear and where on the combined statement of comprehensive income for the year ending December 31, 2011.

## SOLUTION TO EXERCISE 17-4

(a) Unrealized Loss—Income ........................................................ 8,000

        Securities Fair Value Adjustment (Trading) ..................... 8,000

Unrealized Loss—Equity ........................................................ 25,000

        Securities Fair Value Adjustment (Available-for-Sale) ..... 25,000

**Explanation:** Investments in marketable equity securities are to be accounted for by the equity method if the investor has significant influence over the investee. When the equity method is inappropriate, the securities are recorded at cost and are reported at fair value. With this latter method, the securities are first grouped into one of two portfolios: the trading portfolio or the available-for-sale portfolio. Each portfolio is to be reported at fair value. Thus, the total market value of the trading portfolio at the balance sheet date ($222,000) is compared with the total cost of the trading portfolio ($230,000) to determine the balance needed in the related valuation (market adjustment) account. If market value is lower than cost, a credit balance is needed in the valuation account for the excess of cost over market ($8,000 in this case). Thus, the market adjustment account is credited and an unrealized loss account is debited. The same comparison is made for the available-for-sale portfolio. The journal entry to establish a valuation account for the available-for-sale portfolio looks very similar to the journal entry to establish a valuation account for the trading portfolio but a major difference lies in the reporting of the unrealized loss (or gain) account [see part (b) of this exercise].

(b)
## Balance Sheet

Current assets
Trading securities, at fair value                                              $222,000

Investments
Available-for-sale securities, at fair value                                   $545,000

Stockholders' equity
Common stock                                                               $ 400,000
Retained earnings                                                             600,000
   Total paid-in capital and retained earnings                   1,000,000
Accumulated other comprehensive income
     Unrealized gains (losses) on securities              (25,000)
   Total stockholders' equity                                  $ 975,000

## Income Statement

Income from operations                                                        $100,000
Other expenses and losses:
   Unrealized loss on valuation of trading
     marketable equity securities                          (8,000)
Net income                                                                      92,000
Other comprehensive income
   Unrealized holding loss                                        (25,000)
Comprehensive income                                                         $ 67,000

**Explanation:** Changes in the valuation account for the trading portfolio of marketable securities go through net income but changes in the valuation account for an available-for-sale portfolio are reflected as a component of other comprehensive income and as a separate component in stockholders' equity (i.e. in a contra stockholders' equity account in this case).

> **TIP:** If there had been transactions involving the available-for-sale securities in prior periods, the amount of unrealized holding gains or losses reflected in accumulated other comprehensive income on the balance sheet would very likely be **unequal** to the amount of unrealized holding gains or losses running through the other comprehensive income section of the combined statement of comprehensive income for the current period.

(c)

**January 7, 2011**

Cash.............................................................................    94,000
   Stock Investments—Trading ........................................               70,000
   Gain on Sale of Investments ........................................              24,000

### January 8, 2011

| | | |
|---|---|---|
| Cash............................................................................... | 141,000 | |
| Loss on Sale of Investments ...................................................... | 19,000 | |
|    Stock Investments—Available-for-Sale ........................ | | 160,000 |

The sale of an investment (short-term or long-term) at a price other than its cost will result in a realized gain or loss to be reported in the Other Revenues and Gains or Other Expenses and Losses section of a multiple-step income statement. Thus, the $24,000 gain will be reported in the Other Revenues and Gains section and the $19,000 loss will be reported in the Other Expenses and Losses section of Accolades' income statement for the year of 2011. It is permissible to net the realized gains and losses for a period, in which case Accolades would report a gain of $5,000 in the Other Revenues and Gains classification on its income statement for the year of 2011.

---

**TIP:** The valuation account is not involved in recording the purchase or sale of securities during the period. The valuation account is adjusted **only** at the end of an accounting period.

**TIP:** Because $22,000 of the above $24,000 realized gains associated with DEF stock was reported as an unrealized holding gain in the prior year (as a part of net income and, therefore, a component of comprehensive income for 2010) and a loss of $24,000 ($160,000 - $136,000) was reported as an unrealized holding loss in the prior year (as a part of other comprehensive income for 2010), reclassification adjustments are to be made to avoid double counting these items in comprehensive income. These reclassification adjustments will result in the following being reported in a combined statement of comprehensive income for the year of 2011:

| | |
|---|---|
| Net income | ? |
| Other comprehensive income: | |
|    Total holding gains or losses arising during | |
|     the period | ? |
|    Reclassification adjustment for gains included | |
|     in net income | (22,000) |
|    Reclassification adjustment for losses included | |
|     in net income | 24,000 |
| Comprehensive income | $  ? |

# EXERCISE 17-5

**Purpose:**    (L.O. 1) This exercise will review the accounting procedures appropriate for an investment in debt securities classified as available-for-sale or held-to-maturity.

A five-year $100,000 bond with a 7% stated interest rate and a 5% yield rate is purchased on December 31, 2009 for $108,660. The bond matures on December 31, 2014. Interest is to be received at the end of each year. The following amortization schedule reflects interest to be received, interest revenue, amortization of bond premium, and amortized cost of the bond investment at year end.

| Date | Stated Interest | Effective Interest | Amortization | Amortized Cost |
|---|---|---|---|---|
| 12/31/09 | | | | $108,660 |
| 12/31/10 | $ 7,000 | $ 5,433 | $1,567 | 107,093 |
| 12/31/11 | 7,000 | 5,354 | 1,646 | 105,447 |
| 12/31/12 | 7,000 | 5,272 | 1,728 | 103,719 |
| 12/31/13 | 7,000 | 5,186 | 1,814 | 101,905 |
| 12/31/14 | 7,000 | 5,095 | 1,905 | 100,000 |
| Totals | $35,000 | $26,340 | $8,660 | |

The following presents a comparison of the amortized cost and market value (assumed) of the bond at year end.

| Date | Amortized Cost | Market Value | Difference |
|---|---|---|---|
| 12/31/09 | $108,660 | $108,660 | $0 |
| 12/31/10 | 107,093 | 106,000 | (1,093) |
| 12/31/11 | 105,447 | 107,500 | 2,053 |
| 12/31/12 | 103,719 | 105,500 | 1,781 |
| 12/31/13 | 101,905 | 103,000 | 1,095 |
| 12/31/14 | 100,000 | 100,000 | 0 |

## Instructions

(a)    Record the journal entries at December 31, 2009, December 31, 2010, and December 31, 2011, assuming the bond is classified as held-to-maturity.

(b)    Assuming the bond is classified as held-to-maturity, describe what will be reflected in the income statement and balance sheet prepared at December 31, 2010 and December 31, 2011 with regard to this investment.

(c)    Record the journal entries at December 31, 2009, December 31, 2010, and December 31, 2011, assuming the bond is classified as available-for-sale.

(d)    Assuming the bond is classified as available-for-sale, describe what will be reflected in the income statement and balance sheet prepared at December 31, 2010 and December 31, 2011 with regard to this investment.

(e)    Assuming the bond is classified as held-to-maturity, prepare the journal entry to record the sale of the investment if it is sold on January 2, 2012 for $107,250.

(f)    Assuming the bond is classified as available-for-sale, prepare the journal entry to record the sale of the investment if it is sold on January 2, 2012 for $107,250.

## Solution to Exercise 17-5

(a)                          **December 31, 2009**
Held-to-Maturity Securities...................................................................... 108,660
    Cash   .......................................................................................... 108,660

> **TIP:** Although the issuer of the bonds sets up a separate account for premium or discount on bonds, an investor typically does **not** set up a separate account; rather, any discount or premium is reflected in the investment account.

                             **December 31, 2010**
Cash   ........................................................................................7,000
    Interest Revenue............................................................... 5,433
    Held-to-Maturity Securities.............................................. 1,567

                             **December 31, 2011**
Cash   ........................................................................................7,000
    Interest Revenue............................................................... 5,354
    Held-to-Maturity Securities.............................................. 1,646

(b)    The bond investment would be reported in the long-term investment section of the balance sheet at amortized cost of $107,093 at December 31, 2010 and $105,447 at December 31, 2011. Interest revenue of $5,433 would be reported in the income statement for the year ending December 31, 2010 and interest revenue of $5,354 would be reported in the income statement for the year ending December 31, 2011. Interest revenue is classified as "other revenue" on a multiple-step income statement.

> **TIP:** Only debt securities can be classified as held-to-maturity because only debt securities have a maturity date; equity securities do not have a maturity date. Held-to-maturity debt securities are always reported at amortized cost. Held-to-maturity securities are always a noncurrent asset classification (long-term investments) unless their maturity date is within one year of the balance sheet date; then they are classified as a current asset.

(c)                          **December 31, 2009**
Available-for-Sale Securities................................................... 108,660
    Cash   .......................................................................... 108,660

                             **December 31, 2010**
Cash   ........................................................................................7,000
    Interest Revenue............................................................... 5,433
    Available-for-Sale Securities ........................................... 1,567

Unrealized Holding Gain or Loss—Equity................................ 1,093
    Securities Fair Value Adjustment (Available-for-Sale) .................. 1,093

                             **December 31, 2011**
Cash   ........................................................................................7,000
    Interest Revenue............................................................... 5,354
    Available-for-Sale Securities ........................................... 1,646

| | | |
|---|---|---|
| Securities Fair Value Adjustment (Available-for-Sale) ............................. | 3,146[a] | |
|    Unrealized Holding Gain or Loss—Equity ...................................... | | 3,146 |

    [a]$107,500 market value - $105,447 amortized cost = $2,053 debit balance
    desired in valuation account.
    $2,053 debit balance desired + $1,093 credit balance existing = $3,146
    debit adjustment required for the valuation account.

(d)    An investment in an available-for-sale security is reported in the current asset or long-term investment section of the balance sheet at fair value at a balance sheet date. It is a current asset classification if the item is readily marketable and if there is a lack of management intent to hold on to it for a long-term purpose; otherwise, it is classified as a long-term investment. The investment in this exercise would be reported at the fair value of $106,000 at December 31, 2010 and $107,500 at December 31, 2011. An unrealized loss of $1,093 would be shown as a negative item (loss) in other comprehensive income and as a separate component of stockholders' equity (Accumulated Other Comprehensive Income) at December 31, 2010; an unrealized gain of $3,146 would be shown as a positive item in other comprehensive income and a net unrealized gain of $2,053 would be shown as a separate component of stockholders' equity at December 31, 2011. Interest revenue of $5,433 would be reported in the income statement for the year ending December 31, 2010 and interest revenue of $5,354 would be reported in the income statement for the year ending December 31, 2011.

(e)                                **January 2, 2012**

| | | |
|---|---|---|
| Cash  .....................................................................107,250 | | |
|    Held-to-Maturity Securities........................................... | | 105,447[a] |
|    Gain on Sale of Securities............................................ | | 1,803 |

    [a]$108,660 - ($1,567 + $1,646) = $105,447 balance

(f)                                  **January 2, 2012**

| | | |
|---|---|---|
| Cash  .....................................................................107,250 | | |
|    Available-for-Sale Securities ....................................... | | 105,447 |
|    Gain on Sale of Securities........................................... | | 1,803 |

> **TIP:**    At the end of 2012, there would no longer be any need for the valuation account, so the following entry would be made:
>
> | | | |
> |---|---|---|
> | Unrealized Holding Gain or Loss—Equity ................... | 2,053 | |
> |    Securities Fair Value Adjustment | | |
> |       (Available-for-Sale)............................................ | | 2,053 |

> **TIP:** The realized gain of $1,803 from the sale of the investment will be reported in the "other revenues and gains" section of the income statement for the year ending December 31, 2012. The $2,053 would be reflected as a debit type reclassification adjustment in other comprehensive income. This adjustment is needed to "back out" the net cumulative unrealized gains reflected in other comprehensive income in the current and prior years related to this security. This is appropriate because the realized gain of $1,803 is a component of net income this period and we don't want duplication of reported gains and losses (see **Illustration 17-4**).

## EXERCISE 17-6

**Purpose:** (L.O. 1) This exercise will review the factors involved in computing interest revenue using the straight-line method of amortization for bonds purchased at a discount between interest payment dates.

Tennie Pumps Corporation purchased bonds to be held as a long-term investment; they are classified as held-to-maturity. Tennie uses the straight-line method of amortization, and a calendar year reporting period. Other facts are as follows:

| | |
|---|---|
| Par value of bonds | $300,000 |
| Stated rate of interest | 10% |
| Purchase price | $287,960 |
| Purchase date | March 1, 2010 |
| Interest payment dates | January 1 and July 1 |
| Maturity date | January 1, 2016 |

### Instructions
(a) Compute the interest revenue to be reported on the income statement for the year ending December 31, 2010.
(b) Compute the interest revenue to be reported on the income statement for the year ending December 31, 2011.
(c) Compute the interest revenue to be reported on the income statement for the year ending December 31, 2012.

> **TIP:** Recall that the straight-line method of amortization is not a generally acceptable accounting method. It can be used and not be considered a departure from GAAP when the results of its use are not materially different from the results of using the preferable effective interest method of amortization. This problem assumes an immaterial difference exists.

## Solution to Exercise 17-6

**Approach:** Draw a T-account. Make all the entries that would be reflected in the Interest Revenue account for the period in question.

(a)

Interest Revenue

| | | | |
|---|---|---|---|
| 3/1/10 | 5,000 | 7/1/10 | 15,000 |
| | | 12/31/10 | 15,000 |
| | | 12/31/10 | 1,720 |
| | | 12/31/10 Bal. | 26,720 |

**Explanation:**

3/1/10      **Payment of accrued interest at date of purchase.** A purchaser of bonds must pay the seller any interest accrued between the last interest payment date and the purchase date. This amount can be debited to the Interest Revenue account or to the Interest Receivable account on the purchaser's books. This solution assumes the former.

$300,000 x 10% = $30,000 interest per year.
$30,000 ÷ 12 = $2,500 interest per month.
$2,500 x 2 = $5,000 accrued interest at 3/1/10.

7/1/10      **Receipt of interest at interest payment date.** A full six months interest is received every interest payment date. Because the accrued interest at 3/1/10 was recorded in the revenue account, the entire receipt on 7/1/10 can be credited to the revenue account.

$2,500 x 6 months = $15,000.

12/31/10      **Accrual of interest at year end.** Six months have passed since the last interest receipt.

$2,500 x 6 months = $15,000.

12/31/10      **Amortization of discount for the year.** The discount is to be amortized over the 70 months that are between the purchase date (March 1, 2010) and the maturity date (January 1, 2016). Ten months of amortization pertain to 2010 (March 1 to December 31).

$300,000 - $287,960 = $12,040 discount.
$12,040 ÷ 70 months = $172 amortization per month.
$172 x 10 months = $1,720 amortization for 2010.

(b)

Interest Revenue

| | | | |
|---|---|---|---|
| | | 7/1/11 | 15,000 |
| | | 12/31/11 | 15,000 |
| | | 12/31/11 | 2,064 |
| | | 12/31/11 Bal. | 32,064 |

**Explanation:**

| | | |
|---|---|---|
| 7/1/11 | **Receipt of interest at interest payment date.** | $2,500 x 6 months = $15,000. |
| 12/31/11 | **Accrual of interest at year end.** | $2,500 x 6 months = $15,000. |
| 12/31/11 | **Amortization of discount for the year.** | $172 x 12 months = $2,064. |

> **TIP:** The receipt of $15,000 on January 1, 2011 covered the interest that was earned and accrued at the end of the last accounting period. Assuming reversing entries are not made, this receipt would be recorded by a debit to Cash and a credit to Interest Receivable. Thus, it has no effect on the interest revenue amount for 2011. If reversing entries are made by the company, a reversing entry at January 1, 2011 would have put a debit in the Interest Revenue account that would then offset the $15,000 credit that would have been recorded to the same Interest Revenue account for the $15,000 cash received on January 1, 2011. Thus, whether reversing entries are made or not, the $15,000 cash received in January 2011 has no net effect on revenue for 2011.

(c)     <u>$32,064</u>.          Same explanation and solution as for part (b) of this exercise.


# EXERCISE 17-7

**Purpose:**     (L.O.1) This exercise will illustrate (1) the computations and journal entries for a bond investment purchased at a discount and (2) the accounting procedures required when the bond investment is sold prior to the bond's maturity date.

John and Martha Hitt Company purchased bonds to be held to maturity. The following details pertain:

| | |
|---|---|
| Face value | $100,000.00 |
| Stated interest rate | 7% |
| Yield rate | 10% |
| Maturity date | January 1, 2013 |
| Date of purchase | January 1, 2010 |
| Interest receipts due | Annually on January 1 |
| Method of amortization | Effective interest |
| Purchase price | $92,539.95 |

## Instructions
(a)     Compute the amount of purchase premium or discount.
(b)     Prepare the journal entry for the purchase of the bonds. Do not record the premium or discount separately in the accounts.
(c)     Prepare the amortization schedule for these bonds.
(d)     Prepare all of the journal entries (subsequent to the purchase date) for 2010 and 2011 that relate to these bonds. Assume the accounting period coincides with the calendar year. Assume reversing entries are not used.
(e)     Prepare the journal entry to record the sale of the bonds, assuming they are sold on January 1, 2012 for $102,000.00. Assume the sale occurs immediately after the annual interest receipt.

## Solution to Exercise 17-7

(a)    Face value                                                              $100,000.00
Purchase price                                                                92,539.95
Discount on investment in bonds                                       $   7,460.05

(b)                                              **January 1, 2010**
Held-to-Maturity Securities............................................................   92,539.95
    Cash. . . .     ............................................................................   92,539.95

> **Explanation:** The discount of $7,460.05 is reflected in the investment account because the instructions indicate the discount is not to be shown separately in the accounts. If a separate account were to be used, the entry would have included a debit to Held-to-Maturity Securities for $100,000.00, a credit to Discount on Held-to-Maturity Securities for $7,460.05, and a credit to Cash for $92,539.95.

(c)

| Date | 7% Stated Interest | 10% Interest Revenue | Discount Amortization | Carrying Value |
|---|---|---|---|---|
| 1/1/10 | | | | $   92,539.95 |
| 1/1/11 | $   7,000.00 | $   9,254.00 | $ 2,254.00 | 94,793.95 |
| 1/1/12 | 7,000.00 | 9,479.40 | 2,479.40 | 97,273.35 |
| 1/1/13 | 7,000.00 | 9,726.65[a] | 2,726.65 | 100,000.00 |
| | $ 21,000.00 | $ 28,460.05 | $ 7,460.05 | |

[a]Includes rounding error of $.69.

**Explanation:** Stated interest is determined by multiplying the par value ($100,000) by the contract rate of interest (7%). Interest revenue is computed by multiplying the carrying value at the beginning of the interest period by the effective interest rate (10%). The amount of discount amortization for the period is the excess of the interest revenue over the stated interest (cash interest) amount. The carrying value at an interest receipt date is the carrying value at the beginning of the interest period plus the discount amortization for the interest period.

> **TIP:**   The amount of interest revenue of $9,479.40 appearing on the "1/1/12" receipt line is the amount of interest revenue for the interest period ending on that date. Thus, in this case, $9,479.40 is the interest revenue for the twelve months preceding the date 1/1/12 which would be the calendar year of 2011.
>
> **TIP:**   Any rounding error should be plugged to (included in) the interest revenue amount for the last period. Otherwise, there would be a small balance left in the Investment in Bonds account after the bonds are extinguished.
>
> **TIP:**   Notice that the total interest revenue ($28,460.05) over the three-year period equals the total cash interest ($21,000.00) plus the total purchase discount ($7,460.05). Thus, you can see that the purchase discount represents an additional amount of interest to be recognized over the time the bonds are held.

(d)     12/31/10     Held-to-Maturity Securities ................................     2,254.00
                              Interest Receivable..........................................     7,000.00
                                     Interest Revenue ...................................                           9,254.00

**Explanation:** This entry records (1) the accrual of interest for twelve months, and (2) the amortization of discount for the first twelve months the bonds are held. This compound entry could be replaced with two single entries to accomplish the same objectives. The first entry would include a debit to Interest Receivable and a credit to Interest Revenue for $7,000.00. The second entry would include a debit to Held-to-Maturity Securities and a credit to Interest Revenue for $2,254.00. The two entry approach is sometimes easier to employ when reversing entries are used, a subject that was covered in **Appendix 3A**, because the first of the two single entries can be reversed, but the second of the two single entries (the one to record the amortization of discount or premium) should **never** be reversed.

1/1/11          Cash   ................................................................7,000.00
                              Interest Receivable.....................................                           7,000.00

12/31/11       Held-to-Maturity Securities .............................     2,479.40
                      Interest Receivable..........................................     7,000.00
                              Interest Revenue ....................................                           9,479.40

(e)     1/1/12          Cash .................................................................     7,000.00
                              Interest Receivable.....................................                           7,000.00

                      Cash   ................................................................102,000.00
                              Held-to-Maturity Securities .....................                           97,273.35[a]
                              Gain on Sale of Securities.......................                           4,726.65[b]
                                     [a]($92,539.95 + $2,254.00 + $2,479.40
                                       = $97,273.35 carrying amount)
                                     [b]($102,000.00 - $97,273.35
                                       = $4,726.65 gain)

**TIP:**     Gains or losses on the sale of investments are to be classified in the "other revenues, gains, expenses, and losses" section of a multiple-step income statement. They very rarely meet the criteria to be classified as an extraordinary item.

## EXERCISE 17-8

**Purpose:**    (L.O. 4) This exercise will allow you to compare the results of using the fair value and equity methods of accounting for an investment in stock.

On January 1, 2010, Magic Johnson Corporation acquired 100,000 of the 400,000 outstanding shares of common stock of Wilt Chamberlain Corporation as a long-term investment at a cost of $50 per share. The fair value and the book value of the investee's net assets were both $20,000,000 at January 1, 2010. Wilt Chamberlain Corporation paid a cash dividend of $2.00 per common share on September 5, 2010 and reported net income of $1,400,000 for the year ending December 31, 2010. The market value of the Wilt Chamberlain stock was $47 at December 31, 2010.

### Instructions
(a)    Assuming Magic Johnson does **not** exercise significant influence over the investee, determine the following:
(1)    Amount to report as investment (dividend) revenue for the year ending December 31, 2010.
(2)    Amount to report as the carrying value of the investment at December 31, 2010.
(b)    Assuming Magic Johnson **does** exercise significant influence over the investee, determine the following:
(1)    Amount to report as investment revenue for the year ending December 31, 2010.
(2)    Amount to report as the carrying value of the investment at December 31, 2010.

## Solution to Exercise 17-8

**Approach:** Mentally reconstruct the journal entries to record the transactions above. Draw T-Accounts for the investment and the investment revenue accounts. Enter the amounts as they would be posted to those accounts.

(a)    (1)    $200,000.    (2) $4,700,000.

| Available-for-Sale Securities | | Dividend Revenue | |
|---|---|---|---|
| 1/1/10    5,000,000[1] | | | 9/5/10    200,000[2] |

[1]100,000 shares x $50 = $5,000,000.
[2]100,000 shares x $2 = $200,000.

**Explanation:** Because the investor does not exert significant influence over the investee, the investor should use the fair value method (as opposed to the equity method) to account for the investment. The investment should be reported at fair value at each balance sheet date. At December 31, 2010, the market value ($47 x 100,000 = $4,700,000) is lower than the cost ($50 x 100,000 = $5,000,000) of the shares held; thus a valuation account with a $300,000 credit balance is needed.

> **TIP:** In general, investments accounted for under the **fair value method** are maintained in the investment account at acquisition cost until partially or entirely liquidated. (A writedown of cost is appropriate when [a] a dividend received represents a liquidating dividend, or [b] operating losses of the investee significantly reduce its net assets and greatly impair its earning potential.) A valuation account (Securities Fair Value Adjustment) is used to record the difference between cost and fair (market) value so that the investment in stock is reported at fair value at each balance sheet date. A change in the valuation account is a component of other comprehensive income. Cash dividends received from the investee are usually recorded as dividend revenue. However, when the dividends received by the investor in periods subsequent to the purchase exceed the investor's share of the investee's earnings for the same periods, the dividends are to be accounted for as a return of capital; thus, the investor is to record a reduction of the investment's carrying value rather than revenue.

(b)    (1)    $350,000. (2) $5,150,000.

| Investment in Wilt Chamberlain Stock | | | | | Revenue From Investment | | |
|---|---|---|---|---|---|---|---|
| 1/1/10 | 5,000,000 | 9/5/10 | 200,000[3] | | | 12/31/10 | 350,000[4] |
| 12/31/10 | 350,000[4] | | | | | | |
| 12/31/10 Bal. | 5,150,000 | | | | | 12/31/10 Bal. 350,000 | |

[3]100,000 shares x $2 = $200,000.
[4]100,000 ÷ 400,000 = 25% ownership; 25% x $1,400,000 = $350,000.

**Explanation:** When the investment allows the investor to exercise significant influence over the investee, the investor should use the equity method (or elect the fair value option). The investor recognizes its proportionate share of the investee's earnings by a debit to the investment account and a credit to investment revenue. When the investee distributes earnings, the investor records an increase in cash and a decrease in the carrying value of the investment. Because the cost of the investment was equal to the carrying value of the investee's underlying net assets, there is no amortization to be considered (which would affect investment revenue and the investment account balance) in this case. The market value of the shares at the balance sheet date is not relevant when the equity method is used.

> **TIP:** Under the **equity method**, the investment is originally recorded at cost and then subsequently adjusted by the investor's **proportionate share** of the investee's earnings and dividend payments. Income earned by the investee results in investment revenue and an increase in the investment account on the books of the investor. An investee's net loss or dividend payments reduce the investment account. When the investor acquires the stock at a price unequal to the book value of the investee's underlying net assets, the investor must amortize the difference between the investor's cost and the investor's proportionate share of the underlying book value of the investee at the date of acquisition. This amortization affects investment revenue and the investment account balance.
>
> **TIP:** The **fair value option** can be elected under case (a) or (b). Then dividends would be recorded as divided revenue and the change in the fair value of the stock ($3 decrease x 100,000 shares = $300,000) would be recorded by a credit to the investment account and a debit to an unrealized loss account that is a component of net income.

## EXERCISE 17-9

**Purpose:**    (L.O. 4) This exercise will illustrate how to use the equity method of accounting for an investment in stock.

Deloitte Corporation acquired 30% of the 1,000,000 outstanding shares of Touche Corporation on January 1, 2010 for $3,240,000.

Touche Corporation reported net income of $1,600,000 for 2010 and $2,000,000 for 2011. Touche paid dividends of $400,000 on December 6, 2010 and $500,000 on December 5, 2011.

### Instructions
(a)    Prepare all  journal entries for Deloitte Corporation for 2010 and 2011 that relate to this investment.
(b)    Indicate the amount that should appear as investment income on Deloitte's income statement for (1) the year ending December 31, 2010, and (2) the year ending December 31, 2011.
(c)    Indicate the amount that should appear as the balance of Deloitte's investment on: (1) the balance sheet at December 31, 2010, and (2) the balance sheet at December 31, 2011.

## Solution to Exercise 17-9

(a)    1/1/10    Investment in Touche Company Stock.................    3,240,000
                 Cash      ...........................................................3,240,000

12/6/10    Cash..................................................................................120,000
                 Investment in Touche Company Stock.................                    120,000
                 (30% x $400,000 = $120,000)

12/31/10    Investment in Touche Company Stock..........................    480,000
                 Revenue from Investment ......................................                    480,000
                 (30% x $1,600,000 = $480,000)

12/5/11    Cash.................................................................................150,000
                 Investment in Touche Company Stock..................                    150,000
                 (30% x $500,000 = $150,000)

12/31/11    Investment in Touche Company Stock..........................    600,000
                 Revenue from Investment ......................................                    600,000
                 (30% x $2,000,000 = $600,000)

**Explanation:** The equity method is an accrual method of accounting for an investment in stock. A portion of the investee's earnings is recorded as income by the investor in the same time period the investee earns it. Dividends received are recorded as a recovery of investment, not as income. (To record dividends as income would "double count" the amount already recorded as a share of the investee's earnings.)

(b)    (1)    $480,000 for the year ending December 31, 2010.
(2)    $600,000 for the year ending December 31, 2011.

**Approach:** Post the amounts from the entries in part (a) to a T-account to solve.

Revenue from Investment

|  |  |  |  |
|---|---|---|---|
|  |  | 12/31/10 | 480,000 |
| 12/31/10 To close | 480,000 | 12/31/10 Balance | 480,000 |
|  |  | 12/31/11 | 600,000 |
|  |  | 12/31/11 Balance | 600,000 |

(c)    (1)    $3,600,000 at December 31, 2010.
(2)    $4,050,000 at December 31, 2011.

**Approach:** Post the amounts from the entries in part (a) to a T-account to solve.

Investment in Touche Company

|  |  |  |  |
|---|---|---|---|
| 1/1/10 | 3,240,000 | 12/6/10 | 120,000 |
| 12/31/10 | 480,000 |  |  |
| 12/31/10 Balance | 3,600,000 |  |  |
| 12/31/11 | 600,000 | 12/5/11 | 150,000 |
| 12/31/11 Balance | 4,050,000 |  |  |

## ILLUSTRATION 17-5
## FAIR VALUE OPTION TO REPORT FINANCIAL INSTRUMENTS (L.O. 5)

Companies have the option to report financial instruments at fair value, with all gains and losses related to changes in fair value reported in net income. This option is applied on an instrument-by-instrument basis and is generally available only at the time a company first purchases the financial asset or incurs the financial liability. When the fair value option is elected for an instrument, the election is irrevocable and the company is required to use the fair value option for that instrument until the company no longer has that instrument.

Election of the fair value option is relevant for:
a.    a company's investment in debt or equity security classified as available-for-sale.
b.    a company's investment in debt or equity security classified as held-to-maturity.
c.    a company's investment in equity security that qualifies for use of the equity method.
d.    a company's own debt instruments.

Use of the fair value election for a financial instrument results in a change in the fair value of the instrument being reflected as a component of net income for the period.

For examples:
1.    An available-for-sale security (stock in Rafael Company) is purchased for $300,000. The fair value of the security at the end of the fiscal period is $335,000. Using the fair value option, the following entries would apply:

| Investment in Rafael Company | 300,000 | |
| Cash | | 300,000 |
| (To record purchase of investment in stock) | | |

| Investment in Rafael Company | 35,000 | |
| Unrealized Holding Gain or Loss—Income | | 35,000 |
| (To record unrealized holding gain from increase in fair value) | | |

This treatment differs from how this security would be accounted for if the fair value option were **not** elected in the following ways:
(a)    There is no use of a Securities Fair Value Adjustment account for a change in fair value here because the accounting for a security using the fair value option is on an investment-by-investment basis rather that a portfolio basis so the Investment account is adjusted directly for the change in fair value.
(b)    With the fair value option election, the unrealized gain or loss (gain in this case) is reported as part of **net income** rather than a component of **other comprehensive income** on the income statement.

2.    A held-to-maturity security (bonds of Halle Corporation) is purchased for $100,000. The fair value of the security at the end of the period is $95,000. Using the fair value option, the following entries would apply:

| Investment in Halle Corp. Bonds | 100,000 | |
| Cash | | 100,000 |
| (To record purchase of investment in bonds) | | |

| Unrealized Holding Gain or Loss—Income | 5,000 | |
| Investment in Halle Corp. Bonds | | 5,000 |
| (To record unrealized holding loss from decrease in fair value) | | |

This treatment differs from how this security would be accounted for if the fair value option were **not** elected in the following ways:

(a) The asset is adjusted to fair value using the fair value option whereas the asset would be reflected on the balance sheet at unamortized cost if there was no election of the fair value option.

(b) The unrealized holding loss will reduce net income (earnings) by $5,000 using the fair value option whereas there would be no impact on net income or other comprehensive income if there was no election of the fair value option.

3. Stock in Baxter Corp. is purchased for $800,000 that qualifies for use of the equity method. The fair value of the stock at the end of the period is $942,000. Using the fair value option, the following entries would apply:

| | | |
|---|---|---|
| Investment in Baxter Stock | 800,000 | |
| Cash | | 800,000 |
| (To record purchase of stock) | | |

| | | |
|---|---|---|
| Investment in Baxter Stock | 142,000 | |
| Unrealized Holding Gain or Loss | | 142,000 |
| (To record increase in fair value of stock) | | |

This treatment differs from how this security would be accounted for if the fair value option were **not** elected in the following ways:

(a) The asset is adjusted to fair value using the fair value option whereas the asset would be reflected on the balance sheet at cost adjusted for the investor's proportionate share of the earnings (losses) of the investee and the dividends received by the investor using the equity method **without** election of the fair value election.

(b) Using the fair value option, the change in fair value is reported as a component of net income. Also, dividends received from the investee are credited to Dividend Revenue and reported as a component of net income. In contrast, the equity method would call for the investor's pro rata share of the investee's earnings to be reported as a component of net income, dividends received to be recorded as a reduction in the investment account, and for the fair value to be ignored in all of the investor's accounting for the investee.

4. Woodrow Corp. issued $750,000 of 6% bonds at face value on September 1, 2010. At December 31, 2010, the fair value of the bonds is $770,000 because interest rates have decreased in the market place. Under the fair value option, the following entry would be made:

| | | |
|---|---|---|
| Unrealized Holding Gain or Loss—Income | 20,000 | |
| Bonds Payable | | 20,000 |
| (To record increase in fair value of bond liability) | | |

The unrealized holding loss of $20,000 will reduce net income and the liability will be reported at $770,000 on the balance sheet.

## ILLUSTRATION 17-6
## INVESTMENTS—ACCOUNTING FOR
## TRANSFERS BETWEEN CATEGORIES (L.O. 7)

| Type of Transfer | Measurement Basis | Impact of Transfer on Stockholders' Equity | Impact of Transfer on Net Income |
|---|---|---|---|
| Transfer from Trading to Available-for-Sale* | Security transferred at fair value at the date of transfer, which is the new cost basis of the security. | None. | None (The unrealized gain or loss at the date of transfer will have already been recognized in income and should not be reversed). |
| Transfer from Available-for-Sale to Trading* | Security transferred at fair value at the date of transfer, which is the new cost basis of the security. | The unrealized gain or loss at the date of transfer carried as a separate component of stockholders' equity is reversed. | The unrealized gain or loss at the date of transfer is recognized in net income. |
| Transfer from Held-to-Maturity to Available-for-Sale* | Security transferred at fair value at the date of transfer. | The separate component of stockholders' equity is increased or decreased by the unrealized gain or loss at the date of transfer. | None (The unrealized holding gain or loss will be included in other comprehensive income). |
| Transfer from Available-for-Sale to Held-to-Maturity | Security transferred at fair value at the date of transfer. | The unrealized gain or loss at the date of transfer carried as a separate component of stockholders' equity is amortized over the remaining life of the security. | None |

*GAAP states that these types of transfers should be rare.

# EXERCISE 17-10

**Purpose:**    (L.O. 8) This exercise will apply the proper accounting procedures for reclassification of securities.

The Heath Corporation has the following securities at December 31, 2009, a balance sheet date:

### Trading Securities

|  | Cost | Fair Value | Net Unrealized Gain (Loss) |
|---|---|---|---|
| U.S. government bonds | $ 110,000 | $ 103,000 | $ (7,000) |

### Available-for-Sale Securities

|  | Cost | Fair Value | Net Unrealized Gain (Loss) |
|---|---|---|---|
| Equity securities | $ 174,000 | $ 195,000 | $ 21,000 |
| Corporate bonds | 150,000 | 168,000 | 18,000 |

All securities were purchased during 2009.

## Instructions

(a)    Assume that on January 1, 2010 Heath decides to transfer its equity securities to the trading portfolio. Prepare the journal entry(ies) necessary to record this transfer.

(b)    Assume that on January 1, 2010 Heath decides to transfer its U.S. government bonds to the available-for-sale portfolio. Prepare the journal entry necessary to record this transfer.

(c)    Assume that on January 1, 2010 Heath decides to transfer its corporate bonds to a held-to-maturity portfolio. Prepare the journal entry(ies) necessary to record this transfer.

## Solution to Exercise 17-10

(a)    Unrealized Holding Gain or Loss—Equity ........................................ 21,000
　　　Unrealized Holding Gain or Loss—Income ....................................... 　　　　21,000

Trading Securities    ...................................................................................195,000
　　　Available-for-Sale Securities ............................................................. 174,000
　　　Securities Fair Value Adjustment (Available-for-Sale) ....................... 21,000

**Explanation:** The equity securities are transferred to the trading security category at fair value, which establishes the new cost basis of that security. When this transfer occurs, the unrealized holding gain of $21,000 reflected in stockholders' equity related to the equity securities is eliminated by recognizing the unrealized gain in income of 2010. The cost of the securities ($174,000) is removed from the Available-for-Sale Securities account and the balance of the Securities Fair Value Adjustment account related to these securities is eliminated. A reclassification adjustment is needed to reflect a charge of $21,000 in other comprehensive income because the $21,000 reflected as a realized gain in net income of the current period (2010) also had been included in other comprehensive income as an unrealized holding gain in the prior period (2009) in which the holding gain arose. The $21,000 is deducted through comprehensive income in 2010 (which is the same year the $21,000 gain is included in net income) to avoid including it in comprehensive income twice.

| | | |
|---|---|---|
| (b) Available-for-Sale Securities | 103,000 | |
| Securities Fair Value Adjustment (Trading) | 7,000 | |
|     Trading Securities | | 110,000 |

**Explanation:** The U.S. government bonds are transferred to the available-for-sale category at fair value, which is the new cost basis of the security. When this transfer occurs, stockholders' equity and net income are not affected. The $7,000 net unrealized loss that was recognized in income in 2009 is not reversed. The trading securities account for these bonds and the related fair value adjustment account are eliminated.

| | | |
|---|---|---|
| (c) Held-to-Maturity Securities | 150,000 | |
| Securities Fair Value Adjustment (Held-to-Maturity) | 18,000 | |
|     Available-for-Sale Securities | | 150,000 |
|     Securities Fair Value Adjustment (Available-for-Sale) | | 18,000 |

**Explanation:** The corporate bonds are transferred to the held-to-maturity category at fair value at the date of transfer. Upon transfer, the carrying value in the balance sheet and the net unrealized holding gain of $18,000 reported in stockholders' equity will remain the same. In this case, both the Securities Fair Value Adjustment (Held-to-Maturity) balance of $18,000 and the Unrealized Holding Gain—Equity of $18,000 (a stockholders' equity account that is one possible component of the classification Accumulated Other Comprehensive Income) are to be amortized over the remaining life of the bonds.

> **TIP:** Refer to **Illustration 17-6** for a summary of guidelines in accounting for transfers of securities from one category to another.

## *ILLUSTRATION 17-7
## SUMMARY OF DERIVATIVES ACCOUNTING (L.O. *10, *11, *12, and *13)

| Accounting for Derivative Use | Accounting for Derivative | Hedged Item | Common Example |
|---|---|---|---|
| Speculation ized holding gains and losses recorded in income. | At fair value with unreal- | Not applicable. an equity security. | Call or put option on |
| Hedging Fair Value recorded in income. | At fair value with holding gains and losses in income. | At fair value with gains and losses recorded | Put option to hedge an equity investment. |
| Cash Flow holding gains and losses from the hedge recorded in other comprehensive income, and reclassified in income when the hedged transaction's cash flows affect earnings. | At fair value with unrealized | Use other generally accepted accounting principles for the for the hedged item. | Use of a futures contract to hedge a forecasted purchase of inventory. |

# ANALYSIS OF MULTIPLE-CHOICE TYPE QUESTIONS

**QUESTION**

1.    (L.O. 1) An investor purchased bonds with a face amount of $100,000 between interest payment dates. The investor purchased the bonds at 102, paid incidental costs of $1,500, and paid accrued interest for three months of $2,500. The amount to record as the cost of this long-term investment in bonds is:
a.    $100,000.
b.    $102,000.
c.    $103,500.
d.    $106,000.

**Explanation:** The cost is determined as follows:

|  |  |
|---|---|
| Purchase price (102% x $100,000 par) | $ 102,000 |
| Incidental costs to acquire | 1,500 |
| Total acquisition cost of investment | $ 103,500 |

The cost of an investment includes its purchase price and all incidental costs to acquire the item, such as brokerage commissions and taxes. Any accrued interest is to be recorded by a debit to Interest Receivable or by a debit to Interest Revenue; it is **not** an element of the investment's cost. Accrued interest increases the cash outlay to acquire an investment but does not increase the investment's cost. (Solution = c.)

**QUESTION**

2.    (L.O. 1) Refer to the facts in **Question 1** above. The amount of cash outlay required to acquire the investment is:
a.    $100,000.
b.    $102,000.
c.    $103,500.
d.    $106,000.

**Explanation:** The amount of cash required to acquire the investment is determined as follows:

|  |  |
|---|---|
| Purchase price (102% x $100,000 par) | $ 102,000 |
| Incidental costs to acquire | 1,500 |
| Total acquisition cost of investment | 103,500 |
| Accrued interest for three months | 2,500 |
| Total cash required to acquire investment | $ 106,000 |

(Solution = d.)

**QUESTION**

3.    (L.O. 1) When an investor's accounting period ends on a date that does not coincide with an interest receipt date for bonds held as an investment, the investor must:
a.    make an adjusting entry to debit Interest Receivable and to credit Interest Revenue for the amount of interest accrued since the last interest receipt date.
b.    notify the issuer and request that a special payment be made for the appropriate portion of the interest period.
c.    make an adjusting entry to debit Interest Receivable and to credit Interest Revenue for the total amount of interest to be received at the next interest receipt date.
d.    do nothing special and ignore the fact that the accounting period does not coincide with the bond's interest period.

**Approach:** Think of the requirements of the accrual basis of accounting: revenues are to be recognized when they are earned and expenses are to be recognized (recorded and reported) when they are incurred. Interest is earned by the passage of time and is usually collected after the time period for which it pertains. Thus, to comply with the revenue recognition principle, an adjusting entry is necessary to record the accrued revenue (revenue earned but not yet received). (Solution = a.)

---

## QUESTION

4.   (L.O. 1) The market value of Security A exceeds its cost, and the market value of Security B is less than its cost at a balance sheet date. Both securities are held as investments in debt securities; Security A is classified as trading and Security B is classified as available-for-sale. How should each of these assets be reported on the balance sheet?

|     | Security A | Security B |
| --- | --- | --- |
| a.  | Market value | Market value |
| b.  | Amortized cost | Amortized cost |
| c.  | Amortized cost | Market value |
| d.  | Market value | Amortized cost |

**Approach and Explanation:** Mentally review the accounting requirements for debt securities. They are summarized in **Illustration 17-1**. Investments in debt and equity securities classified as trading or available-for-sale are to be reported at fair value. Market value, if one is available, is used as a measure of fair value. Investments in debt securities classified as held-to-maturity are to be reported at amortized cost. (Solution =a.)

## QUESTION

5.   (L.O. 1) At December 31, 2009, Bithlo Corporation reported the following for its portfolio of investment in marketable debt securities:

| | |
| --- | --- |
| Investment in bonds, at cost | $ 400,000 |
| Less securities fair value adjustment | 39,000 |
| | $ 361,000 |

At December 31, 2010 the market value of the portfolio was $389,000. The cost remained at $400,000. Under what circumstances would Bithlo report a $28,000 credit on its income statement for 2010 as a result of the increase in the market price of the investment in 2010?

a.   When the security is classified in the trading category.
b.   When the security is classified in the available-for-sale category.
c.   When the security is classified in the held-to-maturity category.
d.   No circumstances would call for such a credit of $28,000 on the 2010 income statement.

**Approach and Explanation:** Quickly review the guidelines in accounting for an investment in debt securities; they are:

**Trading category:** Report at fair value on the balance sheet. Changes in fair value are reported on the income statement.

**Available-for-sale category:** Report at fair value on the balance sheet. Changes in fair value are reflected in a separate component of stockholders' equity rather than as a component of income.

**Held-to-maturity category:** Report at amortized cost on the balance sheet. Changes in fair value are ignored. (Solution = a.)

**QUESTION**

6.   (L.O. 3) ABC Studios holds four available-for-sale equity securities at December 31, 2010. They are all classified as long-term investments. All securities were purchased in 2010. The portfolio of securities appears as follows at December 31, 2010:

| | Cost | Market Value | Difference |
|---|---|---|---|
| Barbara Walters Corp. $100,000 | $ 80,000 | $(20,000) | |
| Harry Reasoner Corp. | 220,000 | 230,000 | 10,000 |
| David Brinkley Corp. | 210,000 | 150,000 | (60,000) |
| Hugh Downs Corp. | 140,000 | 145,000 | 5,000 |
| Totals | $670,000 | $605,000 | $(65,000) |

Assuming the decline in the market value of David Brinkley Corp. stock is considered to be other than temporary, the amounts of realized loss and unrealized loss to report as a component of net income for the year ending December 31, 2010 are:

| | **Realized Loss** | **Unrealized Loss** |
|---|---|---|
| a. | $60,000 | $5,000 |
| b. | $60,000 | $0 |
| c. | $0 | $65,000 |
| d. | $0 | $60,000 |

**Explanation:** A decline in fair value that is other than temporary is referred to as an **impairment**. Regardless of the category in which the security is classified, the security is written down to fair value. The amount of the writedown is accounted for as a realized loss and, therefore, included in net income. The fair value at the date of writedown is used as a new cost basis for the security. Temporary changes in the fair value of securities in the available-for-sale category are reflected as a component of other comprehensive income and in a separate stockholders' equity account rather than a component of net income. Thus, the $60,000 reduction in market value of David Brinkley Corp. stock is recorded as an impairment (charge to the income statement as a realized loss) and the remaining net unrealized loss [($20,000) + $10,000 + $5,000 = ($5,000)] is reported as a component of other comprehensive income and as a separate component of stockholders' equity and **not** a component of net income. (Solution = b.)

> **TIP:**   If the same facts above were for securities classified in the trading category, the answer would be "a" because the temporary changes in fair value of a trading portfolio are recognized as an element of net income.

**QUESTION**

7.   (L.O. 3) During 2009, Colquitt Company purchased 4,000 shares of Eichner Corp. common stock for $63,000 as an available-for-sale investment. The fair value of these shares was $60,000 at December 31, 2009. Colquitt sold all of the Eichner stock for $17 per share on December 3, 2010, incurring $2,800 in brokerage commissions. Colquitt Company should report a realized gain on the sale of stock in 2010 of:

a.   $8,000.
b.   $5,200.
c.   $5,000.
d.   $2,200.

**Explanation:** The gain is computed as follows:

| | |
|---|---|
| Selling price ($17 x 4,000 shares) | $ 68,000 |
| Cost of sale—commissions | (2,800) |
| Net proceeds (or net selling price) | 65,200 |
| Cost | 63,000 |
| Realized gain on sale | $ 2,200 |

(Solution = d.)

> **TIP:**   The valuation account balance existing at the end of 2009 would have no effect on this computation.

**QUESTION**

8. (L.O. 3) On its December 31, 2009 balance sheet, Simpson Company appropriately reported a $4,000 credit balance in its Securities Fair Value Adjustment (Available-for-Sale) account. There was no change during 2010 in the composition of Simpson's portfolio of marketable equity securities held as available-for-sale securities. The following information pertains to that portfolio:

| Security | Cost | Fair value at 12/31/10 |
|---|---|---|
| A | $ 50,000 | $ 65,000 |
| B | 40,000 | 38,000 |
| C | 70,000 | 50,000 |
| | $160,000 | $153,000 |

What amount of unrealized loss on these securities should be included in Simpson's shareholders' equity section of the balance sheet at December 31, 2010?
a. $0
b. $3,000
c. $4,000
d. $7,000

**Explanation:** The Securities Fair Value Adjustment (Available-for-Sale) account would be increased by $3,000 to a $7,000 credit balance; hence the Unrealized Holding Gain or Loss account would be also adjusted to a $7,000 debit balance. The Unrealized Holding Gain or Loss account is reported as a separate line item in stockholders' equity; it reflects the **net** unrealized loss of $7,000 on this portfolio ($160,000 cost - $153,000 fair value = $7,000). It is one possible component of Accumulated Other Comprehensive Income. (Solution = d.)

**QUESTION**

9. (L.O. 3) Refer to the facts of **Question 8** above. The amount of unrealized loss to appear as a component of comprehensive income for the year ending December 31, 2010 is:
a. $0.
b. $3,000.
c. $4,000.
d. $7,000.

**Explanation:** The $3,000 change in fair value during the current year goes on the comprehensive income statement for the year; whereas, the $7,000 **net** change in fair value since the acquisition date is reflected as a separate component of stockholders' equity. Because the change in fair value this period was a decrease, it appears as an unrealized holding loss (a debit) on the comprehensive income statement. Because the total fair value of the investment securities is less than the total cost, the $7,000 difference represents a **net** unrealized holding loss. The $7,000 appears as a separate component in stockholders' equity; in this case it is a debit item (contra stockholders' equity). (Solution = b.)

**QUESTION**

10. (L.O. 4) An investor has a long-term investment in stocks. Regular cash dividends received by the investor are recorded as:

| | Fair Value Method | Equity Method |
|---|---|---|
| a. | Income | Income |
| b. | A reduction of the investment | A reduction of the investment |
| c. | Income | A reduction of the investment |
| d. | A reduction of the investment | Income |

**Approach and Explanation:** Write down the journal entry to record the receipt of cash dividends (other than liquidating dividends) under both the fair value and equity methods. Observe the effects of the entries. Find the answer selection that correctly describes those effects.

| **Fair Value Method** | | | **Equity Method** | | |
|---|---|---|---|---|---|
| Cash | XX | | Cash | XX | |
| Dividend Revenue | | XX | Investment in Investee Stock | | XX |

(Solution = c.)

## QUESTION

11. (L.O. 4)   The Higgins Corporation purchased 6,000 shares of common stock of the Barnett Corporation for $40 per share on January 2, 2010. The Barnett Corporation had 60,000 shares of common stock outstanding during 2010, paid cash dividends of $30,000 during 2010, and reported net income of $120,000 for 2010.  The Higgins Corporation should report revenue from investment for 2010 in the amount of:
    a.   $3,000.
    b.   $9,000.
    c.   $12,000.
    d.   $15,000.

**Explanation:**  Because the Higgins Corporation owns only 10% of the outstanding common stock of the investee, it is assumed that Higgins Corporation cannot exercise significant influence over the financing and operating policies of the investee and must keep track of the cost of the investment and use the fair value method to report the investment. Using the fair value method, the investor will report dividend revenue equal to the amount of cash dividends received during the period.  ($30,000 X 10% = $3,000). (Solution = a.)

## QUESTION

12. (L.O. 4)   When the equity method is used to account for an investment in common stock of another corporation, the journal entry on the investor's books to record the receipt of cash dividends from the investee will:
    a.   include a debit to Cash and a credit to Dividend Revenue.
    b.   reduce the carrying value of the investment.
    c.   increase the carrying value of the investment.
    d.   be the same journal entry that would be recorded if the cost method were used to account for the investment.

**Explanation:**  The journal entry will be a debit to Cash and a credit to Investment in Stock. The credit portion of this entry reduces the balance of the investment account and, therefore, it reduces the carrying value of the investment.  (Solution = b.)

## QUESTION

13. (L.O. 5)   After electing the fair value option for the acquisition of an available-for-sale security, a change in the fair value of the security will be reported:
    a.   as a component of net income.
    b.   as a component of other comprehensive income.
    c.   both as a component of net income and as a component of other comprehensive income.
    d.   neither as a component of net income nor as a component of other comprehensive income.

**Explanation:** With the election of the fair value option, the security is reported at fair value on the balance sheet and all changes in fair value go thru net income.   (Solution =  a.)

**QUESTION**
14.   (L.O. 8) A debt security is transferred from one category to another. Generally acceptable accounting principles require that for this particular reclassification  (1) the security be transferred at fair value at the date of transfer, and (2) the unrealized gain or loss at the date of transfer currently carried as a separate component of stockholders' equity be amortized over the remaining life of the security. What type of transfer is being described?
a.    transfer from trading to available-for-sale
b.    transfer from available-for-sale to trading
c.    transfer from held-to-maturity to available-for-sale
d.    transfer from available-for-sale to held-to-maturity

**Approach:** Mentally review the accounting requirements for transfers from one investment category to another. Refer to **Illustration 17-6** for a summary of these requirements. (Solution = d.)


**QUESTION**
15.   (L.O. 7) An investment in debt or equity securities may be transferred from one category to another. Assuming the fair value differs from cost at the date of transfer, which of the following will immediately result in reporting an amount on the income statement?
   I.   Transfer from available-for-sale to trading.
   II.   Transfer from held-to-maturity to available-for-sale.
   III.   Transfer from available-for-sale to held-to-maturity.
a.    item I only
b.    items I and II only
c.    items I and III only
d.    items II and III only
e.    items I, II, and III

**Approach and Explanation:** Mentally review the accounting requirements for transfers from one investment category to another. Also review the effects of those requirements. Refer to **Illustration 17-6** for a summary of those requirements. (Solution = a.)


**QUESTION**
*16.   (L.O. 10)  Derivatives such as forwards and options are assets and liabilities and should be reported in the balance sheet at:
   a.    zero.
   b.    historical cost.
   c.    the creator's book value.
   d.    fair value.

**Explanation:** Derivatives such as forwards and options are assets and liabilities and should be reported in the balance sheet at fair value. Relying on some other basis of valuation, such as historical cost, does not make sense because many derivatives have a historical cost of zero. (Solution = d.)


**QUESTION**
*17.   (L.O. 11)  A call option gives the holder the:
   a.    right to buy an item at a present (or exercise) price.
   b.    obligation to buy an item at a present (or exercise) price.
   c.    right to sell an item at a present (or exercise) price.
   d.    obligation to sell an item at a present (or exercise) price.

**Explanation:** A call option gives the holder the right, but not the obligation, to buy at a present price (often referred to as the strike price or the exercise price). A put option gives the holder the option (right) to sell an item at a present (exercise) price. (Solution = a.)

# CHAPTER 18

# REVENUE RECOGNITION

## OVERVIEW

The revenue recognition principle provides that revenue is to be recognized when (1) it is realized or realizable and (2) it is earned. This rule sounds simple enough, but the many methods of marketing products and services make it extremely difficult to apply in certain situations. Although a large percentage of entities find it appropriate to recognize revenue at the point of sale (delivery) of a good or service, other entities find it appropriate to use some other basis of revenue recognition which may result in recognizing revenue prior to delivery or at a point in time after delivery. In this chapter, we discuss accounting guidelines for the recognition of revenue.

## SUMMARY OF LEARNING OBJECTIVES

1.  **Apply the revenue recognition principle.** The revenue recognition principle provides that revenue is recognized when (1) it is realized or realizable and (2) it is earned. Revenues are **realized** when goods and services are exchanged for cash or claims to cash. Revenues are **realizable** when assets received in exchange are readily convertible to known amounts of cash or claims to cash. Revenues are **earned** when the entity has substantially accomplished what it must do to be entitled to the benefits represented by the revenues, that is, when the earning process is complete or virtually complete.

2.  **Describe accounting issues involved with revenue recognition at point of sale.** The two conditions for recognizing revenue are usually met by the time a product or merchandise is delivered or services are rendered to customers. Companies commonly recognize revenue from manufacturing and selling activities at the time of sale. Problems of implementation can arise because of (1) sales with buyback agreements, (2) revenue recognition when right of return exists, and (3) trade loading and channel stuffing.

3.  **Apply the percentage-of-completion method for long-term contracts.** To apply the percentage-of-completion method to long-term contracts, a company must have some basis for measuring the progress toward completion at particular interim dates. One of the most popular input measures used to determine the progress toward completion is the cost-to-cost basis. Using this basis, a company measures the percentage of completion by comparing costs incurred to date with the most recent estimate of the total costs associated with the contract. The percentage that costs incurred to date bear to total estimated costs is applied to the total revenue or the estimated total gross profit on the contract, to arrive at the amount of revenue or gross profit to be recognized to date.

4. **Apply the completed-contract method for long-term contracts.** Under this method, companies recognize revenue and gross profit only at point of sale—that is, when the company completes the contract. The company accumulates costs of long-term contracts in process and current billings. It makes no interim charges or credits to income statement accounts for revenues, costs, and gross profit. The entries to record costs of construction, progress billings, and collections from customers would be identical to those for the percentage-of-completion method—with the significant exclusion of the recognition of revenue and gross profit.

5. **Identify the proper accounting for losses on long-term contracts.** Two types of losses can become evident under long-term contracts: (1) **Loss in current period on a profitable contract:** Under the percentage-of-completion method only, the estimated cost increase requires a current period adjustment of excess gross profit recognized on the project in prior periods. The company records this adjustment as a loss in the current period because it is a change in accounting estimate. (2) **Loss on an unprofitable contract:** Under both the percentage-of-completion and the completed-contract methods, the company must recognize the entire expected contract loss in the current period.

6. **Describe the installment sales method of accounting.** The installment-sales method (sometimes called the installment method) recognizes income in the periods of collection rather than in the period of sale. The installment-sales method of accounting is justified on the premise that when there is no reasonable basis for estimating the degree of collectibility, a company should not recognize revenue until it has collected cash.

7. **Explain the cost recovery method of accounting.** Under the cost recovery method, companies do not recognize profit until cash payments by the buyer exceed the seller's cost of the merchandise sold. After the seller has recovered all costs, it includes in income any additional cash collections. The income statement for the period of sale reports sales revenue, the cost of goods sold, and the gross profit—both the amount that is recognized during the period and the amount that is deferred. The deferred gross profit is offset against the related receivable on the balance sheet. Subsequent income statements report the gross profit as a separate item of revenue when it is recognized as earned.

*8. **Explain revenue recognition for franchises and consignment sales.** In a franchise arrangement, the franchisor records as revenue the initial franchise fee as it makes substantial performance of the services it is obligated to perform and collection of the fee is reasonably assured. Franchisors recognize continuing franchise fees as revenue when they are earned and receivable from the franchisee. In a consignment sale, the consignor recognizes revenue when it receives cash and notification of a sale from the consignee.

   *This material is covered in Appendix 18A in the text.

# TIPS ON CHAPTER TOPICS

**TIP:** All revenues cause an increase in net assets (owners' equity); thus, a revenue item also results in either an increase in assets or a decrease in liabilities. **Revenues** are defined in *SFAC No. 6* as: "Inflows of assets and/or settlements of liabilities from delivering or producing goods, rendering services, or other earning activities that constitute an enterprise's ongoing major or central operations during a period."

**TIP:** The amount of revenue for a period is generally determined independently of expenses. The **revenue recognition principle** is applied to determine in what period(s) revenue transactions are to be reported. Then the **matching principle** is applied to determine in what period(s) expense transactions are to be reported; expenses are to be recognized in the same period as the revenues to which the expenses contributed.

**TIP:** To **recognize** means to give expression in the accounts. To recognize a revenue means to record an item as revenue in the accounts; thus, the item will get reported as revenue in the financial statements. Likewise, to recognize an asset means to record an increase in an asset account. **Recognition** is "the process of formally recording or incorporating an item in the accounts and financial statements of an entity" (*SFAC No. 6*, par. 143). "Recognition includes depiction of an item in both words and numbers, with the amount included in the totals of the financial statements" (*SFAC No. 5*, par. 6). For an asset or liability, recognition involves recording not only acquisition or incurrence of the item but also later changes in it, including removal from the financial statements.

**TIP:** Recognition is **not** the same as realization, although the two are sometimes used interchangeably in accounting literature and practice. **Realization** is "the process of converting noncash resources and rights into money and is most precisely used in accounting and financial reporting to refer to sales of assets for cash or claims to cash" (*SFAC No. 6*, par. 143).

**TIP:** In accordance with the revenue recognition principle: (a) revenue from selling products is recognized at the date of sale, usually interpreted to mean the date of delivery to customers; (b) revenue from services rendered is recognized when services have been performed and are billable; (c) revenue from permitting others to use enterprise assets such as interest, rent, and royalties, is recognized as time passes or as the assets are used; and, (d) revenue from disposing of assets other than products is recognized at the date of sale.

**TIP:** The term **income** is sometimes used to refer to a gross amount (such as dividend income, rent income, interest income) which makes its usage synonymous with revenue. The term income is also used to refer to a net amount, such as net income for a period. Thus, if an exam question asks for the computation of income to be recognized for the current period for a long-term construction contract using the percentage-of-completion method, it may be unclear whether the question is using "income" to mean "revenue" or if "income" means "gross profit" (revenue **net** of related costs). If it is a multiple choice question, compute both revenue and gross profit and you may quickly solve the mystery.

**TIP:** **Revenue** is a **gross** amount (an amount before costs are deducted); whereas, **gain** is a **net** amount (an amount after costs are subtracted). Gains (as contrasted to revenues) commonly result from transactions and other events that do not involve an earning process. For gain recognition, being earned is generally less significant than being realized or realizable. Gains are commonly recognized at the time of sale of an asset, disposition of a liability, or when prices of certain assets change. The following example illustrates how revenue is a gross concept, and gain is a net concept.

A company sells two assets for $1,000 each. The first asset is an inventory item which cost $600. The second asset is a piece of equipment which cost $900 and has been depreciated $300 thus far. The first item would cause the following to be reflected in the income statement:

| | |
|---|---|
| Sales revenue | $1,000 |
| Cost of goods sold | 600 |
| Gross profit | $ 400 |

The second item would cause the following to be reflected in the "other income" section of a multiple-step income statement:

Gain on sale of equipment $400*
*$900 cost - $300 accumulated depreciation = $600 carrying value
$1,000 selling price - $600 carrying value = $400 gain

In the case of the second item, it is not an item held for sale in the main course of business. The proceeds ($1,000) and the related cost (carrying value of $600) are netted off the statement, and only the net amount ($400 gain) appears on the face of the income statement.

**TIP:** The revenue recognition bases or methods, the criteria for their use, and the reasons for departing from the sale basis when accounting for the sale of a product are summarized in **Illustration 18-3**. Review those methods and be able to explain when and why they are used.

**TIP:** The percentage of completion method is used for long-term construction contracts where revenue is appropriately recognized during production (prior to completion and delivery). Justification for recognition of revenue during the construction period is based on the fact that the ultimate sale and the selling price are assured by the contract. The percentage-of-completion method recognizes revenue, costs, and gross profit as progress is made toward completion on a long-term contract. The progress made during a period may be supplied by engineering estimates or determined by the cost-to-cost method (the latter method is used in most textbook situations). Companies use various methods to determine the extent of progress toward completion. The most common are the **cost-to-cost method** (used in most homework and exam questions– see **Exercise 1** and **Exercise 2** and **multiple choice Questions 4 and 5** in this book for examples) and the units-of-delivery method (units of delivery may be measured as tons produced, miles of highway completed, or floors of a building completed, for example). Using the **cost-to-cost method,** the amounts of revenue and gross profit to be recognized each period are computed using the following formula:

$$\left[ \frac{\text{Costs incurred to date}}{\text{Estimate of total costs}} \times \begin{array}{c} \text{Estimated total} \\ \text{revenue (or} \\ \text{gross profit)} \end{array} \right] - \begin{array}{c} \text{Total revenue (or gross} \\ \text{profit) recognized} \\ \text{in prior periods} \end{array} = \begin{array}{c} \text{Current period} \\ \text{revenue (or} \\ \text{gross profit)} \end{array}$$

In this formula, estimated total revenue is determined by the contract price, and estimated total gross profit is determined by the contract price reduced by an estimate of total costs. The estimate of total costs includes costs incurred to date **plus** an estimate of remaining costs to be incurred to complete the contract. Costs incurred to date include costs incurred in prior periods **plus** costs incurred in the current period.

## ILLUSTRATION 18-1
## SALES WHEN RIGHT OF RETURN EXISTS (L.O. 2)

Some companies experience such a high rate of sales returns that they find it necessary to postpone reporting sales until the return privilege has substantially expired. Among the types of companies that experience these high rates of return by customers are publishers, perishable food dealers, distributors who sell to retail outlets, recording industry companies, toy and sporting goods manufacturers.

Three alternative revenue recognition methods are available when the right of return exposes the seller to continued risks of ownership. These are: (1) not recording a sale until all return privileges have expired; (2) recording the sale, but reducing sales by an estimate of future returns; and (3) recording the sale and accounting for the returns as they occur. The FASB concluded that if a company sells its product but gives the buyer the right to return it, the company should recognize revenue from the sales transactions at the time of sale **only if all of the following six conditions** have been met.
1. The seller's price to the buyer is substantially fixed or determinable at the date of sale.
2. The buyer has paid the seller, or the buyer is obligated to pay the seller, and the obligation is not contingent on resale of the product.
3. The buyer's obligation to the seller would not be changed in the event of theft or physical destruction or damage of the product.
4. The buyer acquiring the product for resale has economic substance apart from that provided by the seller.
5. The seller does not have significant obligations for future performance to directly bring about resale of the product by the buyer.
6. The seller can reasonably estimate the amount of future returns.

What if the six conditions are not met? In that case, the company must recognize sales revenue and cost of sales either when the return privilege has substantially expired or when those six conditions subsequently are met, **whichever occurs first.**

| | |
|---|---|
| **TIP:** | **Trade loading** and **channel stuffing** are practices that get customers to buy more than they can sell so that the manufacturer can report inflated revenue numbers. These practices distort operating results and "window dress" financial statements. An appropriate allowance for expected sales returns is necessary for fair reporting. |

**ILLUSTRATION 18-2**
**JOURNAL ENTRIES FOR LONG-TERM**
**CONSTRUCTION CONTRACTS (L.O. 3, 4)**

| ENTRY | PERCENTAGE-OF-COMPLETION METHOD | COMPLETED-CONTRACT METHOD |
|---|---|---|
| To record costs of construction | Construction in Process<br>    Materials, Cash, Payables, etc. | Construction in Process<br>    Materials, Cash, Payables, etc. |
| To record progress billings | Accounts Receivable<br>    Billings on Construction in Process | Accounts Receivable<br>    Billings on Construction in Process |
| To record collections | Cash<br>    Accounts Receivable | Cash<br>    Accounts Receivable |
| To recognize revenue and gross profit | Construction in Process    GP**<br>Construction Expenses    COSTS<br>    Revenue from Long-Term Contracts    REV | No Entry.* |
| To record final approval of the contract | Billings on Construction in Process<br>    Construction in Process | Billings on Const. in Process    REV<br>    Revenue from Long-Term Contracts    REV<br>Costs of Construction***  COSTS<br>    Construction in Process    COSTS |

GP = Gross Profit    COSTS = Costs Incurred    REV = Revenue

*A loss on an unprofitable contract is recognized, in full, immediately under either method. A loss would be recorded under the completed-contract method by a debit to Loss from Long-Term Contracts and a credit to Construction in Process for the estimated amount of loss.
**When a loss is estimated, this account (Construction in Process) gets credited for the estimated amount of loss. The rest of the entry is the same as what is shown for a profitable situation.
***The account Construction Expenses can be titled Construction Costs or Costs of Construction.

**TIP:** An estimated loss on a long-term construction contract is to be recognized in the period it is determined there will ultimately be a loss on completion of the contract, regardless of the method being used to account for the contract. The justification for recognizing the loss before completion even under the completed-contract method lies with the conservatism constraint and the axiom—anticipate no profits but provide for all losses.

## ILLUSTRATION 18-3
## REVENUE RECOGNITION BASES OTHER THAN
## THE SALE BASIS FOR PRODUCTS (L.O. 3, 4, 6, 7)

| Recognition Basis (or Method of Applying a Basis) | Criteria for Use of Basis | Reason(s) for Departing from Sale Basis |
| --- | --- | --- |
| Percentage-of-completion method | Long-term construction of property; dependable estimates of extent of progress and cost to complete; reasonable assurance of collectibility of contract price; expectation that both contractor and buyer can meet obligations; and absence of inherent hazards that make estimates doubtful. | Availability of evidence of ultimate proceeds; better measure of periodic income; avoidance of fluctuations in revenues, expenses, and income; performance is a "continuous sale" and therefore not a departure from the sale basis. |
| Completed-contract method | Use on short-term contracts, and whenever percentage-of-completion criteria are not met for long-term contracts. | Existence of inherent hazards in the contract beyond the normal, recurring business risks; conditions for using the percentage-of-completion method are absent. |
| Completion-of-production basis | Immediate marketability at quoted prices; unit interchangeability; difficulty of determining costs; and no significant distribution costs. | Known or determinable revenues; inability to determine costs and thereby defer expense recognition until sale. |
| Installment sales method | Absence of a reasonable basis for estimating degree of collectibility and costs of collection. | Collectibility of the receivable is so uncertain that gross profit is not recognized until cash is actually received. |
| Cost recovery method | Absence of a reasonable basis for estimating degree of collectibility and cost of collection. | Collectibility of the receivable is so doubtful that no income is recognized until the amount of cash received exceeds the cost of the good sold. |
| Deposit method | Cash received before the sales transaction is completed. | No recognition of revenue and income because there is not sufficient transfer of the risks and rewards of ownership. |

> **TIP:** The revenue recognition principle provides that companies should recognize revenue (1) when it is realized or realizable and (2) when it is earned. Revenues are **realized** when a company exchanges goods and services for cash or claims to cash (receivables). Revenues are **realizable** when assets a company receives in exchange are readily convertible to known amounts of cash or claims to cash. Revenues are **earned** when a company has substantially accomplished what it must do to be entitled to the benefits represented by the revenues–that is, when the earnings process is complete or virtually complete.

**Source:** Adapted from *Survey of Present Practices in Recognizing Revenues, Expenses, Gains, and Losses*, FASB, 1981, pp. 12 and 13.

## EXERCISE 18-1

**Purpose:**   (L.O. 3, 4) This exercise will allow you to compare the results of using the percentage-of-completion method versus the results of applying the completed-contract method to compute the amount of gross profit to be recognized in each year of a three-year contract.

At the beginning of 2010, Buildalot Construction Company signed a fixed-price contract to construct a sports arena at a price of $26,000,000. Information relating to the costs and billings for this contract is as follows:

|  | 2010 | 2011 | 2012 |
|---|---|---|---|
| Costs incurred during the period | $ 8,320,000 | $11,360,000 | $ 3,520,000 |
| Estimated costs to complete, as of December 31 | 12,480,000 | 4,320,000 | -0- |
| Billings during the year | 3,900,000 | 15,900,000 | 6,200,000 |
| Collections during the year | 3,120,000 | 12,000,000 | 10,880,000 |

## Instructions

(a)   Assuming the completed-contract method is used, compute the gross profit to be recognized in (1) 2010, (2) 2011, and (3) 2012.

(b)   Assuming the percentage-of-completion method is used, compute the gross profit to be recognized in (1) 2010, (2) 2011, and (3) 2012.

(c)   Assuming the percentage-of-completion method is used, show how the details related to this construction contract would be disclosed on the balance sheet at December 31, 2011.

## Solution to Exercise 18-1

(a) (1)  2010                    -0-
(2) 2011                    -0-
(3) 2012            $2,800,000*

    *Computations:
    Total revenue          $26,000,000
    Total costs incurred              23,200,000**
    Total gross profit        $ 2,800,000

        **Costs incurred in 2010          $ 8,320,000
        Costs incurred in 2011            11,360,000
        Costs incurred in 2012             3,520,000
        Total costs incurred           $23,200,000

**Explanation:** When the completed-contract method is used, the recognition of all revenue and related costs (and, therefore, resulting gross profit) is deferred until the period of completion (2012 in this case). The only exception to this guideline is in the case where a loss is expected. A loss should be recognized immediately in the period in which it is determined that a loss will result.

(b) (1)  2010          $2,080,000
    (2) 2011          $ (440,000)
    (3) 2012          $1,160,000

**Computations:**

**2010:**  Costs incurred to date (12/31/10)                          $  8,320,000
            Estimated costs to complete as of 12/31/10              12,480,000
            Estimate of total costs as of 12/31/10                  $ 20,800,000

            Total revenue (contract price)                          $ 26,000,000
            Estimate of total costs                                  20,800,000
            Estimated total gross profit                            $  5,200,000

$$\frac{\$8,320,000}{\$20,800,000} \times \$5,200,000 = \underline{\$2,080,000} \quad \text{Gross profit to be recognized in 2010}$$

**2011:**  Costs incurred to date (12/31/11)($8,320,000 + $11,360,000)   $ 19,680,000
            Estimated costs to complete as of 12/31/11               4,320,000
            Estimate of total costs as of 12/31/11                  $ 24,000,000

            Total revenue (contract price)                          $26,000,000
            Estimate of total costs                                  24,000,000
            Estimated total gross profit                            $ 2,000,000

$$\frac{\$19,680,000}{\$24,000,000} \times \$2,000,000 - \$2,080,000 = \underline{\$(440,000)} \quad \text{Loss to be recognized in 2011}$$

**2012:**  Costs incurred in 2010                                   $  8,320,000
            Costs incurred in 2011                                  11,360,000
            Costs incurred in 2012                                   3,520,000
            Total costs incurred   23,200,000

            Total revenue (contract price)                          $26,000,000
            Total costs incurred   23,200,000
            Total gross profit earned on contract                    2,800,000
            Gross profit recognized in 2010                         (2,080,000)
            Loss recognized in 2011                                    440,000
            Gross profit to be recognized in 2012                   $ 1,160,000

**Approach and Explanation:** Gross profit to be recognized in a particular year can be determined by applying the following formula:

$$\left[ \frac{\text{Costs incurred}}{\text{to date}} \middle/ \text{Estimate of} \atop \text{total costs} \times \text{Estimated total} \atop \text{gross profit} \right] - \text{Total gross} \atop {\text{profit recognized} \atop \text{in prior periods}} = \text{Current period} \atop \text{gross profit}$$

In the computation for estimated total gross profit, the current (most up-to-date) estimate of total costs is deducted from total revenue (the contract price). The estimate of total costs is likely to change every year which will cause the estimated total gross profit to change each year. Such is the case in this exercise.

In the second year of the contract, Buildalot's cost estimates increased dramatically, which caused the gross profit recognized to date (2010's gross profit of $2,080,000) to exceed the $1,640,000 total gross profit earned to date ($19,680,000 ÷ $24,000,000 x $2,000,000 = $1,640,000). This excess is recognized as a loss of $440,000 in 2011 to bring the total gross profit recognized by the end of 2011 to $1,640,000.

In the last year of the contract, total costs incurred on the contract are deducted from total revenue on the contract to arrive at total gross profit earned on the contract. The amounts reported on prior income statements as gross profit (loss) are deducted from (added to) this amount to arrive at the gross profit to recognize in the last period.

In the situation at hand, the costs incurred in 2012 are less than what was expected, according to the cost estimates at the end of 2011, which results in more total gross profit than was predicted at the end of 2011.

**TIP:** Notice that **neither** the amount of billings **nor** the amount of cash collections during the year has an impact on the amount of gross profit to be recognized.

**TIP:** Notice that a loss was recognized in the second year using the percentage-of-completion method but no loss was recognized using the completed-contract method. The reasons for this is that the loss was an interim loss, not an overall loss on the contract. An interim loss refers to the loss that results when the total gross profit to date (at the end of 2011) is less than the amount of gross profit recognized in prior periods (2010). It is a loss in the current period (2011) on a profitable contract. It results from an increase in estimated costs which requires a current period adjustment of excess gross profit recognized on the contract in prior periods. This adjustment is recorded in the current period because it is a change in accounting estimate. If an overall loss is expected on a contract, it must also be recognized immediately even under the completed-contract method.

(c)     Current assets:

| | | |
|---|---|---|
| Accounts receivable | | $4,680,000 |
| Inventories | | |
|    Construction in process | $21,320,000 | |
|    Less: Billings on construction in process | 19,800,000 | |
|       Costs and recognized profit in excess of billings | | $1,520,000 |

**Approach and Explanation:** Draw T-accounts. Mentally think through the journal entries that would be recorded for the facts given. Post these amounts to the T-accounts on paper.

| Accounts Receivable | | | |
|---|---|---|---|
| 2010 | 3,900,000 | 2010 | 3,120,000 |
| 2011 | 15,900,000 | 2011 | 12,000,000 |
| | | | |
| 12/31/11 | | | |
| Bal. | 4,680,000 | | |

| Construction in Process | | | |
|---|---|---|---|
| 2010 | 8,320,000 | 2011 | 440,000 |
| 2010 | 2,080,000 | | |
| 2011 | 11,360,000 | | |
| 12/31/11 | | | |
| Bal. | 21,320,000 | | |

| Billings on Construction in Process | | | |
|---|---|---|---|
| | | 2010 | 3,900,000 |
| | | 2011 | 15,900,000 |
| | | 12/31/11 | |
| | | Bal. | 19,800,000 |

**TIP:** Notice that the amounts reflected in the balance sheet at Dec. 31, 2011, for accounts receivable ($4,680,000) and inventories ($1,520,000) when combined with the increase in cash from collections of billings ($15,120,000 collections to date) equals $21,320,000 (the balance in the Construction in Process account) which also equals the percentage of the total contract revenue earned to date ($19,680,000/ $24,000,000 x $26,000,000 = $21,320,000). The balance of the Billings on Construction in Process account is deducted from the balance in the Construction in Process account so as not to double count assets related to accounting for construction contracts. The total amount billed thus far ($19,800,000) is either collected ($15,120,000 has been collected so the Cash account has increased which is not shown here) or uncollected ($4,680,000 balance in Accounts Receivable).

**TIP:** Regardless of whether the percentage-of-completion method or the completed-contract method is used, the difference between the balance of the Construction in Process account and the balance of the Billings on Construction in Process account is reported as a current liability (if Billings on Construction in Process has the larger balance) or as a current asset (if Construction in Process has the larger balance). The balance of the Billings on Construction in Process account is offset against the balance of the inventory account (Construction in Process) because the inventory amount should not be double counted (i.e., the inventory account was not removed when the Accounts Receivable account was increased at the date of a billing to a customer).

**TIP:** When comparing the completed contract method with the percentage-of-completion method at any particular balance sheet date, the percentage-of-completion method will yield a higher balance in the Construction in Process account, assuming a profit is expected on the overall contract. If a loss is expected on the contract, both methods will yield the same balance in the Construction in Process account. For the above situation, the completed-contract method would result in a balance of $19,680,000 in the Construction in Process account at the end of 2011. The balances of the Accounts Receivable and Billings on Construction in Process accounts do not differ between the methods used.

## EXERCISE 18-2

**Purpose:**   (L.O. 3, 4) This exercise will illustrate the computations, journal entries, and balance sheet presentations involved in the use of the completed-contract and percentage-of-completion methods of accounting for long-term construction contracts.

The Nifty Construction Company entered into a long-term contract in 2010. The contract price was $1,600,000, and the company initially estimated the total costs of the project to be $1,150,000. The following data pertains to the three years that the contract was in process:

| Year | Costs Incurred During the Year | Estimated Costs at End of the Year to Complete Contract | Billings During the Year | Collections During the Year | Operating Expenses |
|---|---|---|---|---|---|
| 2010 | $224,000 | $896,000 | $ 200,000 | $170,000 | $80,000 |
| 2011 | 712,000 | 264,000 | 1,000,000 | 900,000 | 82,000 |
| 2012 | 344,000 | -0- | 400,000 | 430,000 | 74,000 |

## Instructions

(a)   Compute the gross profit to be reported in each of the three years using the completed-contract method.

(b)   Compute the gross profit to be reported in each of the three years using the percentage-of-completion method based on the costs incurred to date and the estimated costs to complete the contract. (Also compute the amount of revenue and cost of sales reflected in each gross profit figure.)

(c)   Prepare the related journal entries for all three years using the completed-contract method.

(d)   Prepare the related journal entries for all three years using the percentage-of-completion method.

(e)   Prepare a partial balance sheet at the end of each of the three years assuming (1) the completed-contract method is used and (2) the percentage-of-completion method is used.

| TIP: | The use of T-accounts is helpful here to determine the balances of accounts at the balance sheet date. |
|---|---|

## Solution to Exercise 18-2

(a)   2010                -0-
2011              -0-
2012   $1,600,000 - ($224,000 + $712,000 + $344,000) = $320,000

(b)   **2010**   Estimate of total costs = $224,000 + $896,000 = $1,120,000
        Estimate of total gross profit = $1,600,000 - $1,120,000 = $480,000

        Gross profit to be recognized in 2010 = $\dfrac{\$224,000}{\$1,120,000}$ x $480,000 = $96,000

**2011**   Costs incurred to date = $224,000 + $712,000 = $936,000
Estimate of total costs = $936,000 + $264,000 = $1,200,000
Estimate of total gross profit = $1,600,000 - $1,200,000 = $400,000
Gross profit to be recognized in 2011 =

$$\left[ \frac{\$936,000}{\$1,200,000} \quad ,000 \quad - \$96,000 \right] = \underline{\$216,000}$$

**2012**   Total costs incurred for project = $224,000 + $712,000 + $344,000
     = $1,280,000
Contract price of $1,600,000 minus total costs incurred of $1,280,000
    equals total gross profit on project of $320,000
Gross profit to be recognized in 2012 = $320,000 - ($96,000 + $216,000)
    = $\underline{\$8,000}$

**2010**   Revenue for 2010 = $\dfrac{\$224,000}{\$1,120,000}$ x $1,600,000 = $\underline{\$320,000}$

Costs to match with revenue for 2010 = $\underline{\$224,000}$

Gross profit for 2010 = $320,000 - $224,000 = $96,000

**2011**   Revenue for 2011 = $\left[ \dfrac{\$936,000}{\$1,200,000} \quad 00,000 \quad - \$320,000 \right] = \underline{\$928,000}$

Costs to match with revenue for 2011 = $\underline{\$712,000}$

Gross profit for 2011 = $928,000 - $712,000 = $216,000

**2012**   Revenue for 2012 = $1,600,000 - ($320,000 + $928,000) = $\underline{\$352,000}$

Costs to match with revenue for 2012 = $\underline{\$344,000}$

Gross profit for 2007 = $352,000 - $344,000 = $8,000

---

**TIP:**   iGAAP prohibits the use of the completed-contract method of accounting for long-term construction contracts. Companies must use the percentage-of-completion method. If revenues and costs are difficult to estimate, then companies recognize revenue only to the extent of the costs incurred—a zero-profit approach.

(c)    **Journal Entries—Completed Contract Method**

|  | 2010 | | 2011 | | 2012 | |
|---|---|---|---|---|---|---|
| **Accounts** | **Dr.** | **Cr.** | **Dr.** | **Cr.** | **Dr.** | **Cr.** |
| Const. in Process | 224,000 | | 712,000 | | 344,000 | |
| Operating Expenses | 80,000 | | 82,000 | | 74,000 | |
| Materials, Cash, Payables, Etc. | | 304,000 | | 794,000 | | 418,000 |
| | | | | | | |
| Accounts Receivable | 200,000 | | 1,000,000 | | 400,000 | |
| Billings on Const. in Process | | 200,000 | | 1,000,000 | | 400,000 |
| | | | | | | |
| Cash | 170,000 | | 900,000 | | 430,000 | |
| Accounts Rec. | | 170,000 | | 900,000 | | 430,000 |
| | | | | | | |
| Billings on Const. in Process | | | | | 1,600,000 | |
| Revenue from Long-term Contracts | | | | | | 1,600,000 |
| | | | | | | |
| Construction Exp. | | | | | 1,280,000 | |
| Const. in Process | | | | | | 1,280,000 |

(d)    **Journal Entries—Percentage-of-Completion Method**

|  | 2010 | | 2011 | | 2012 | |
|---|---|---|---|---|---|---|
| **Accounts** | **Dr.** | **Cr.** | **Dr.** | **Cr.** | **Dr.** | **Cr.** |
| Const. in Process | 224,000 | | 712,000 | | 344,000 | |
| Operating Expenses | 80,000 | | 82,000 | | 74,000 | |
| Materials, Cash, Payables, Etc. | | 304,000 | | 794,000 | | 418,000 |
| | | | | | | |
| Accounts Receivable | 200,000 | | 1,000,000 | | 400,000 | |
| Billings on Const. in Process | | 200,000 | | 1,000,000 | | 400,000 |
| | | | | | | |
| Cash | 170,000 | | 900,000 | | 430,000 | |
| Accounts Rec. | | 170,000 | | 900,000 | | 430,000 |
| | | | | | | |
| Const. Expenses | 224,000 | | 712,000 | | 344,000 | |
| Const. in Process | 96,000 | | 216,000 | | 8,000 | |
| Revenue from Long-Term Contracts | | 320,000 | | 928,000 | | 352,000 |
| | | | | | | |
| Billings on Const. in Process | | | | | 1,600,000 | |
| Const. in Process | | | | | | 1,600,000 |

(e)   1.    **Partial Balance Sheet—Completed-Contract Method**

|  | End of 2010 | End of 2011 | End of 2012 |
|---|---|---|---|
| **Current assets:** | | | |
| Accounts receivable | $30,000 | $130,000 | $100,000 |
| Inventories | | | |
|    Construction in process | $224,000 | | |
|    Less: Billings on const. in process | 200,000 | | |
|    Unbilled contract costs | $24,000 | | |
| | | | |
| **Current liabilities:** | | | |
| Billings on const. in process | | $1,200,000 | |
| Less: Construction in process | | 936,000 | |
| Billings in excess of costs and recognized profit | | $264,000 | |

**Approach:** Draw T-accounts and post journal entries to determine account balances.

2.    **Partial Balance Sheet—Percentage-of-Completion Method**

|  | End of 2010 | End of 2011 | End of 2012 |
|---|---|---|---|
| **Current assets:** | | | |
| Accounts receivable | $30,000 | $130,000 | $100,000 |
| Inventories | | | |
|    Construction in process | $320,000 | $1,248,000 | |
|    Less: Billings on const. in process | 200,000 | 1,200,000 | |
|    Costs and recognized profit in excess of billings | $120,000 | $48,000 | |

**Approach:** Draw T-accounts and post journal entries to determine account balances.

# EXERCISE 18-3

**Purpose:**   (L.O. 6, 7) This exercise will (1) illustrate the computations involved with the installment method of accounting, (2) examine the classification of the Deferred Gross Profit account and (3) apply the cost recovery method.

Arnie Sagar Company has appropriately used the installment method of accounting since it began business in 2010. The following data were obtained for the years 2010 and 2011:

|  | 2010 | 2011 |
|---|---|---|
| Installment sales | $800,000 | $900,000 |
| Cost of installment sales | 592,000 | 684,000 |
| Cash collections on sales of 2010 | 280,000 | 320,000 |
| Cash collections on sales of 2011 | -0- | 400,000 |

## Instructions

(a)   Compute the amount of realized gross profit to report for (1) 2010, and (2) 2011.

(b)   Compute the balance in the deferred gross profit accounts on (1) December 31, 2010, and (2) December 31, 2011.

(c)   Explain the classification of the total deferred gross profit on the balance sheet at December 31, 2011.

(d)   Prepare the journal entry to record the repossession of merchandise because of a defaulting customer. Assume that at the date of default in 2011, the balance on the related installment receivable (which originated in 2010) was $14,000 and the fair value of the merchandise was $8,500.

(e)   Assume the cost recovery method is used rather than the installment method. Compute the amount of realized gross profit that would be recognized (1) on the 2010 income statement, and (2) on the 2011 income statement.

## Solution to Exercise 18-3

(a)   (1)   Gross Profit Ratio—2010:

| | |
|---|---:|
| Installment sales for 2010 | $ 800,000 |
| Cost of installment sales for 2010 | (592,000) |
| Gross profit on installment sales for 2010 | $ 208,000 |

$$\frac{\$208,000 \text{ Gross Profit}}{\$800,000 \text{ Sales}} = \underline{26\%} \text{ Gross profit ratio on 2010 sales}$$

| | |
|---|---:|
| Cash collections in 2010 on sales of 2010 | $ 280,000 |
| Gross profit ratio for 2010 sales | 26% |
| Gross profit realized in 2010 on 2010 sales | $  72,800 |

(2)   Gross Profit Ratio—2011:

| | |
|---|---:|
| Installment sales for 2011 | $ 900,000 |
| Cost of installment sales for 2011 | (684,000) |
| Gross profit on installment sales for 2011 | $ 216,000 |

$$\frac{\$216,000 \text{ Gross profit}}{\$900,000 \text{ Sales}} = \underline{24\%} \text{ Gross profit ratio on 2011 sales}$$

| | |
|---|---:|
| Cash collections in 2011 on sales of 2011 | $ 400,000 |
| Gross profit ratio for 2011 sales | 24% |
| Gross profit realized in 2011 on 2011 sales | $  96,000 |

| | |
|---|---:|
| Cash collections in 2011 on sales of 2010 | $ 320,000 |
| Gross profit ratio for 2010 sales | 26% |
| Gross profit realized in 2011 on 2010 sales | $  83,200 |

| | |
|---|---:|
| Gross profit realized in 2011 on 2011 sales | $  96,000 |
| Gross profit realized in 2011 on 2010 sales | 83,200 |
| Total gross profit realized in 2011 | $ 179,200 |

> **TIP:** Always compute a separate gross profit ratio for each year in which there are installment sales. Clearly label each ratio so it is ready for use in subsequent computations. For any given year, the cash collections during the year on Year 1 installment sales multiplied by the gross profit ratio on Year 1 installment sales will yield the gross profit realized during that given year on Year 1 installment sales. The balance of Installment Accounts Receivable, Year 1, at a balance sheet date, multiplied by the gross profit ratio for Year 1 installment sales will yield the appropriate adjusted balance for the related Deferred Gross Profit, Year 1 account at the same date.

(b)     (1)

**Deferred Gross Profit, 2010**

| 2010 | 72,800[b] | 2010 | 208,000[a] |
|------|-----------|------|------------|
|      |           | 12/31/10 Bal. | 135,200 |

(2)

**Deferred Gross Profit, 2006**

| 2011 | 83,200[c] | 12/31/10 Bal. | 135,200 |
|------|-----------|---------------|---------|
|      |           | 12/31/11 Bal. | 52,000 |

**Deferred Gross Profit, 2011**

| 2011 | 96,000[e] | 2011 | 216,000[d] |
|------|-----------|------|------------|
|      |           | 12/31/11 Bal. | 120,000 |

[a] Gross profit on 2010 installment sales = $800,000 - $592,000 = $208,000.
[b] Gross profit realized in 2010 on 2010 sales = $280,000 collections x 26% = $72,800.
[c] Gross profit realized in 2011 on 2010 sales = $320,000 collections x 26% = $83,200.
[d] Gross profit on 2011 installment sales = $900,000 - $684,000 = $216,000.
[e] Gross profit realized in 2011 on 2011 sales = $400,000 collections x 24% = $96,000.

> **TIP:** The $52,000 balance in the Deferred Gross Profit, 2010 account at December 31, 2011 can be independently verified by multiplying the balance of Installment Accounts Receivable, 2010 at December 31, 2011 [$800,000 - ($280,000 + $320,000) = $200,000] by the gross profit ratio for 2010 installment sales (26%).

(c)     Per the answers to part (b) (2) above, the total deferred gross profit at December 31, 2011 amounts to $172,000 [$52,000 + $120,000 = $172,000]. In *SFAC No. 6*, par. 232-234, the FASB states that "deferred gross profit on installment sales is conceptually an asset valuation—that is, a reduction of an asset." However, in practice, deferred gross profit on installment sales is generally treated as unearned revenue and is classified as a current liability (because the operating cycle is longer than the installment period).

(d)     **Approach:**

| | | |
|---|---|---|
| *Do Second* | Deferred Gross Profit (26% x $14,000) .......................... | 3,640 |
| *Do Third* | Repossessed Merchandise ........................................... | 8,500 |
| *Plug* | Loss on Repossession ................................................. | 1,860 |
| *Do First* |     Installment Accounts Receivable........................... | 14,000 |

**Explanation:** The amount of the loss is determined by (1) subtracting the deferred gross profit from the amount of the account receivable to determine the unrecovered cost (or book value) of the merchandise repossessed ($14,000 - $3,640 = $10,360), and (2) subtracting the estimated fair value of the merchandise repossessed from the unrecovered cost to get the amount of the loss on repossession ($10,360 - $8,500 = $1,860). As an alternative, the loss on repossession can be charged to the Allowance for Doubtful Accounts account.

(e)  (1)  Using the cost recovery method, no gross profit would be recognized on the 2010 income statement because the $280,000 cash collections did not exceed the $592,000 cost of the merchandise sold.

(2)  Using the cost recovery method of revenue recognition, gross profit of $8,000 would be reported in 2011 due to installment sales made in 2010. No gross profit would be recognized on 2011 sales because cash collections did not exceed the cost of the merchandise sold.

**Computations:**

| | |
|---|---:|
| Cumulative cash collections on 2010 sales | $ 600,000* |
| Cost of 2010 installment sales | (592,000) |
| Gross profit to be recognized in 2011 using cost recovery method | $    8,000 |

*$280,000 + $320,000 = $600,000

**Explanation:** The cost recovery method provides for gross profit to be recognized **only** after all costs of related sales have been recovered. All subsequent cash collections are recognized as profit.

## *EXERCISE 18-4

**Purpose:**  (L.O. 8) This exercise will examine the treatment for an initial franchise fee under three scenarios.

Ma's Best Cookies Inc. charges an initial franchise fee of $110,000. Upon the signing of the agreement, a payment of $50,000 is due; thereafter, three annual payments of $20,000 are required. The credit rating of the franchisee is such that it would have to pay interest at 10% to borrow money.

## Instructions
Prepare the entries to record the initial franchise fee on the books of the franchisor under the following assumptions:
(a)  The down payment is not refundable, no future services are required by the franchisor, and collection of the note is reasonably assured.
(b)  The franchisor has substantial services to perform, and the collection of the note is very uncertain.
(c)  The down payment is not refundable, collection of the note is reasonably certain, the franchisor has yet to perform a substantial amount of services, and the down payment represents a fair measure of the services already performed.

## Solution to Exercise 18-4

(a)     Cash................................................................ 50,000
Notes Receivable........................................................ 60,000
        Discount on Notes Receivable .......................................... 10,263
          [$60,000 - ($20,000 x 2.48685*)]
        Revenue from Franchise Fees.......................................... 99,737
          ($50,000 + $60,000 - $10,263)

(b)     Cash................................................................ 50,000
        Unearned Franchise Fees................................................ 50,000

(c)     Cash................................................................ 50,000
Notes Receivable........................................................ 60,000
        Discount on Notes Receivable .......................................... 10,263
        Revenue from Franchise Fees.......................................... 50,000
        Unearned Franchise Fees ($20,000 x 2.48685*)................. 49,737

*The factor for the present value of an ordinary annuity of 1 for $n = 3$,
  $i = 10\%$ is 2.48685.

| | |
|---|---|
| **TIP:** | The amount of revenue recognized and the carrying value of the note receivable recorded by the franchisor upon the receipt of the franchise agreement and the initial franchise fee depend upon several factors, including: (1) whether or not the fee may be refundable, (2) an estimate of the collectibility of the note, (3) a measure of the future services to be performed by the franchisor, and (4) the incremental borrowing rate of the franchisee. |

# *EXERCISE 18-5

**Purpose:**     (L.O. 8) This exercise will review computations involved with consignment sales.

On April 15, 2010, Stayfit Company consigned 70 treadmills, costing $600 each, to Higley Company. The cost of shipping the treadmills amounts to $800 and was paid by Stayfit Company. On December 30, 2010, an account sales was received from the consignee, reporting that 35 treadmills had been sold for $700 each. Remittance was made by the consignee for the amount due, after deducting a commission of 6%, advertising of $200, and total delivery costs of $300 on the treadmills sold.

## Instructions
(a)     Compute the inventory value of the units unsold in the hands of the consignee.
(b)     Compute the profit for the consignor for the units sold.
(c)     Compute the amount of cash that will be remitted by the consignee.

## Solution to Exercise 18-5

(a)   Inventoriable Costs:

| | |
|---|---:|
| 70 units shipped at cost of $600 each | $ 42,000 |
| Freight to consignee | 800 |
| Total inventoriable cost | $ 42,800 |
| | |
| 35 units on hand (1/2 x $42,800) | $ 21,400 |

(b)   Computation of Consignment Profit:

| | |
|---|---:|
| Consignment sales (35 x $700) | $ 24,500 |
| Cost of units sold (1/2 x $42,800) | (21,400) |
| Commission charged by consignee (6% x $24,500) | (1,470) |
| Advertising costs | (200) |
| Delivery costs to customers | (300) |
| Profit on consignment sales | $   1,130 |

(c)   Remittance of Consignee:

| | | |
|---|---:|---:|
| Consignment sales | | $ 24,500 |
| Less:  Commissions | $ 1,470 | |
|           Advertising | 200 | |
|           Delivery | 300 | 1,970 |
|           Remittance from consignee | | $ 22,530 |

---

**TIP:** Goods on consignment should be reported as inventory by the consignor, not the consignee.

---

## ANALYSIS OF MULTIPLE-CHOICE TYPE QUESTIONS

**QUESTION**
1.(L.O. 1) The process of formally recording or incorporating an item in the financial statements of an entity is:
a.    allocation.
b.    articulation.
c.    realization.
d.    recognition.

**Approach and Explanation:** Write down a brief definition of each term listed. Select the one that matches the description in the stem of the question. **Allocation** is the accounting process of assigning or distributing an amount according to a plan or formula. Allocation is a broad term and includes amortization, which is the accounting process of reducing an amount by periodic payments or writedowns. **Articulation** refers to the interrelation of elements of the financial statements. **Realization** means the process of converting noncash resources and rights into money (such as the sale of assets for cash or claims to cash). **Recognition** is defined in *SFAC No. 6* as the process of formally recording or incorporating an item in the financial statements of an entity. (Solution = d.)

**QUESTION**

2.    (L.O. 1) Dot Point, Inc. is a retailer of washers and dryers and offers a three-year service contract on each appliance sold. Although Dot Point sells the appliances on an installment basis, all service contracts are cash sales at the time of purchase by the buyer. Collections received for service contracts should be recorded as:
a.    service revenue.
b.    deferred service revenue.
c.    a reduction in installment accounts receivable.
d.    a direct addition to retained earnings.

**Approach and Explanation:** Recall the revenue recognition principle and think about how it would apply to this situation. Revenue is to be recognized when it is realized (or realizable) and earned. The service contract revenue is realized at the date the cash is received; however, it is earned over the three-year period to which the contract pertains. Therefore, at the point of collection, the cash should be recorded by a credit to a Deferred (Unearned) Service Revenue account. The revenue will be earned over the three-year period as the company performs the services it promises by the contract. (Solution = b.)

**QUESTION**

3.(L.O. 3) L. Mahoney Corporation sells equipment. On December 31, 2010, Mahoney sold a piece of equipment to C. Bailey for $30,000 with the following terms: 2% cash discount if paid within 30 days, 1% discount if paid between 31 and 60 days of purchase, or payable in full within 90 days if not paid within a discount period. Bailey had the right to return this equipment to Mahoney if Bailey could not resell it before the end of the 90-day payment period, in which case Bailey would no longer be obligated to Mahoney. How much should be included in Mahoney's net sales for 2010 because of the sale of this machine?
a.    $30,000
b.    $29,700
c.    $29,400
d.    $0

**Explanation:** Per the terms of the sale/purchase, Bailey has the right to return the equipment to the seller if Bailey is not able to resell the equipment before expiration of the 90-day payment period. According to *SFAS No. 48*, if an enterprise sells its product but gives the buyer the right to return the product, revenue from the sales transaction is **not** recognized at the time of the sale **if** the buyer's obligation to pay the seller is contingent upon resale of the product. (Solution = d.)

**QUESTION**

4.    (L.O. 3) Bella Construction Co. uses the percentage-of-completion method. In 2010, Bella began work on a contract for $2,200,000; it was completed in 2011. The following cost data pertain to this contract:

|  | Year Ended December 31 | |
|---|---|---|
|  | 2010 | 2011 |
| Costs incurred during the year | $780,000 | $560,000 |
| Estimated costs to complete at end of year | 520,000 | -- |

The amount of gross profit to be recognized on the income statement for the year ended December 31, 2010 is:
a.    $0.
b.    $516,000.
c.    $540,000.
d.    $900,000.

**Approach and Explanation:** Write down the formula used to compute the gross profit recognized to date at the end of 2010. Use the data given to compute the gross profit.

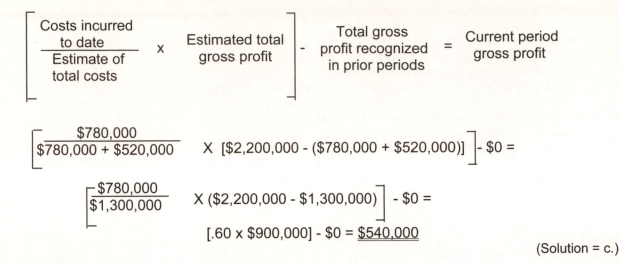

$$\left[\frac{\$780,000}{\$780,000 + \$520,000} \times [\$2,200,000 - (\$780,000 + \$520,000)]\right] - \$0 =$$

$$\left[\frac{\$780,000}{\$1,300,000} \times (\$2,200,000 - \$1,300,000)\right] - \$0 =$$

$$[.60 \times \$900,000] - \$0 = \underline{\$540,000}$$

(Solution = c.)

**QUESTION**
5. (L.O. 3) Refer to the facts for **Question 4** above. The amount of gross profit to be recognized on the income statement for the year ended December 31, 2011 is:
a. $860,000.
b. $360,000.
c. $344,000.
d. $320,000.

**Explanation:** Use the formula shown for **Question 4** and plug in the data for 2011.

$$\left[\frac{\$780,000 + \$560,000}{\$780,000 + \$560,000 + \$0} \times [\$2,200,000 - (\$780,000 + \$560,000)]\right] - \$540,000 =$$

$$\left[\frac{\$1,340,000}{\$1,340,000} \times (\$2,200,000 - \$1,340,000)\right] - \$540,000 =$$

$$\$860,000 - \$540,000 = \underline{\$320,000}$$

(Solution = d.)

**QUESTION**
6. (L.O. 3) Refer to the data for **Question 4** above. If the completed-contract method of accounting was used, the amount of gross profit to be reported for years 2010 and 2011 would be:

|  | **2010** | **2011** |
|---|---|---|
| a. | $0 | $860,000 |
| b. | $0 | $900,000 |
| c. | $900,000 | $(40,000) |
| d. | $860,000 | $0 |

**Explanation:** The completed-contract method calls for deferral of all revenue and costs related to a contract (project) until the period of completion. Thus, the entire gross profit ($2,200,000 total revenue − $1,340,000 total costs = $860,000 total gross profit) is recognized in the period the contract is completed. (Solution = a.)

| TIP: | The percentage-of-completion method is the generally accepted preferable method. The completed-contract method is acceptable under certain circumstances, such as in the case where estimates of costs etc. are not dependable. |
|------|---|

## QUESTION

7.  (L.O. 3) Designer Homes Construction Company uses the percentage-of-completion method. The costs incurred to date as a proportion of the estimated total costs to be incurred on a project are used as a measure of the extent of progress made toward completion of the project. During 2010, the company entered into a fixed-price contract to construct a mansion for Donald Thrumper for $24,000,000. The following details pertain to that contract:

|  | At December 31, 2010 | At December 31, 2011 |
|---|---|---|
| Percentage of completion | 25% | 60% |
| Estimated total costs of contract | $18,000,000 | $20,000,000 |
| Gross profit recognized to date | 1,500,000 | 2,400,000 |

The amount of construction costs incurred during 2011 was:
a.  $2,000,000.
b.  $4,500,000.
c.  $7,500,000.
d.  $12,000,000.

**Approach and Explanation:** Write down the formula used to compute the gross profit recognized to date at the end of 2011. Look at the components of the fraction.

$$\frac{\text{Costs incurred to date}}{\text{Estimate of total costs}} \times \frac{\text{Estimated total}}{\text{gross profit}} = \frac{\text{Total gross profit}}{\text{earned to date}}$$

According to the facts given, the fraction at December 31, 2011 is equal to 60%. Therefore, the costs incurred by the end of 2011 = 60% x $20,000,000 = $12,000,000. According to the facts given, the fraction for the same formula at the end of 2010 is equal to 25%. Therefore, the costs incurred by the end of 2010 = 25% x $18,000,000 = $4,500,000. The difference between the cumulative costs at the end of 2011 ($12,000,000) and the cumulative costs at the end of 2010 ($4,500,000) equals the costs incurred during 2011 of $7,500,000. (Solution = c.)

## QUESTION

8.  (L.O. 6, 7) A manufacturer of large equipment sells on an installment basis to customers with questionable credit ratings. Which of the following methods of revenue recognition is **least** likely to overstate the amount of gross profit reported?
a.  at the time of completion of the equipment (completion of production method)
b.  at the date of delivery (sale method)
c.  the installment sales method
d.  the cost recovery method

**Explanation:** Recognition of income at the time the equipment is completed would be the method **most** likely to overstate gross profit. The recognition of gross profit at the time the equipment is completed or at the date the equipment is delivered would provide for the recognition of profits before any or much of the cash has been received; thus, these methods are not appropriate for situations where there is doubt about the collectibility of the selling price. The use of the installment sales method would allow for the recognition of profits in proportion to the amount of the revenue collected in cash. The cost recovery method defers the recognition of all gross profit until cash collections of revenue are equal to the cost of the item sold; all remaining cash collections are reported as profit. Therefore, the cost recovery method is **least** likely to overstate the amount of gross profit reported. (Solution = d.)

## QUESTION

9.  (L.O. 6) Eazy-Pay Sales Company has appropriately used the installment method of accounting since it began operations at the beginning of 2011. The following information pertains to its operations for 2011:

| | |
|---|---|
| Installment sales | $ 600,000 |
| Cost of installment sales | 420,000 |
| Collections on installment sales | 240,000 |
| General and administrative expenses | 60,000 |

The amount to be reported on the December 31, 2011 balance sheet as Deferred Gross Profit should be:
a.   $360,000.
b.   $144,000.
c.   $108,000.
d.   $72,000.

**Explanation:** The $360,000 balance of Installment Accounts Receivable, 2011 ($600,000 - $240,000 = $360,000) is multiplied by the 2011 gross profit ratio of 30% ($600,000 - $420,000 = $180,000; $180,000 ÷ $600,000 = 30%) to arrive at deferred gross profit of $108,000 ($360,000 x 30% = $108,000) at the balance sheet date. (Solution = c.)

| | |
|---|---|
| **TIP:** | General and administrative expenses have no effect on the computations of realized gross profit or deferred gross profit. They are to be classified as operating expenses on the income statement of the period in which they are incurred. |
| **TIP:** | The **installment sales method of revenue recognition** emphasizes collection of the selling price rather than the sale. It recognizes income in the periods of collection rather than in the period of sale. The installment sales method is **not** a generally accepted method; it is to be used only for situations where uncollectible accounts cannot be reasonably estimated at the time of sale. |

## QUESTION

10.   (L.O. 6) Kayla Inc. appropriately uses the installment method of accounting to recognize income in its financial statements. Some pertinent data relating to this method of accounting include:

| | 2010 | 2011 |
|---|---|---|
| Installment sales | $ 300,000 | $ 360,000 |
| Cost of sales | 180,000 | 252,000 |
| Gross profit | $ 120,000 | $ 108,000 |
| | | |
| Collections during year: | | |
| On 2010 sales | 100,000 | 100,000 |
| On 2011 sales | | 120,000 |

What amount of realized gross profit should be reported on Kayla's income statement for 2011?
a.   $108,000
b.   $88,000
c.   $76,000
d.   $66,000
e.   None of the above

**Approach and Explanation:** (1) Compute the gross profit percentages for 2010 and 2011. (2) Apply the appropriate gross profit percentage to the amount of collections of installment receivables during 2011.

**Computations:**

(1)     $120,000 ÷ $300,000 = 40% gross profit percentage for 2010 installment sales

$108,000 ÷ $360,000 = 30% gross profit percentage for 2011 installment sales

(2)

| | |
|---|---:|
| Collections in 2011 on 2010 installment sales | $ 100,000 |
| Gross profit percentage for 2010 installment sales | 40% |
| Gross profit realized in 2011 on 2010 installment sales | $ 40,000 |
| | |
| Collections in 2011 on 2011 installment sales | $ 120,000 |
| Gross profit percentage for 2011 installments sales | 30% |
| Gross profit realized in 2011 on 2011 installment sales | $ 36,000 |
| | |
| Gross profit realized in 2011 on 2010 installment sales | $ 40,000 |
| Gross profit realized in 2011 on 2011 installment sales | 36,000 |
| Total gross profit realized in 2011 | $ 76,000 |

(Solution = c.)

> **TIP:** When using the **installment sales method of accounting**, the amount of gross profit to be recognized for a particular period is determined by multiplying the amount of cash collected during the period on installment receivables by the appropriate gross profit percentage(s). A rather difficult exam question may give the amount of gross profit recognized along with the gross profit percentage and require the examinee to solve for the amount of cash collected. For example, if gross profit recognized for 2011 is $90,000 and the gross profit percentage is 30%, cash collections during the period amount to $300,000 ($90,000 ÷ 30% = $300,000).

**QUESTION**

11.     (L.O. 6) Marvel Mart sells large-screen televisions on an installment basis and appropriately uses the installment sales method of accounting. A customer with an account balance of $4,000 refuses to make any more payments and the merchandise is repossessed. The gross profit rate on the original sale is 40%. Marvel estimates that the television can be sold as is for $1,250, or for $1,500 if $100 is spent to refurbish the cabinet. The loss on repossession is:

a.     $1,000.
b.     $1,150.
c.     $1,600.
d.     $2,750.

**Approach and Explanation:** Prepare the journal entry to record the repossession; it is as follows:

| | | |
|---|---:|---:|
| Deferred Gross Profit ($4,000 x 40%) .................................................... | 1,600 | |
| Repossessed Merchandise ($1,500 - $100).................................... | 1,400 | |
| Loss on Repossession ........................................................................ | 1,000 | |
| [($4,000 - $1,600) - ($1,500 - $100)] | | |
| Installment Accounts Receivable................................................. | | 4,000 |

The book value of the receivable is removed from the accounts ($4,000 - $1,600), the repossessed merchandise is recorded at its fair value (or net realizable value of $1,400 in this case), and a loss ($1,000) is recorded for the excess of the receivable's book value ($4,000 - $1,600 = $2,400) over its net realizable value ($1,400) (a measure of fair value). (Solution = a.)

# CHAPTER 19

# ACCOUNTING FOR INCOME TAXES

## OVERVIEW

Most revenue type transactions are **taxable amounts** (they increase taxable income) in some time period, and most expense type transactions are **deductible amounts** (they decrease taxable income) in some time period. Interperiod income tax allocation procedures are required when a revenue or expense item is reported on the tax return in one year but is reported on the income statement in a different time period. Thus, the income tax consequences of revenues and expenses are reflected on the income statement in the **same** year that the revenues and expenses are reported on the financial statements, regardless of when the revenues and expenses appear on the tax return. Accounting for income taxes in a manner that properly measures income tax expense and related liabilities and/or assets is the subject of this chapter.

## SUMMARY OF LEARNING OBJECTIVES

1.  **Identify differences between pretax financial income and taxable income.** Companies compute pretax financial income (or income for book purposes) is computed in accordance with generally accepted accounting principles. They compute taxable income (or income for tax purposes) in accordance with prescribed tax regulations. Because tax regulations and GAAP differ in many ways, so frequently do pretax financial income and taxable income. Differences may exist, for example, in the timing of revenue recognition and the timing of expense recognition. That is, revenues are recognized on the income statement in the period they are earned, but they may be taxable in a different period. Also, expenses are reported on the income statement in the period incurred, but they may be tax deductible in a different period.

2.  **Describe a temporary difference that results in future taxable amounts.** A credit sale that is recognized as revenue for book purposes in the period it is earned but is deferred and reported as revenue for tax purposes in the period it is collected will result in future taxable amounts. A deferred tax liability is to be recognized for the deferred tax consequences of the revenue and related account receivable already reflected in the financial statements. The recording of the deferred tax liability causes the total income tax expense to exceed the amount of income tax payable for the period in which the credit sale occurs. The future taxable amounts will occur in the periods the related account receivable for book purposes is recovered and the collections are reported as revenue for tax purposes. These future taxable amounts increase taxable income in the later periods in which they occur.

3.  **Describe a temporary difference that results in future deductible amounts.** An accrued warranty expense that is paid for and is deductible for tax purposes in a period later than the period in which it is recognized for book purposes will result in future deductible amounts. A deferred tax asset is to be recognized for the deferred tax consequences of the warranty expense and related warranty liability already reflected in the financial statements. The recording of the deferred tax asset causes the total income tax expense to be less than the amount of income tax payable for the period in which the warranty expense is recognized for book purposes. The future deductible amounts will occur in the periods the related warranty liability for book purposes is

settled and the expenditures are reported as expense for tax purposes. These future deductible amounts decrease taxable income in the later periods in which they occur.

4.    **Explain the purpose of a deferred tax asset valuation allowance.** A deferred tax asset should be reduced by a valuation allowance if, based on all available evidence, it is more likely than not (a level of likelihood that is at least slightly more than 50%) that some portion or all of the deferred tax asset will **not** be realized. All available evidence, both positive and negative, should be carefully considered to determine whether, based on the weight of available evidence, a valuation allowance is needed.

5.    **Describe the presentation of income tax expense in the income statement.** The significant components of income tax expense should be disclosed in the income statement or in the notes to the financial statements. The most commonly encountered components are the current tax expense (or current tax benefit) and the deferred tax expense (or deferred tax benefit).

6.    **Describe various temporary and permanent differences.** Examples of situations that give rise to temporary differences are: (1) revenue or gains that are taxable **after** they are recognized in financial income, (2) expenses or losses that are deductible **after** they are recognized in financial income, (3) revenues or gains that are taxable **before** they are recognized in financial income, and (4) expenses or losses that are deductible **before** they are recognized in financial income. Permanent differences arise from situations where: (1) items are recognized for financial reporting purposes but **not** for tax purposes, and (2) items are recognized for tax purposes but **not** for financial reporting purposes.

7.    **Explain the effect of various tax rates and tax rate changes on deferred income taxes.** The tax rate that is used to measure deferred tax liabilities and deferred tax assets (called the **applicable tax rate**) is the enacted tax rate(s) expected to apply to taxable income in the years that the related future taxable amounts and future deductible amounts are expected to occur. Presently enacted changes in tax rates that become effective for a particular future year or years must be considered when determining the tax rate to apply to temporary differences reversing in that year or years. Tax rates for the current year are used to tax effect cumulative temporary differences if no changes have been enacted for future years. When a change in the tax rate is enacted into law, its effect on the existing deferred income tax accounts should be recorded immediately; this effect is reported as an adjustment to income tax expense in the period of the rate change.

8.    **Apply accounting procedures for a loss carryback and a loss carryforward.** A company may carry a net operating loss back 2 years and receive funds for income taxes paid in those years. The loss must be applied to the earliest year first and then to the second prior year. Any loss remaining after the 2-year carryback may be carried forward up to 20 years to offset future taxable income. A company may elect to forgo the loss carryback and use the loss carryforward, offsetting future taxable income for up to 20 years. For financial reporting purposes, the benefits of a loss carryback are recognized by a debit to a receivable account and a credit to the income statement in the loss year. The benefits of a loss carryforward are recognized by a debit to Deferred Tax Asset and a credit to the income statement in the loss year; a valuation allowance is established against the deferred tax asset if it is more likely than not that a portion or all of the related tax benefits will not be realized.

9.    **Describe the presentation of deferred income taxes in financial statements.** Companies report deferred tax accounts on the balance sheet as assets and liabilities. These deferred tax assets and liabilities are classified as a **net** current and a **net** noncurrent amount. An individual deferred tax liability or asset is classified as current or noncurrent based on the classification of the related asset or liability for financial reporting purposes. A deferred tax liability or asset that is not related to an asset or liability for financial reporting purposes, including a deferred tax asset related to a loss carryforward, shall be classified according to the expected reversal date of the temporary difference.

10.　　**Indicate the basic principles of the asset-liability method.** Companies apply the following basic principles in accounting for income taxes at the date of the financial statements: (1) Recognize a current tax liability or asset for the estimated taxes payable or refundable on the tax return for the current year; (2) Recognize a deferred tax liability or asset for the estimated future tax effects attributable to temporary differences and carryforwards using the applicable tax rate; (3) Base the measurement of current and deferred tax liabilities and assets ion provisions of the enacted tax law; and (4) Reduce the measurement of deferred tax assets, if necessary, by the amount of any tax benefits that, based on available evidence, the company does not expect to realize.

*11.　　**Understand and apply the concepts and procedures of interperiod tax allocation.** Accounting for deferred taxes involves the following steps: (1) Calculate taxable income and income tax payable for the year (or refundable, in case of an operating loss being carried back). (2) Compute deferred income taxes at the end of the year. (3) Determine deferred income tax expense (or deferred income tax benefit). (4) Make the journal entry(s) to record income taxes. (5) Classify deferred tax assets and liabilities as current or noncurrent in the financial statements.
　　　　　*This material is covered in Appendix 19-A in the text.

# TIPS ON CHAPTER TOPICS

**TIP:**　Reread the Summary of Learning Objectives on Pages 19-1 thru 19-3 in this manual before you attempt to do the rest of the chapter. After completing the chapter, reread these same learning objectives in this *Problem Solving Survival Guide.* This should help to tie the pieces of the chapter together.

**TIP:**　The term **pretax financial income (loss)** refers to the difference between revenues earned and expenses incurred (other than income tax expense) on the accrual basis income statement for a given year. The term **taxable income (loss)** refers to the difference between taxable amounts and tax deductible amounts on the tax return for a given year. Pretax financial income appears on the income statement with the caption "Income before income taxes." **Pretax financial income** is often referred to as **income for book purposes**, **accounting income**, or **income for financial reporting purposes**.

**TIP:**　An excess of tax deductible expenses over taxable revenues on an entity's tax return is often called a **net operating loss (NOL).** The tax law provides that an NOL may be carried back two years and forward twenty years. In the carryback situation, the NOL is first applied to the **earliest** of the two years prior to the loss year. Any remaining NOL is then carried to the most recent prior year. Any remaining NOL is then carried forward to future years. (Although a corporation can elect to forego the carryback and use only a carryforward, do not assume this election is used in doing homework problems.) The provisions of the tax law must be applied in accounting for the tax benefits of an NOL.

**TIP:**    **Income tax payable for a period** is also the amount of **current tax expense** and is determined by applying the provisions of the tax law to the taxable income (or loss) figure for the period. In the case where an NOL results in a carryback, the entity will have **income tax refundable** (rather than income tax payable) which results in a **current tax benefit**.

**TIP:**    A revenue or an expense amount that appears on the income statement or the tax return in one year but **never** appears on the other report is called a **permanent difference**. Deferred income taxes are **never** recorded for permanent differences because these differences will never reverse (i.e., they will neither cause future taxable nor future deductible amounts). Examples of permanent differences appear in **Illustration 19-1**.

**TIP:**    A **temporary difference** is a difference between the tax basis of an asset or liability and its reported amount (book value or carrying amount) in the financial statements that will result in taxable or deductible amounts in future years when the reported amount of the asset is recovered or the liability is settled. Temporary differences that will result in taxable amounts when the related assets are recovered are often called **taxable temporary differences**; temporary differences that will result in deductible amounts in future years when the related liabilities are settled are often called **deductible temporary differences**. **Taxable temporary differences give rise to recording deferred tax liabilities; deductible temporary differences give rise to recording deferred tax assets.**

**TIP:**    A temporary difference originates in one or more periods and then reverses in one or more later periods. An **originating temporary difference** is the initial difference between the book basis and the tax basis of an asset or liability regardless of whether the tax basis of the asset or liability exceeds or is exceeded by the book basis of the asset or liability. An originating difference results in increasing a deferred tax account on the balance sheet. A **reversing temporary difference** occurs when an existing temporary difference is eliminated. The related deferred tax account is reduced in the time period a temporary difference reverses.

**TIP:**    Most temporary differences are caused by reporting a revenue or an expense in one year for financial reporting purposes and reporting the same revenue or expense in a different year for income tax purposes. Examples of these situations appear in **Illustration 19-2**. Other causes of temporary differences are not addressed in this book.

**TIP**    **Deferred tax expense (or benefit) for a period results from changes in the deferred tax asset and liability accounts.** A **deferred tax expense** results from an increase in a deferred tax liability or a decrease in a deferred tax asset; a **deferred tax benefit** results from an increase in a deferred tax asset or a decrease in a deferred tax liability. This is true because the other half of the journal entry dealing with a deferred tax account (a balance sheet item) is the income tax expense account (an income statement item). A deferred tax expense **increases** total income tax expense for the period; a deferred tax benefit **reduces** total income tax expense for the period.

**TIP:** **Total income tax expense (or benefit)** is the sum of **current tax expense (or benefit)** and **deferred tax expense (or benefit)**. Income tax expense is often referred to as "provision for income taxes." Hence, there is usually both a current portion and a deferred portion of the income tax provision. The meaning of the word "current" in this text bears **no relationship** to the meaning of the term "current" as used to refer to a balance sheet classification of deferred taxes.

**TIP:** A temporary difference originating in the current period that causes an increase in a deferred tax liability will also cause a debit (charge) to the provision for deferred income taxes on the income statement; an increase in a deferred tax asset will result in a credit to the provision for deferred taxes.

**TIP:** Pay close attention to terminology in this chapter and be careful not to confuse the many terms introduced. When describing deferred taxes from a balance sheet perspective, we speak about deferred tax assets and deferred tax liabilities. Whereas, when talking about the effects of deferred taxes on the income statement, we speak about deferred tax expense or deferred tax benefit. There is a correlation, however, because it is changes in deferred tax assets and liabilities on the balance sheet that result in deferred tax expense or benefit on the income statement.

**TIP:** A corporation often makes estimated tax payments during the year and charges them to an account called Prepaid Income Taxes. The balance of this account is used to offset the balance of the Income Tax Payable account for reporting purposes. The net amount is classified as a current asset if the prepaid account has the larger balance; the net amount is classified as a current liability if the payable account has the larger balance.

**TIP:** The **effective tax rate** for a period is calculated by dividing total income tax expense on the income statement by income before income taxes on the income statement. The effective tax rate for a period may differ from the statutory tax rate for the same period because of (a) permanent differences, and (b) changes in cumulative temporary differences that have been tax effected at statutory tax rates enacted for future (or prior) periods.

**TIP:** Deferred tax accounts are **not** to be reported at discounted amounts.

**TIP:** **Future deductible amounts** are often called **future tax deductible amounts**.

## ILLUSTRATION 19-1
## EXAMPLES OF PERMANENT DIFFERENCES (L.O. 6)

1.   **Revenues that are recognized for financial reporting purposes but are never included for tax purposes:**
   a.   Interest received on state and municipal obligations.
   b.   Proceeds from life insurance carried by the company on key officers or employees.

2.   **Expenses that are recognized for financial reporting purposes but are never included for tax purposes:**
   a.   Expenses incurred in obtaining tax-exempt income.
   b.   Premiums paid for life insurance carried by the company on key officers or employees (company is beneficiary).
   c.   Fines and expenses resulting from a violation of law.

3.   **Revenues that are recognized for tax purposes but are never included in financial statements:**
   a.   No examples exist at the current time.

4.   **Expenses or other deductions that are recognized for tax purposes but are never included in financial statements:**
   a.   "Percentage depletion" of natural resources in excess of their cost.
   b.   The deduction for dividends received from U.S. corporations, generally 70% to 80%.

# ILLUSTRATION 19-2
# EXAMPLES OF TEMPORARY DIFFERENCES (L.O. 6)

1.   **Revenues or gains that are taxable after they are included in financial income.** An asset (e.g. accounts receivable or investment) may be recorded in the process of the recognition of revenues or gains that will result in **future taxable amounts** when the asset is recovered.

Examples include:

- Accrued revenues that are reported on the income statement in the period earned but included on the tax return in the period collected. Includes sales accounted for on the accrual basis for financial reporting purposes and on the installment (cash) basis for tax purposes.
- Contracts which are accounted for under the percentage-of-completion method for financial reporting purposes, but a portion of the related gross profit is deferred for tax purposes.
- Investments which are accounted for under the equity method for financial reporting purposes and under the cost method for tax purposes.
- Gain on involuntary conversion of a nonmonetary asset which is recognized for financial reporting purposes but is deferred for tax purposes.
- Unrealized holding gains for financial reporting purposes (including use of the fair value option) but deferred for tax purposes (such as an unrealized holding gain on investment in trading securities).

> **TIP:** One of the most commonly illustrated examples in this category is the use of the accrual method in accounting for installment sales for financial reporting purposes and the use of the installment (cash) method for tax purposes. This situation causes an excess of the reported amount of an asset (receivable) over its tax basis that will result in a taxable amount in a future year(s) when the asset is recovered (when the cash is collected).

2.   **Expenses or losses that are deductible after they are included in financial income.** A liability (or contra asset) may be recorded in the process of the recognition of expense or loss that will result in **future tax deductible amounts** when the liability is later settled.

Examples include:

- Product warranty liabilities.
- Estimated liabilities related to discontinued operations or restructurings.
- Litigation accruals.
- Bad debt expense recognized using the allowance method for financial reporting purposes and the direct write-off method used for tax purposes.
- Stock-based compensation expense.
- Unrealized holding losses for financial reporting purposes (including use of the fair value option) but deferred for tax purposes (such as an unrealized holding loss on investment in trading securities).

> **TIP:** Let's look again at the example of the accrual of an expense or loss contingency (e.g., litigation accrual) in computing pretax financial income. This item is deductible for tax purposes only when it is realized. This situation causes a liability's reported amount to exceed its tax basis (zero) which will result in deductible amounts in future year(s) when the liability (estimated litigation obligation) is settled.

3. **Revenues or gains that are taxable before they are included in financial income.** A liability may be recognized for an advance receipt for goods and services to be provided in future years. For tax purposes, the advance receipt is included in taxable income upon the receipt of the cash. Future sacrifices to provide goods or services (or future refunds to those who cancel their orders) that settle the liability will result in **future tax deductible amounts**.

    Examples include:
    - Sales and leasebacks for financial reporting purposes (income deferral) and sales for tax purposes.
    - Prepaid contracts and royalties received in advance.

> **TIP:** Examine again the example where revenue is received in advance for rent or subscriptions. For tax purposes, the revenue is taxable in the period the related cash is received, but the revenue is not included in the computation of pretax financial income until the period in which it is earned. This type of case causes the reported amount for a liability (unearned revenue) on the balance sheet to exceed its tax basis (zero) which will result in future tax deductible amounts when the liability is settled. This situation is said to result in future tax deductible amounts because of the future sacrifices required to provide goods or services or to provide refunds to those who cancel their orders.

4. **Expenses or losses that are deductible before they are included in financial income.** The cost of an asset may have been deducted for tax purposes faster than it was expensed for financial reporting purposes. Amounts received upon recovery of the asset for financial reporting (through use or sale) will exceed the remaining tax basis of the asset and thereby will result in **future taxable amounts**.

    Examples include:
    - Depreciable property which may be depreciated faster for tax purposes.
    - Depletable resources and intangibles which may be amortized faster for tax purposes.
    - Deductible pension funding which exceeds the amount of pension expense.
    - Prepaid expenses that are deducted on the tax return in the period paid but are deducted on the income statement in the period incurred.

> **TIP:** The most common example of this category is the situation where a depreciable asset is depreciated faster for tax purposes than it is depreciated for financial accounting purposes. This causes the asset's reported value to exceed its tax basis. Amounts received upon the future recovery of the asset's reported value (through use or sale) will exceed its tax basis, and the excess will be taxable when the asset is recovered. Therefore, this situation results in taxable amounts in future years.

# ILLUSTRATION 19-3
# RECONCILIATION OF PRETAX FINANCIAL INCOME
# TO TAXABLE INCOME (L.O. 6)

**Pretax financial income**

<table>
<tr><td rowspan="5">P<br>E<br>R<br>M<br>A<br>N<br>E<br>N<br>T</td><td rowspan="5">D<br>I<br>F<br>F<br>E<br>R<br>E<br>N<br>C<br>E<br>S</td><td>–</td><td>Revenue recognized for books this period, but never recognized for tax purposes</td></tr>
<tr><td>+</td><td>Expense recognized for books this period, but never recognized for tax purposes</td></tr>
<tr><td>+</td><td>Revenue recognized for tax purposes this period, but never recognized for books.</td></tr>
<tr><td>–</td><td>Expense recognized for tax purposes this period, but never recognized for books.</td></tr>
</table>

<table>
<tr><td rowspan="4">O<br>R<br>I<br>G<br>I<br>N<br>A<br>T<br>I<br>N<br>G</td><td rowspan="4">T<br>E<br>M<br>P<br>O<br>R<br>A<br>R<br>Y</td><td rowspan="4">D<br>I<br>F<br>F<br>E<br>R<br>E<br>N<br>C<br>E<br>S</td><td>–</td><td>Revenue recognized for books this period, but recognized later for tax purposes</td></tr>
<tr><td>+</td><td>Expense recognized for books this period, but recognized later for tax purposes</td></tr>
<tr><td>+</td><td>Revenue recognized for tax purposes this period, but recognized later for books.</td></tr>
<tr><td>–</td><td>Expense recognized for tax purposes this period, but recognized later for books.</td></tr>
</table>

<table>
<tr><td rowspan="4">R<br>E<br>V<br>E<br>R<br>S<br>I<br>N<br>G</td><td rowspan="4">T<br>E<br>M<br>P<br>O<br>R<br>A<br>R<br>Y</td><td rowspan="4">D<br>I<br>F<br>F<br>E<br>R<br>E<br>N<br>C<br>E<br>S</td><td>–</td><td>Revenue recognized for books this period, but recognized earlier for tax purposes</td></tr>
<tr><td>+</td><td>Expense recognized for books this period, but recognized earlier for tax purposes</td></tr>
<tr><td>+</td><td>Revenue recognized for tax purposes this period, but recognized earlier for books.</td></tr>
<tr><td>–</td><td>Expense recognized for tax purposes this period, but recognized earlier for books.</td></tr>
</table>

= **Taxable income**

**TIP:** **No** deferred taxes are to be recognized for permanent differences because they will not have any future tax consequences.

## ILLUSTRATION 14-3 (Continued)

**TIP:** Temporary differences that **originate** in the current period and give rise to **future taxable amounts** are to be **deducted** from pretax financial income in this reconciliation. These differences will result in an increase in **deferred tax liabilities** during the current period for the deferred tax consequences of those future taxable amounts.

**TIP:** Temporary differences that **originate** in the current period and give rise to **future deductible amounts** are to be **added** to pretax financial income in this reconciliation. These differences will result in an increase in **deferred tax assets** during the current period for the deferred tax consequences of those future deductible amounts.

**TIP:** Refer to **Illustration 19-1** for examples of permanent differences; refer to **Illustration 19-2** for examples of temporary differences. The four types of examples addressed in those two illustrations appear in the same order there as they are referenced in this illustration. Thus, the first type of permanent difference listed in **Illustration 19-3** corresponds to the first type described in **Illustration 19-1**. Also, the first type of the temporary differences listed in **Illustration 19-3** corresponds to the first type described in **Illustration 19-2**.

**TIP:** This reconciliation will aid you in solving some homework assignments and exam questions, but it is not relevant to all situations. The temporary differences used in this reconciliation are **only** the ones that originated or reversed during the current year. The reconciliation does **not** use cumulative temporary differences. This reconciliation can be used to solve for taxable income, pretax financial income, or changes in cumulative temporary differences for a given period of time.

## CASE 19-1

**Purpose:**    (L.O.6) This case will provide practice in distinguishing between temporary differences and permanent differences. It will also provide practice in distinguishing between taxable type and deductible type temporary differences.

In reviewing the records of a client, you find the items listed below pertain to the current year.

### Instructions

For each item in the list, use the appropriate letter to indicate if it is:
a.    A temporary difference which gives rise to future deductible amounts.
b.    A temporary difference which gives rise to future taxable amounts.
c.    A permanent difference.

_____    1.    MACRS depreciation was used for tax purposes, and straight-line depreciation was used for accounting purposes for some depreciable assets.

_____    2.    The client is a landlord and collected some rents in advance.

_____ 3. An installment sale of an investment was accounted for by the accrual method for books and the installment method for tax purposes.

_____ 4. Interest was received on an investment in municipal obligations.

_____ 5. The costs of guarantees and warranties were estimated and accrued for accounting purposes.

_____ 6. Expenses were incurred in obtaining tax-exempt income.

_____ 7. Proceeds were received from a life insurance company because of the death of a key officer (the company carries a policy on key officers).

_____ 8. For some assets, straight-line depreciation was used for both accounting purposes and tax purposes, but the assets' lives were shorter for tax purposes.

_____ 9. The tax return reports a deduction for 70% of the dividends received from U.S. corporations. For accounting purposes, the fair value method was used in accounting for the related investments in available-for-sale securities.

_____ 10. Estimated losses on pending lawsuits and claims were accrued for books. These losses will be tax deductible in the year(s) they are realized.

_____ 11. Interest and property taxes were incurred during construction of a building. The building is being constructed for the company's own use and is expected to have a service life of 40 years. For tax purposes, the interest and property taxes incurred during construction are capitalized as a part of the basis of the related asset. For tax purposes, the building will be depreciated over 27 years.

_____ 12. The company paid a fine for violation of a law.

_____ 13. Plant assets were acquired in the current year. The depreciation taken for book purposes exceeded the depreciation reported for tax purposes for the current year.

_____ 14. The company recognized a loss on the income statement due to a temporary decline in the fair value of the trading portfolio of investment in marketable equity securities.

_____ 15. "Percentage depletion" of natural resources was in excess of the cost of natural resources.

_____ 16. The income statement reports earnings from investments in stock accounted for by the equity method. No dividends were received during the year from the investee. When dividends are received in future years, 70% will be eligible for the dividends received deduction.

_____ 17. The company has a construction division which uses the percentage-of-completion method for books and the completed-contract method for tax purposes.

_____   18.  The company paid $8,000 in premiums for life insurance which it carries on key officers. The cash surrender value of the related policies increased $1,200.

_____   19.  An accrued revenue was reported on the income statement for the current year; the revenue will be taxable when it is collected.

_____   20.  Prepaid advertising expense is deferred and amortized for accounting purposes and deducted as an expense when paid for tax purposes.

_____   21.  The company received a condemnation award from the state for land and a building that it owned which lay in the path of a proposed highway. The award of $500,000 exceeded the property's carrying value (and tax basis) of $220,000. The company used the entire proceeds received to replace the property within two years and, therefore, was able to defer the related gain for tax purposes.

_____   22.  The corporation owns a patent and allows another company to use the rights embodied in the patent in exchange for royalty payments which are collected in advance.

_____   23.  A transaction accounted for as a sale and leaseback for accounting purposes was treated as a sale for tax purposes. A gain resulted from the sale.

_____   24.  The amount funded for the company pension plan this year was less than the amount expensed for financial reporting purposes. Only the amount funded was deductible on this year's tax return.

_____   25.  The company collected subscriptions in advance for a magazine it publishes.

_____   26.  The accrual for postretirement benefits other than pensions was made in accordance with *SFAS No. 106*. This amount will be charged to the tax returns of the years in which amounts are paid for these benefits.

# Solution to Case 19-1

1.  b
2.  a
3.  b  •The use of the accrual method for books causes the entire gross profit from the installment sale to be reflected in the income statement of the period of sale. The use of the installment method for tax purposes causes the gross profit to be allocated over the collection period; the amount of gross profit recognized in a period is proportionate to the amount of sales price collected in the period.
4.  c  •The interest is tax exempt revenue.
5.  a
6.  c
7.  c
8.  b
9.  c
10. a
11. b  •Interest and property taxes incurred during construction are also capitalized for financial reporting purposes. *SFAS No. 34* requires that avoidable interest cost during construction be capitalized. Therefore, the interest and property taxes will be amortized to income via the depreciation process. The amortization (depreciation) period is shorter for tax purposes in this particular case, causing a net future taxable amount.
12. c
13. a
14. a  •This loss will not be deductible for tax purposes until the future period in which the loss is realized (that is, in the period the securities are sold).
15. c  •Percentage depletion is often referred to as statutory depletion.
16. b & c  •The 70% is a permanent difference and 30% of the total difference is a temporary difference.
17. b
18. c  •The amount of the permanent difference is $6,800, which is the amount expensed on the income statement. The $1,200 increase in cash surrender value of life insurance is reflected as an increase in assets on the GAAP basis balance sheet and does not result in either a permanent or temporary difference.
19. b
20. b
21. b  •A gain of $280,000 must be recognized for financial reporting purposes. (*FIN No. 30*); the entire gain is deferred for tax purposes because all proceeds received were reinvested in replacement property within two years of the involuntary conversion of nonmonetary assets to monetary assets.
22. a  •The royalty receipts are to be included in taxable income in the period they are received.
23. a  •The gain is generally deferred for accounting purposes but reported currently for tax purposes.
24. a
25. a  •The collections are included in taxable income in the period received. The related revenue is deferred for financial reporting purposes until it is earned.
26. a

# ILLUSTRATION 19-4

## COMPOUND JOURNAL ENTRY TO RECORD INCOME TAXES (L.O. 1, 2, 3, 5)

In recording income taxes, the best approach is to perform the following steps in order:

1.    **Compute the amount of income tax payable for the current period.** This is always based on the amount of taxable income and the tax rate for the current year. This amount is also referred to as "current tax expense"; it is recorded by a credit to Income Tax Payable. If there is a net operating loss for the current year, then the benefits of a loss carryback are called "current tax benefit" and are recorded by a debit to a receivable account.

2.    **Compute the change required in the deferred tax account(s).** To do this, the appropriate balance of the deferred tax account(s) at the balance sheet date must be determined and this may require a scheduling process. The appropriate balance represents the deferred tax consequences of cumulative temporary differences and operating loss carryforwards existing at the balance sheet date. The difference between the ending balance and the beginning balance of a deferred tax account is called "deferred tax expense" or "deferred tax benefit" or "benefits of loss carryforward," whichever is appropriate. It is recorded by a debit or a credit to a deferred tax asset or liability account.

3.    **Record income tax expense** which is the total of current tax expense (or benefit) and deferred tax expense (or benefit). In a compound journal entry, it is the "plug" figure required to make the journal entry balance.

**TIP:**    In computing deferred income taxes at a balance sheet date, the amount of cumulative temporary differences must be determined. Information on when those differences originated is **not** needed; some or all of the differences could have originated in prior periods. Information about the individual future years in which these differences are expected to reverse is generally **not** needed because the tax rate is usually the same flat rate year after year. One case in which this information **is** needed is the situation where there are different tax rates enacted for the individual future years in which existing temporary differences are expected to cause taxable and deductible amounts to occur. Thus, if a single tax rate applies to all future years, an aggregate computation for deferred income taxes is appropriate. However, if different tax rates apply to individual future years, a scheduling of future taxable and deductible amounts (due to temporary differences at the balance sheet date) with a separate computation for each future year affected is required.

**TIP:**    Single entries (rather than one compound journal entry) can be used to record income taxes. With this approach, you could perform Step 1 above and record the results by either a credit to Income Tax Payable (if there is taxable income for the current period) or a debit to Income Tax Refund Receivable (if there is a loss on the current tax return and a carryback is appropriate). The other half of this first entry is a debit or credit (whichever is needed to make the entry balance) to Income Tax Expense. A second entry would be recorded for the results of Step 2 above. In this second entry, a debit or credit would be recorded to Deferred Tax Asset or Deferred Tax Liability, whatever is needed to properly report deferred taxes on the balance sheet. The other half of this second entry would be either a debit or credit to Income Tax Expense, as appropriate, to make the entry balance. Step 2 is repeated (and another single entry is recorded) if there is more than one reason for having temporary differences. Thus, if one entity has three types of temporary differences, Step 2 is performed three times and there would be a total of four single entries to record income taxes for the period. (This single entries approach to recording income taxes is illustrated in parts (a) and (b) of the **Solution to Exercise 19-1**).

> **TIP:** The recording of income taxes is an estimate in that the people who prepare the tax return are interpreting how the law pertains to the transactions of the corporation. The IRS audits a portion of the tax returns filed each year and in many cases disagrees with a position taken by the taxpayer and, therefore, disallows a deduction (which causes an increase in the taxes due for that period). An **uncertain tax position** is a tax position for which the tax authority may disallow a deduction in whole or in part. It can come about when a company takes an aggressive approach in its tax planning because the tax law is unclear or where the company may believe that the risk of audit in that area is low. Uncertain tax positions give rise to tax benefits either by reducing income tax expense or related payables or increasing an income tax refund receivable or deferred tax asset. The rules for recording contingencies must be probable and subject to reasonable estimation) apply to the recognition of the benefits from uncertain tax positions. The FASB has rules that require a company to determine whether it is "more likely than not" that tax positions will be sustained upon audit. Applying the "more likely than not" criteria means that if the probability is more than 50 percent, a company may reduce its recorded tax liability.

## CASE 19-2

**Purpose:**    (L.O. 2, 5, 10) This case examines the focus of the liability method and the steps in the annual computation of deferred tax assets and liabilities.

The objectives of accounting for income taxes are to recognize (a) the amount of taxes payable or refundable for the current year, and (b) deferred tax liabilities and assets that arise because of the future tax consequences of events that have been recognized in an enterprise's financial statements or tax returns.

## Instructions
(a)    If a revenue item is reported on the income statement in 2010, but is included on the tax return in 2011, explain whether the related income tax effect should be reflected on the income statement in 2010 or 2011, and why.
(b)    Explain whether the liability method of accounting for deferred taxes focuses on the proper valuation of assets and liabilities (balance sheet orientation) or on income determination (income statement orientation).
(c)    List the steps to be included in the annual computation of deferred tax liabilities and assets.

## Solution to Case 19-2

(a)     The tax consequences of a transaction or event are to be recognized in the same period that the transaction or event is recognized in the financial statements. This is the essence of the comprehensive income tax allocation approach. Thus, the income tax effect of revenue recognized in 2010 should also be recognized on the income statement in 2010, even though the payment of the resulting tax is deferred until a later year.

(b)     At any given balance sheet date, deferred income taxes are computed by applying the applicable tax rate(s) to future taxable and deductible amounts stemming from temporary differences existing at the balance sheet date. Thus, a deferred tax liability (or asset) is recognized for taxes payable (or a reduction in taxes payable) in future years due to existing temporary differences. The amount of deferred tax expense (or benefit) for the income statement is determined by the change in deferred tax accounts from one balance sheet date to another; thus, deferred income tax expense (or benefit) is a residual figure (commonly called a plug figure). Therefore, the liability method is said to be balance sheet oriented.

(c)     The procedures in the computation of deferred income taxes are as follows:

1.     Identify (a) the types and amounts of existing temporary differences, and (b) the nature and amount of each type of operating loss and tax credit carryforward and the remaining length of the carryforward period.

2.     Measure the total deferred tax liability for taxable temporary differences using the applicable tax rate.

3.     Measure the total deferred tax asset for deductible temporary differences and operating loss carryforwards using the applicable tax rate.

4.     Measure deferred tax assets for each type of tax credit carryforward.

5.     Reduce deferred tax assets by a **valuation allowance** if, based on the weight of available evidence, it is **more likely than not** (a likelihood of more than 50 percent) that some portion or all of the deferred tax assets will **not** be realized. The valuation allowance should be sufficient to reduce the deferred tax assets to the amount that is more likely than not to be realized.

# EXERCISE 19-1

**Purpose:** (L.O. 1, 2, 5) This exercise will illustrate how to record current tax expense and deferred tax expense when one taxable temporary difference exists. It will also illustrate the effect of the reversal of the same temporary difference on income tax expense.

Gary Winarski, Inc. has pretax financial income for 2010 of $400,000. There were no deferred taxes at the beginning of 2010. At the end of 2010, temporary differences of $85,000 exist which are expected to result in taxable amounts in 2012. The enacted tax rates are as follows:

| Year | Tax Rate |
|------|----------|
| 2009 | 50% |
| 2010-2011 | 40% |
| 2012 and later | 30% |

## Instructions
(a) Compute taxable income for 2010 and record income tax payable.
(b) Compute deferred taxes at December 31, 2010 and record the change in deferred taxes, assuming taxable income is expected in all future years.
(c) Draft the income tax expense section of the income statement for 2010 (beginning with "Income before income taxes").
(d) Draft the income tax expense section of the income statement for 2012 assuming taxable income for 2012 is $360,000 (begin with the line "Income before income taxes").

## Solution to Exercise 19-1

(a)

| | |
|---|---:|
| Pretax financial income | $ 400,000 |
| Originating temporary difference resulting in future taxable amounts | (85,000) |
| Taxable income | $ 315,000 |

| | | |
|---|---:|---:|
| Income Tax Expense ................................................................ | 126,000 | |
|     Income Tax Payable ($315,000 x 40%) ............................. | | 126,000 |
|       (To record current tax expense) | | |

**Approach and Explanation:** Use the reconciliation format in **Illustration 19-3** to compute taxable income. Because there was no deferred taxes (and, thus, no temporary differences) existing at the beginning of 2010, all $85,000 of temporary differences existing at the end of 2010 must have originated (came about) during 2010. Because these originating temporary differences will result in future taxable amounts, they cause taxable income to be lower than pretax financial income in 2010.

(b)  Future taxable amounts                                                                $ 85,000
Enacted tax rate for applicable future year                                          30%
Balance needed for deferred tax liability at December 31, 2010        25,500
Balance of deferred tax liability at January 1, 2010                             0
Increase in deferred tax liability during 2010                              $ 25,500

Income Tax Expense .........................................................................   25,500
    Deferred Tax Liability ...............................................................                25,500*
       (To record the change in deferred taxes)

    *See computation above.

**Explanation:** The deferred tax liability at December 31, 2010 is measured by using the tax rate enacted for the future year (2012) in which the underlying temporary difference will result in future taxable amounts.

> **TIP:** Refer to **Illustration 19-4** and the last **TIP** for that illustration. This exercise makes use of the single entry approach to recording income taxes. The entries for parts (a) and (b) of this exercise are often combined for a compound journal entry as follows:
>
> Income Tax Expense.................................................   151,500
>     Income Tax Payable.......................................                126,000
>     Deferred Tax Liability....................................                 25,500

(c)  Income before income taxes                                                    $ 400,000
Income tax expense:
    Current tax expense                        $ 126,000
    Deferred tax expense                          25,500        151,500
Net income                                                                  $ 248,500

> **TIP:** Notice that the effective tax rate for 2010 is 37.875% ($151,500 ÷ $400,000 = .37875). This rate is lower than the 40% statutory tax rate for 2010 because $315,000 of the $400,000 is tax effected at 40% and $85,000 of the $400,000 is tax effected at 30%.

(d)  Income before income taxes                                                    $ 275,000[a]
Income tax expense:
    Current tax expense                        $ 108,000[b]
    Deferred tax benefit                          (25,500)[c]       82,500
Net income                                                                  $ 192,500

    [a]Pretax financial income                    $        X
    Reversing taxable temporary difference            85,000
    Taxable income                               $ 360,000
        Solving for X:   X + $85,000 = $360,000
                X = $360,000 - $85,000
                X = $275,000 = Pretax financial income

    [b]Taxable income for 2012                        $ 360,000
    Enacted tax rate                                      30%
    Income tax payable for 2012                    $ 108,000

$^c$There is no temporary difference existing at the end of 2012, so the balance in the deferred tax liability account would be eliminated. A decrease in a deferred tax liability results in a deferred tax benefit on the income statement.

| | | | |
|---|---|---|---|
| **TIP:** | Notice that the effective tax rate for 2012 is 30% ($82,500 ÷ $275,000 = .30), which equals the statutory tax rate for 2012. | | |
| **TIP:** | Think about the journal entry(s) that would be required in 2012 to record income taxes. Using single entries (as opposed to one compound entry), they would appear as follows: | | |
| | Income Tax Expense ............................................... | 108,000 | |
| | Income Tax Payable ($360,000 X 30%) ........ | | 108,000 |
| | (To record current tax expense) | | |
| | Deferred Tax Liability ............................................. | 25,500 | |
| | Income Tax Expense ...................................... | | 25,500 |
| | (To record the change in deferred taxes) | | |

# EXERCISE 19-2

**Purpose:**    (L.O. 1, 2, 3, 5, 6) This exercise illustrates how to account for income taxes when there are both permanent and temporary differences involved and a flat tax rate is enacted for all periods affected.

The Monte Neece Corporation has pretax financial income of $200,000 for 2010 (the first year of operations). The difference between revenues and expenses reported on the tax return for 2010 and the income statement for 2010 are as follows:

| | Tax Return | Income Statement |
|---|---|---|
| Depreciation expense | $ 80,000 | $ 62,000 |
| Insurance premiums expense | | 8,000 |
| Warranty expense | 10,000 | 19,000 |
| Interest revenue from municipal bonds | | 2,000 |
| Rent revenue | 6,200 | 5,000 |

The insurance premiums pertain to life insurance on the lives of corporate officers, and the beneficiary is the corporation.

The tax rate for 2010 is 40%, and no new rate has been enacted for future years.

## Instructions
(a)    Compute taxable income for 2010.
(b)    Prepare the journal entry to record income taxes for 2010.
(c)    Prepare the portion of the income statement for 2010 that reports income taxes. Begin with the caption "Income before income taxes."

## Solution to Exercise 19-2

(a)     Pretax financial income for 2010                                                                    $ 200,000
Nondeductible expense—life insurance on officers                                      8,000
Nontaxable revenue—interest on municipal bonds                                    (2,000)
Excess depreciation per tax return for 2010                                            (18,000)
Excess warranty expense per books for 2010                                             9,000
Excess rent revenue per tax return for 2010                                               1,200
Taxable income for 2010                                                                      $ 198,200

(b)     Income Tax Expense ...........................................................     82,400$^e$
Deferred Tax Asset—Warranties ....................................................     3,600$^d$
Deferred Tax Asset—Rents .........................................................     480$^c$
        Deferred Tax Liability—Depreciation....................................                    7,200$^b$
        Income Tax Payable .................................................................                    79,280$^a$

$^a$$198,200 x 40% = $79,280.
$^b$$18,000 x 40% = $7,200.
$^c$$1,200 x 40% = $480.
$^d$$9,000 x 40% = $3,600.
$^e$$79,280 + $7,200 - $480 - $3,600 = $82,400.

> **TIP:**     Although some people may choose to use only one deferred tax asset account in the above entry, the use of a separate deferred tax account for each type of temporary difference (as illustrated above) is helpful when later classifying deferred taxes on the balance sheet.

(c)     Income before income taxes                                                                    $ 200,000
Provision for income taxes:
        Current tax expense                            $ 79,280
        Deferred tax expense                              3,120*          82,400
Net income                                                        $ 117,600

        *Deferred tax expense of $7,200, deferred tax benefit of $480, and deferred
         tax benefit of $3,600, net to a deferred tax expense of $3,120.

> **TIP:**     The amount reported for total income tax expense ($82,400 in this exercise) should agree with the balance of the Income Tax Expense account before closing.

## EXERCISE 19-3

**Purpose:** (L.O. 1, 2, 3, 5, 7) This exercise illustrates the steps involved in computing and recording income taxes when two types of temporary differences exist and there is a phased-in change in tax rates.

T&C Benyon Corporation has the following facts available:
1. Pretax financial income for Year 1 is $105,000.
2. Year 1 is the first year of operations.
3. One temporary difference exists at the end of Year 1 that will result in deductible amounts of:     $20,000 in Year 2.
            $30,000 in Year 3.
4. Another temporary difference exists at the end of Year 1 which will result in taxable amounts of:     $11,000 in Year 2.
            $14,000 in Year 3.
5. Tax rates enacted by the end of Year 1 are:     50% for Year 1.
            40% for Year 2.
            30% for Year 3.
6. Taxable income is expected in all future years.

## Instructions
(a) Compute taxable income for Year 1.
(b) Compute the deferred taxes to be reported on the balance sheet at the end of Year 1.
(c) Prepare the journal entry to record income taxes for Year 1.
(d) Draft the income tax expense section of the income statement for Year 1.

## Solution to Exercise 19-3

| (a) | |
|---|---:|
| Pretax financial income for Year 1 | $ 105,000 |
| Temporary differences originating: | |
|     Deductible temporary difference | 50,000 |
|     Taxable temporary difference | (25,000) |
| Taxable income for Year 1 | $ 130,000 |

(b) At December 31, Year 1, a deferred tax asset of $17,000 and a deferred tax liability of $8,600 should be reflected on the balance sheet. Deferred taxes are computed by a scheduling process as follows:

|  | Current Year | Future Years | | |
|---|---|---|---|---|
|  | Year 1 | Year 2 | Year 3 | Total |
| Taxable income | $130,000 | | | |
| Future deductible amounts | | ($20,000) | ($30,000) | ($50,000) |
| Future taxable amounts | | 11,000 | 14,000 | 25,000 |
| Enacted tax rates | 50% | 40% | 30% | |
| Deferred tax (asset) | | | | |
| liability | | ($8,000) | ($9,000) | ($17,000) |
| | | 4,400 | 4,200 | $ 8,600 |

| (c) Deferred Tax Asset ............................................................. | 17,000 | |
|---|---|---|
| Income Tax Expense ..................................................................... | 56,600 | |
| Income Tax Payable ................................................................ | | 65,000 |
| Deferred Tax Liability .............................................................. | | 8,600 |

**Computations:**

Step 1:
| Taxable income | $ 130,000 |
|---|---|
| Tax rate for Year 1 | 50% |
| Income tax payable | $ 65,000 |

Step 2: See the scheduling in part (b) for determination of the $17,000 ending balance for deferred tax asset and $8,600 ending balance for deferred tax liability.

The change in deferred taxes is computed as follows:
| Balance of deferred tax asset at end of Year 1 | $ 17,000 |
|---|---|
| Balance of deferred tax asset at beginning of Year 1 | 0 |
| Increase in deferred tax asset (which is a deferred tax benefit) | $ 17,000 |

| Balance of deferred tax liability at end of Year 1 | | $ 8,600 |
|---|---|---|
| Balance of deferred tax liability at beginning of Year 1 | | 0 |
| Increase in deferred tax liability (a deferred tax expense) | $ 8,600 | |

Step 3:
| Deferred tax benefit | $(17,000) | |
|---|---|---|
| Deferred tax expense | 8,600 | |
| Net deferred tax benefit | | (8,400) |
| Current tax expense | 65,000 | |
| Total income tax expense for Year 1 | $ 56,600 | |

> **TIP:** The three following single entries are equivalent to the one compound journal entry above. Notice the first one records the current tax expense and a current tax obligation of $65,000. The second entry adjusts the deferred tax asset account and records a deferred tax benefit of $17,000; a deferred tax benefit reduces total income tax expense. The third one adjusts the deferred tax liability account and records a deferred tax expense of $8,600; a deferred tax expense increases total income tax expense. These three entries can be used in place of the one compound entry.

| | | |
|---|---|---|
| Income Tax Expense............................................. | 65,000 | |
| Income Tax Payable................................ | | 65,000 |
| | | |
| Deferred Tax Asset.............................................. | 17,000 | |
| Income Tax Expense............................... | | 17,000 |
| | | |
| Income Tax Expense............................................. | 8,600 | |
| Deferred Tax Liability............................... | | 8,600 |

(d)    The relevant section of the income statement would appear as follows:

| | | |
|---|---|---|
| Income before income taxes | | $ 105,000 |
| Income tax expense: | | |
| Current tax expense | $ 65,000 | |
| Deferred tax benefit | (8,400) | 56,600 |
| Net income | $  48,400 | |

# EXERCISE 19-4

**Purpose:**    (L.O. 2, 3, 5) This exercise will review a situation that involves both a deferred tax asset and a deferred tax liability, one with a beginning balance. It also reviews the relationships existing in the reconciliation of pretax financial income and taxable income.

The following facts relate to the Tasty Bits Corporation:
1.    Deferred tax liability, January 1, 2010, $80,000.
2.    Deferred tax asset, January 1, 2010, $0.
3.    Taxable income for 2010, $164,000.
4.    There are no permanent differences in 2010.
5.    Cumulative temporary difference at December 31, 2010, giving rise to future taxable amounts, $440,000.
6.    Cumulative temporary difference at December 31, 2010, giving rise to future deductible amounts, $70,000.
7.    Tax rate for all years, 40%.
8.    The company is expected to operate profitably in all future years.

## Instructions
(a)    Prepare the journal entry to record income tax payable, deferred income taxes, and income tax expense for 2010.
(b)    Draft the income tax expense section of the income statement for 2010, beginning with the line "income before income taxes."

## Solution to Exercise 19-4

(a)     Journal entry:

| | | |
|---|---:|---:|
| Income Tax Expense | 133,600 | |
| Deferred Tax Asset | 28,000 | |
|     Income Tax Payable ($164,000 x 40%) | | 65,600 |
|     Deferred Tax Liability | | 96,000 |

**Computations:**

| Temporary Difference | Future Taxable (Deductible) Amounts | Tax Rate | Deferred Tax (Asset) | Deferred Tax Liability |
|---|---:|---:|---:|---:|
| Taxable type | $ 440,000 | 40% | | $176,000 |
| Deductible type | (70,000) | 40% | $(28,000) | |
|   Totals | $ 370,000 | 40% | $(28,000) | $176,000** |

**Because of a flat tax rate, these totals can be reconciled:
$370,000 x 40% = ($28,000) + $176,000

| | |
|---|---:|
| Deferred tax liability, 12/31/10 | $ 176,000 |
| Deferred tax liability, 12/31/09 | 80,000 |
| Deferred tax expense, 2010 | $ 96,000 |
|    (net increase required in a deferred tax liability) | |

| | |
|---|---:|
| Deferred tax asset, 12/31/10 | $ 28,000 |
| Deferred tax asset, 12/31/09 | 0 |
| Deferred tax expense (benefit), 2010 | $ (28,000) |
|    (net increase required in a deferred tax asset) | |

| | |
|---|---:|
| Deferred tax expense for 2010 | $ 96,000 |
| Deferred tax benefit for 2010 | (28,000) |
| Net deferred tax expense for 2010 | 68,000 |
| Current tax expense, 2010 | 65,600 |
| Total income tax expense, 2010 | $ 133,600 |

| | | |
|---|---:|---:|
| (b)     Income before income taxes | | $ 334,000* |
| Income tax expense: | | |
|    Current tax expense | $ 65,600 | |
|    Deferred tax expense | 68,000 | 133,600 |
| Net income | $ 200,400 | |

*Because of the flat tax rate for all years, the amount of cumulative temporary difference existing at the beginning of the year can be calculated by dividing the $80,000 beginning balance in Deferred Tax Liability by 40%, which equals $200,000. This information may now be combined with the other facts given in the exercise to reconcile pretax financial income with taxable income for 2010 as follows:

| | |
|---|---|
| Pretax financial income | $    X |
| Net originating temporary difference giving rise to future taxable amounts ($440,000 - $200,000) | (240,000) |
| Originating temporary difference giving rise to future deductible amounts | 70,000 |
| Taxable income | $ 164,000 |

Solving for X:        X - $240,000 + $70,000 = $164,000;
        X = $334,000

# EXERCISE 19-5

**Purpose:**    (L.O. 9) This exercise illustrates the application of guidelines for the classification of deferred income taxes.

The Chicone Corporation has several temporary differences existing at December 31, 2010. The following information pertains:

1.    The carrying value of plant assets exceeds the tax basis of those assets by $500,000.
2.    A long-term pension liability of $700,000 appears on the balance sheet due to the accrual of pension costs. Only the amounts funded have been deducted on the tax returns over the years.
3.    For tax purposes, $400,000 of income on contracts has been deferred until 2011.
4.    The company recognized a loss of $80,000 in 2010 associated with a contingency. A related accrued liability is classified as a current liability on the balance sheet.
5.    An allowance for doubtful accounts of $220,000 appears on the GAAP basis balance sheet. Uncollectible accounts are tax deductible only when individual accounts are written off. All accounts receivable are classified as current assets.
6.    An estimated liability for litigation settlements of $130,000 appears in the long-term liability section of the balance sheet. This liability has a tax basis of zero.

A flat tax rate of 40% is enacted for all years.

# Instructions

Compute the deferred tax assets and liabilities to appear on the balance sheet at December 31, 2010. Indicate how they are to be classified.

| TIP: | Deferred income tax assets and liabilities are to be reported on the balance sheet in a **net** current and a **net** noncurrent amount. Deferred tax liabilities and assets are to be classified as current or noncurrent based on the classification of the related asset or liability for financial reporting. A deferred tax liability or asset that is **not** related to an asset or liability for financial reporting, including deferred tax assets related to carryforwards, should be classified according to the expected reversal date of the temporary difference. |
|---|---|

## Solution to Exercise 19-5

| Temporary Difference | Resulting Deferred Tax (Asset) | Liability | Related Balance Sheet Account | Deferred Tax Classification |
|---|---|---|---|---|
| 1. Excess depreciation for tax purposes. | | $200,000 | Plant Assets | Noncurrent |
| 2. Excess pension expense for book purposes. | $(280,000) | | Pension Liability | Noncurrent |
| 3. Excess contract income for book purposes. | | 160,000 | None | Current |
| 4. Accrual of plant closing costs for books. | (32,000) | | Accrued Liability for Contingency | Current |
| 5. Accrual of uncollectible accounts for books. | (88,000) | | Allowance for Doubtful Accounts | Current |
| 6. Accrual of litigation settlements. | (52,000) | | Estimated Obligation for Lawsuits | Noncurrent |
| | $(452,000) | $360,000 | | |

**Summary:** The net current amount is a liability of $40,000 [$160,000 - ($32,000 + $88,000) = $40,000]. The net noncurrent amount is an asset of $132,000 ($280,000 - $200,000 + $52,000 = $132,000).

**Explanation:**

1. $500,000 future taxable amounts x 40% = $200,000 deferred tax liability. There is a related asset on the books, Plant Assets, and its classification is noncurrent. Therefore, the resulting deferred tax liability account is noncurrent.

2. $700,000 future deductible amounts x 40% = $280,000 deferred tax asset. There is a related Pension Liability on the GAAP balance sheet, and its classification is noncurrent. Therefore, the resulting deferred tax asset is noncurrent.

3. $400,000 future taxable amounts x 40% = $160,000 deferred tax liability. There is no asset or liability on the balance sheet that is related to the deferral of contract income for tax purposes. The classification of the deferred taxes is, therefore, dependent on the expected reversal date of the temporary difference. The expected reversal date (2011) is the year immediately following the balance sheet date; hence, the classification of the deferred tax account is current.

4.      $80,000 future deductible amounts x 40% = $32,000 deferred tax asset. There is a related liability on the balance sheet, Accrued Liability for Contingency, and its classification is current. Therefore, the resulting deferred tax asset is current.

5.      $220,000 future deductible amounts x $40% = $88,000 deferred tax asset. There is a related contra asset account, Allowance for Doubtful Accounts, in the current asset section of the balance sheet. Hence, the related deferred tax account is a current asset.

6.      $130,000 future deductible amounts x 40% = $52,000 deferred tax asset. There is a related accrued liability account, Estimated Obligation for Lawsuits, reported as a long-term liability on the balance sheet. The related deferred tax asset is therefore a noncurrent asset.

---

**TIP:** A commonly confusing point stems from the fact that the term **current** is used in association with **two totally unrelated amounts** involved with accounting for income taxes. These two amounts are the **current portion of income tax expense on the income statement** and the **current portion of deferred taxes on the balance sheet**. On the income statement, income tax expense is comprised of both current and deferred portions. On the balance sheet, deferred taxes are classified as either current or noncurrent. A change during the period in both current and noncurrent deferred taxes on the balance sheet results in the deferred portion of income tax expense for the same period on the income statement. The current portion of income tax expense on the income statement refers to the amount of taxes generated by the tax return for the current period. Taxable income produces a tax due (payable) and, therefore, current tax expense; a net operating loss on the tax return for the current period that calls for a carryback of the NOL results in a current tax benefit to be reported as the current portion of income tax expense on the income statement.

---

## EXERCISE 19-6

**Purpose:**     (L.O. 8) This exercise reviews the accounting procedures for an actual net operating loss.

The T. Evans Corporation has had no permanent or temporary differences since it began operations. Information regarding taxable income and taxes paid is as follows:

| Year | Taxable Income (Loss) | Tax Rate | Taxes Paid |
|------|-----------------------|----------|------------|
| 1    | $  60,000             | 40%      | $ 24,000   |
| 2    | 100,000               | 40%      | 40,000     |
| 3    | 80,000                | 35%      | 28,000     |
| 4    | 160,000               | 35%      | 56,000     |
| 5    | (300,000)             | 30%      |            |

The tax rate enacted for Year 6 and subsequent years is 25%.

## Instructions

(a)   Assuming the NOL (net operating loss) in Year 5 is carried back to the extent possible, prepare the journal entry to record the benefits of the carryback and the journal entry to record the expected benefits of any related NOL carryforward. Assume it is likely that the benefits of any carryforward will be fully realized.

(b)   Explain how all of the accounts in the entries above are to be reported in the financial statements for Year 5. Draft the income tax expense section of the income statement for Year 5, beginning with the line "Operating loss before income taxes."

(c)   Assuming taxable income is $100,000 (before considering the NOL carryforward) in Year 6, prepare the journal entry to record income taxes. Also, draft the income tax expense section of the income statement for Year 6, beginning with the line "Income before income taxes."

## Solution to Exercise 19-6

(a)   Income Tax Refund Receivable ................................................   84,000
      Benefits Due to Loss Carryback............................................              84,000
         ($28,000 + $56,000 = $84,000)

Deferred Tax Asset   .....................................................................15,000
      Benefits Due to Loss Carryforward ........................................              15,000
         ($300,000 - $80,000 - $160,000 = $60,000)
            ($60,000 x 25% = $15,000)

> **TIP:**   The expected benefits of an operating loss carryforward are recognized in the year of the loss which gives rise to the carryforward. The tax rate enacted for the future year in which the benefits are expected to be realized is used to calculate the related deferred tax asset.
>
> **TIP:**   Benefits Due to Loss Carryback and Benefits Due to Loss Carryforward are both negative components of total income tax expense; therefore, they are credits to the income statement. The Benefits Due to Loss Carryback represent a current tax benefit, and the Benefits Due to Loss Carryforward are a deferred tax benefit.
>
> **TIP:**   If it is **more likely than not** that a portion or all of the deferred tax asset will **not** be realized, a valuation allowance should be established by a charge to income tax expense and a credit to an allowance account. For example, in the case above, if one-half of the benefits of the operating loss carryforward were not expected to be realized within the carryforward period, an adjusting entry for $7,500 would be recorded by a debit to Benefits Due to Loss Carryforward and a credit to Allowance to Reduce Deferred Tax Asset to Expected Realizable Value.

(b)   The Income Tax Refund Receivable account is to be classified as a current asset on the balance sheet. The Deferred Tax Asset relates to an NOL carryforward so it is to be classified as a current asset **if** the benefits of the carryforward are expected to be realized in the year that immediately follows the balance sheet date. If the benefits are expected in a later year, the Deferred Tax Asset is to be classified as a noncurrent asset (in the Other Assets classification).

The other two accounts are negative components of income tax expense. The income statement would reflect them as follows:

| | |
|---|---|
| Operating loss before income taxes | $(300,000) |
| Benefits due to loss carryback | 84,000 |
| Benefits due to loss carryforward | 35,000 |
| Net loss | $(181,000) |

(c)
| | | |
|---|---|---|
| Income Tax Expense ................................................. | 25,000 | |
| Income Tax Payable ................................................. | | 10,000* |
| Deferred Tax Asset ($60,000 x 25%)......................... | | 15,000 |

*$100,000 - $60,000 = $40,000 taxable income for Year 6.
$40,000 x 25% = $10,000 income tax payable.

| | | |
|---|---|---|
| Income before income taxes | | $ 100,000 |
| Income tax expense: | | |
| Current tax expense | $ 10,000 | |
| Deferred tax expense | 15,000 | 25,000 |
| Net income | | $ 75,000 |

# EXERCISE 19-7

**Purpose:**    (L.O. 2, 3, 5, 7) This comprehensive exercise will illustrate how the interperiod allocation of income taxes affects the financial statements.

The following facts pertain to the Michael Hess Corporation:
- There were no deferred taxes on the December 31, 2009 balance sheet.
- Pretax financial income for 2010 is $113,000.
- Revenue of $20,000 reported on the 2010 income statement will be included on the 2011 income tax return.
- Expense of $7,000 reported on the 2010 income statement will be reported on the 2012 income tax return.
- There are no differences between pretax financial income and taxable income for 2010, other than the two items mentioned above.
- Enacted tax rates are as follows as of December 31, 2010:

| Year | Rate |
|---|---|
| 2010 | 50% |
| 2011 | 40% |
| 2012 | 30% |

- Taxable income is expected in all future years.

## Instructions

(a)   Compute the amount of taxable income for the year ending December 31, 2010.

(b)   Compute the amount of income tax payable for the year ending December 31, 2010.

(c)   Describe how each of the two temporary differences will impact future income tax returns.

(d)   Compute the deferred taxes to be reported on the balance sheet at December 31, 2010. Describe how they will affect the income statement for the year ending December 31, 2010.

(e)   Prepare the journal entry(ies) to record income taxes for 2010.

(f)   Describe how the deferred tax accounts will be reported on the balance sheet at December 31, 2010.

(g)   Prepare the section of the 2010 income statement involving income tax expense, beginning with "Income before income taxes."

## Solution to Exercise 19-7

(a)   Pretax financial income for 2010                                        $ 113,000

Temporary difference originating that gives rise to
   a future taxable amount                           (20,000)

Temporary difference originating that gives rise to a
   future deductible amount                        7,000
            Taxable income for 2010             $ 100,000

(b)   Taxable income for 2010                          $ 100,000

Enacted tax rate for 2010                           50%

Income tax payable for 2010                        $  50,000

(c)   The revenue of $20,000 that is being deferred for tax purposes will result in a **taxable amount** (an amount which increases taxable income) on the 2011 income tax return. The expense of $7,000 that is being deferred for tax purposes will result in a **deductible amount** (an amount which reduces taxable income) on the 2012 income tax return.

(d)

| | Current Year | Future Years | | |
|---|---|---|---|---|
| | **2010** | **2011** | **2012** | **Total** |
| Taxable income | $100,000 | | | |
| Future taxable (deductible) amounts | | | | |
|   Revenue deferred for tax purposes | | $20,000 | | $20,000 |
|   Expense deferred for tax purposes | | | $(7,000) | $ (7,000) |
| Enacted tax rate | 50% | 40% | 30% | |
| Deferred tax liability | | $ 8,000 | | $ 8,000 |
| Deferred tax asset | | | $(2,100) | $ (2,100) |

There is no balance in the Deferred Tax Liability account at the beginning of 2010. Therefore, the journal entry(ies) to record income taxes for 2010 will include an increase in Deferred Tax Liability (credit) of $8,000. This will cause a corresponding increase in Income Tax Expense (debit) of $8,000, which is referred to as **deferred tax expense** of $8,000. There is no balance in the Deferred Tax Asset account at the beginning of 2010. Therefore, the journal entry(ies) to record income taxes for 2010 will include an increase in Deferred Tax Asset (debit) of $2,100. This will cause a corresponding decrease in Income Tax Expense (credit) of $2,100, which is referred to as **deferred tax benefit** of $2,100. The deferred tax expense of $8,000 is combined with the deferred tax benefit of $2,100 on the income statement to produce a net deferred tax expense of $5,900.

---

**TIP:**  Notice that the future tax consequences of the $20,000 revenue item being deferred for tax purposes are recognized in the income statement in 2010 (which is the year in which that revenue item appears in the income statement). Those tax consequences are an increase in taxes of $8,000. Also, notice that the future tax consequences of the $7,000 expense item being deferred for tax purposes are recognized in the income statement in 2010 (which is the year in which that expense item appears in the income statement). Those tax consequences are a reduction in taxes of $2,100.

**TIP:**  Examine the definition of "taxable temporary difference," "deferred tax liability," and "deferred tax expense" and how they apply to this situation. Those definitions and applications are as follows:

**Taxable temporary difference:** *Definition*—a temporary difference that results in taxable amounts in a future year(s) when the related asset or liability is recovered or settled, respectively. *Application*—a revenue item of $20,000 is being recognized for financial reporting purposes in 2010 but is being deferred for tax purposes. Thus, it may be an accrued revenue for book purposes which results in recording an account receivable or accrued receivable. In 2011, this asset (receivable) will be recovered (through collection of the receivable) which will result in reporting the $20,000 revenue item on the future (2011) tax return; that is, a taxable amount of $20,000 will appear on the 2011 tax return. Thus, at December 31, 2010, there is a temporary difference giving rise to a future taxable amount of $20,000.

**Deferred tax liability:** *Definition*—the deferred tax consequences attributable to taxable type temporary differences. *Application*—the taxable temporary difference of $20,000 existing at December 31, 2010 will cause an increase of $8,000 in income taxes payable in the future when the related taxable amount is reported on the 2008 tax return. Thus, a deferred tax liability of $8,000 is to be reported on the balance sheet at December 31, 2010.

**Deferred tax expense:** *Definition*—an increase in a deferred tax liability or a reduction in a deferred tax asset during the period. *Application*—the increase of $8,000 during 2010 in a deferred tax liability account on the balance sheet results in a deferred tax expense of $8,000 on the income statement for 2010.

---

**TIP:**  Examine the definitions of "deductible temporary difference," "deferred tax asset," and "deferred tax benefit" and how they apply to this situation. Those definitions and applications are as follows:

> **Deductible temporary difference:** *Definition*—a temporary difference that results in deductible amounts in a future year(s) when the related asset or liability is recovered or settled, respectively. *Application*—an expense item of $7,000 is being recognized for financial reporting purposes in 2010 but is being deferred for tax purposes. Thus, it may be an accrued expense for book purposes which results in recording an account payable or accrued payable. In 2012, this accrued payable will be settled (by payment of the payable) which will result in reporting the $7,000 expense item on the future (2012) tax return; that is, a deductible amount of $7,000 will appear on the 2012 tax return. Thus, at December 31, 2010, there is a temporary difference giving rise to a future deductible amount of $7,000.
>
> **Deferred tax asset:** *Definition*—the deferred tax consequences attributable to deductible type temporary differences and loss carryforwards. *Application*—the deductible temporary difference of $7,000 existing at December 31, 2010 will cause a decrease of $2,100 in taxes payable in the future when the related deductible amount is reported on the 2012 tax return. Thus, a deferred tax asset of $2,100 is to be reported on the balance sheet at December 31, 2010.
>
> **Deferred tax benefit:** *Definition*—an increase in a deferred tax asset or a reduction in a deferred tax liability during the period. *Application*—the increase of $2,100 during 2010 in a deferred tax asset account on the balance sheet results in a deferred tax benefit of $2,100 on the income statement for 2010.

(e)   The journal entry to record current tax expense (the amount of income taxes payable) for 2010 as determined by applying the provisions of the enacted tax law to the taxable income for 2010 is as follows:

| | | |
|---|---|---|
| Income Tax Expense | 50,000 | |
| Income Tax Payable ($100,000 x 50%) | | 50,000 |

The journal entry to record the increase in deferred tax liability during 2010 is as follows:

| | | |
|---|---|---|
| Income Tax Expense | 8,000 | |
| Deferred Tax Liability | | 8,000 |

The journal entry to record the increase in deferred tax asset during 2010 is as follows:

| | | |
|---|---|---|
| Deferred Tax Asset | 2,100 | |
| Income Tax Expense | | 2,100 |

| TIP: | The three entries above are usually combined to form one compound journal entry as follows: | | |
|---|---|---|---|
| | Income Tax Expense........................................................... | 55,900 | |
| | Deferred Tax Asset............................................................ | 2,100 | |
| | Deferred Tax Liability.................................................... | | 8,000 |
| | Income Tax Payable...................................................... | | 50,000 |

(f)    The deferred tax accounts on the balance sheet are classified as current or noncurrent, based on the classification of any related asset or liability. Assuming the $20,000 temporary difference has a related accrued receivable on the books classified as a current asset, the resulting $8,000 deferred tax liability will be classified as a current liability. Assuming the $7,000 temporary difference has a related accrued payable on the books classified as a noncurrent liability, the resulting $2,100 deferred tax asset will be classified under "other assets" on the balance sheet. Deferred tax assets and liabilities are netted for reporting purposes **only** where they are both current or both noncurrent classification.

(g)    Income before income taxes                                                         $ 113,000
Income tax expense:
    Current expense                                         $ 50,000
    Deferred expense                                            5,900
        Total income tax expense                                                 55,900
Net income                                                             $  57,100

| TIP: | Notice that the effective tax rate for 2010 ($55,900 ÷ $113,000) is not equal to the statutory tax rate for 2010 (50%) because a $20,000 revenue item reflected in the $113,000 is tax effected at 40% in determining the related increase in 2010 income tax expense and a $7,000 expense item reflected in the $113,000 is tax effected at 30% in determining the related reduction in 2010 income tax expense. |
|---|---|
| TIP: | Recall the objectives of the asset-liability method of accounting for income taxes and review the solution above to see how these objectives are met. These objectives are: |
| | (1)     to recognize the amount of taxes payable (or refundable) for the current year, and |
| | (2)     to recognize deferred tax liabilities and assets for the **future tax consequences** of events that have been recognized in the financial statements or tax returns. |

> **TIP:** Think about what will happen in 2011 when the $20,000 **taxable temporary difference is eliminated (reverses).** In 2011, the $20,000 will appear as a revenue item on the tax return but not on the income statement for that year. Therefore, there will be no deferred tax liability on the December 31, 2011 balance sheet. The reduction in the deferred tax liability (a debit) in 2011 will result in a deferred tax benefit (a credit) of $8,000 on the 2011 income statement and current tax expense for 2011 will exceed total income tax expense for that year because the tax consequences of the $20,000 revenue item were reflected in the total income tax expense amount in 2010.
>
> **TIP:** Think about what will happen in 2012 when the $7,000 **deductible temporary difference is eliminated (reverses).** In 2012, the $7,000 will appear as an expense item (deduction) on the tax return but not on the income statement for that year. Therefore, there will be no deferred tax asset on the December 31, 2012 balance sheet. The reduction in the deferred tax asset (a credit) in 2012 will result in a deferred tax expense (a debit) of $2,100 on the 2012 income statement and current tax expense for that year will be less than total tax expense for 2012 because the tax consequences (a tax savings) of the $7,000 expense item were reflected in the total income tax expense amount in 2012.

## ANALYSIS OF MULTIPLE-CHOICE TYPE QUESTIONS

**QUESTION**

1. (L.O. 2, 3,) A temporary difference arises when a revenue item is reported for tax purposes in a period

| | After it is reported in financial income | Before it is reported in financial income |
|---|---|---|
| a. | Yes | Yes |
| b. | Yes | No |
| c. | No | Yes |
| d. | No | No |

**Explanation:** Revenue that is taxable **after** it is recognized in financial income creates a difference between the tax basis of an asset (zero) and its reported amount in the financial statements. This difference will result in a taxable amount in a future period(s) when the reported amount of the asset is settled. (An example situation is when revenue is earned and accrued to a period in advance of the period in which the related cash is collected and taxed. A receivable is reported on a GAAP basis balance sheet until the period in which the cash collection occurs. The cash collection is a taxable event.)

Revenue that is taxable **before** it is recognized in financial income creates a difference between the tax basis of a liability (zero) and its reported amount in the financial statements. This difference will result in a deductible amount in a future period(s) when the reported amount of the related liability is settled. (An example situation is when revenue is collected in a period in advance of the period it is earned. The cash collection triggers a taxable event. Unearned revenue is reported on a GAAP basis balance sheet until the period in which the revenue is earned.) (Solution = a.)

**QUESTION**

2. (L.O. 2, 3) Which of the following should be recognized for the amount of deferred tax consequences attributable to temporary differences that will result in deductible amounts in future years?

| | **Deferred Tax Asset** | **Deferred Tax Liability** |
|---|---|---|
| a. | Yes | Yes |
| b. | Yes | No |
| c. | No | Yes |
| d. | No | No |

**Explanation:** A temporary difference giving rise to future deductible amounts requires the recognition of a deferred tax asset for the amount of the future tax consequences related to the existing temporary difference. A temporary difference giving rise to future taxable amounts requires the recognition of a deferred tax liability for the amount of the future tax consequences related to the existing temporary difference. (Solution = b.)

**QUESTION**

3. (L.O. 2, 6) Assuming a 40% statutory tax rate applies to all years involved, which of the following situations will give rise to reporting a deferred tax liability on the balance sheet?
   I.    A revenue is deferred for financial reporting purposes but not for tax purposes.
   II.   A revenue is deferred for tax purposes but not for financial reporting purposes.
   III.  An expense is deferred for financial reporting purposes but not for tax purposes.
   IV.   An expense is deferred for tax purposes but not for financial reporting purposes.
   a.    item II only
   b.    items I and II only
   c.    items II and III only
   d.    items I and IV only

**Approach and Explanation:** Notice that each situation described involves a difference in the timing of revenue or expense recognition for financial reporting purposes (accounting purposes or book purposes) and tax purposes (tax reporting purposes). Thus, each situation involves a temporary difference. For each, determine if future taxable or deductible amounts will occur. Because a flat tax rate applies to all periods involved, a temporary difference resulting in net future taxable amounts will give rise to reporting a deferred tax liability, and a temporary difference giving rise to net future deductible amounts will result in reporting a deferred tax asset. Items II and III will give rise to future taxable amounts; items I and IV will give rise to future deductible amounts. (Solution = c.)

**QUESTION**

4. (L.O. 2, 5) At the December 31, 2010 balance sheet date, Garth Brooks Corporation reports an accrued receivable for financial reporting purposes but **not** for tax purposes. When this asset is recovered in 2011, a future taxable amount will occur and:
   a.    pretax financial income will exceed taxable income in 2011.
   b.    Garth will record a decrease in a deferred tax liability in 2011.
   c.    total income tax expense for 2011 will exceed current tax expense for 2011.
   d.    Garth will record an increase in a deferred tax asset in 2011.

**Explanation:** The receivable stems from a revenue earned but not received; the revenue has been booked for accounting purposes but not for tax purposes. When this asset (receivable) is recovered through collection of the receivable in 2011, it will result in a taxable amount (taxable revenue on the 2011 income tax return). Thus, in 2011, pretax financial income will be less than taxable income because of the elimination (reversal) of the temporary difference. Also in 2011, Garth will record a decrease in the deferred tax liability, resulting in a deferred tax benefit on the 2011 income statement (which causes current tax expense in 2011 to exceed total tax expense for 2011). (Solution = b.)

**QUESTION**

5.(L.O. 3) The Mary Colson Corporation collects rent revenue in advance from tenants. The collection of $50,000 in 2010 is reported as revenue for tax purposes; it will be reported on the income statement in 2011 when it is earned. This situation will:

a.  result in future deductible amounts.
b.  result in reporting a deferred tax liability on the balance sheet at the end of 2010.
c.  cause total income tax expense to be less than income tax payable in 2011.
d.  cause pretax financial income to exceed taxable income in 2010.

**Explanation:** The collection and reporting of revenue for tax purposes in a period before it is earned and recognized for book purposes will result in future deductible amounts. A deferred tax asset is to be recognized for the deferred tax consequences of the revenue already reflected in the income tax return. In a later period, the unearned revenue per books (a liability) will be settled by delivering goods or services to the customers or by refunding the customers' money; the related outlays are, therefore, tax deductible in the later period in which the revenue is earned. In that later period, pretax financial income will exceed taxable income. Also, in that later period, total income tax expense will exceed income tax payable (current tax expense) by the amount of the decrease in the related Deferred Tax Asset account due to the reversal of the temporary difference. (Solution = a.)

**QUESTION**

6.  (L.O. 2, 3, 5) Kaminsky Company reported deferred tax expense of $70,000 on its income statement for the year ended December 31, 2010. This could be the result of an increase in a:

|     | **Deferred Tax Asset** | **Deferred Tax Liability** |
| --- | --- | --- |
| a.  | Yes | Yes |
| b.  | No | No |
| c.  | Yes | No |
| d.  | No | Yes |

**Approach and Explanation:** Think about the journal entry to record deferred tax expense. The entry involves a debit to Income Tax Expense and a credit to a balance sheet account for deferred taxes. Thus, this credit is either an increase in the Deferred Tax Liability account or a decrease in the Deferred Tax Asset account. (Solution = d.)

**QUESTION**

7.(L.O. 2, 7) Mixner Corporation reported $50,000 in revenues in its 2010 financial statements, of which $22,000 will **not** be included in the tax return until 2011. The enacted tax rate is 40% for 2010 and 35% for 2011. What amount should Mixner report for deferred income tax liability in its balance sheet at December 31, 2010?

a.  $7,700
b.  $8,800
c.  $9,800
d.  $11,200

**Approach and Explanation:** At the balance sheet date, December 31, 2010, there is a temporary difference of $22,000. That temporary difference will result in a taxable amount of $22,000 in 2011. The taxes payable on that amount will be $7,700 ($22,000 x 35%). The deferred tax consequences are to be reflected in the financial statements for 2010. The journal entry to record these consequences (assuming no balance of deferred taxes at the beginning of the period) would include a credit to Deferred Tax Liability and a debit to Income Tax Expense for $7,700. Therefore: (1) revenue of $50,000; and (2) a current tax expense of $11,200 ($28,000 x 40%) and a deferred tax expense of $7,700 ($22,000 x 35%) will be reflected on the 2010 income statement. Thus, the tax consequences of the full $50,000 appear on the same income statement as the $50,000 revenue, regardless of when the taxes are to be paid. (Solution = a.)

**QUESTION**

8. (L.O. 2, 7) Garver Inc. uses the accrual method of accounting for financial reporting purposes and appropriately uses the installment method of accounting for income tax purposes. Profits of $500,000 recognized for books in 2010 will be collected in the following years:

| Collection of Profits | |
|---|---|
| 2011 | $ 50,000 |
| 2012 | 100,000 |
| 2013 | 150,000 |
| 2014 | 200,000 |

The enacted tax rates are: 40% for 2010, 35% for 2011, 30% for 2012 and 2013, and 25% for 2014. Taxable income is expected in all future years. What amount should be included in the December 31, 2010, balance sheet for the deferred tax liability related to the above temporary difference?

a. $0
b. $17,500
c. $125,000
d. $142,500
e. $200,000

**Explanation:** The temporary difference will cause future taxable amounts. The future taxable amounts are to be tax effected at the appropriate enacted tax rates for future periods. The computation is as follows:

| | | | |
|---|---|---|---|
| 2011 | $ 50,000 x 35% | = | $ 17,500 |
| 2012 | 100,000 x 30% | = | 30,000 |
| 2013 | 150,000 x 30% | = | 45,000 |
| 2014 | 200,000 x 25% | = | 50,000 |
| Balance of deferred tax liability, Dec. 31, 2010 | | | $142,500 |

(Solution = d.)

**QUESTION**

9. (L.O. 2, 5, 6, 7) CPA-CPE Corporation prepared the following reconciliation for its first year of operations:

| | |
|---|---|
| Pretax financial income for 2010 | $ 600,000 |
| Tax exempt interest | (50,000) |
| Originating temporary difference | (150,000) |
| Taxable income | $ 400,000 |

The temporary difference will reverse evenly over the next two years at an enacted tax rate of 40%. The enacted tax rate for 2010 is 28%. What amount should be reported in its 2010 income statement for total income tax expense?

a. $52,000
b. $112,000
c. $168,000
d. $172,000
e. $192,000

**Explanation:**

| | |
|---|---|
| Current tax expense ($400,000 x 28%) | $112,000 |
| Deferred tax expense ($150,000 x 40%) | 60,000 |
| Total income tax expense for 2010 | $172,000 |

The temporary difference is originating and is causing taxable income to be lower than pretax financial income in the current period; therefore, the temporary difference will result in future taxable amounts. An increase in the related deferred tax liability account causes a deferred tax expense to be reported on the income statement. No deferred taxes are recorded for the tax exempt interest (a permanent difference). (Solution = d.)

**QUESTION**
10.    (L.O. 2, 5, 6, 7) Refer to the facts of **Question 9** above. In CPA-CPE's 2010 income statement, what amount should be reported as the deferred portion of its provision for income taxes?
a.    $80,000 debit
b.    $60,000 debit
c.    $60,000 credit
d.    $56,000 credit
e.    $42,000 debit

**Explanation:** The temporary difference existing at December 31, 2010 will result in future taxable amounts and thus gives rise to a deferred tax liability of $60,000 ($150,000 cumulative temporary difference x 40%) to be reported on the balance sheet at that date. There was no beginning deferred tax liability (2010 is the first year of operations). Thus, the $60,000 increase in deferred tax liability results in deferred tax expense (debit) of $60,000 on the 2010 income statement. No deferred taxes are recorded for a permanent difference (the tax exempt interest) because it will never reverse. (Solution = b.)

> **TIP:**    Recall that "provision for income taxes" is another name for "income tax expense."

**QUESTION**
11.(L.O. 5) Refer to the facts of **Question 9** above. In CPA-CPE's 2010 income statement, what amount should be reported as the current portion of its provision for income taxes?
a.    $112,000
b.    $160,000
c.    $168,000
d.    $240,000

**Explanation:** The taxable income of $400,000 multiplied by the tax rate of 28% for the current year yields a current tax expense of $112,000. (Solution = a.)

**QUESTION**
12.    (L.O. 6, 7) The Kay Bryan Company has the following cumulative taxable temporary differences:

| **12/31/10** | **12/31/09** |
|---|---|
| $ 450,000 | $ 320,000 |

The tax rate enacted for 2010 is 40%, while the tax rate enacted for future years is 30%. Taxable income for 2010 is $800,000 and there are no permanent differences. Kay Bryan's pretax financial income for 2010 is:
a.    $350,000.
b.    $670,000.
c.    $930,000.
d.    $1,250,000.

**Approach and Explanation:** Use the format for the reconciliation of pretax financial income with taxable income (see **Illustration 19-3** and its accompanying **TIP**). Enter the data given. Solve for the unknown. (Solution = c.)

| | |
|---|---|
| Pretax financial income | $         X |
| Temporary differences originating this period which will result in future taxable amounts ($450,000 - $320,000) | (130,000) |
| Taxable income | $ 800,000 |

Solving for X:    X - $130,000 = $800,000
                          X = $930,000

| TIP: | No tax rates were used in this solution. |
|---|---|

## QUESTION

13.     (L.O. 4) Norman Corporation has a deferred tax asset at December 31, 2010 of $50,000 due to the recognition of potential tax benefits of an operating loss carryforward. The enacted tax rates are as follows: 40% for 2007-2009; 35% for 2010; and 30% for 2011 and thereafter. Assuming that management expects that only 50% of the related benefits will actually be realized, a valuation account should be established in the amount of:

a.     $25,000.
b.     $10,000.
c.     $8,750.
d.     $7,500.

**Approach and Explanation:** Prepare the journal entry to record the necessary valuation account for the portion of the deferred tax asset that more likely than not will not be realized. That entry is as follows:

Benefit Due to Loss Carryforward
   (or Income Tax Expense) ................................................................... 25,000
      Allowance to Reduce Deferred Tax Asset
         to Expected Realizable Value................................................ 25,000

Because only 50% of the benefits are expected to be realized, a valuation account is needed for the 50% (50% x $50,000 = $25,000) that is not expected to be realized. The tax rates are not relevant in this question. The future tax rate (30%) was used to apply to the NOL carryforward amount in computing the $50,000 of potential benefits reflected in the Deferred Tax Asset account. (Solution = a.)

| TIP: | From the facts given, we can determine that the NOL carryforward amount was $166,666.67 ($50,000 ÷ 30% = $166,666.67). |
|---|---|

## QUESTION

14.     (L.O. 7) At December 31, 2009 Malcohm Corporation reported a deferred tax liability of $60,000 which was attributable to a taxable type temporary difference of $200,000. The temporary difference is scheduled to reverse in 2010. During 2010, a new tax law increased the corporate tax rate from 30% to 40%. Which of the following entries will correctly account for the effect of this change on deferred taxes?

a.     Retained Earnings    .......................................................................20,000
      Deferred Tax Liability................................................................. 20,000
b.     Retained Earnings    .......................................................................6,000
      Deferred Tax Liability................................................................. 6,000
c.     Income Tax Expense    .......................................................................6,000
      Deferred Tax Liability................................................................. 6,000
d.     Income Tax Expense    .......................................................................20,000
      Deferred Tax Liability................................................................. 20,000

**Approach and Explanation:** Deferred tax liabilities and assets are to be adjusted in the period of enactment for the effect of an enacted change in tax laws or rates. The effect is included in income from continuing operations as a component of income tax expense [$200,000 x (40% - 30%) = $20,000]. (Solution = d.)

**QUESTION**

15.(L.O. 8) Carrie Freeman Corporation began operations in 2006. There have been no permanent differences or temporary differences to account for since the inception of the business. The following data are available:

| Year | Enacted Tax Rate | Taxable Income | Taxes Paid |
|------|------|------|------|
| 2006 | 50% | $100,000 | $ 50,000 |
| 2007 | 40% | 200,000 | 80,000 |
| 2008 | 40% | 250,000 | 100,000 |
| 2009 | 30% | 300,000 | 90,000 |
| 2010 | 25% | | |
| 2011 | 20% | | |

In 2010, Carrie Freeman has an NOL of $310,000. What amount of income tax benefits should be reported on the 2010 income statement due to this NOL?

a.    $77,500
b.    $93,000
c.    $94,000
d.    $118,000

**Explanation:** The loss is carried back two years and must be applied to the earliest year first. The $310,000 loss is therefore applied as follows:

| | | | |
|------|------|------|------|
| 2008 | $250,000 x 40% | = | $100,000 |
| 2009 | 60,000 x 30% | = | 18,000 |
| | Benefits of NOL carryback | | $ 118,000 |

The future rate (2011 and beyond) would only be used to compute the benefits of an NOL carryforward. An NOL carryforward will result when the NOL is larger than the combined taxable income for the two years involved in the carryback period or when a company elects to forego the carryback procedure and use only the carryforward. The tax rate for the current period (2010) is not used to compute the benefits of an NOL carryback or carryforward. (Solution = d.)

CHAPTER 20

# ACCOUNTING FOR PENSIONS AND POSTRETIREMENT BENEFITS

## OVERVIEW

A pension plan is an arrangement whereby an employer provides benefits to employees after they retire. A defined benefit plan defines the benefits the employees will receive at the time of retirement. The accounting for a defined benefit plan is complex. Pension cost is a function of service cost, interest on the pension liability, return on plan assets, amortization of prior service cost, and recognition of gains and losses. Numerous disclosures are required. Accounting on an employer's books for a defined-benefit pension plan is the focus of this chapter. The accounting for health care and other benefits provided to retirees is similar to the accounting for pension plans. The topic "other postretirement benefit plans" is also covered in this chapter.

## SUMMARY OF LEARNING OBJECTIVES

1. **Distinguish between accounting for the employer's pension plan and accounting for the pension fund.** The company or employer is the organization sponsoring the pension plan. It incurs the cost and makes contributions to the pension fund. The fund or plan is the entity that receives the contributions from the employer, administers the pension assets, and makes the benefit payments to the pension recipients (retired employees). The fund should be a separate legal and accounting entity; it maintains a set of books and prepares financial statements.

2. **Identify types of pension plans and their characteristics.** The two most common types of pension arrangements are: (1) **Defined contribution plans:** The employer agrees to contribute to a pension trust a certain sum each period based on a formula. This formula may consider such factors as age, length of employee service, employer's profits, and compensation level. Only the employer's contribution is defined; no promise is made regarding the ultimate benefits paid out to the employees. (2) **Defined benefit plans:** These plans define the benefits that the employee will receive at the time of retirement. The formula typically provides for the benefits to be a function of the employee's years of service and the employee's compensation level when he or she nears retirement.

3. **Explain alternative measures for valuing the pension obligation.** One measure bases the pension obligation only on the benefits vested to the employees. Vested benefits are those that the employee is entitled to receive even if he or she renders no additional services under the plan. The **vested benefits pension obligation** is computed using current salary levels and includes only vested benefits. Another measure of the obligation, called the **accumulated benefit obligation**, computes the deferred compensation amount based on all years of service performed by employees under the plan—both vested and nonvested— using current salary levels. A third measure, called the **projected benefit obligation**, bases the computation of the deferred compensation amount on both vested and nonvested service using expected future salaries.

4.    **List the components of pension expense.** Pension expense is a function of the following components: (1) service cost, (2) interest on the pension liability, (3) actual return on plan assets, (4) amortization of unrecognized prior service cost, and (5) gain or loss.

5.    **Use a work sheet for employer's pension plan entries.** Companies may use a work sheet unique to pension accounting. This worksheet records both the formal entries and the memo entries to keep track of all the employer's relevant pension plan items and components.

6.    **Describe the amortization of prior service cost.** Prior service cost is the cost of retroactive benefits granted in a plan amendment. An actuary computes the amount of the prior service cost, and the company records it as an adjustment to the projected benefit obligation (which affects the balance of the Pension Asset/Liability account) and other comprehensive income. The FASB prefers a "years-of-service" amortization method that is similar to a units-of-production computation. First, the company computes the total estimated number of service-years to be worked by all of the participating employees. Second, it divides the accumulated unrecognized prior service cost by the total number of service-years to obtain a cost per service-year (the unit cost). Third, the company multiplies the number of service-years consumed each year by the cost per service-year to obtain the annual amortization charge. The FASB does allow an alternative method of computing amortization of unrecognized prior service cost; employers may use straight-line amortization over the average remaining service life of the employees.

7.    **Explain the accounting procedure for recognizing unexpected gains and losses.** In estimating the projected benefit obligation (the liability), actuaries make assumptions about such items as mortality rate, retirement rate, turnover rate, disability rate, and salary amounts. Any change in these actuarial assumptions affects the amount of the projected benefit obligation. These unexpected gains or losses from changes in the projected benefit obligation are liability gains and losses. Liability gains result from unexpected decreases in the liability balance; liability losses result from unexpected increases. Companies also incur asset gains or losses. Both types of actuarial gains or losses are recorded in other comprehensive income and adjust either the projected benefit obligation or the plan assets balance which is then reflected in the Pension Asset/Liability account balance.

8.    **Explain the corridor approach to amortizing unrecognized gains and losses.** The FASB set a limit for the size of an accumulated net gain or loss balance. That arbitrarily selected limit (called a **corridor)** is 10% of the larger of the beginning balances of the projected benefit obligation or the market-related value of the plan assets. Beyond that limit, an accumulated net gain or loss balance is considered to be too large and must be amortized. If the balance of the accumulated net gain or loss account stays within the upper and lower limits of the corridor, no amortization is required.

9.    **Describe the requirements for reporting pension plans in financial statements.** Currently, companies must disclose the following pension plan information in their financial statements: (1) The components of net periodic pension expense for the period. (2) A schedule showing changes in the benefit obligation and plan assets during the year. (3) The amount of prior service cost and net gains and losses in accumulated OCI, including the estimated prior service cost and gains and losses that will affect net income in the next year. (4) The weighted-average assumed discount rate, the rate of compensation increase used to measure the projected benefit obligation, and the weighted-average expected long-term rate of return on plan assets. (5) A table showing the allocation of pension plan assets by category and the percentage of the fair value to total plan assets. (6) The expected benefit payments for current plan participants for each of the next five fiscal years and for the following five years in aggregate, along with an estimate of expected contributions to the plan during the next year.

*10.    **Identify the differences between pension plans and postretirement health care benefit plans.** Pension plans are generally funded, but health care benefit plans are generally not funded. Pension benefits are generally well-defined and level in amount; health care benefits are generally uncapped and variable. Pension benefits are payable monthly; health care benefits are paid as needed and used. Pension plan variables are reasonably predictable, whereas health care plan variables are difficult to predict.

*11. **Contrast accounting for pensions to accounting for other postretirement benefits.** Many of the basic concepts and much of the accounting terminology and measurement methodology applicable to pensions also apply to other postretirement benefit accounting. Because other postretirement benefit plans are unfunded, large obligations can occur. Two significant concepts peculiar to accounting for other postretirement benefits are (a) expected postretirement benefit obligation (EPBO) and (b) accumulated postretirement benefit obligation (APBO).

      *This material is covered in Appendix 20A in the text.

## TIPS ON CHAPTER TOPICS

**TIP:** The **pension fund** is the entity that receives the contributions from the employer, administers the pension assets, and makes the benefit payments to the retired employees (pension recipients). The pension fund, as a separate legal and accounting entity, maintains a set of books and prepares financial statements. This chapter does **not** discuss the accounting procedures for the fund; it focuses on the reporting problems of the employer as the sponsor of a pension plan. The amount in the fund affects the balance of the Pension Asset/Liability account that gets reported on the employer's balance sheet and changes in the fund balance will affect Pension Expense on the employer's income statement and may affect Accumulated Other Comprehensive Income on the employer's statements.

**TIP:** In a **defined-contribution plan**, the employer agrees to contribute a certain sum (based on a formula) each period to a pension trust. The plan makes no promise regarding the ultimate benefits to be paid to retirees. The accounting for this type of plan is simple. Each period, a journal entry to record the employer's contribution to the fund includes only a debit to Pension Expense and a credit to Cash for the amount being funded.

**TIP:** A **defined-benefit plan** outlines the benefits that employees will receive when they retire. These benefits are the responsibility of the employer and typically are a function of an employee's years of service and of the compensation level in the years approaching retirement. Estimates must be made regarding how much money must be put into the fund periodically to provide for the payment of the promised benefits for all covered employees. These estimates are also affected by other estimates, such as the rate of return that will be earned by fund assets while on deposit, the life span of employees, employee turnover rates and future salary levels. This causes the accounting for these plans to be very complex.

**TIP:** Recall in an earlier chapter when we discussed the accounting for services received from salaried employees prior to the date they are paid for those services. That situation calls for an accrual of Salaries Expense and a credit to Salaries Payable. In this chapter, we extend that concept to the more complicated situation where employees are subject to a pension plan whereby the employees will receive benefits after retirement for services they are providing currently in their capacity of being employees. These complications arise from things including: (1) the employer sets aside funds to later take care of those benefits (2) those funds earn interest and dividends and often suffer/enjoy unexpected losses or gains (3) the pension benefits to be paid to the employees in the future must be estimated by an actuary and that estimate is dependent on a number of factors including employee turnover rates, future salaries levels and interest rates which have to be estimated. In the end, our job is to sort out all the details so we still recognize compensation expense in the period the employee works and record any related liability for future payment.

**TIP:** The **accumulated benefit obligation (ABO)** measures the pension obligation at a balance sheet date using current salary levels. The **projected benefit obligation (PBO)** measures the same obligation using future salary levels. Notice that the PBO is used in the following computations:
1. The **beginning** balance of the **PBO** is used to compute the interest component of pension expense for the period. (L.O.4)
2. The greater of the **beginning** balance of the **PBO or market-related value of plan assets** (beginning of period) is used to compute the 10% corridor in determining the need for amortization of the balance of accumulated net gain or loss. (L.O.8)

**TIP:** At the end of an accounting period, the balance of the Pension Asset/Liability account reflects the underfunded or overfunded status of the pension plan which gets reported on the employer's balance sheet. That is, the difference between the projected benefit obligation amount at a balance sheet date and the fair value of the plan assets amount at the same date is the pension asset or liability amount.

A caption such as Excess of the Fair Value of Pension Plan Assets over the Projected Benefit Obligation (overfunded status) will be reported as a noncurrent asset (noncurrent because of the restricted nature of plan assets—restricted to fund the PBO) whereas an Excess of Projected Benefit Obligation over Fair Value of Plan Assets (underfunded status) will be reported as a liability. The current portion of a net pension liability represents the amount of benefit payments to be paid in the next 12 months (or operating cycle, if longer) if that amount cannot be funded from existing plan assets. Otherwise the pension liability is classified as a noncurrent liability.

## ILLUSTRATION 20-1
## COMPONENTS OF PENSION EXPENSE (L.O. 4)

**COMPUTATION OF PENSION EXPENSE:**

|     | SERVICE COST |
| --- | --- |
| + | INTEREST ON THE PBO LIABILITY |
| - | ACTUAL RETURN ON PLAN ASSETS |
| + | AMORTIZATION OF PRIOR SERVICE COST |
| +/- | EFFECTS OF GAINS OR LOSSES |
| = | **PENSION EXPENSE** |

**DEFINITIONS OF COMPONENTS:**

**Service Cost.** The expense caused by the increase in pension benefits payable (the projected benefit obligation) to employees because of their services rendered during the current year. Actuaries compute **service cost** as the present value of the additional benefits that an employer must pay under the plan's benefit formula as a result of the employees' current year's service.

**Interest on the Liability.** Because a pension is a deferred compensation arrangement, there is a time value of money factor. As a result, it is recorded on a discounted basis. **Interest accrues each year on the projected benefit obligation just as it does on any discounted debt.** The accountant receives help from the actuary in selecting the interest rate, called for this purpose the **settlement rate**.

**Actual Return on Plan Assets.** The return earned by the accumulated pension fund assets in a particular year is relevant in measuring the net cost to the employer of sponsoring an employee pension plan. Therefore, **annual pension expense should be adjusted for interest and dividends that accumulate within the fund as well as increases and decreases in the market value of fund assets**.

**Amortization of Prior Service Cost.** Pension plan amendments (including initiation of a pension plan) often include provisions to increase benefits (in rare situations to decrease benefits) for employee service provided in prior years. Because plan amendments are granted with the expectation that the employer will realize economic benefits in future periods, **the cost (prior service cost) of providing these retroactive benefits is allocated to pension expense in the future, specifically to the remaining service-years of the affected employees**.

**Gain or Loss.** Volatility in pension expense can be caused by sudden and large changes in the market value of plan assets and by changes in the projected benefit obligation (which changes when actuarial assumptions are modified or when actual experience differs from expected experience). Two items comprise this gain or loss: (1) unexpected asset or liability gains or losses arising in the current period and (2) amortization of the accumulated net gain or loss from previous periods. This computation is complex.

**In summary,** the components of pension expense and their effect are as follows:
- Service cost (increases pension expense).
- Interest on the liability (increases pension expense).
- Actual return on plan assets (decreases pension expense if positive).
- Amortization of prior service cost (generally increases pension expense).
- Gain or loss (decreases or increases pension expense).

## ILLUSTRATION 20-1 (Continued)

**TIP:** Plan adoptions or amendments often include provisions to increase benefits for employee service provided in prior years. These increased benefits result in **prior service costs** and are provided for employees with the expectation that the employer company will receive benefits (enhanced services from the employees) in the future. Therefore, these costs are to be recognized as expense over the current and future periods. This is accomplished by the following: In the year the prior service costs (PSC) are initiated, the employer records the prior service cost as an adjustment to Other Comprehensive Income (which does not affect current net income). The employer then recognizes the prior service cost as a component of pension expense over the remaining service lives of the employees who are expected to benefit from the change in the plan. The years-of-service amortization method is typically used to compute the amount going into the pension calculation for the current period.

**TIP:** **Unexpected gains and losses** result from changes in the market value of plan assets (often called **asset gains and losses**) or from changes in the projected benefit obligation caused by changes in actuarial assumptions (often called **liability gains and losses**). Unexpected gains and losses arising in the current period (both asset and liability types) are recorded in the Other Comprehensive Income account which when closed to the Accumulated Other Comprehensive Income account combines them with gains and losses accumulated in prior years. This treatment is similar to that for prior service costs described above. The net **accumulated** gain or loss is amortized by the **corridor approach**; the net accumulated gain or loss is amortized when it exceeds 10% of the larger of the beginning balances of the projected benefit obligation or the market-related value of the plan assets.

**TIP:** For the gain or loss component of the pension expense calculation: (1) an unexpected asset or liability gain occurring in the current period will be added; an unexpected asset or liability loss will be deducted; and, (2) amortization of an accumulated net gain from previous periods will be deducted; amortization of an accumulated net loss from previous periods will be added in computing pension expense.

**TIP:** **Unexpected asset gains or losses** often arise in the current period from the actual return on fund assets differing from the expected return. (An excess of actual return over expected return gives rise to an unexpected asset gain.) **Unexpected liability gains or losses** often arise from actual experience differing from actuarial assumptions related to items such as mortality, employee turnover, interest rates, and salary levels. (A change in an actuarial assumption that causes an unexpected increase in the projected benefit obligation gives rise to an unexpected liability loss.)

**TIP:** The **expected return on plan assets** is calculated by multiplying the expected rate of return times the market-related asset value at the beginning of the year. If the actual return is higher than the expected return (called an unexpected asset gain), the unexpected gain is added to pension expense; and when the actual return is lower (called an unexpected asset loss), the unexpected loss is deducted from pension expense. As a result, the **expected return** is the amount actually used to compute pension expense.

Reread this **TIP** (it contains a confusing aspect) and review the computation for pension expense. Notice that the actual return on plan assets is deducted in the computation of pension expense for the current period. Assume the actual return is $80,000 which includes an unexpected gain of $9,000. Thus, the $80,000 actual return would be deducted and the $9,000 unexpected gain would be added in the pension expense computation; thus, only the $71,000 expected return is reflected in the pension expense balance.

TIP: Throughout the FASB literature, the term "periodic pension cost" is used rather than "pension expense" because part of the cost recognized in a period may be capitalized along with other costs as part of an asset such as inventory. For example, pension cost related to factory workers in a manufacturing company is charged to Factory Labor, which is accounted for as a product cost; thus, it is incorporated in the cost of inventory until the period the related product is sold, at which time it is charged to Cost of Goods Sold. "Pension expense" is used in this chapter as a means of simplification; its use is appropriate when the pension cost relates to employees whose salaries and wages are expensed rather than capitalized (i.e., employees such as sales clerks and most executives). "Pension Expense" is sometimes classified as "Employee Benefits" on the income statement.

# EXERCISE 20-1

**Purpose:** (L.O. 4) This exercise will enable you to practice computing pension expense.

The following data relate to Kleen Company's pension plan for the year 2010:

| | |
|---|---:|
| Actual and expected return on plan assets | $ 60,000 |
| Benefits paid | 40,000 |
| Contributions to plan | 105,000 |
| Plan assets at January 1, 2010 | 684,000 |
| Prior service cost amortization | 15,000 |
| Projected benefit obligation at January 1, 2010 | 850,000 |
| Service cost | 90,000 |
| Accumulated OCI (PSC) at January 1, 2010 | 160,000 |
| Settlement rate | 10% |

## Instructions
Compute the pension expense for 2010.

## Solution to Exercise 20-1

| | |
|---|---:|
| Service cost | $ 90,000 |
| Interest cost ($850,000 x 10%) | 85,000 |
| Actual return on plan assets | (60,000) |
| Amortization of prior service cost | 15,000 |
| Pension expense for 2010 | $ 130,000 |

**Approach:** Whenever you are to compute pension expense, use the format in **Illustration 20-1**. Select or solve for the data needed. Ignore the data not needed.

TIP: The **actual return on plan assets** is the increase in plan assets from interest, dividends, and realized and unrealized changes in the market value of the plan assets. If the actual return is positive (gain), it is subtracted in the computation of pension expense. The return on plan asset is **deducted** in the expense calculation because it is an amount that the fund generated itself (on fund assets) so it will reduce a cost that otherwise would have to be borne by the employer corporation.

TIP: Because the actual return on plan assets equals the expected return on plan assets for 2010, there was no difference (unexpected gain or loss) to include in the expense computation.

## ILLUSTRATION 20-2
## CHANGES IN THE PROJECTED BENEFIT OBLIGATION
## AND PLAN ASSETS (L.O. 4, 5)

|   | Projected benefit obligation, balance at beginning of the period |
|---|---|
| + | Service cost for the period |
| + | Interest for the period on beginning projected benefit obligation balance |
| - | Benefits paid to employees during the period |
| +/- | Liability gains and losses due to changes in actuarial assumptions |
| = | Projected benefit obligation, balance at end of the period |

|   | Plan assets, fair value at beginning of the period |
|---|---|
| + | Contributions to plan during the period |
| - | Benefits paid to employees during the period |
| +/- | Actual return on plan assets during the period* |
| = | Plan assets, fair value at end of the period |

*Includes realized earnings such as dividends and interest, realized gains and losses due to sales of plan assets, and unrealized asset gains and losses from changes in the fair value of plan assets.

**TIP:** It is helpful to know the various reasons for changes in the projected benefit obligation and plan assets over the course of time. For example, if you are given the amounts funded by the employer during the year, the benefits paid from the pension fund during the year, and the net increase in fair value of plans assets for the year, you can solve for the actual return on plan assets for the period.

**TIP:** Although the balance of the projected benefit obligation and the balance of plan assets are **not** reported on the employer's balance sheet, these balances are used in determining certain amounts that do appear in the financial statements. An excess of plan assets over projected benefit obligation (PBO) indicates an **overfunded** situation and will result in a debit balance in the Pension Asset/Liability account to be reported as an asset on the employer's balance sheet. An excess of PBO over fair value of plan assets indicates an **underfunded** situation and will result in a credit balance in the Pension Asset/Liability account to be reported as a liability on the employer's balance sheet.

**TIP:** One of the reasons for a change in the balance of the projected benefit obligation is "liability gains and losses due to changes in actuarial assumptions." Liability **gains reduce** the PBO balance, whereas liability **losses increase** the PBO balance.

**TIP:** One of the reasons for a change in the plan assets' fair value balance is the "actual return on plan assets during the period." This actual return includes unexpected asset gains and losses. Asset **gains increase** the plan assets' fair value balance, whereas asset **losses reduce** the plan assets' fair value balance.

## EXERCISE 20-2

**Purpose:**　　(L.O. 5) This exercise illustrates the mechanics of the pension work sheet.

**Instructions**

(a)　　Using the data in **Exercise 20-1,** prepare a pension work sheet. Insert January 1, 2010 balances and show the journal entry for pension expense for 2010 and the December 31, 2010 balances.

(b)　　Prepare the journal entry to record pension expense for 2010.

In preparation of the pension work sheet and the related reconciliation schedule:

**TIP:**　Although the balances of the projected benefit obligation and plan assets do **not** appear on the employer's balance sheet, they have an impact on the determination of amounts that do appear on the employer's income statement and balance sheet and amounts that appear in the notes to those financial statements.　The "Memo Record" columns maintain balances of these **unrecognized (noncapitalized)** pension items. These items are "off balance sheet" pension items and are therefore outside the formal general ledger accounting system. These items must be disclosed in the notes to the financial statements.

**TIP:**　In using the work sheet, the Pension Asset/Liability account balance (which **is** reported on the balance sheet)  equals the net of the balances in the memo accounts. If the net of the memo record balances is a **credit**, the reconciling amount in the Pension Asset/Liability column will be a **credit** equal in amount.

**TIP:**　A pension work sheet includes both formal entries and memo entries. The formal journal entry to record pension expense and the annual contribution to the pension fund is a debit to Pension Expense for the appropriate amount computed, a credit to Cash for the amount funded for the period, and a debit or credit to Pension Asset/Liability for the difference. When there are unexpected gains or losses and/or prior service cost, then there are additional components in the aforementioned journal entry to account for these items.

**TIP:**　The reconciliation schedule reconciles the balances of the off-balance-sheet items with the Pension Asset/Liability account balance reported in the balance sheet.

(a)

**Kleen Company**
**PENSION WORK SHEET – 2010***

| | General Journal Entries | | | | Memo Record | |
|---|---|---|---|---|---|---|
| | Annual Pension Expense | Cash | OCI – Prior Service Cost | Pension Asset/Liability | Projected Benefit Obligation | Plan Assets |
| Balance, January 1, 2010 | | | | | | |
| (1) Service cost | | | | | | |
| (2) Interest cost | | | | | | |
| (3) Actual return | | | | | | |
| (4) Amortization of PSC | | | | | | |
| (5) Contributions | | | | | | |
| (6) Benefits | | | | | | |
| Journal entry for 2010 | | | | | | |
| Accumulated OCI, Dec. 31, 2009 | | | | | | |
| Balance, December 31, 2010 | | | | | | |

# Solution to Exercise 20-2

(a)

## Kleen Company
### PENSION WORK SHEET* – 2010

| | General Journal Entries | | | | Memo Record | |
|---|---|---|---|---|---|---|
| | Annual Pension Expense | Cash | OCI -- Prior Service Cost | Pension Asset/Liability | Projected Benefit Obligation | Plan Assets |
| Balance, January 1, 2010 | | | | 166,000 Cr. | 850,000 Cr. | 684,000 Dr. |
| (1) Service cost | 90,000 Dr. | | | | 90,000 Cr. | |
| (2) Interest cost | 85,000 Dr. | | | | 85,000 Cr. | |
| (3) Actual return | 60,000 Cr. | | | | | 60,000 Dr. |
| (4) Amortization of PSC | 15,000 Dr. | | 15,000 Cr. | | | |
| (5) Contributions | | 105,000 Cr. | | | | 105,000 Dr. |
| (6) Benefits | | | | | 40,000 Dr. | 40,000 Cr. |
| Journal entry for 2010 | 130,000 Dr. | 105,000 Cr. | 15,000 Cr. | 10,000 Cr. | | |
| Accumulated OCI, Dec. 31, 2009 | | | 160,000 Dr. | | | |
| Balance, December 31, 2010 | | | 145,000 Dr. | 176,000 Cr. | 985,000 Cr. | 809,000 Dr. |

*The use of this pension entry work sheet is recommended and illustrated by Paul B. W. Miller. "The New Pension Accounting (Part 2)." *Journal of Accountancy* (February 1987), pp. 86-94.

(b)

| | | |
|---|---|---|
| Pension Expense | 130,000 | |
| Cash | | 105,000 |
| Other Comprehensive Income (PSC) | 15,000 | |
| Pension Asset/ Liability | | 10,000 |

## EXERCISE 20-3

**Purpose:**  (L.O. 4, 5, 6, 7) This exercise will review the components of pension expense, the completion of a worksheet, and the relationship of the items involved in the preparation of a pension worksheet.

A partially completed pension worksheet appears below for Griggs Pharmacy Inc.

**Instructions:**

(a)  Determine the missing amounts (identified by letters in parentheses) in the pension worksheet for 2010. Label each amount as a debit or a credit.

(b)  Prepare the journal entry to record pension expense for 2010.

(c)  Indicate what amounts will be reported for pensions in the financial statements and the proper classification for each amount.

(a)

### Griggs Pharmacy Inc.
### PENSION WORKSHEET

| | General Journal Entries | | | | | Memo Record | |
|---|---|---|---|---|---|---|---|
| | Annual Pension Expense | Cash | OCI -- Prior Service Cost | OCI -- Gain/Loss | Pension Asset/Liability | Projected Benefit Obligation | Plan Assets |
| Balance, Jan. 1, 2010 | | | | | 158,000 Cr. | 426,000 Cr. | 268,000 Dr. |
| Service Cost | (a) | | | | | 27,000 Cr. | |
| Interest cost | (b) | | | | | 40,000 Cr. | |
| Actual return | (c) | | | | | | 24,000 Dr. |
| Unexpected gain | 18,000 Dr. | | | (d) | | | |
| Amortization of PSC | (e) | | 36,000 Cr. | | | | |
| Contributions | | 47,000 Cr. | | | | | 47,000 Dr. |
| Benefits | | | | | | 21,000 Dr. | 21,000 Cr. |
| Liability increase | | | | (f) | | 55,000 Cr. | |
| Journal entry | (g) | (h) | (i) | (j) | (k) | | |
| Accum. OCI, 12/31/09 | | | | 3,000 Cr. | | | |
| | | | 100,000 Dr. | 34,000 Dr. | 209,000 Cr. | | |
| Balance, Dec. 31, 2010 | | | | | | 527,000 Cr. | |

# SOLUTION TO EXERCISE 20-3

(a)

## Griggs Pharmacy Inc.
## PENSION WORKSHEET

| | General Journal Entries | | | | | Memo Record | |
| --- | --- | --- | --- | --- | --- | --- | --- |
| | Annual Pension Expense | Cash | OCI – Prior Service Cost | OCI – Gain/Loss | Pension Asset/Liability | Projected Benefit Obligation | Plan Assets |
| Balance, Jan. 1, 2010 | | | | | 158,000 Cr. | 426,000 Cr. | 268,000 Dr. |
| Service Cost | 27,000 Dr. | | | | | 27,000 Cr. | |
| Interest cost | 40,000 Dr. | | | | | 40,000 Cr. | |
| Actual return | 24,000 Cr. | | | | | | 24,000 Dr. |
| Unexpected gain | 18,000 Dr. | | | 18,000 Cr. | | | |
| Amortization of PSC | 36,000 Dr. | | 36,000 | | | | |
| Contributions | | 47,000 Cr. | | | | | 47,000 Dr. |
| Benefits | | | | | | 21,000 Dr. | 21,000 Cr. |
| Liability increase | | | | 55,000 Dr. | | 55,000 Cr. | |
| Journal entry | 97,000 Dr. | 47,000 Cr. | 36,000 Cr. | 37,000 Dr. | 51,000 Cr. | | |
| Accum. OCI, 12/31/09 | | | 100,000 Dr. | 3,000 Cr. | | | |
| Balance, Dec. 31, 2010 | | | | 34,000 Dr. | 209,000 Cr. | 527,000 Cr. | 318,000 Dr. |

Accumulated OCI (PSC) .......... 64,000 Dr.  
Accumulated OCI (G/L) .......... 34,000 Dr.  
Accumulated OCI, Dec. 31, 2010 .......... 98,000 Dr.

(b)

| | | | |
|---|---|---|---|
| Pension Expense | 97,000 | | |
| Other Comprehensive Income-G/L | 55,000 | | |
| Cash | | 47,000 | |
| Other Comprehensive Income-PSC | | 36,000 | |
| Other Comprehensive Income-G/L | | 18,000 | |
| Pension Asset/Liability | | 51,000 | |

---

**TIP:** In the worksheet, notice the following:
1. On the first line, the excess of credits over debits in the "Memo Record" columns at Jan. 1, 2010 equals the beginning balance in the Pension Asset/Liability column at that same date ($158,000 credit).
2. For the next 8 lines, the total debits on each line equal the total credit entries on that same line.
3. For the "Journal entry" line, total debits equals total credits.
4. Each column "foots" or balances.
5. On the "Balance, Dec. 31, 2010" line, the excess of credits over debits in the "Memo Record" columns at Dec. 31, 2010 equals the ending balance in the Pension Asset/Liability column at that same date ($209,000 credit).

---

(c) Pension expense of 97,000 will be classified with compensation expense on the income statement for 2010. The $209,000 pension liability (excess of projected benefit obligation over the fair value of plan assets) will be classified as a long-term liability on the balance sheet at December 31, 2010. (There can be a current portion of a net pension liability if the amount of benefits to be paid in the next 12 months [or operating cycle, if longer] cannot be funded from existing plan assets. Any current portion will be classified as a current liability.) The $98,000 debit balance in the Accumulated Other Comprehensive Income will be classified as a contra equity item and is listed as the last item in the stockholders' equity section of the balance sheet. The $36,000 credit to Other Comprehensive income-PSC for the current period's amortization of prior service cost, the $55,000 debit to "Other Comprehensive Income-G/L, due to the unexpected liability loss (liability increase) from the increase in the PBO (from changes in actuarial assumptions and differences between actual experience and actuarial assumptions), and the $18,000 credit to Other Comprehensive Income-G/L due to the unexpected gain will appear as three components of other comprehensive income for the year ending December 31, 2010. The components of other comprehensive income must be reported in one of three ways: (1) in a second income statement, (2) in a combined statement of comprehensive income, or (3) as a part of a statement of changes in stockholders' equity. Regardless of the format used, other comprehensive income must be added to net income to arrive at comprehensive income. For homework purposes, use the second income statement approach unless otherwise stated. In this case, the $55,000 would reduce comprehensive income of the current period and the $36,000 along with the $18,00 would both increase comprehensive income of the current period.

Additionally, there are many footnote disclosures required for various details on pension accounting.

---

**TIP:** See **Illustration 4-4** in your *Problem Solving Survival Guide* for examples of the three ways to report components of Other Comprehensive Income. The Other Comprehensive Income-PSC and Other Comprehensive Income-G/L accounts (nominal accounts) are closed to Accumulated Other Comprehensive Income account (real account) at the end of the accounting period.

# EXERCISE 20-4

**Purpose:**    (L.O. 8) This exercise illustrates the use of the corridor approach to amortizing accumulated gains and losses.

Beginning-of-the-year present values for Learn Company's projected benefit obligation and beginning-of-the-year market-related values for its pension plan assets are:

|  | Projected Benefit Obligation | Market-Related Value of Plan Assets |
|---|---|---|
| 2010 | $ 3,200,000 | $ 3,600,000 |
| 2011 | 3,700,000 | 3,900,000 |
| 2012 | 4,300,000 | 4,200,000 |
| 2013 | 5,000,000 | 4,800,000 |

The accumulated net gain is $300,000 on January 1, 2010. The unrecognized net gain or loss that occurred during the year is: 2010, $210,000 gain; 2011, $25,000 loss; 2012, $50,000 loss; and 2013, $100,000 gain. The average remaining service life per employee is 12 years in 2010 and 2011, and is 15 years in 2012 and 2013.

# Instructions

Set up an appropriate schedule to compute the amount of accumulated net gain or loss to be amortized to pension expense each year using the corridor approach.

# Solution to Exercise 20-4

### Corridor Amortization Schedule

| Year | Projected Benefit Obligation (1) | Market-Related Value of Plan Assets (1) | 10% Corridor (2) | Accumulated OCI (G/L) | Minimum Amortization of Gain |
|---|---|---|---|---|---|
| 2010 | $ 3,200,000 | $3,600,000 | $360,000 | $300,000 | $    -0- |
| 2011 | 3,700,000 | 3,900,000 | 390,000 | 510,000 | 10,000 (3) |
| 2012 | 4,300,000 | 4,200,000 | 430,000 | 475,000  (4) | 3,000 (5) |
| 2013 | 5,000,000 | 4,800,000 | 500,000 | 422,000  (6) | - 0- |

(1)    All as of the beginning of the year.
(2)    10% of the greater of projected benefit obligation or plan assets' market-related value.
(3)    ($510,000 - $390,000) ÷ 12 = $10,000.
(4)    $510,000 - $10,000 net gain amortized - $25,000 loss = $475,000.
(5)    ($475,000 - $430,000) ÷ 15 = $3,000.
(6)    $475,000 - $3,000 net gain amortized - $50,000 loss = $422,000.

> **TIP:** Unexpected gains or losses from changes in the balance of the projected benefit obligation due to changes in actuarial assumptions are called "liability gains and losses" by the FASB. These liability gains and losses (liability gains result from unexpected decreases in the liability balance and liability losses result from unexpected increases) recorded in an Other Comprehensive Income account.
>
> If the balance of the accumulated net gains or losses amount stays within the upper and lower limits of the corridor, no amortization is required—the net gain or loss balance is carried forward unchanged. If the balance grows large enough to exceed the boundaries of the corridor, amortization is required. Then the minimum amortization amount is the excess (beyond the corridor) gain or loss divided by the average remaining service life to expected retirement of all active employees. Likewise, asset gains and losses (see **Illustration 20-1**).
>
> for a description of asset gains and losses) are recorded in an Other Comprehensive Income account. At the end of an accounting period all asset and liability gains and losses arising from the current period are grouped with asset and liability gains and losses from prior periods in Accumulated Other Comprehensive Income on the balance sheet in stockholders' equity.

## EXERCISE 20-5

**Purpose:** (L.O. 4) This exercise requires calculation of actual return on plan assets.

White Company reports the following pension plan data:

| | |
|---|---:|
| Fair value of plan assets, January 1, 2010 | $ 3,200,000 |
| Fair value of plan assets, December 31, 2010 | 3,600,000 |
| Benefits paid during 2010 | 460,000 |
| Contributions to the plan during 2010 | 640,000 |

## Instructions
Compute the actual return on plan assets for 2010.

## Solution to Exercise 20-5

| | |
|---|---:|
| Plan assets, fair value at beginning of the year | $ 3,200,000 |
| Contributions to plan during the year | 640,000 |
| Benefits paid to employees during the year | (460,000) |
| Actual return on plan assets during the year | + X |
| Plan assets, fair value at end of the year | $ 3,600,000 |

Solving for X: X = $220,000

**Approach:** Write down the format for reconciling beginning and ending balances of plan assets at fair value (see **Illustration 20-2**). Enter the data given. Solve for the unknown.

# EXERCISE 20-6

**Purpose:**     (L.O. 4) This exercise requires calculation of the expected return on plan assets and examines its use in determining pension expense.

White Company (from **Exercise 20-5**) also reports:

| | |
|---|---|
| Market-related asset value, January 1, 2010 | $ 3,000,000 |
| Market-related asset value, December 31, 2010 | 3,300,000 |
| Expected return on plan assets | 10% |

## Instructions

(a)     Compute the expected return on plan assets during 2010 and the unexpected gain or loss.

(b)     Explain how the actual return and the unexpected gain or loss enter into the calculation of pension expense for 2010.

## Solution to Exercise 20-6

(a)     10% x $3,000,000 = $300,000 expected return on plan assets.

| | |
|---|---|
| Expected return | $ 300,000 |
| Actual return (**Exercise 20-5**) | 220,000 |
| Unexpected loss | $ 80,000 |

(b)     The actual return on plan assets of $220,000 is deducted in the calculation of pension expense because earnings generated by the plan assets reduce the total pension cost to the employer. The unexpected loss of $80,000 is also deducted in the pension expense computation because **unexpected gains and losses are to be handled in a manner that does not cause a dramatic change in pension expense from one period to another**. As a result, **the expected return** of $300,000 **is the amount actually used to compute current pension expense.** (If the unexpected loss was not deducted, the current period's pension expense would be higher which would reflect recognition of the unexpected loss in the current period.)

**Explanation:** The expected return on plan assets is determined by multiplying the expected rate of return on plan assets times the beginning-of-the-year market-related asset value. Differences between the expected return and the actual return, often referred to as the unexpected gain or loss, are called "asset gains and losses" by the FASB and are amortized over future periods when the cumulative amount becomes excessive.

---

**TIP:**     The market-related asset value is used in two calculations: (1) the expected return on plan assets, and (2) the determination of the corridor. In both cases, it is the market-related asset value at the beginning of the year.

**TIP:**     The gain or loss component of pension expense for a period is the sum of (a) the difference between the actual return on plan assets and the expected return on plan assets, and (b) the amortization of the unrecognized net gain or loss from previous periods.

## EXERCISE 20-7

**Purpose:**    (L.O. 10) This exercise illustrates the nature of the Pension Asset/Liability balance.

Steele Company provided the following data at December 31, 2010:

| | |
|---|---|
| Accumulated benefit obligation | $ 770,000 |
| Market-related asset value | 610,000 |
| Plan assets (at fair value) | 590,000 |
| Projected benefit obligation | 850,000 |
| Accumulated net asset gains | 30,000 |
| Accumulated prior service cost | 190,000 |

### Instructions
Compute the balance of Pension Asset/Liability at December 31, 2010.

## Solution to Exercise 20-7

| | |
|---|---|
| Projected benefit obligation | $850,000 |
| Plan assets at fair value | 590,000 |
| Pension liability reported on the balance sheet | $260,000 |

## *EXERCISE 20-8

**Purpose:**    (L.O. 11) This exercise is related to postretirement benefits other than pensions.

Handy Company reports the following data related to postretirement benefits for 2010:

| | |
|---|---|
| APBO at January 1, 2010 | $ 480,000 |
| EPBO at January 1, 2010 | 540,000 |
| Actual return on plan assets in 2010 | 27,000 |
| Expected return on plan assets in 2010 | 30,000 |
| Service cost | 88,000 |
| Discount rate | 10% |
| Benefits paid | 43,000 |
| Contributions (funding) | 60,000 |
| Amortization of accumulated net gain | 2,000 |

### Instructions
(a)    Compute the amount of postretirement expense for 2010.
(b)    Prepare the journal entry to record postretirement expense and Handy's contribution for 2010.
(c)    Compute the amount of APBO at December 31, 2010.

---

**TIP:**    EPBO stands for Expected Postretirement Benefit Obligation. EPBO is the actuarial present value of all benefits expected to be paid after retirement to employees and their dependents.

**TIP:**    APBO stands for Accumulated Postretirement Benefit Obligation. APBO is the actuarial present value of future benefits attributed to employees' services rendered to date. The EPBO includes an additional amount related to services to be rendered by employees before they are fully eligible for benefits.

## Solution to Exercise 20-8

| (a)   Service cost | $ 88,000 |
|---|---|
| Interest cost (10% x $480,000) | 48,000 |
| Actual return on plan assets | (27,000) |
| Unexpected loss ($27,000 - $30,000) | (3,000) |
| Amortization of accumulated net gain | (2,000) |
| Postretirement expense—2010 | $ 104,000 |

**Explanation:** Postretirement expense consists of many of the same components used to compute pension expense.

> **TIP:**   Service cost is the portion of the EPBO attributed to employee service during the period.
>
> **TIP:**   Interest cost is the discount rate times the APBO at the beginning of the year.
>
> **TIP:**   When the expected return is greater than the actual return, there is an unexpected loss. In the computation of postretirement expense, the actual return is deducted and an unexpected loss is also deducted so that the expected return is the amount actually reflected in the current expense. An unexpected gain would be added in the expense computation.
>
> **TIP:**   A net gain ultimately reduces the cost to the employer of postretirement benefits; therefore, the amortization of a net gain reduces postretirement expense.

| (b)   Other Comprehensive Income (G/L) | 3,000 | |
|---|---|---|
| Other Comprehensive Income (G/L) | 2,000 | |
| Postretirement Expense (Computed above) | 104,000 | |
| Postretirement Asset/Liability | | 49,000 |
| Cash | 60,000 | |

**Explanation:** The journal entry to record postretirement expense is similar to the entry to record pension expense. The credit to Postretirement Asset/Liability account in this journal entry is a "plug" figure in that the rest of the entry is recorded and the "difference" is an amount to make the entry balance. Thus, $104,000 + $2,000 + $3,000 - $60,000 = $49,000.

| (c)   APBO at January 1, 2010 | $ 480,000 |
|---|---|
| Service cost for 2010 | 52,000 |
| Interest cost for 2010 | 48,000 |
| Benefits paid in 2010 | (43,000) |
| APBO at December 31, 2010 | $ 537,000 |

**Explanation:** Examine the APBO column in a postretirement benefits work sheet in your text. Note that service cost and interest cost increase the APBO and benefits paid decrease the APBO.

## ANALYSIS OF MULTIPLE-CHOICE TYPE QUESTIONS

**QUESTION**

1. (L.O. 4) The Mighty Minnow Corp. has a defined benefit pension plan. Information for the plan for 2010 is as follows:

| | | |
|---|---|---|
| Service cost | $320,000 | |
| Actual and expected return on plan assets | | 70,000 |
| Amortization of prior service cost | 10,000 | |
| Annual interest on pension obligation | 100,000 | |

What amount should Mighty Minnow report as pension expense in its income statement for 2010?
a. $500,000.
b. $420,000.
c. $360,000.
d. $340,000.

**Explanation:** The pension expense is determined by the following computation:

| | |
|---|---|
| Service cost | $320,000 |
| Actual and expected return on plan assets | (70,000) |
| Amortization of prior service cost | 10,000 |
| Annual interest on pension obligation | 100,000 |
| Total pension expense for 2010 | $360,000 |

(Solution = c.)

**QUESTION**

2. (L.O. 4) Which of the following items should be included in the net pension cost calculated by an employer who sponsors a defined benefit pension plan for its employees?

| | Fair value of plan assets | Amortization of prior service cost |
|---|---|---|
| a. | Yes | Yes |
| b. | Yes | No |
| c. | No | Yes |
| d. | No | No |

**Approach and Explanation:** Mentally list the components of pension expense (refer to **Illustration 20-1**). Compare the items in the question with the items in the list. Amortization of prior service cost is a component of net pension cost. While the actual return on plan assets is a component, the fair value of the plan assets is not used in the net pension cost calculation. Prior service cost comes about when a pension plan is initiated or amended. Typically, a plan gives existing employees credit for their service prior to the initiation/amendment date which causes an increase in the projected benefit obligation. This increase is recognized as expense over the remaining service lives of the employees who are expected to benefit from the change in the plan. The Accumulated Other Comprehensive Income (PSC) account balance is the amount at any certain date that remains to be amortized. The preferable method of amortization is the years-of-service amortization method that is similar to a units-of-production computation. (Solution = c.)

## QUESTION

3.(L.O. 4) The following information is related to the pension plan of Jay, Inc. for 2010.

| | |
|---|---|
| Actual return on plan assets | $ 80,000 |
| Amortization of accumulated net gain | 33,000 |
| Amortization of accumulated prior service cost | 60,000 |
| Expected return on plan assets | 92,000 |
| Interest on projected benefit obligation | 145,000 |
| Service cost | 320,000 |

Pension expense for 2010 is:
a.      $400,000.
b.      $412,000.
c.      $466,000.
d.      $478,000.

**Explanation:** Service cost and interest cost increase pension expense. Remember that the adjustment of actual return on plan assets for an unexpected gain or loss means that the amount of the expected return on plan assets is used to compute the pension expense ($80,000 actual return + $12,000 unexpected loss = $92,000 expected return). The amortization of an accumulated net gain reduces pension expense. Amortization of prior service cost increases pension expense. The computation is:

| | | |
|---|---|---|
| Service cost | | $ 320,000 |
| Interest cost | | 145,000 |
| Actual return on plan assets | | (80,000) |
| Unexpected loss ($80,000 - $92,000) | (12,000) | |
| Amortization of accumulated net gain | (33,000) | |
| Amortization of accumulated prior service cost | 60,000 | |
| Pension expense for 2010 | | $ 400,000 |

(Solution = a.)

## QUESTION

4.     (L.O. 4) The following data are for the pension plan for the employees of Chip Company.

| | 1/1/09 | 12/31/09 | 12/31/10 |
|---|---|---|---|
| Market-related asset value | $2,200,000 | $2,900,000 | $3,100,000 |
| Plan assets (at fair value) | 2,300,000 | 3,000,000 | 3,300,000 |
| Accumulated benefit obligation | 2,500,000 | 2,600,000 | 3,400,000 |
| Projected benefit obligation | 2,700,000 | 2,800,000 | 3,700,000 |
| Accumulated net loss | -0- | 480,000 | 500,000 |
| Settlement rate (for year) | | 10% | 9% |
| Expected rate of return (for year) | | 8% | 7% |

Chip's contribution was $420,000 in 2010 and benefits paid were $375,000. Chip estimates that the average remaining service life is 15 years. The actual return on plan assets in 2010 is:
a.      $155,000.
b.      $200,000.
c.      $255,000.
d.      $300,000.

**Approach and Explanation:** Recall that the actual return is found by (1) computing the change in plan assets (at fair value), (2) deducting contributions, and (3) adding benefits paid. The calculation is:

| | |
|---|---|
| Plan assets, 12/31/10 | $ 3,300,000 |
| Plan assets, 12/31/09 | 3,000,000 |
| Increase during 2010 | 300,000 |
| Deduct contributions | (420,000) |
| Add benefits paid | 375,000 |
| Actual return, 2010 | $ 255,000 |

(Solution = c.)

**QUESTION**
5.   (L.O. 4, 7) Refer to the data in **Question 4.** You know that the actual return on plan assets in 2010 is $255,000. The unexpected gain or loss on plan assets in 2010 is:
a.   $24,000 gain.
b.   $38,000 gain.
c.   $45,000 gain.
d.   $52,000 gain.

**Explanation:** The expected return is the expected rate of return times the market-related asset value at the beginning of the year. For 2010, the expected return is $203,000 (7% x $2,900,000). Since the actual return is $255,000, there is an unexpected gain of $52,000 ($255,000 - $203,000). (Solution = d.)

**QUESTION**
6.   (L.O. 8) Refer to the data in **Question 4.** The corridor for amortization of accumulated net gain or loss in 2010 is:
    a.   $280,000.
    b.   $290,000.
    c.   $300,000.
    d.   $370,000.

**Explanation:** The corridor is 10% of the larger of the beginning balances of the projected benefit obligation ($2,800,000) or the market-related value of the plan assets ($2,900,000). Chip's corridor in 2010 is $290,000 (10% x $2,900,000). (Solution = b.)

> **TIP:**   The accumulated net gain or loss is the result of both asset gains and losses and liability gains and losses experienced to date that have not been amortized to pension expense and therefore have not yet had an impact on net income.

**QUESTION**
7.   (L.O. 8) Refer to the data in **Question 4**. You know that the corridor for 2010 is $290,000. The amount of accumulated net loss amortized in 2010 is:
a.   $12,667.
b.   $14,000.
c.   $32,000.
d.   $33,333.

**Explanation:** The amount of accumulated net loss subject to being amortized is the portion of the accumulated net loss at the beginning of the period that is greater than the corridor. The minimum amortization is computed by dividing the excess over the corridor by the average remaining service life. The amount of accumulated net loss in excess of the corridor is $190,000 ($480,000 - $290,000). The accumulated net loss amortized in 2010 is $12,667 ($190,000 ÷ 15). (Solution = a.)

**QUESTION**
8.   (L.O. 5) A corporation has a defined benefit plan. A pension liability will result at the end of the first year if:
    a.   The accumulated benefit obligation exceeds the fair value of the plan assets.
    b.   The fair value of the plan assets exceeds the accumulated benefit obligation.
    c.   The amount of employer contributions exceeds the net periodic pension cost.
    d.   The amount of net periodic pension cost exceeds employer contributions.

**Explanation:** The journal entry to record the employer contributions and annual pension expense is balanced by either a debit to Pension Asset or a credit to Pension Liability, depending on the relationship of the amount of net periodic pension cost (debit to Pension Expense) and the amount being funded (credit to Cash). For there to be a credit to Pension Liability, the debit to Pension Expense exceeds the credit to Cash in this entry.

Pension Expense                                                    Expense Computation
Pension Asset                                                               Difference
   **or**  Pension Liability                                                                  Difference
       Cash                                                              Amount Funded

(Solution = d.)

# QUESTION

9. (L.O. 9) The following pension plan information is for Kent Company at December 31, 2010.

| | | |
|---|---|---|
| Projected benefit obligation | | $ 5,600,000 |
| Accumulated benefit obligation | 5,000,000 | |
| Plan assets (at fair value) | | 4,100,000 |
| Market-related asset value | | 4,300,000 |
| Accumulated other comprehensive income-prior service cost | | 360,000 |
| Pension expense for 2010 | | 2,000,000 |
| Contribution for 2010 | | 1,600,000 |

The amount to be reported as the total liability for pensions on the December 31, 2010 balance sheet is:

a. $700,000.
b. $900,000.
c. $1,300,000.
d. $1,500,000.

**Explanation:**

| | |
|---|---|
| Projected benefit obligation | $5,600,000 |
| Plan assets (at fair value) | (4,100,000) |
| Total liability for pensions | $1,500,000 |

The liability for pensions is the excess of the projected benefit obligation over the fair value of plan assets. (Solution = d.)

# QUESTION

10. (L.O. 9) Laramie Corp., has a defined benefit plan for its employees. All of the following must be disclosed (either in the body of the financial statements or in the notes) **except**:
a. All of the major components of pension expense.
b. A schedule of the changes in employees covered by the plan.
c. A reconciliation showing how the projected benefit obligation changed from the beginning to the end of the period.
d. The funded status of the plan.

**Approach and Explanation:** Before reading the answer choices, briefly think of the list of items that must be disclosed with regard to a pension plan. Then companre your list with the answer selections. The disclosure requirements for pensions are extensive. The following information, if not disclosed in the body of the financial statements, should be disclosed in the notes:

1. A schedule showing all the major components of pension expense.
2. A reconciliation showing how the projected benefit obligation and the fair value of the plan assets changed from the beginning of to the end of the period.
3. A disclosure of the rates used in measuring the benefit amounts (discount rate, expected return on plan assets, rate of compensation).
4. A table indicating the allocation of pension plan assets by category (equity securities, debt securities, real estate, and other assets), and showing the percentage of the fair value to total plan assets.

5.    The expected benefit payments to be paid to current plan participants for each of the next five fiscal years and in the aggregate for the five fiscal years thereafter. Also, the best estimate of expected contributions to be paid to the plan during the next year.

6.    The nature and amount of changes in plan assets and benefit obligations recognized in net income and in other comprehensive income of each period.

7.    The accumulated amount of changes in plan assets and benefit obligations that have been recognized in other comprehensive income and that will be recycled into net income in future periods.

8.    The amount of estimated net actuarial gains and losses and prior service costs and credits that will be amortized from accumulated other comprehensive income into net income over the next fiscal year.                                                    (Solution = b.)

**QUESTION**
*11.    (L.O. 11) The following data relate to the Boyd Company postretirement benefits plan for 2010:

| | |
|---|---|
| APBO at January 1, 2010 | $ 300,000 |
| EPBO at January 1, 2010 | 400,000 |
| Service cost | 82,000 |
| Discount rate | 8% |
| Actual return on plan assets in 2010 | 13,000 |
| Expected return on plan assets in 2010 | 17,000 |

The amount of postretirement expense for 2010 is:
a.    $89,000.
b.    $93,000.
c.    $97,000.
d.    $106,000.

**Explanation:** Recall that postretirement expense includes service cost, interest cost, an adjustment for return on plan assets, amortization of prior service cost (if any), and a possible adjustment for a gain or loss component. The interest cost is the discount rate times the APBO at the beginning of the year. A positive actual return is deducted in the calculation. Because the postretirement expense is credited for an unexpected loss or debited for an unexpected gain on plan assets (the difference between the actual and the expected return), this component is really the expected return. No information was given about prior service cost.

| | |
|---|---|
| Service cost | $ 82,000 |
| Interest cost (8% x $300,000) | 24,000 |
| Actual return during 2010 | (13,000) |
| Unexpected loss ($13,000 - $17,000) | (4,000) |
| Postretirement expense | $ 89,000 |

(Solution = a.)

# CHAPTER 21

# ACCOUNTING FOR LEASES

## OVERVIEW

Many entities lease assets. Leasing will often offer tax and cash flow advantages when compared to the purchase of these assets. Some leases are pure rentals; others are, in substance, an installment purchase of the asset by the lessee. This chapter will discuss both operating and nonoperating type leases but will focus on the nonoperating type where we must account for substance over form. That is, even though it is legally a rental situation, in substance the transaction is an installment purchase of the asset by the lessee and an installment sale of the asset by the lessor.

## SUMMARY OF LEARNING OBJECTIVES

1.  **Explain the nature, economic substance, and advantages of lease transactions.** A lease is a contractual agreement between a lessor and a lessee that conveys to the lessee the right to use specific property (real or personal), owned by the lessor, for a specified period of time. In return for this right, the lessee periodically pays cash (rents) to the lessor. The advantages of lease transactions are: (1) 100% financing, (2) protection against obsolescence, (3) flexibility, (4) less costly financing, (5) possible tax advantages, and (6) off-balance-sheet financing.

2.  **Describe the accounting criteria and procedures for capitalizing leases by the lessee.** A lease is a capital lease if it meets one or more of the following four (Group I) criteria: (1) The lease transfers ownership of the property to the lessee. (2) The lease contains a bargain purchase option. (3) The lease term is equal to 75% or more of the estimated economic life of the leased property. (4) The present value of the minimum lease payments (excluding executory costs) equals or exceeds 90% of the fair value of the leased property. For a capital lease, the lessee records an asset and a liability at the lower of (1) the present value of the minimum lease payments or (2) the fair market value of the leased asset at the inception of the lease. If a lease does not meet the criteria to be classified as a capital lease, it is an operating lease from the lessee's standpoint.

3.  **Contrast the operating and capitalization methods of recording leases.** The total charges to operations are the same over the span of time the asset is used by the lessee whether the lease is accounted for as a capital lease or as an operating lease. Under the capital lease treatment, the charges are higher in the earlier years and lower in the later years. If an accelerated method of depreciation is used, the differences between the amounts charged to operations under the two methods would be even larger in the earlier and later years. The following occurs if a capital lease instead of an operating lease is employed: (1) an increase in the amount of reported debt (both short-term and long-term), (2) an increase in the amount of total assets (specifically long-lived assets), and (3) a lower net income early in the life of the lease and, therefore, lower retained earnings.

4.     **Identify the classifications of leases for the lessor.** A lessor may classify leases for accounting purposes as follows: (1) operating leases, (2) direct- financing leases, or (3) sales-type leases. The lessor should classify and account for an arrangement as a direct-financing lease or a sales-type lease if, at the date of the lease agreement, the lease meets one or more of the Group I criteria (which are the same four criteria as listed in learning objective 2 for lessees) and **both** of the following Group II criteria. *Group II:* (1) Collectibility of the payments required from the lessee is reasonably predictable, and (2) no important uncertainties surround the amount of unreimbursable costs yet to be incurred by the lessor under the lease. All leases that fail to meet the criteria are classified and accounted for by the lessor as operating leases.

5.     **Describe the lessor's accounting for direct-financing leases.** Leases that are in substance the financing of an asset purchase by a lessee require the lessor to substitute a "lease receivable" for the leased asset on the lessor's books. The amount recorded in the Lease Receivable account is equal to the present value of the minimum lease payments plus the present value of the unguaranteed residual value relevant to the lessor (i.e., if the lessor expects to get the asset back at the end of the lease term). A guaranteed residual value, if any, is a component of minimum lease payments. Therefore, the present value of any residual value relevant to the lessor (whether guaranteed or unguaranteed) is included in the Lease Receivable account. Payments received from the lessee reduce the Lease Receivable. Interest revenue is accrued by applying the effective interest rate to the Lease Receivable balance.

6.     **Identify special features of lease arrangements that cause unique accounting problems**. The features of lease arrangements that cause unique accounting problems are: (1) residual value, (2) sales-type lease (lessor), (3) bargain purchase option, (4) initial direct costs, (5) current versus noncurrent classification, and (6) disclosures.

7.     **Describe the effect of a residual value, guaranteed or unguaranteed, on lease accounting.** Whether an estimated residual value is guaranteed by the lessee or unguaranteed is of both economic and accounting consequences to the lessee. The accounting difference is that the minimum lease payments computation, the basis for capitalization, includes a guaranteed residual value but excludes any unguaranteed residual value. If the lessee is the party agreeing to guarantee a residual value, the guaranteed residual value affects the lessee's computation of minimum lease payments and, therefore, the amounts capitalized as a leased asset and a lease obligation. In effect, it is an additional lease payment that will be paid in property or cash, or both, at the end of the lease term. An unguaranteed residual value has no effect upon the computation of the minimum lease payments, the lessee's cost of the leased asset, or the lessee's reported amount for the lease liability. To the lessee, an unguaranteed residual value is the same as no residual value.

8.     **Describe the lessor's accounting for sales-type leases.** A sales-type lease is distinguished from a direct-financing type lease by the relationship between the fair value of the leased asset and the cost of the leased asset; in a sales-type lease they are unequal; whereas, in a direct-financing type lease, they are equal. The computations for Lease Receivable and periodic interest revenue reflect any residual value involved (a guaranteed residual or an unguaranteed residual that will be available to the lessor). When recording sales revenue and cost of goods sold, there is a difference in the accounting for a guaranteed or an unguaranteed residual value. A guaranteed residual value can be considered part of sales revenue because the lessor knows that the entire asset has been sold. There is less certainty that the unguaranteed residual portion of the asset has been "sold;" therefore, sales and cost of goods sold are recognized only for the portion of the asset for which realization is assured. However, the gross profit amount on the sale of the asset is the same whether a guaranteed or unguaranteed residual value is involved.

9.     **List the disclosure requirements for leases.** The disclosure requirements for the lessees and lessors vary based upon the type of lease (capital or operating) and whether the issuer is the lessor or lessee. These disclosure requirements provide investors with the following information:

(1) general description of the nature of leasing arrangements, (2) the nature, timing and amount of cash inflows and outflows associated with leases, including payments to be paid or received for each of the five succeeding years, (3) the amount of lease revenues and expenses reported in the income statement each period, (4) description and amounts of leased assets by major balance sheet classification and related liabilities, and (5) amounts receivable and unearned revenues under lease agreements.

*10. **Understand and apply lease accounting concepts to various lease arrangements**. The classification of leases by lessees and lessors is based on criteria that assess whether the lessor has transferred substantially all of the risks and benefits of ownership of the asset to the lessee. In addition, lessors assess two additional criteria to ensure that payment is assured and that there are not uncertainties about lessor's future costs. Lessees capitalize leases that meet any of the criteria, recording a lease asset and related lease liability. For leases that are in substance a financing of an asset purchase, lessors substitute a lease receivable for the leased asset. In a sales-type lease, the fair value of the leased asset is greater than the cost, and lessors record gross profit. Leases that do not meet capitalization criteria are classified as operating leases, on which rent expense (revenue) is recognized by lessees (lessors) for lease payments.
      *This material is covered in Appendix 21A in your text.

**11. **Describe the lessee's accounting for a sale-leaseback transaction.** If the lease meets one of the four criteria for treatment as a capital lease, the seller-lessee accounts for the transaction as a sale and the lease as a capital lease. The seller-lessee defers any profit it experiences from the sale of an asset that is leased back under a capital lease. The seller-lessee amortizes any profit over the lease term (or the remaining economic life of the asset if either criterion 1 or 2 of Group I is satisfied) in proportion to the amortization of the leased asset. If none of the capital lease criteria are satisfied, the seller-lessee accounts for the transaction as a sale and the lease as an operating lease. Under an operating lease, the lessee generally defers such profit on the sale of the asset and amortizes it in proportion to the rental payments over the period of time that it expects to use the assets.
      **This material is covered in Appendix 21B in your text.

## TIPS ON CHAPTER TOPICS

> **TIP:** For a nonoperating type lease, **always draw a time line** and enter on that diagram all the cash flows associated with the lease which are expected by the party for whom you are accounting. For a lessee, those will be the minimum lease payments. For a lessor, those will be the minimum lease payments plus any unguaranteed residual value to the lessor.
>
> **TIP:** **Minimum lease payments** include the following:
> 1. Regular periodic rental payments, excluding executory costs (an annuity).
> 2. Bargain purchase option (a single sum), if any.
> 3. Guaranteed residual value (a single sum), if any.
> 4. Penalty for failure to renew, if any.
>
> **TIP:** The **cost** (and initial amount of liability) **for an asset under a capital lease** is determined by the present value of the minimum lease payments (excluding executory costs included therein). However, the amount recorded should not exceed the fair market value of the asset at the inception date. The rate to use in the discounting process is the lessee's incremental borrowing rate or the lessor's implicit rate. The lessor's rate is used when it is known and when it is the **lower** of the two rates.

**TIP:**    The time period to be used for depreciation of an asset under capital lease depends on which criteria the lease meets in determining that it is a capital lease. If there is automatic transfer of title of the asset at the end of the lease term or if there is a bargain purchase option, the asset is expected to be with the lessee for the remainder of its economic life; therefore, to comply with the matching principle, the asset should be depreciated over its remaining useful life. If the lease contract does not provide for the automatic transfer of title and there is no bargain purchase option, the asset will be used by the lessee only for the lease term; therefore, to comply with the matching principle, the asset should be depreciated over the lease term.

**TIP:**    A **bargain purchase option** is defined as an option to purchase at a bargain price. A bargain price is a price substantially below the expected market value of the asset at the date the option becomes exercisable. If the option price is 30% of the expected market value, accountants would agree that the price constitutes a bargain. If the option price is 90% of the expected market value, accountants would agree that the price does **not** constitute a bargain. The range that lies between these two extremes provides room for controversy. A question appearing on a CPA examination considered a 50% relationship to constitute a bargain. But what about 70% or 80%? Judgment is required in this area.

**TIP:**    The amount representing net investment in lease for a lessor is recorded in the lessor's books in the account Lease Receivable. The amount of **net investment** is the present value of all future cash flows (excluding executory costs) to the lessor from the lease situation. Thus, net investment in lease largely is the present value of the minimum lease payments. If the asset reverts back to the lessor at the end of the lease term and there is an unguaranteed residual value, the present value of that residual value must be included in net investment in lease on the lessor's books. Minimum lease payments include a guaranteed residual value, if any. Thus, both guaranteed residual value (because it is included as part of minimum lease payments) and unguaranteed residual value (because it is added in the net investment) are included as part of lease receivable if a portion of the residual value is guaranteed in the lease agreement and if the unguaranteed portion is relevant to the lessor (that is, if the lessor expects to get the asset back).

**TIP:**    You will need present value factors to work the exercises in this book. These factors can be found on the Kieso student web-site (www.wiley.com\college\kieso).

# ILLUSTRATION 21-1
# CLASSIFICATION OF LEASES (L.O. 2, 4)

## CLASSIFICATION OF LEASES BY THE LESSEE

From the standpoint of the lessee, all leases may be classified for accounting purposes as follows:

- (a)     Operating leases.
- (b)     Capital leases.

If at the inception of a noncancelable lease agreement the lease meets **one or more** of the following four criteria, the lessee shall classify and account for the arrangement as a **capital lease**:

1.     The lease transfers ownership of the property to the lessee.
2.     The lease contains a bargain purchase option.
3.     The lease term is equal to 75% or more of the estimated economic life of the leased property.
4.     The present value of the minimum lease payments (excluding executory costs) equals or exceeds 90% of the fair value of the leased property.

## CLASSIFICATION OF LEASES BY THE LESSOR

From the standpoint of the **lessor**, all leases may be classified for accounting purposes as follows:

- (a)     Operating leases.
- (b)     Direct financing leases.
- (c)     Sales-type leases.

If at the inception of a lease agreement the lessor is party to a lease that meets **one or more** of the following Group I criteria (1, 2, 3, and 4) and **both** of the following Group II criteria (1 and 2), the lessor shall classify and account for the arrangement as a **direct financing lease** or as a **sales-type lease**.  (If the lessor's net investment at inception equals the asset's carrying value, the lease is a direct financing lease; if the net investment is unequal to the asset's carrying value, the lease is a sales-type lease.)

### GROUP I
1.     The lease transfers ownership of the property to the lessee.
2.     The lease contains a bargain purchase option.
3.     The lease term is equal to 75% or more of the estimated economic life of the leased property.
4.     The present value of the minimum lease payments (excluding executory costs) equals or exceeds 90% of the fair value of the leased property.

### GROUP II
1.     Collectibility of the payments required from the lessee is reasonably predictable.
2.     No important uncertainties surround the amount of unreimbursable costs yet to be incurred by the lessor under the lease (i.e., lessor's performance is substantially complete and future costs are reasonably predictable).

## ILLUSTRATION 21-1 (Continued)

**TIP:**    Note that the Group I criteria are identical to the criteria that must be met for a lease to be classified as a capital lease by a lessee.

**TIP:**    In certain cases, the lessee may capitalize the lease while the lessor does not. This situation results because the lease meets one or more Group I criteria, but the lease does not meet both Group II criteria; thus, the lease meets the qualifications required for capitalization by the lessee but the lease does not meet the qualifications required for capitalization by the lessor. Therefore, both parties will report the leased asset on their balance sheets, and both parties will record depreciation each period for financial reporting purposes. They must agree who is to take depreciation for tax purposes because the IRS will not allow both parties to report depreciation on the leased asset.

## ILLUSTRATION 21-2
## STEPS IN EVALUATING AND ACCOUNTING
## FOR A LEASE SITUATION FOR A LESSEE (L.O. 2, 7)

**STEP 1:**    **Examine the facts regarding the lease agreement.**
Determine if the lease meets the criteria to capitalize the lease (the criteria are listed in **Illustration 21-1**). If so, perform the rest of the steps below; if not, account for the lease as an operating lease.

**STEP 2:**    **Draw the time line.**

**STEP 3:**    **Compute the present value of the minimum lease payments.**
- The minimum lease payments include:
  - (a)    periodic rental payments
  - (b)    bargain purchase option, if any
  - (c)    guaranteed residual value, if any residual value is guaranteed by the lessee
  - (d)    penalty for failure to renew, if any.
- Use the lessee's incremental borrowing rate or the lessor's implicit rate, whichever is lower. (The lessor's rate must be known for it to be used.)

**STEP 4:**    **Determine the cost of the asset under capital lease.**
- The cost is the **lower** of the present value of the minimum lease payments (Step 3) or the asset's fair value.
- If the fair value is the lower, a new effective interest rate must be determined. That new rate is the interest rate which sets the minimum lease payments equivalent to the fair value of the asset, giving effect to the time value of money.

## ILLUSTRATION 21-2 (Continued)

**STEP 5:**   **Prepare the lessee's amortization schedule.**
The beginning obligation balance is the amount determined in Step 4. (The interest rate for Step 5 is the rate used in Step 3, unless that rate was replaced in Step 4.)

**STEP 6:**   **Prepare journal entries to record the transactions related to the lease on the lessee's books.**

## ILLUSTRATION 21-3
## STEPS IN EVALUATING AND ACCOUNTING
## FOR A LEASE SITUATION FOR A LESSOR (L.O. 7, 8)

**STEP 1:**   **Examine the facts regarding the lease agreement.**
Determine if the lease meets the criteria for the lessor to capitalize the lease (the criteria are listed in **Illustration 21-1**). If so, perform the rest of the steps below; if not, account for the lease as an operating lease.

**STEP 2:**   **Determine the periodic rental payments required by the lessor to yield the desired rate of return on the investment if that payment is not given data.**
- The future cash flows to the lessor from the leased asset are to allow the lessor to recover the asset's fair value or its cost.
- The present value of any single sum expected by the lessor at the end of the lease term (bargain purchase option or guaranteed residual value or unguaranteed residual value) is deducted from the asset's fair value (or cost) to arrive at the present value of the periodic rents. The amount of a single rent is determined by solving for Rent in the following formula:

Present Value of an Annuity = Rent (Present Value Factor)

**STEP 3:**   **Draw the time line.**

**STEP 4:**   **Compute the net investment at inception.**
- Net investment is the present value of the minimum lease payments plus the present value of any unguaranteed residual value that will be available to the lessor.
- Use the lessor's implicit rate in the discounting process.

## ILLUSTRATION 21-3 (Continued)

STEP 5:    **Prepare the lessor's amortization schedule.**
The beginning net investment (computed in Step 4) is the starting point for this schedule. Use the lessor's implicit rate to compute interest revenue.

STEP 6:    **Prepare the journal entries to record the transactions related to the lease on the lessor's books.**

## EXERCISE 21-1

**Purpose:**    (L.O. 2, 5) This exercise illustrates how a lessee and a lessor are to account for a lease when the contract allows for automatic transfer of title to the leased asset at the end of the lease term.

The following facts pertain to a lease between Sun Bank Leasing and JMJ Schmitt Printers for an electronic laser printer:

1.    The lease is for a five-year term, beginning January 1, 2010. The remaining economic life of the asset is five years.
2.    The lessor's implicit rate is 10%; the lessee's incremental borrowing rate is 10%.
3.    The fair value of the leased asset is $100,000. The lessor's cost is $100,000.
4.    The annual rent payments are $25,981.62; the first one is due on January 1, 2010. This amount includes $2,000.00 for executory costs.
5.    The title to the asset automatically transfers to the lessee at the end of the lease term. The asset is expected to have zero residual value at that date.
6.    Both the lessee and the lessor use the calendar year for their accounting periods.

## Instructions
(a)    Describe the type of lease from the viewpoint of the: (1) lessee and (2) lessor.
(b)    Prepare an amortization schedule for use by the lessee and the lessor. Explain why they could both use the same schedule in this situation. Also, draw a time line for the lessor.
(c)    Prepare the journal entry to record the inception of the lease on the lessee's books.
(d)    Prepare the journal entry to record the inception of the lease on the lessor's books.
(e)    Indicate the amount(s) to appear in the lessee's December 31, 2011 balance sheet for this lease. Also indicate the portion that will appear in the current liability section, and the portion that will appear in the long-term liability classification. Explain how to determine these amounts.
(f)    Indicate the amount to appear in the lessor's December 31, 2011 balance sheet for net investment in lease. Also indicate the portion that will appear in the current asset section, and the portion that will appear in the long-term investment section of the balance sheet.

## Solution to Exercise 21-1

(a)    The lease is a capital lease for the lessee because the title to the leased asset automatically transfers to the lessee at the end of the lease term. (The lease also meets two other criteria required by the lessee for capitalization.) Assuming that uncollectible lease payments are reasonably estimable and there are no important uncertainties surrounding future unreimbursable costs to be incurred by the lessor with respect to the lease, the lessor has a nonoperating type lease because of the automatic transfer of the title of the leased asset at the end of the lease term. The lessor has a direct financing type lease (rather than a sales type) because the net investment at inception of $100,000 equals the lessor's carrying value of $100,000 cost.

**Computations:**
$25,981.62 - $2,000.00 executory costs = $23,981.62
$23,981.62 x present value factor for an annuity due for $n = 5$, $i = 10\%$ = net
    investment
$23,981.62 x 4.16986 = $100,000.00 net investment

(b)                             **AMORTIZATION SCHEDULE**

| Date | Rent Excluding Executory Costs | 10% Interest | Reduction of Present Value | Present Value Balance |
|---|---|---|---|---|
| 1/1/10 | | | | $ 100,000.00 |
| 1/1/10 | $ 23,981.62* | $ -0- | $ 23,981.62 | 76,018.38 |
| 1/1/11 | 23,981.62 | 7,601.84 | 16,379.78 | 59,638.60 |
| 1/1/12 | 23,981.62 | 5,963.86 | 18,017.76 | 41,620.84 |
| 1/1/13 | 23,981.62 | 4,162.08 | 19,819.54 | 21,801.30 |
| 1/1/14 | 23,981.62 | 2,180.32** | 21,801.30 | -0- |
| | $ 119,908.10 | $19,908.10 | $ 100,000.00 | |

*$25,981.62 - $2,000.00 = $23,981.62
**Includes rounding error of $.19.

The lessor and the lessee can use the same amortization schedule in this situation because they are using the same interest rate to account for the lease, and the lessor has no unguaranteed residual value for which to account. For these same reasons, both parties have the same time line for the lease which is depicted as follows:

PV = ?   $23,981.62      $23,981.62      $23.981.62      $23,981.62      $23,981.62

1/1/10        1/1/11   1/1/12        1/1/13        1/1/14        12/31/14

$$n = 5, i = 10\%$$

PV = $100,000

| TIP: | In this situation, there is no interest expense for the lessee and no interest revenue for the lessor for the last year of the lease because all amounts are fully paid by the lessee and totally received by the lessor as of the beginning of the fifth year. |
|------|------|

(c)     Leased Printer Under Capital Lease ....................................    100,000.00

        Lease Liability ........................................................................                        100,000.00

(d)     Lease Receivable...........................................................    100,000.00

        Printer  ...................................................................    100,000.00

(e)     The asset Leased Printer Under Capital Lease for $100,000 will appear in the property, plant, and equipment section of the lessee's balance sheet. Accumulated depreciation of $40,000 would also appear in that section. In computing the periodic depreciation, the cost of the asset under capital lease ($100,000) is spread over the useful life to the lessee (5 years) giving $20,000 depreciation per year. The present value of the obligation under capital lease at December 31, 2011 is $65,602.46 ($59,638.60 + $5,963.86 = $65,602.46). The present value amount will be reported on the lessee's balance sheet at this date as follows:

**Current liabilities**
       Interest payable                                    $   5,963.86
       Lease Liability                                      18,017.76
**Long-term liabilities**
       Lease Liability                                      41,620.84

To determine these amounts, look at the amortization schedule. Find the date on the schedule that is the balance sheet date (December 31, 2011). If the balance sheet date is not on the schedule (as is the case here), locate the date that most recently precedes the balance sheet date. That date is January 1, 2011 in this exercise. Find the balance on that payment line (which is $59,638.60) and add any interest that has accrued since that date (i.e., $59,638.60 x 10% = $5,963.86). The total is the present value of the remaining minimum lease payments at the balance sheet date. The liability due to the accrued interest expense belongs in the current liability classification. The portion of the principal that is to be shown in current liabilities is the amount on the **next** payment line (1/1/12) of the amortization schedule in the "Reduction of Present Value" column ($18,017.76); the portion of the principal that is noncurrent is on that same (1/1/12) line in the "Present Value Balance" column ($41,620.84).

(f)     The net investment in lease at December 31, 2011 is $65,602.46 ($59,638.60 + $5,963.86 = $65,602.46). This will appear on the lessor's December 31, 2011 balance sheet as follows:

**Current assets**
| | |
|---|---|
| Interest receivable | $  5,963.86 |
| Lease receivable | $ 18,017.76 |

**Long-term investments**
| | |
|---|---|
| Lease receivable | $ 41,620.84 |

> **TIP:** To check on the accuracy of the current and noncurrent portions, add the two portions together; that total ($5,963.86 + $18,017.76 + $41,620.84 = $65,602.46) should equal the present value of the lease at the balance sheet date ($59,638.60 + $5,963.86 = $65,602.46). It does in this case.
>
> To determine the amounts to appear in the current asset section, refer to the amortization schedule and the explanation for the solution to part (e) above.

# EXERCISE 21-2

**Purpose:**     (L.O. 2, 5) This exercise is a comprehensive illustration of the accounting procedures for a lease where the lessee guarantees a residual value. This exercise illustrates (1) how the lessor determines the amount of the periodic lease payment, (2) the lessor's computations for recording the transactions associated with the lease, (4) the meaning of the term "net investment," (5) the lessee's computations for recording the transactions associated with the lease, (6) the journal entries on the lessor's books, and (7) the journal entries on the lessee's books. This exercise is long but not too difficult. Take it one part at a time.

On January 1, Year 1, Leaseco has a piece of equipment with a cost of $80,000 and a fair value of $80,000. On that date, Leaseco leases the asset to Rentco for a five-year term at an implicit rate of 10%. The annual lease payment is due at the beginning of each year, and the first payment is to be collected at the inception date. The leased asset will revert back to Leaseco at the end of the lease term; the lessee guarantees a residual value of $7,000. Both Leaseco and Rentco have a calendar-year reporting period. Rentco is aware of the lessor's implicit rate; Rentco's incremental borrowing rate is 12%. Leaseco can reasonably estimate uncollectible lease payments and has no important uncertainties regarding future unreimbursable costs associated with this lease.

## Instructions

Assuming the lease is a capital lease to the lessee and a direct financing lease to the lessor:

(a)     Compute the amount of the annual lease payment (excluding executory costs) to be collected by the lessor.

(b)     Draw the time line for the lessor.

(c)     For the lessor, compute the net investment in lease at the inception of the lease.

(d)     Compute the amount of interest revenue to be reported by the lessor for: (1) Year 1, (2) Year 2, and (3) Year 5.

(e)     Prepare the amortization schedule for the lessor.

(f)     Compute the cost of the lessee's asset under capital lease.

(g)     Draw the time line for the lessee.

(h)     Compute the amount of interest expense to be reported by the lessee for (1) Year 1, (2) Year 2, and (3) Year 5.

(i)     Prepare the amortization schedule for the lessee.

(j)     Explain why the lessee's amortization schedule is the same as the lessor's amortization schedule. Under what circumstances will the two parties be able to use the same amortization schedule?

(k)     Prepare all of the journal entries for the lessor's books for Years 1 and 2 (assuming reversing entries are not used).

(l)     Prepare all of the journal entries for the lessee's books for Years 1 and 2 (assuming reversing entries are not used).

(m)     Compare and contrast the journal entries for the lessee [part (l)] with the journal entries for the lessor [part (k)].

## Solution to Exercise 21-2

| | |
|---|---:|
| (a)     Total amount to be recovered | $80,000.00 |
| Present value of residual ($7,000 x .62092[1]) | (4,346.44) |
| Present value of annual payments | 75,653.56 |
| Factor for present value of an annuity due of 1 for $n = 5$, $i = 10$ | ÷ 4.16986 |
| **Annual rent required** | $18,142.95 |

[1].62092 is the factor for present value of 1 for $n = 5$, $i = 10\%$.

> **TIP:**   In this case, the asset's fair value (or cost) is to be recovered through annual payments by the lessee and through a guaranteed residual value ($7,000.00) at the end of the lease. Today's cash equivalent of $7,000.00 due in five years is less than $7,000.00, due to the time value of money.

(b)

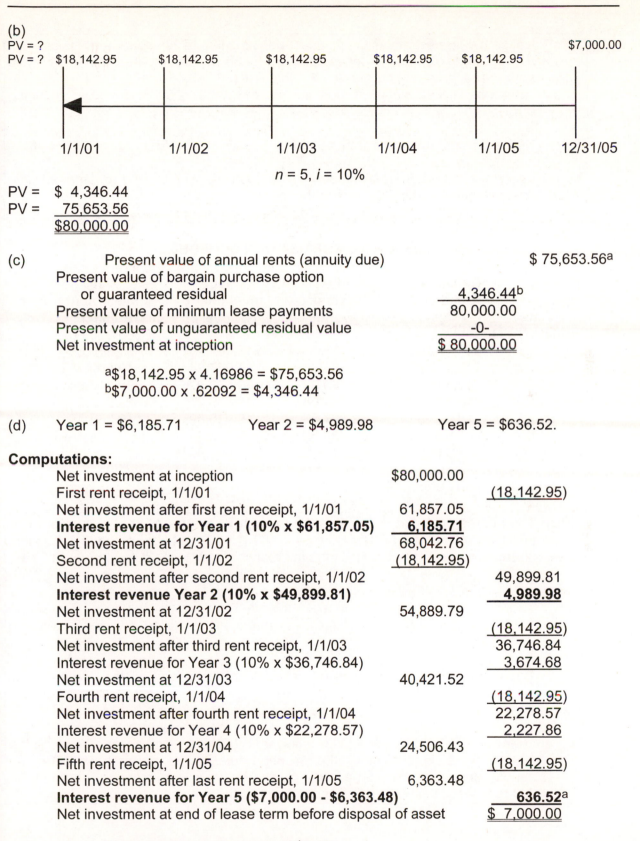

PV = ?

PV = ?  $18,142.95     $18,142.95     $18,142.95     $18,142.95     $18,142.95     $7,000.00

1/1/01     1/1/02     1/1/03     1/1/04     1/1/05     12/31/05

$n = 5, i = 10\%$

PV = $ 4,346.44
PV =   75,653.56
     $80,000.00

(c)

| | |
|---|---:|
| Present value of annual rents (annuity due) | $ 75,653.56[a] |
| Present value of bargain purchase option or guaranteed residual | 4,346.44[b] |
| Present value of minimum lease payments | 80,000.00 |
| Present value of unguaranteed residual value | -0- |
| Net investment at inception | $ 80,000.00 |

     [a]$18,142.95 x 4.16986 = $75,653.56
     [b]$7,000.00 x .62092 = $4,346.44

(d)     Year 1 = $6,185.71       Year 2 = $4,989.98       Year 5 = $636.52.

**Computations:**

| | | |
|---|---:|---:|
| Net investment at inception | $80,000.00 | |
| First rent receipt, 1/1/01 | | (18,142.95) |
| Net investment after first rent receipt, 1/1/01 | 61,857.05 | |
| **Interest revenue for Year 1 (10% x $61,857.05)** | **6,185.71** | |
| Net investment at 12/31/01 | 68,042.76 | |
| Second rent receipt, 1/1/02 | (18,142.95) | |
| Net investment after second rent receipt, 1/1/02 | | 49,899.81 |
| **Interest revenue Year 2 (10% x $49,899.81)** | | **4,989.98** |
| Net investment at 12/31/02 | 54,889.79 | |
| Third rent receipt, 1/1/03 | | (18,142.95) |
| Net investment after third rent receipt, 1/1/03 | | 36,746.84 |
| Interest revenue for Year 3 (10% x $36,746.84) | | 3,674.68 |
| Net investment at 12/31/03 | 40,421.52 | |
| Fourth rent receipt, 1/1/04 | | (18,142.95) |
| Net investment after fourth rent receipt, 1/1/04 | | 22,278.57 |
| Interest revenue for Year 4 (10% x $22,278.57) | | 2,227.86 |
| Net investment at 12/31/04 | 24,506.43 | |
| Fifth rent receipt, 1/1/05 | | (18,142.95) |
| Net investment after last rent receipt, 1/1/05 | 6,363.48 | |
| **Interest revenue for Year 5 ($7,000.00 - $6,363.48)** | | **636.52[a]** |
| Net investment at end of lease term before disposal of asset | | $ 7,000.00 |

     [a]Includes a rounding error of $0.17.

> **TIP:** Notice the interest amount for the last period ($636.52 for Year 5, in this case) is a "plug" figure. When the derived amount ($636.52) is compared with what would have been a calculated amount for interest ($6,363.48 x 10% = $636.35), the difference is the amount of rounding error ($636.52 - $636.35 = $.17 rounding error).
>
> **TIP:** Notice that **net investment in lease is a present value (discounted) amount**.
>
> **TIP:** Interest is a function of (a) present value balance, (b) rate, and (c) time. As time passes, interest accrues (due to the time value of money). Interest **increases** the present value balance; payments **decrease** the present value balance.

(e)

### LESSOR'S AMORTIZATION SCHEDULE

| Date | Receipts Residual Value | 10% Interest Revenue | Net Investment Recovery | Net Investment Balance |
|------|-------------------------|----------------------|-------------------------|------------------------|
| 1/1/01 | | | | $80,000.00 |
| 1/1/01 | $18,142.95 | | $18,142.95 | 61,857.05 |
| 1/1/02 | 18,142.95 | $ 6,185.71 | 11,957.24 | 49,899.81 |
| 1/1/03 | 18,142.95 | 4,989.98 | 13,152.97 | 36,746.84 |
| 1/1/04 | 18,142.95 | 3,674.68 | 14,468.27 | 22,278.57 |
| 1/1/05 | 18,142.95 | 2,227.86 | 15,915.09 | 6,363.48 |
| 12/31/05 | 7,000.00 | 636.52* | 6,363.48 | -0- |
| | $97,714.75 | $17,714.75 | $80,000.00 | |

*Includes a rounding error of $0.17.

> **TIP:** The interest included in a rent is the interest for the period that occurs **prior** to the due date of the rent. Thus, the $4,989.98 for interest shown on the 1/1/03 line on the amortization schedule is the interest charged for the calendar year of Year 2.
>
> **TIP:** The heading for the third money column may be titled "Lease Receivable Recovery" and the fourth money column may be called "Lease Receivable Balance".
>
> **TIP:** The amounts on the amortization schedule were derived by the computations performed in part (d) above. However, the components are arranged a little differently on the amortization schedule.
>
> **TIP:** There is no interest included in the first rent receipt in this exercise because the first rent is to be received on the inception date (hence, the rents constitute an annuity due). There is no passage of time between the inception date and the first rent receipt date; therefore, no interest is earned.

**TIP:** The rounding error is always to be plugged in the interest column on the last line of the amortization schedule. If all computations are performed correctly and are rounded to the nearest cent, the rounding error will be small—usually less than $10.00. Therefore, a rounding error larger than this will generally indicate that there are errors in the schedule. There may be math errors or more serious procedural errors.

**TIP:** All items that appear on the time line in part (b) are to appear in the "Receipts" column of the amortization schedule.

**TIP:** The total of the "Net Investment Recovery" column is equal to the beginning figure in the "Net Investment Balance" column.

**TIP:** Notice how the net investment amount at December 31, Year 1, as derived from the appropriate numbers on the amortization schedule, can be proved by an independent present value calculation as of that date.

**Computations:**
*From the amortization schedule:*

| | |
|---|---:|
| Net investment balance at 1/1/01 | $ 61,857.05 |
| Interest for Year 1 | 6,185.71 |
| Net investment balance at 12/31/01 | $ 68,042.76 |

*Present value computations:*
Present value of an annuity due of 1, $n = 4$, $i = 10\% = 3.48685$
Present value of 1, $n = 4$, $i = 10\% = .68301$

| | |
|---|---:|
| $18,142.95 x 3.48685 | $ 63,261.75 |
| $7,000.00 x .68301 | x 4,781.07 |
| Present value at end of Year 1 | $ 68,042.82 |

The 6 cents difference between $68,042.76 and $68,042.82 is due to rounding errors.

(f)

| | |
|---|---:|
| Annual rent payment | $ 18,142.95 |
| Present value of an annuity due of 1, $n = 5$, $i = 10$ | x 4.16986 |
| Present value of annual rents | 75,653.56 |
| Present value of bargain purchase option or guaranteed residual | 4,346.44[a] |
| Present value of minimum lease payments | $ 80,000.00 |

[a] $7,000 X .62092 = $4,346.44

**TIP:** The lessee's cost of asset under capital lease is the lower of the asset's fair value or the present value of the minimum lease payments. The interest rate to be used in determining the present value of the minimum lease payments is the lessee's incremental borrowing rate or the lessor's implicit rate, whichever is lower. (The lessor's rate cannot possibly be used if it is unknown.)

> **TIP:**  When the leased asset is to revert back to the lessor at the end of the lease term rather than remain with the lessee, and the lessee does not guarantee a residual value, the lessee does not find the residual value of any relevance; hence, under those circumstances, the lessee would **not** use the residual value for any of its accounting.

(g)

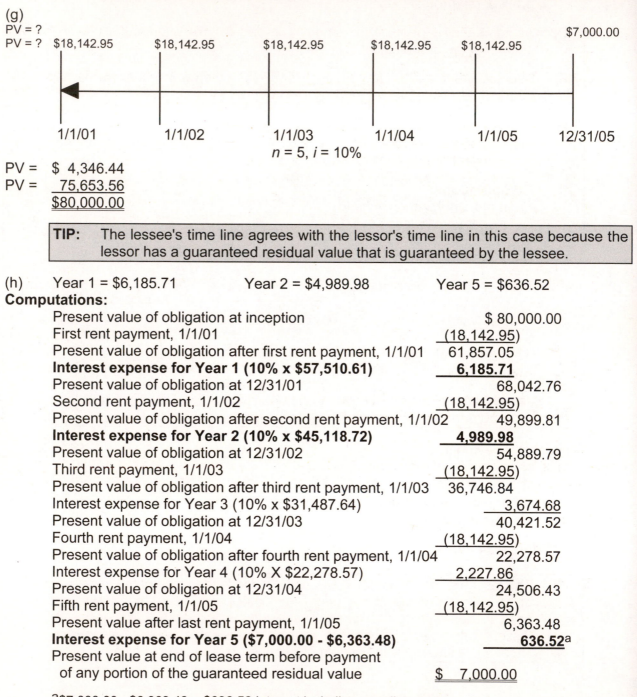

PV = ?
PV = ?

PV = $ 4,346.44
PV =   75,653.56
        $80,000.00

> **TIP:**  The lessee's time line agrees with the lessor's time line in this case because the lessor has a guaranteed residual value that is guaranteed by the lessee.

(h)    Year 1 = $6,185.71          Year 2 = $4,989.98          Year 5 = $636.52
**Computations:**

| | |
|---|---:|
| Present value of obligation at inception | $ 80,000.00 |
| First rent payment, 1/1/01 | (18,142.95) |
| Present value of obligation after first rent payment, 1/1/01 | 61,857.05 |
| **Interest expense for Year 1 (10% x $57,510.61)** | **6,185.71** |
| Present value of obligation at 12/31/01 | 68,042.76 |
| Second rent payment, 1/1/02 | (18,142.95) |
| Present value of obligation after second rent payment, 1/1/02 | 49,899.81 |
| **Interest expense for Year 2 (10% x $45,118.72)** | **4,989.98** |
| Present value of obligation at 12/31/02 | 54,889.79 |
| Third rent payment, 1/1/03 | (18,142.95) |
| Present value of obligation after third rent payment, 1/1/03 | 36,746.84 |
| Interest expense for Year 3 (10% x $31,487.64) | 3,674.68 |
| Present value of obligation at 12/31/03 | 40,421.52 |
| Fourth rent payment, 1/1/04 | (18,142.95) |
| Present value of obligation after fourth rent payment, 1/1/04 | 22,278.57 |
| Interest expense for Year 4 (10% X $22,278.57) | 2,227.86 |
| Present value of obligation at 12/31/04 | 24,506.43 |
| Fifth rent payment, 1/1/05 | (18,142.95) |
| Present value after last rent payment, 1/1/05 | 6,363.48 |
| **Interest expense for Year 5 ($7,000.00 - $6,363.48)** | **636.52**[a] |
| Present value at end of lease term before payment of any portion of the guaranteed residual value | $   7,000.00 |

[a]$7,000.00 - $6,363.48 = $636.52 interest including rounding error.
$6,363.48 x 10% = $636.35 interest if there was no rounding error.
$636.52 - $636.35 = $.17 rounding error.

(i)
## LESSEE'S AMORTIZATION SCHEDULE

| Date | Payments | 10% Interest Expense | Reduction of Liability | Lease Liability Balance |
|---|---|---|---|---|
| 1/1/01 | | | | $80,000.00 |
| 1/1/01 | $18,142.95 | | $18,142.95 | 61,857.05 |
| 1/1/02 | 18,142.95 | $ 6,185.71 | 11,957.24 | 49,899.81 |
| 1/1/03 | 18,142.95 | 4,989.98 | 13,152.97 | 36,746.84 |
| 1/1/04 | 18,142.95 | 3,674.68 | 14,468.27 | 22,278.57 |
| 1/1/05 | 18,142.95 | 2,227.86 | 15,915.09 | 6,363.48 |
| 12/31/05 | 7,000.00 | 636.52* | 6,363.48 | -0- |
| | $97,714.75 | $17,714.75 | $80,000.00 | |

*Includes a rounding error of $0.17.

> **TIP:** The total of the "Payments" column minus the total of the "Interest Expense" column equals the total of the "Reduction of Liability" column, and the total of the "Reduction of Liability" column equals the obligation's present value at inception (the beginning amount for the schedule).

(j) The lessor and the lessee have the same amortization schedule in this case. The lessor and the lessee can use the same amortization schedule when they use the same interest rate and when there is one of the following: (1) an automatic transfer of title, or (2) a bargain purchase option, or (3) a residual value guaranteed by the lessee to the lessor, or (4) an unguaranteed residual value for the lessor of zero. The lessee and the lessor will **not** be able to use the same amortization schedule when (a) they have different interest rates, or (b) there is a guaranteed residual value guaranteed by a party other than the lessee, or (c) an unguaranteed residual value is relevant to the lessor.

> **TIP:** If the $7,000 residual value was an unguaranteed residual, the lessor would start its amortization schedule with the $80,000 as shown above; however, the lessee would start its amortization schedule (and initially record a liability) with $75,653.56 (the present value of the minimum lease payments in that case).

(k) 1/1/01

| | | | |
|---|---|---|---|
| Lease Receivable | | 80,000.00 | |
| Equipment | | | 80,000.00 |
| Cash | | 18,142.95 | |
| Lease Payments Receivable | | | 18,142.95 |

12/31/01

| Interest Receivable | 6,185.71 | |
|---|---|---|
| Interest Revenue—Leases | | 6,185.71 |

1/1/02

| Cash | 18,142.95 | | |
|---|---|---|---|
| Lease Receivable | | | 11,957.24 |
| Interest Receivable | | | 6,185.71 |

12/31/02

| Interest Receivable | 4,989.98 | |
|---|---|---|
| Interest Revenue—Leases | | 4,989.98 |

| (l) | 1/1/01 | Leased Equipment Under Capital Leases .......... | 80,000.00 | |
| | | Lease Liability ..................................................... | | 80,000.00 |
| | | | | |
| | | Lease Liability ..................................................... | 18,142.95 | |
| | | Cash ................................................................... | | 18,142.95 |
| | 12/31/01 | Interest Expense ................................................. | 6,185.71 | |
| | | Interest Payable ................................................. | | 6,185.71 |
| | | | | |
| | | Depreciation Expense ......................................... | 14,600.00 | |
| | | Accumulated Depreciation .................................. | | 14,600.00 |
| | | [($80,000 - $7,000) ÷ 5 = $14,600] | | |

---

**TIP:** If the lessee guarantees a residual value, that guaranteed residual value is subtracted from the cost of the leased asset for the purpose of computing depreciation.

---

| | 1/1/02 | Interest Payable ................................................. | 6,185.71 | |
| | | Lease Liability ..................................................... | 11,957.24 | |
| | | Cash ................................................................... | | 18,142.95 |
| | 12/31/02 | Interest Expense ................................................. | 4,989.98 | |
| | | Interest Payable ................................................. | | 4,989.98 |
| | | | | |
| | | Depreciation Expense ......................................... | 14,600.00 | |
| | | Accumulated Depreciation .................................. | | 14,600.00 |

(m) The lease is a capitalized lease (nonoperating type lease) for both the lessee and the lessor. Both the lessor and the lessee account for interest, **but** only the lessee accounts for depreciation. The interest is an expense to the lessee and a source of revenue to the lessor. The asset that is legally owned by the lessor is accounted for as an installment purchase by the lessee and an installment sale by the lessor. Thus the lessee has a liability for the lease and the lessor has a receivable for the lease.

# EXERCISE 21-3

**Purpose:**    (L.O. 8) This exercise will provide an example of: (1) the accounting procedures for a lessor with a sales-type lease, (2) lease periods that do not coincide with accounting periods, and (3) a lease with a purchase option.

The following facts relate to a lease made by the Wandie Warmus Company to the Harker Marina Corporation.

| | |
|---|---|
| Inception of lease | May 1, 2010 |
| Annual payment due at beginning of each lease year, first one is due on May 1, 2010 | $10,000 |
| Lease term | 5 years |
| Remaining economic life of asset | 7 years |
| Residual value at end of lease term | $8,000 |
| Purchase option at end of lease term | $2,000 |
| Lessor's cost | $40,000 |
| Lessor's implicit rate | 10% |
| Annual accounting period | Calendar year |

## Instructions
(a)    Prepare the amortization schedule and draw the time line for the lessor.
(b)    Answer the following questions from the viewpoint of the lessor:
(1)    What is the net investment at inception?
(2)    What amount of gross profit should be reported on the income statement for 2010?
(3)    What amount of gross profit should be reported on the income statement for 2011?
(4)    What amount should be reported as interest revenue on the income statement for 2010?
(5)    What amount should be reported as interest revenue on the income statement for 2011?
(c)    Prepare the following journal entries for the lessor:
(1)    Inception of the lease on May 1, 2010.
(2)    Rent receipt on May 1, 2010.
(3)    Adjusting entry at December 31, 2010.
(4)    Rent receipt on May 1, 2011.
(5)    Adjusting entry at December 31, 2011.
(d)    If the lessee has an incremental borrowing rate of 10%, can the lessee use the same amortization schedule as the lessor in this situation?
(e)    Explain how the entry in part (c)(1) would be different for the lessor if there was no purchase option and the estimated residual value to the lessor (unguaranteed) at the end of the lease term was $2,000. Also, explain whether the lessee could use the same amortization schedule as the lessor in this latter instance.

## Solution to Exercise 21-3

(a)                    AMORTIZATION SCHEDULE FOR LESSOR

| Date | Rents Plus BPO[a] | 10% Interest | Reduction of Present Value | Present Value Balance |
|---|---|---|---|---|
| 5/1/10 | | | | $42,940.44 |
| 5/1/10 | $10,000.00 | | $10,000.00 | 32,940.44 |
| 5/1/11 | 10,000.00 | $3,294.04 | 6,705.96 | 26,234.48 |
| 5/1/12 | 10,000.00 | 2,623.45 | 7,376.55 | 18,857.93 |
| 5/1/13 | 10,000.00 | 1,885.79 | 8,114.21 | 10,743.72 |
| 5/1/14 | 10,000.00 | 1,074.37 | 8,925.63 | 1,818.09 |
| 4/30/15 | 2,000.00 | 181.91* | 1,818.09 | -0- |
| | $52,000.00 | $9,059.56 | $42,940.44 | |

[a]BPO is an abbreviation for "bargain purchase option." The option to purchase is deemed to constitute a bargain purchase option because the option price is only 25% ($2,000 ÷ $8,000 = 25%) of the estimated market value of the asset at the date the option is exercisable.

*Includes a rounding error of $0.10.

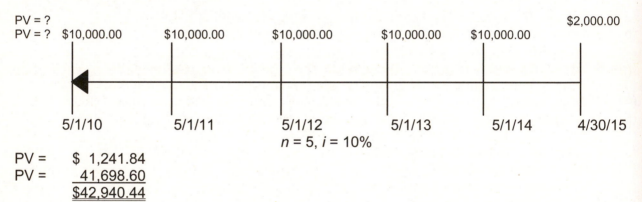

PV = ?
PV = ?  $10,000.00    $10,000.00    $10,000.00    $10,000.00    $10,000.00    $2,000.00

5/1/10    5/1/11    5/1/12    5/1/13    5/1/14    4/30/15
$n = 5, i = 10\%$

PV =  $ 1,241.84
PV =    41,698.60
       $42,940.44

(b)    (1)    Present value of rents ($10,000 x 4.16986[a])    $ 41,698.60
Present value of BPO ($2,000 x .62092[b])    1,241.84
Present value of minimum lease payments    42,940.44
Present value of unguaranteed residual value    -0-
Net investment at inception    $ 42,940.44

    [a]Factor for present value of an annuity due for n=5, i=10%.
    [b]Factor for present value of a single sum for n=5, i=10%.

(2)    Sales price    $ 42,940.44[a]
Cost of goods sold    40,000.00[b]
Gross profit to be recognized during 2010    $ 2,940.44

    [a]The sale price is equal to the present value of the minimum lease payments:

        Present value of rents ($10,000 x 4.16986)    $41,698.60
        Present value of BPO ($2,000 x .62092)    1,241.84
        Present value of minimum lease payments    $42,940.44

    [b]Cost of goods sold is equal to the lessor's carrying value less the present value of any unguaranteed residual value for the lessor:

        Carrying value    $40,000.00
        Present value of unguaranteed residual value    -0-
        Cost of goods sold    $40,000.00

(3)    None. All of the gross profit attributable to a sales-type lease is to be recognized in the year in which the inception of the lease occurs. In this case, that year is 2007.

(4)    $3,294.04 x 8/12 = $2,196.03 interest for 2010

There are eight months between May 1, 2010 and December 31, 2010. The interest for those eight months are reflected on the 5/1/11 payment line of the amortization schedule. The $3,294.04 interest showing on that 5/1/11 payment line is for the twelve-month period preceding 5/1/08. The interest for the last eight months of 2010 is therefore 8/12 x $3,294.04.

(5)    $3,294.04 x 4/12                           $ 1,098.01
       $2,623.45 x 8/12                             1,748.97
       Interest for 2008                          $ 2,846.98

> **TIP:** The amortization schedule is **always** prepared using the interest dates (which are dictated by the lease periods). The interest amount appearing on a given payment line is then apportioned to the appropriate accounting period(s). In examining the amortization schedule in part (a), the interest appearing on the 5/1/11 line is the interest for 5/1/10 through 4/30/11. Thus, 8/12 of it belongs on the 2010 income statement and 4/12 of it is reported on the 2011 income statement. Likewise, the $2,623.45 appearing on the 5/1/12 payment line reflects the interest for 5/1/11 through 4/30/12. Thus, 8/12 of it is reported on the 2011 income statement.

(c)    (1)    5/1/10
       Lease Receivable.................................................................   42,940.44
       Cost of Goods Sold .............................................................   40,000.00
              Inventory..................................................................                      40,000.00
              Sales Revenue .......................................................                           42,940.44

(2)    5/1/10
       Cash          10,000.00
              Lease Receivable.......................................................                         10,000.00

(3)    12/31/10
       Interest Receivable ...............................................................   2,196.03
              Interest Revenue--Leases ..........................................                              2,196.03
              ($3,294.04 x 8/12 = $2,196.03)

(4)    5/1/11
       Cash          10,000.00
              Lease Receivable.......................................................                          6,705.96
              Interest Receivable.....................................................                         2,196.03
              Interest Revenue—Leases...........................................                              1,098.01
              ($3,294.04 x 4/12 = $1,098.01)

(5)    12/31/11
       Interest Receivable ...............................................................   1,748.97
              Interest Revenue--Leases ..........................................                              1,748.97
              ($2,623.45 x 8/12 = $1,748.97)

(d)    Yes. The lessee will record the asset under capital lease and the obligation under capital lease at $42,940.44. The lessee's amortization schedule will appear exactly like the lessor's amortization schedule.

> **TIP:** The lessee will depreciate the entire $42,940.44 cost of the asset under capital lease over the useful life of the asset to the lessee, which is 7 years. Due to the existence of the bargain purchase option, the lessee is expected to use the asset for its entire remaining economic life. Thus, the matching principle will dictate that the asset's cost be allocated over the 7 years.

(e)   If there was no bargain purchase option, but there was a $2,000.00 unguaranteed residual value relevant to the lessor, the lessor's journal entry at inception would be:

| | | |
|---|---|---|
| Lease Receivable | 42,940.44[a] | |
| Cost of Goods Sold | 38,758.16[b] | |
| Inventory | | 40,000.00 |
| Sales Revenue | | 41,698.60[c] |

| [a]Present value of minimum lease payments | $41,698.60 |
|---|---|
| Present value of unguaranteed residual | 1,241.84 |
| Net investment in lease | $42,940.44 |

| [b]Carrying value of the asset | $40,000.00 |
|---|---|
| Present value of unguaranteed residual value | (1,241.84)[1] |
| Cost of goods sold | $38,758.16 |

[1]$2,000.00 x .62092 = $1,241.84

| [c]Present value of rents | $41,698.60[3] |
|---|---|
| Present value of BPO or GRV | -0- |
| Present value of minimum lease payments | $41,698.60 |

[3]$10,000.00 x 4.16986 = $41,698.60

The entry differs from part (c) (1) in that both Sales Revenue and Cost of Goods Sold are reduced by the cash equivalent value of the $2,000.00 unguaranteed residual value to be received in five years. In this instance, a portion of the asset ($2,000.00) is considered **not** to be sold to the lessee; the remainder of the asset is treated as a sale.

The lessor's amortization schedule would be the same as it appears now in part (a), except that the column heading "Rents Plus BPO" would be changed to "Rents Plus Residual Value;" however, the lessee's amortization schedule would differ, even if both parties are using a 10% interest rate.

The lessor's amortization schedule would include accounting for the $2,000.00 unguaranteed residual value. The lessee's schedule would **not** include any accounting for the $2,000.00 unguaranteed residual value to the lessor. The lessee's schedule would begin with $41,698.60, rather than $42,940.44.

## ILLUSTRATION 21-4
## USE OF RESIDUAL VALUE IN NONOPERATING LEASE SITUATIONS
  (L.O. 7)

Residual value is the estimated value of an asset at some given future point in time. Residual value may be estimated at the end of the lease term or at the end of the asset's useful life, depending on which, if either, is relevant to the party for whom you are accounting.

The residual value at the end of the lease term is used by the lessor in determining the amount to charge the lessee as the periodic rent if either of the following is true:
- The asset will revert back to the lessor at the end of the lease and the residual value is guaranteed.
- The asset will revert back to the lessor at the end of the lease and the residual value is unguaranteed.

The residual value at the end of the lease term is used by the lessor in determining the net investment in the lease if either of the following is true:
- The asset will revert back to the lessor at the end of the lease and the residual value is guaranteed.
- The asset will revert back to the lessor at the end of the lease and the residual value is unguaranteed.

The residual value at the end of the lease term is used by the lessee in determining the cost of the asset under capital lease and the initial amount of lease liability **only** if the following is true:
- The asset will revert back to the lessor at the end of the lease and the residual value is guaranteed by the lessee.

The residual value at the end of the lease term (or at the end of the asset's life) is used by the lessee in determining the periodic depreciation if either of the following is true:
- The asset will revert back to the lessor at the end of the lease and the residual value is guaranteed by the lessee. (Use the residual value at the end of the lease term.)
- The asset will transfer to the lessee at the end of the lease term either through an automatic transfer clause or a bargain purchase option. (Use the residual at the end of the asset's life.)

> **TIP:** When a lessor has a sales-type lease to account for, the present value of any unguaranteed residual value is deducted from the asset's carrying value to determine the amount to record for Cost of Goods Sold. In essence, the lessor accounts for the situation as if he sold most of the asset; only a portion of the asset (today's cash equivalent of the residual value estimated at the end of the lease term) is continuing to be reflected as an asset on the lessor's books. It is reflected as an asset by way of fact that the present value of the unguaranteed residual is added to the present value of the minimum lease payments in recording the initial amount of net investment in lease in the Lease Receivable account.

# CASE 21-1

**Purpose:** (L.O. 7) This case will review the lessee's and lessor's accounting procedures for a lease with a guaranteed residual value.

## Instructions

Refer to the facts of **Exercise 21-3** above. Assume there is no purchase option at the end of the lease term. Further, assume the asset reverts back to the lessor at the end of five years and the lessee guarantees the lessor a residual value of $2,000 at that date.

(a) Explain how the lessor's accounting procedures for a lease with a $2,000 guaranteed residual value will differ from the procedures for a lease containing a $2,000 bargain purchase option.

(b) Explain how the lessee's accounting procedures for a lease requiring the lessee to guarantee a residual value of $2,000 will differ from the procedures for a lease containing a $2,000 bargain purchase option.

## Solution to Case 21-1

(a) From the lessor's standpoint, there is no difference in the computations, time line, or journal entries if the $2,000 is a guaranteed residual value rather than a bargain purchase option. Thus, the **Solution to Exercise 21-3**, parts (a) through (c) would also hold for the $2,000 guaranteed residual value (refer to that solution, and every place you see "bargain purchase option" or "BPO" simply change that phrase to "guaranteed residual value" or "GRV").

(b) From the lessee's standpoint, the time line, journal entries, and most of the computations are the same for a lease containing a guaranteed residual value as those pertaining to a lease that contains a bargain purchase option. The major difference lies in the computation of depreciation:

- If the lease contains a **bargain purchase option,** the cost of the asset under capital lease (reduced by any residual value available to the lessee at the **end of the asset's economic life**) is depreciated over the **remaining economic life** of the asset.

- If the lease contains a **guaranteed residual value**, the cost of the asset under capital lease reduced by the guaranteed residual value at the **end of the lease term** is depreciated over the **lease term**.

Thus, using the data from **Exercise 21-3**, and assuming the lessee uses a 10% interest rate to account for the lease and the straight-line depreciation method, depreciation calculations for the lessee would be as follows:

**Assuming a bargain purchase option of $2,000:**

$$\frac{\$42,940.44 - 0^a}{7 \text{ years}} = \$6,134.35 \text{ depreciation per year for 7 years}$$

[a]Assumes a zero residual value at the end of seven years.

**Assuming a guaranteed residual value of $2,000:**

$$\frac{\$42,940.44 \ - \ \$2,000.00}{5 \ \text{years}} = \$8,188.09 \ \text{depreciation per year for 5 years}$$

> **TIP:** When the $2,000 is assumed to be a guaranteed residual value and the lessee uses the same interest rate as the lessor, the lessee's amortization schedule is the same as the lessor's amortization schedule.

## EXERCISE 21-4

**Purpose:** (L.O. 8, 9) This exercise will illustrate how to classify receivables and payables related to leases on the balance sheet.

The following amortization schedule is properly being used by a lessee and a lessor. The lease contains a bargain purchase option (BPO). Both the lessee and the lessor have a calendar-year reporting period.

| Date | Rent Plus BPO | 10% Interest | Reduction of Present Value | Present Value Balance |
|------|--------------|--------------|---------------------------|----------------------|
| 5/1/10 | | | | $ 42,940.44 |
| 5/1/10 | $ 10,000.00 | | $ 10,000.00 | 32,940.44 |
| 5/1/11 | 10,000.00 | $3,294.04 | 6,705.96 | 26,234.48 |
| 5/1/12 | 10,000.00 | 2,623.45 | 7,376.55 | 18,857.93 |
| 5/1/13 | 10,000.00 | 1,885.79 | 8,114.21 | 10,743.72 |
| 5/1/14 | 10,000.00 | 1,074.37 | 8,925.63 | 1,818.09 |
| 4/30/15 | 2,000.00 | 181.91 | 1,818.09 | -0- |
| | $ 52,000.00 | $9,059.56 | $ 42,940.44 | |

## Instructions
Fill in the blanks that follow. Show computations.

(1)   The amount to be reported in the current liability section of the lessee's balance sheet at December 31, 2011 by the caption "Interest Payable" is $_____.

(2)   The amount to be reported in the current liability section of the lessee's balance sheet at December 31, 2011 by the caption "Lease Liability" is $_____.

(3)   The amount to be reported in the long-term liability section of the lessee's balance sheet at December 31, 2011 by the caption "Lease Liability" is $_____.

(4)     The amount to be reported in the current asset section of the lessor's balance sheet at December 31, 2011 by the caption "Interest Receivable" is $_____.

(5)     The amount of net investment to be reported in the current asset section of the lessor's balance sheet at December 31, 2011 by the caption "Lease Receivable" is $_____.

(6)     The amount of net investment to be reported in the long-term investment section of the lessor's balance sheet at December 31, 2011 by the caption "Lease Receivable" is $_____.

## Solution to Exercise 21-4

| | | |
|---|---|---|
| (1)    Balance of obligation at May 1, 2011 | | $ 26,234.48 |
| Interest rate | | 10% |
| Interest for twelve months, 5/1/11 to 4/30/12 | 2,623.45 | |
| Fraction of year from 5/1/11 to 12/31/11 | | x    8/12 |
| Interest payable for 5/1/11 to 12/31/11, which is a current liability at 12/31/11 | | $  1,748.97 |

(2)     Current portion of Obligations under Capital Leases at 12/31/11        $ 7,376.55

The payment line that follows the balance sheet date (12/31/11) is 5/1/12. The principal portion of the rent payment due on that date ($7,376.55) represents the current portion of the lessee's obligation under capital lease [excluding any accrued interest computed in part (3)] at 12/31/11.

> **TIP:**   The interest portion of a rent payment is for a span of time, so it gets apportioned (allocated) between accounting periods; however, the principal portion of a rent payment falls in only one period and does **not** get allocated. Thus, the interest of $2,623.45 on the 5/1/12 payment line is to be expensed 8/12 in 2011 and 4/12 in 2012. The entire $7,376.55 principal payment appearing on the 5/1/12 rent line becomes due at a point in time and does not get apportioned.
>
> **TIP:**   In published financial statements, the amount of accrued interest payable [solution to part (1)] is often combined with the current portion of the remaining principal [solution to part (2)] and reported as a single line item in current liabilities.

(3)     Noncurrent portion of Obligations Under Capital Leases at 12/31/11        $18,857.93
(This figure is the present value balance on the 5/1/12 rent line.)

| | | |
|---|---|---|
| (4)    Balance of net investment in lease at May 1, 2011 | | $ 26,234.48 |
| Interest rate | | 10% |
| Interest for twelve months, 5/1/11 to 4/30/12 | 2,623.45 | |
| Fraction of year from 5/1/11 to 12/31/11 | | x    8/12 |
| Interest receivable for 5/1/11 to 12/31/11, which is a current asset at 12/31/11 | | $  1,748.97 |

(5)   Current portion of net investment in lease
      (Lease Receivable) at 12/31/11                                      $ 7,376.55

      The receipt line that follows the balance sheet date (12/31/11) is 5/1/12. The principal
      portion of the rent receipt due on that date ($7,376.55) represents the current portion of
      the lessor's net investment in lease [excluding any accrued interest computed in part (3)]
      at 12/31/11.

(6)   The noncurrent portion of the lessor's net investment in lease (Lease Receivable) at
      12/31/11                                                          $18,857.93
      (This figure is the present value balance on the 5/1/12 rent line.)


## ANALYSIS OF MULTIPLE-CHOICE TYPE QUESTIONS

**QUESTION**
1.   (L.O. 2) Max Wells Company leases an airplane from Bill Kennedy Corp. under an agreement
     which meets the criteria to be a capital lease for Max Wells. The ten-year lease requires payment
     of $34,000 at the beginning of each year, including $5,000 per year for maintenance, insurance,
     and taxes. The incremental borrowing rate for the lessee is 15%; the lessor's implicit rate is 12%
     and is known by the lessee. The present value of an annuity due of 1 for ten years at 15% is
     5.77158. The present value of an annuity due of 1 for ten years at 12% is 6.32825. According to
     the accounting guidelines for leases, the lessee should record the leased asset at:
a.   ($29,000) (5.77158) = $167,376.
b.   ($29,000) (6.32825) = $183,519.
c.   ($34,000) (5.77158) = $196,234.
d.   ($34,000) (6.32825) = $215,161.

**Approach and Explanation:** Think through the steps involved in accounting for a lease for a lessee (see
**Illustration 16-2**). Compute the present value of the minimum lease payments (excluding executory
costs). Use the lessee's incremental borrowing rate to do the discounting process, unless the lessor's
implicit rate is known and is lower. In this scenario, the $5,000 executory costs must be deducted from
the $34,000 to arrive at a $29,000 rent excluding executory costs. The lessor's implicit rate of 12% is
known by the lessee and is lower than 15%; therefore, the 12% is to be used to compute the present
value of the minimum lease payments. That present value figure is determined by multiplying the rent
(excluding executory costs) by the factor for present value of an annuity due of 1 for n = 10, i = 12%.
There is no indication that the asset's fair value may be lower than the computed present value amount;
therefore, the asset is to be recorded at the present value figure. (Solution = b.)


**QUESTION**
2.   (L.O. 2) The amount to be recorded as the cost of an asset under capital lease is equal to the:
     a.   present value of the minimum lease payments.
     b.   present value of the minimum lease payments or the fair value of the asset, whichever is
          lower.
     c.   present value of the minimum lease payments plus the present value of any unguaranteed
          residual value.
     d.   carrying value of the asset on the lessor's books.

**Explanation:** For a capital lease, the lessee records an asset and a liability at the lower of (1) the present value of the minimum lease payments or (2) the fair market value of the leased asset at the inception of the lease. An unguaranteed residual value is not relevant to the lessee; the lessee does not account for it. The lessor's carrying value is also irrelevant to the lessee. (Solution = b.)

## QUESTION

3.   (L.O. 2, 5) The following list of items relate to lease accounting:
I.        Annual lease payments
II.       Bargain purchase option
III.      Guaranteed residual value
IV.      Unguaranteed residual value

A lessor has a direct-financing type lease. Minimum lease payments associated with that lease would include items:
a.     I and II only.
b.     I, II, and III only.
c.     I, III, and IV only.
d.     I, II, III, and IV.

**Approach and Explanation:** Mentally list the components of minimum lease payments and compare with the list above. Minimum lease payments may include
- Periodic regular rental payments
- Guaranteed residual value (if any)
- Bargain purchase option (if any)
- Penalty for failure to renew

The minimum lease payments thus includes items I, I, and III only of the list in the stem of the question. (Solution = b.)

> **TIP:**   An unguaranteed residual will be involved in the lessor's accounting for the lease, but it is not part of minimum lease payments. For example, net investment in lease is comprised of the present value of the minimum lease payments plus the present value of any unguaranteed residual value.

## QUESTION

4.   (L.O. 2, 9) On December 31, 2009, Ryan Corporation leased a yacht from Sean Company for an eight-year period expiring December 30, 2017. Equal annual payments of $80,000 are due on December 31 of each year, beginning with December 31, 2009. The lease is properly classified as a capital lease on Ryan's books. The present value at December 31, 2009 of the eight lease payments over the lease term discounted at 10% is $469,474. Assuming all payments are made on time, the amount that should be reported by Ryan Corporation as the total obligation under capital leases on its December 31, 2010 balance sheet is:
a.     $348,421.
b.     $400,063.
c.     $436,421.
d.     $480,000.
e.     none of the above.

**Approach and Explanation:** Compute the information for the first three lines on the lessee's amortization schedule. The schedule will appear as follows: (Solution = a.)

| Date | Rent | Interest | Principal | Present Value Balance |
|------|------|----------|-----------|------------------------|
| 12/31/09 | | | | $469,474.00 |
| 12/31/09 | $80,000.00 | 0 | $80,000.00 | 389,474.00 |
| 12/31/10 | 80,000.00 | $38,947.40 | 41,052.60 | 348,421.40 |

**QUESTION**

5.(L.O. 2, 4) The following facts pertain to a single lease:
1.   A lease provides that the asset will revert back to the lessor at the end of its 7-year term.
2.   The present value of the minimum lease payments is equal to $54,000 and the fair value of the asset at the inception date is $60,000.
3.   The remaining economic life of the leased asset is estimated to be 10 years.
4.   Uncollectible lease payments are subject to a reasonable estimation.
5.   The lessor guarantees the asset against obsolescence.
6.   The fair value of the asset exceeds its cost on the lessor's books.

How should the lease be classified on the books of the lessee and lessor, respectively?

|   | **Lessee** | **Lessor** |
|---|------------|------------|
| a. | Capital | Sales-type |
| b. | Capital | Operating |
| c. | Operating | Sales-type |
| d. | Operating | Operating |

**Approach and Explanation:** Review the facts and determine how the lease should be classified on the books of the lessee. Repeat the process to determine how the lease should be classified on the books of the lessor. Refer to **Illustration 21-1**. The lease meets criterion 4 in Group I. Thus, it is a capital lease from the standpoint of the lessee because it meets at least one criterion in Group I. Because the lease does **not** meet **both** of the criteria in Group II, it is an operating lease from the standpoint of the lessor.

The significance of the facts given is as follows:
1.   The asset will be returned to the lessor at the end of the lease; therefore, the lease does not meet criterion 1 or 2 of Group I.

2.   The present value of the minimum lease payments ($54,000) is equal to 90% of the asset's fair value ($60,000) at the inception date; hence, the lease agreement meets criterion 4 in Group I.

3.   The term of the lease is 7 years, which is only 70% of the remaining economic life of the asset; hence, criterion 3 of Group I is not met.

4.   The lessor can reasonably estimate any uncollectible lease payments; therefore, criterion 1 of Group II is met by the lessor.

5.   The lessor guarantees the asset against obsolescence. This means that the costs of meeting this promise are indeterminable, which further means that an important uncertainty exists surrounding the amount of unreimbursable costs yet to be incurred by the lessor under the lease. Thus, criterion 2 of Group II is not met.

6.   The fair value of the asset (which usually establishes the lessor's initial amount of net investment in lease) exceeds the lessor's carrying value for the asset. This means that the lease would be a sales-type lease on the books of the lessor **if** the lease met one criterion from Group I and both criterion from Group II. (Solution = b.)

## QUESTION

6.(L.O. 2) Danzler Corporation is a lessee with a capital lease. The asset is recorded at $180,000 and has an economic life of 8 years. The lease term is 5 years. The asset is expected to have a market value of $60,000 at the end of 5 years, and a market value of $20,000 at the end of 8 years. The lease agreement provides for the automatic transfer of title of the asset to the lessee at the end of the lease term. What depreciable base and what service life should the lessee use to compute depreciation for the first year of the lease?

| | Depreciable Base | Service Life |
|---|---|---|
| a. | $180,000 - $20,000 | 5 years |
| b. | $180,000 - $20,000 | 8 years |
| c. | $180,000 - $60,000 | 5 years |
| d. | $180,000 - $60,000 | 8 years |

**Approach and Explanation:** Determine what will provide the best matching of costs with revenues. Because of the automatic transfer of title, the lessee is expected to hold and use the asset for eight years. The benefits to be consumed over the eight years are determined by the difference between the asset's recorded cost ($180,000) and its expected value at the end of its useful life to the lessee ($20,000). (Solution = b.)

## QUESTION

7.  (L.O. 2, 5, 7) Three different lease situations are described below:

1.  Lessee's incremental borrowing rate is 12%.
    Lessor's implicit rate is 12%.
    Asset will revert to the lessor at the end of the lease term when the
        asset is expected to have a fair value of $60,000.

2.  Lessee's incremental borrowing rate is 12%.
    Lessor's implicit rate is 12%.
    Lease requires lessee to guarantee a residual value of $30,000 to
        the lessor.

3.  Lessee's incremental borrowing rate is 12%.
    Lessor's implicit rate is 14%.
    Lease contains a bargain purchase option of $20,000.

In which of the above cases will the lessor and the lessee have the same amortization schedule?
a.  1 and 2 only.
b.  2 and 3 only.
c.  1 and 3 only.
d.  1, 2, and 3.
e.  None of the above.

**Approach and Explanation:** The lessee and lessor can use the same amortization schedule when both of the following two conditions exist: (1) the lessee and the lessor both use the same interest rate to account for the lease, and (2) the lessor does **not** have an unguaranteed residual value to account for. The lessee and the lessor have the same rate in case 1 and case 2. The lessee and the lessor will **not** use the same rate in case 3 because the lessee is to use the lower of the two rates, which in this case is **not** the lessor's implicit rate. Therefore, in case 3, the two parties cannot use the same amortization schedule. In case 1, the asset reverts to the lessor at the end of the lease term when the asset has a fair value of $60,000 which constitutes an unguaranteed residual value that will have to be reflected in the lessor's amortization schedule but will not affect the lessee's amortization schedule. Therefore, the two parties cannot use the same amortization schedule for case 1. Thus, case 2 is the only scenario listed in the question in which the two parties can use the same amortization schedule. (Solution = e.)

**QUESTION**

8. (L.O. 3) A lessee with a capital lease containing a bargain purchase option should depreciate the leased asset over the:
   a. asset's remaining economic life.
   b. term of the lease.
   c. life of the asset or the term of the lease, whichever is shorter.
   d. life of the asset or the term of the lease, whichever is longer.

**Explanation:** Depreciation is a cost allocation process which is done to comply with the matching principle—that is, to match expenses with revenues. The period appropriate for depreciation is the period of time the asset will be used in operations. If the lease agreement provides for automatic transfer of title of the asset to the lessee at the end of the lease term or for a bargain purchase option, the assumption is that the lessee will use the asset for its remaining economic life and, therefore, that is the span of time appropriate for depreciation. If the lease does **not** provide for automatic transfer of title of the asset or for a bargain purchase option, the assumption is that the lessee will use the asset only for the term of the lease and, therefore, the lease term is the appropriate period for depreciation. (Solution = a.)

> **TIP:** The cost of leasehold improvements (items such as fences and partitions added to leased premises by a lessee) are to be depreciated (amortized) over the life of the asset (the improvement) or the term of the lease, whichever is the longer.

**QUESTION**

9.(L.O. 5) A lessor has a direct financing type lease. The end of the lessor's accounting period does not coincide with a lease payment date. At the end of the lessor's accounting period, the journal entry to record interest earned since the last rental payment date would be:

| | | | |
|---|---|---|---|
| a. | Cash | XX | |
| | Interest Revenue | | XX |
| b. | Interest Receivable | XX | |
| | Interest Revenue | | XX |
| c. | Interest Revenue | XX | |
| | Interest Receivable | | XX |
| d. | Interest Expense | XX | |
| | Interest Payable | | XX |

**Explanation:** A lessor has interest earned but not received; it is recorded by an increase in a receivable account and an increase in a revenue account. (Solution = b.)

**QUESTION**

10. (L.O. 7) At the inception of a capital lease, a residual value guaranteed by a lessee should be included as part of minimum lease payments on the books of the:

| | Lessee | Lessor |
|---|---|---|
| a. | Yes | Yes |
| b. | Yes | No |
| c. | No | Yes |
| d. | No | No |

**Approach and Explanation:** List the components of minimum lease payments. They are: (a) regular periodic rental payments (excluding executory costs), (b) bargain purchase option, (c) guaranteed residual value, and (d) penalty for failure to renew. If the lessor has a guaranteed residual value, it is included in the lessor's computation of minimum lease payments, regardless of whether the lessee or a third party is the guarantor. The lessee includes a guaranteed residual value in its computation of minimum lease payments only if the lessee is the one providing the guarantee. (Solution = a.)

## QUESTION

11.   (L.O. 5) A lessor has an operating lease with a 5-year term that requires lease payments of $100,000 in 2010, $120,000 in 2011, $140,000 in 2012, $160,000 in 2013 and $180,000 in 2014. In 2012, compared to 2011, the lease will cause the following reported revenues to increase.

| | Rent | Interest |
|---|---|---|
| a. | Yes | Yes |
| b. | Yes | No |
| c. | No | Yes |
| d. | No | No |

**Explanation:** The amount of rent revenue recognized in each accounting period covered by the term of an operating lease is a level amount (straight-line basis) regardless of the lease provisions, unless another systematic and rational basis is more representative of the time pattern in which the benefit is derived from the leased asset. In this situation, an average amount of $140,000 would be recognized as rent revenue in each of the five years. Therefore, the amount of rent revenue is a constant amount. An operating lease has no interest associated with it. Thus, there is no increase in rent revenue or interest revenue from one year to another with an operating lease. (Solution = d.)

| **TIP:** | The journal entry to record the receipt of rent in 2010 would appear as follows: | | |
|---|---|---|---|
| | Cash............................................................ | 100,000 | |
| | Rent Receivable......................................... | 40,000 | |
| | Rent Revenue ..................................... | | 140,000 |

## QUESTION

12.   (L.O. 5) Tom Hanks Leasing Co. has an operating lease. Rents are a constant amount each year. Rent payments collected in 2010 that pertain to use of the leased asset in 2011 should be reported as:
a.   rent revenue in 2010.
b.   accrued rent on the December 31, 2010 balance sheet.
c.   unearned rent on the December 31, 2010 balance sheet.
d.   rent receivable on the December 31, 2010 balance sheet.

**Explanation:** Rent revenue received in advance represents a liability at the December 31, 2010 balance sheet date. Revenue received in advance is often called unearned rent revenue or deferred rent revenue. (Solution = c.)

| **TIP:** | For an operating lease, rents are recognized as revenue by the lessor on a straight-line basis over the lease term as they are earned. If the cash is not received in the period the revenue is earned, a deferral (or an accrual) type adjustment is required. The minimum lease payments are recognized as rental expense by the lessee on a **straight-line basis**, even if not payable on a straight-line basis. Thus, situations involving a lease bonus, scheduled rent increases, or free rent must conform to this guideline. For example: a lessee signs a five-year operating lease and receives ten months of free rent. The cost of the 50 (60 - 10 = 50) rental payments is to be divided by the 60-month lease term to determine the monthly rental expense. |
|---|---|

## QUESTION

13.   (L.O. 8) A lessor with a sales-type lease involving an unguaranteed residual value available to the lessor at the end of the lease term will report sales revenue in the period of inception of the lease at which of the following amounts?
a.   the minimum lease payments plus the unguaranteed residual value
b.   the present value of the minimum lease payments
c.   the cost of the asset to the lessor, less the present value of any unguaranteed residual value
d.   the present value of the minimum lease payments plus the present value of the unguaranteed residual value

**Explanation:** The unguaranteed residual value is viewed as pertaining to a portion of the asset that is not yet sold. Therefore, the sales revenue figure is the present value (today's cash equivalent) of all future cash flows expected to be received by the lessor for the leased asset **except** for the unguaranteed residual value. Therefore, sales revenue is computed by determining the present value of the minimum lease payments. Answer section "a" describes a gross investment calculation, answer selection "c" describes the lessor's cost of goods sold computation, and answer selection "d" describes the lessor's net investment in lease amount. (Solution = b.)

**QUESTION**

14.(L.O. 8) A lease has an 8-year term, and the related asset has a remaining economic life of 10 years. The lease is appropriately classified as a sales-type lease on the books of the lessor. The gross profit related to this lease should be:

a.      recognized wholly in the period of the inception of the lease.

b.      amortized evenly over 8 years.

c.      amortized evenly over 10 years.

d.      amortized over 8 years using the effective interest method of amortization.

**Explanation:** The gross profit related to a sales-type lease is recognized wholly in the period in which the lease's inception date occurs. The lessor's journal entry at the date of inception includes a credit to Sales Revenue (for the present value of the minimum lease payments) and a debit to Cost of Goods Sold (for the asset's carrying value less the present value of any unguaranteed residual value). When these two amounts are reported on the income statement, the resulting difference is the amount of gross profit earned on the lease. (Solution = a.)

**QUESTION**

15.(L.O. 11) Trim Corporation sold a greenhouse to Laventhall Company for $800,000 and realized a gain of $300,000. The buyer immediately leased the asset back to the seller under a capital lease arrangement for the remainder of the asset's economic life of ten years. The lessee uses the straight-line depreciation method. The profit on the sale of the greenhouse should be:

a.      recognized in full in the year of sale.

b.      deferred and amortized over the term of the lease.

c.      deferred and recognized in full at the end of the lease term.

d.      credited directly to retained earnings.

**Explanation:** Any profit or loss experienced by the seller-lessee from the sale of the assets that are leased back under a capital lease should be deferred and amortized over the lease term (or the asset's economic life if criterion 1 or 2 is satisfied) in proportion to the amortization of the leased assets. At a balance sheet date, the balance of the deferred gain is reported as an asset valuation allowance. (Solution = b.)

# CHAPTER 22

# ACCOUNTING CHANGES AND
# ERROR ANALYSIS

## OVERVIEW

In order to have **comparability** of financial statements for successive periods for an entity, the accountant must be consistent in the application of generally accepted accounting principles (**quality of consistency**). However, sometimes there is justification for a change. The accountant must then meet the requirements of **full disclosure** in reporting the change. Accounting changes are discussed in this chapter.

The accountant may be consistent in the application of accounting practices but may make some type of error (such as a math mistake or misapplication of generally accepted accounting principles). When the error is discovered, the effects must be properly reported. Error analysis is also discussed in this chapter.

## SUMMARY OF LEARNING OBJECTIVES

1.  **Identify the types of accounting changes.** The three different types of accounting changes are: (1) **Change in accounting principle:** a change from one generally accepted accounting principle to another generally accepted accounting principle. (2) **Change in accounting estimate:** a change that occurs as the result of new events or additional information or as more experience is acquired. (3) **Change in reporting entity:** a change from reporting as one type of entity to another type of entity.

2.  **Describe the accounting for a change in accounting principle.** A change in accounting principle involves a change from one generally accepted accounting principle to another generally accepted accounting principle. A change in accounting principle is not considered to result from the adoption of a new principle in recognition of events that have occurred for the first time or that were previously immaterial. If the accounting principle previously followed was not acceptable, or if the old principle was applied incorrectly, a change to a generally accepted accounting principle (or to the correct application of the accounting principle) is considered a correction of an error rather than an accounting change.

3.  **Understand how to account for retrospective accounting changes.** The general requirement for changes in accounting principle is retrospective application. Under retrospective application, companies change prior years' financial statements to be on a basis consistent with the newly adopted principle. They treat any part of the effect attributable to years prior to those presented as an adjustment of the earliest retained earnings presented.

4.  **Understand how to account for impracticable changes.** Retrospective application is impracticable if the prior period effect cannot be determined using every reasonable effort to do so. For example, in changing to LIFO, the base-year inventory for all subsequent LIFO calculations is generally the opening inventory in the year the company adopts the method. There is no restatement of prior years' income because it is often too impractical to do so.

5.    **Describe the accounting for changes in estimates.** Companies report changes in estimates prospectively. That is ,companies should make no changes in previously reported results. They do not adjust opening balances nor change financial statements of prior periods.

6.    **Identify and account for a change in a reporting entity.** An accounting change that results in financial statements that are actually the statements of a different entity should be reported by restating the financial statements of all prior periods presented to show the financial information for the new reporting entity for all periods.

7.    **Describe the accounting for a correction of an error.** A company must correct an error as soon as it discovers an error, by a proper entry in the accounts, and report it in the financial statements. The profession requires that a company treat a correction of an error in previously issued financial statements as a prior period adjustment, record it in the year in which the error was discovered, and report it in the financial statements as an adjustment (net of tax) to the beginning balance of retained earnings. If presenting comparative statements, a company should restate the prior period statements affected to correct for the error. The company need not repeat the disclosures in the financial statements of subsequent periods.

8.    **Identify economic motives for changing accounting principles (methods).** Managers might have varying motives for income reporting depending on economic times and whom they seek to impress. Some of the reasons of changing accounting methods are: (1) political costs, (2) capital structure, (3) bonus payments, and (4) smoothing of earnings.

9.    **Analyze the effect of errors.** Three types of errors can occur: (1) *Balance sheet errors* which affect only the asset, liability, or stockholders' equity accounts. (2) *Income statement errors* which affect only the presentation of revenue, expenses, gain, or loss accounts in the income statement. (3) *Balance sheet and income statement errors* which involve both balance sheet and income statement accounts. Errors affecting both balance sheet and income statement accounts are classified into two types: (a) *Counter-balancing errors* will be offset in the period that immediately follows the period in which the error first occurred. (b) *Noncounterbalancing errors* are **not** offset in the accounting period that immediately follows the period in which the error first occurred; they take longer than two periods to correct themselves.

*10.    **Make the computations and prepare the entries necessary to record a change from or to the equity method of accounting.** When changing *from* the equity method to the fair value method, the cost basis for accounting purposes is the carrying amount used for the investment at the date of change. The new method is applied in its entirety once the equity method is no longer appropriate. When changing *to* the equity method, a retroactive adjustment of the carrying amount, of results of current and past operations, and of retained earnings is necessary to restate the accounts as if the equity method had been in effect during all of the periods in which the investment was held. That is, the company adjusts the accounts to be on the same basis as if the equity method had always been used for that investment.
        *This material is covered in Appendix 22A in the text.

# TIPS ON CHAPTER TOPICS

**TIP:** Several items in this chapter are to be reported net of the related income tax effect. The quickest way to compute an amount net of tax is to apply a net-of-tax rate to the amount. The net-of-tax rate is determined by deducting the tax rate from 100%.

**TIP:** If an entity has an error correction, a change in accounting principle, and a change in an accounting estimate all in the same period, the items should be handled in the order in which they are mentioned in this sentence.

# ILLUSTRATION 22-1
# SUMMARY OF ACCOUNTING CHANGES AND ERROR CORRECTION AND REPORTING REQUIREMENTS (L.O. 3, 4, 5, 6, 7)

- **Change in accounting principle**
  Employ the retrospective approach by:
  a. Changing the financial statements of all prior periods presented.
  b. Disclosing in the year of the change the effect on net income and earnings per share for all prior periods presented.
  c. Reporting an adjustment to the beginning retained earnings balance in the retained earnings statement in the earliest year presented.
  If impracticable to determine the prior period effect (e.g., change to LIFO):
  a. Do not change prior years' income.
  b. Use opening inventory in the year the method is adopted as the base-year inventory for all subsequent LIFO computations.
  4. Disclose the effect of the change on the current year, and the reasons for omitting the computation of the cumulative effect and pro forma amounts for prior years.

- **Change in accounting estimate.**
  Employ the current prospective approach by:
  a. Reporting current and future financial statements on the new basis.
  b. Presenting prior period financial statements as previously reported.
  c. Making no adjustments to current-period opening balances for the effects in prior periods.

- **Change in reporting entity.**
  Employ the retrospective approach by:
  a. Recasting (adjusting) the financial statements of all prior periods presented.
  b. Disclosing in the year of change the effect on net income and earnings per share data for all prior periods presented.

- **Change due to error** *(error correction.)*
  Employ the restatement approach (treat as a prior period adjustment) by:
  a. Correcting all prior period statements presented.
  b. Restating the beginning balance of retained earnings for the first period presented when the error effects occur in a period prior to that one.

## ILLUSTRATION 22-1 (Continued)

A **change in accounting principle** occurs when there is a change from one generally acceptable accounting principle to another generally accepted accounting principle or a change in applying an acceptable accounting principle. In this context, an accounting method or policy constitutes an accounting principle. Therefore, a change from one generally acceptable inventory pricing method to another generally accepted inventory pricing method is a change in an accounting principle. A change from an accounting method that is **not** generally accepted to a method that is GAAP is **not** an accounting change—it is a correction of an error.

The term **accounting principle** includes not only accounting principles and practices but also the methods of applying them. Thus, a switch from the aggregate basis to the individual basis for determining the lower-of-cost-or-market valuation of inventory constitutes a change in accounting principle.

A **change in accounting estimate** occurs when an entity has a change from one good faith estimate to another good faith estimate. Accounting estimates change as new events occur, as more experience is acquired, or as additional information is obtained. A change in estimate results from new information or subsequent developments and **not** from oversights or misuse of facts. Companies should consider a careful estimate that later proves to be incorrect as a change in estimate.

**Errors** include mathematical mistakes, oversights, misapplications of accounting principles, and misuse of facts. A correction of an error in previously issued financial statements is not classified as an accounting change; it is a prior period adjustment.

Generally, a change in an accounting principle is to be accounted for **retrospectively.** A change in accounting estimate is to be accounted for **prospectively.** A correction of an error is to be accounted for **retroactively.** Refer to **Illustration 22-1** for a summary of the relevant reporting requirements.

Companies report prospectively a change in an accounting estimate. That is, previously reported results are **not** adjusted for a change in estimate. The effects of a change in estimate are accounted for in (1) the period of change if the change affects that period only (therefore, given current treatment) or (2) the period of change and future periods if the change affects both (in this case, it is said to be given prospective treatment). Changes in estimates are normal recurring corrections and adjustments, the natural result of the accounting process. Retrospective treatment is prohibited for a change in accounting estimate.

In some situations, it is difficult to differentiate between a change in accounting estimate and a change in accounting principle, such as in the case where a company changes from deferring and amortizing marketing costs to expensing them as incurred because future benefits of these costs have become doubtful. This is often referred to as a **change in estimate effected by a change in accounting principle;** it is to be accounted for as a change in estimate.

## ILLUSTRATION 22-1 (Continued)

When a company changes a depreciation method (or method of amortization or depletion), the change is based on changes in estimates about future benefits to be derived from long-lived assets. In such a case, it is not possible to separate the effect of the change in accounting principle (method) from the effect of the change in accounting estimate. Changes of that type often are related to the continuing process of obtaining additional information and revising estimates and, therefore, are considered changes in estimates for accounting purposes; they receive prospective treatment.

---

**TIP:** It is not always possible for companies to determine how they would have reported prior periods' financial information under retrospective application of an accounting principle change. In this case the company **prospectively applies** the new accounting principle as of the earliest date it is practicable to do so.

It is impracticable to apply the retrospective approach if one of the following conditions exists:
1. The company cannot determine the effects of retrospective application.
2. Retrospective application requires assumptions about management's intent in a prior period.
3. Retrospective application requires significant estimates for a prior period, and the company cannot objectively verify the necessary information to develop these estimates.

An example of a situation in which it is usually impracticable to apply the retrospective approach is the change from FIFO to LIFO. Determining prior-period effects of applying the new method would require subjective assumptions about the LIFO layers established in prior periods.

**TIP:** A change in accounting principle, a change in the reporting entity, and a correction of an error require an explanatory paragraph in the auditor's report discussing lack of consistency from one period to the next. A change in accounting estimate does not affect the auditor's opinion relative to consistency; however, if the change in estimate has a material effect on the financial statements, disclosure may still be required. Error correction not involving a change in accounting principle does not require disclosure relative to consistency.

**TIP:** The **retrospective application of a new accounting principle to a prior period is like the restatement of financial statements** for a prior period in that it involves making revisions within the previously prepared statements before they are republished in comparative statements. When restatement or recasting is appropriate, the accountant will restate or recast only those prior periods that are being published again for readers' use. For example, assume a company used LIFO from the company's inception in 2004 through 2009. In 2010, the company changes to FIFO. This change is to receive retrospective treatment. Thus, if at the end of 2010, the company presents income statements for 2008 and 2009 along with 2010 (comparative statements), the income statements previously published for 2008 and 2009 would be recast (that is, changed or revised) to reflect the individual amounts that would have been reported in the body of the statements in prior years if the new method (FIFO) had been used. The effect on the periods prior to the first year being republished (2004 through 2007 are the years prior to 2008 which is the earliest year being presented in the set of comparative reports) would be shown as an adjustment to the balance of Retained Earnings at the beginning of 2008 on the retained earnings statement for 2008 in the comparative retained earnings statement. Thus, computations related to this change involve data from six prior years (2004 through 2009), but only two prior years (2008 and 2009) are formally recast because they are the only years being presented in comparative financial statements. Recast financial statements reflect "as if" type amounts in the body of the statements.

## ILLUSTRATION 22-1 (Continued)

### KEY TERMS RELATED TO ACCOUNTING CHANGES

**ACCOUNTING CHANGE.** A change in (1) an accounting principle, (2) an accounting estimate, or (3) the reporting entity. The correction of an error in previously issued financial statements is not an accounting change.

**CHANGE IN ACCOUNTING PRINCIPLE.** A change from one generally accepted accounting principle to another generally accepted accounting principle when two or more generally accepted accounting principles apply or when the accounting principle formerly used is no longer generally accepted.

**CHANGE IN ACCOUNTING ESTIMATE.** A change that has the effect of adjusting the carrying amount of an existing asset or liability or altering the subsequent accounting for existing or future assets or liabilities. Changes in accounting estimates result from new information.

**CHANGE IN ACCOUNTING ESTIMATE EFFECTED BY A CHANGE IN ACCOUNTING PRINCIPLE.** A change in accounting estimate that is inseparable from the effect of a related change in accounting principle.

**CHANGE IN REPORTING ENTITY.** A change that results in financial statements that, in effect, are those of a different reporting entity.

**DIRECT EFFECTS OF A CHANGE IN ACCOUNTING PRINCIPLE.** Those recognized changes in assets or liabilities necessary to effect a change in accounting principle.

**ERROR IN PREVIOUSLY ISSUED FINANCIAL STATEMENTS.** An error in recognition, measurement, presentation, or disclosure in financial statements resulting from mathematical mistakes, mistakes in the application of GAAP, or oversight or misuse of facts that existed at the time the financial statements were prepared. A change from an accounting principle that is not generally accepted to one that is generally accepted is a correction of an error.

**INDIRECT EFFECTS OF A CHANGE IN ACCOUNTING PRINCIPLE.** Any changes to current or future cash flows of an entity that result from making a change in accounting principle that is applied retrospectively.

**RESTATEMENT.** The process of revising previously issued financial statements to reflect the correction of an error in those financial statements.

**RETROSPECTIVE APPLICATION.** The application of a different accounting principle to one or more previously issued financial statements, or to the statement of financial position at the beginning of the current period, as if that principle had always been used, or a change to financial statements of prior accounting periods to present the financial statements of a new reporting entity as if it had existed in those prior years.

## CASE 22-1

**Purpose:** (L.O. 1 thru 7) This case will provide examples of changes in accounting principles, changes in accounting estimates, and changes from nongenerally accepted methods to accepted methods (error corrections). It will also identify the proper accounting treatment for each.

The following is a list of changes.

## Instructions

For each item in the list:
(a)  Use the appropriate number to indicate if it is:
1.  A change in accounting principle.
2.  A change in reporting entity.
3.  A change in accounting estimate.
4.  An error correction.
5.  None of the above.
(b)  Use the appropriate letter to indicate if it is to be accounted for by the:
R.  Retrospective approach.
P.  Prospective approach.
T.  Restatement approach.
N.  None of the above.

(a)       (b)

_____ _____   1. Change in the estimated residual value used for computing depreciation of a plant asset.

_____ _____   2. Change in the composition of companies included in the consolidated financial statements.

_____ _____   3. Change from completed-contract to percentage-of-completion method in accounting for long-term construction contracts.

_____ _____   4. Change from straight-line to double-declining-balance depreciation method for all assets held.

_____ _____   5. Change from sum-of-the-years'-digits depreciation method to straight-line method for all assets held.

_____ _____   6. Change to straight-line depreciation method for all new assets acquired; 150% declining-balance method will continue to be used for all assets acquired in prior years.

_____ _____   7. Change from double-declining-balance method to straight-line depreciation method; this change was not planned when the asset was acquired and the accelerated method was adopted.

(a)      (b)

_____  _____    8. Change in the total periods used for amortization of an intangible asset.

_____  _____    9. Change from the FIFO cost method to the average cost method for inventory pricing.

_____  _____    10. Change from LIFO to the average cost inventory pricing (cost) method.

_____  _____    11. Change from FIFO to LIFO inventory cost method.

_____  _____    12. Change from LIFO to FIFO for inventory pricing.

_____  _____    13. Change to or from the full cost method as used in the extractive industries.

_____  _____    14. Change from the cash basis to the accrual basis of accounting.

_____  _____    15. Change from the direct write-off method to the allowance method to account for bad debts where bad debts have always been (and continue to be) a material amount.

_____  _____    16. Change from the direct write-off method to the allowance method to account for uncollectible accounts where bad debts have just become a material amount in the current period.

_____  _____    17. Change from direct costing to full absorption costing for a manufacturing company.

_____  _____    18. Change from pay-as-you-go to accrual basis in accounting for pension costs.

_____  _____    19. Change from the installment basis to the accrual basis in accounting for installment sales where uncollectible accounts have always been subject to a reasonable estimation.

_____  _____    20. Change from expensing interest incurred during the construction of a new plant to capitalizing interest incurred during construction.

_____  _____    21. Change in the interest rate used to compute pension expense.

_____  _____    22. Change from capitalizing R & D costs to expensing R & D costs in the period incurred.

_____  _____    23. Adoption of a new accounting method because this is the first time a new type of transaction has occurred.

(a)    (b)

_____ _____ 24. Change from double-declining-balance method to straight-line depreciation method at the midpoint of the asset's life; this change was planned at the time the asset was acquired (and the accelerated depreciation method was adopted) to fully depreciate the cost over the estimated life of the asset.

_____ _____ 25. Change from deferring and amortizing preproduction costs to recording such costs as an expense when incurred because future benefits of the costs have become doubtful.

## Solution to Case 22-1

| Answers | | | Explanation and/or Comment |
|---|---|---|---|
| (a) | (b) | | |
| 3 | P | 1. | |
| 2 | R | 2. | |
| 1 | R | 3. | |
| 3 | P | 4. | A change in accounting estimate effected by a change in accounting principle. |
| 3 | P | 5. | A change in accounting estimate effected by a change in accounting principle. The new method is adopted in partial or complete recognition of a change in the estimated future benefits inherent in the asset, the pattern of consumption of these benefits, or the information available to the entity about those benefits. |
| 5 | N | 6. | Only footnote disclosure is required. New method is used only for new assets. |
| 3 | P | 7. | Assume the change is for all assets held. A change in accounting estimate effected by a change in accounting principle. |
| 3 | P | 8. | |
| 1 | R | 9. | |
| 1 | R | 10. | |
| 1 | R | 11. | The cumulative effect on prior periods and the period-specific effects of this change are generally not determinable; disclose that fact. This is an example of a change in accounting principle where retrospective treatment is usually impracticable. |
| or 1 | N | | |
| 1 | R | 12. | |
| 1 | R | 13. | |
| 4 | T | 14. | The cash basis of accounting is not GAAP. |
| 4 | T | 15. | The direct write-off method is not GAAP where bad debts are a material amount. |
| 5 | N | 16. | Treat like an initial adoption. The initial adoption of an accounting principle is not a change; neither is the adoption or modification of a method due to a substantive change in the kinds of transactions or events being recorded. |

| Answers | | | Explanation and/or Comment |
|---|---|---|---|
| (a) | (b) | | |
| 4 | T | 17. | Direct costing is not GAAP. (The direct costing method is often called variable costing method.) The prime costing and direct costing methods are not generally accepted accounting methods because they treat some elements of manufacturing costs as period costs rather than as product costs. Only the full absorption costing method is GAAP; it assigns all manufacturing costs to inventory. |
| 4 | T | 18. | The pay-as-you-go approach is not GAAP. |
| 4 | T | 19. | The installment basis is not GAAP unless you cannot reasonably estimate uncollectibles. |
| 4 | T | 20. | *SFAS No. 34* requires the capitalization of interest incurred during construction. |
| 3 | P | 21. | Assume both old and new rates are good faith estimates. |
| 4 | T | 22. | In general, *SFAS No. 2* requires that R & D costs be expensed in the period incurred. |
| 5 | N | 23. | The initial adoption of a method is not an accounting change. |
| 5 | N | 24. | This is not an accounting change; rather, the method used is a hybrid or combination method. |
| 3 | P | 25. | A change in estimate effected by a change in accounting principle. |

**Explanation and Approach:** First determine the nature of the change. Then determine how to treat that change. Notice how the answer to part (a) automatically determines the solution to part (b). A change in an accounting principle or a change in the reporting entity is to be accorded the retrospective approach (unless it is impracticable to do so). A change in an accounting estimate is accounted for prospectively. A correction of an error is accounted for by restatement of prior periods. Therefore, an answer of 1 to (a) means a response of R for part (b), an answer of 2 to (a) means a response of R for part (b), an answer of 3 for part (a) calls for an answer of P for part (b), and an answer of 4 to (a) calls for an answer of T for part (b).

# ILLUSTRATION 22-2
# HOW TO COMPUTE, RECORD, AND REPORT THE EFFECTS OF A CHANGE IN ACCOUNTING PRINCIPLE (L.O. 3)

A. Compute the effect of a change in accounting method (principle) on income of periods prior to the change and record it as follows:

1. Determine the effect of the change on retained earnings as of the beginning of the period of change as follows:
   (a) Identify the revenue and/or expense item(s) and amounts that were affected in the prior periods by use of the old method.
   (b) Compute what the amount of those revenue and/or expense item(s) would have been in the prior periods if the new method was used in all periods. Also consider the effect on the amount of taxes reported.
   (c) Compare the amounts in (a) above with those in (b) above. The net difference is the effect of the change on income of prior periods (net of tax effect).

2. Record the cumulative effect of the change on prior periods as follows:
   (a) Determine if the adjustment for the effect on prior periods is a debit or a credit and adjust Retained Earnings.
       (1) If use of the new method would have resulted in higher net incomes in prior years, the adjustment needed is a credit to Retained Earnings.
       (2) If use of the new method would have resulted in lower net incomes in prior years, the adjustment needed is a debit to Retained Earnings.
   (b) Record the rest of the entry so that asset and liability account balances are restated to balances that would have existed at the beginning of the period of change had the new method been used in all prior periods.

B. Report the change in accounting principle in comparative financial statements through retrospective application of the new accounting principle to all prior periods. Retrospective application requires the following:

1. The cumulative effect of the change (to the new accounting principle) on periods prior to those presented shall be reflected in the carrying amounts of assets and liabilities as of the beginning of the first period presented.
2. An offsetting adjustment, if any, shall be made to the opening balance of retained earnings for that first period presented.
3. Financial statements for each individual prior period presented shall be adjusted to reflect the period-specific effects of applying the new accounting principle.

C. Compute the effect of a change in accounting method on the income of the **current** period (period of change) and report it as follows:

1. Identify the amount of revenue and/or expense on the income statement for the current period computed as a result of the use of the new method.
2. Compute what the amount of the particular revenue and/or expense item would be in the current period if the old method was used.
3. Compare the amount(s) in "1" above with the amount(s) in "2" above. The net difference is the effect on the period of change.

> **TIP:** The effect on the period of change does **not** include the cumulative effect on prior periods.

4. Disclose the effect on the period of change (net of tax effect) in the notes to the financial statements of the period of change.

> **TIP:** The mechanics of the restatement approach used for correction of an error is essentially the same as parts (A) and (B) above. With both the retrospective and restatement approaches, prior period financial statements are recast (adjusted) when they are republished in the current period for comparative purposes, and a catch-up adjustment is recorded to Retained Earnings.

## EXERCISE 22-1

**Purpose:** (L.O. 3) This exercise provides an example of the accounting procedures for a change in accounting principle and the retrospective approach.

The Buildaway Construction Company enters into long-term construction contracts. The following data relate to gross profit figures determined first, by use of the completed-contract method, and second, by use of the percentage-of-completion method for Years 1 through 4:

|  | **Pre-Tax Income from Use of** | | |
|---|---|---|---|
|  | **Completed-Contract** | **Percentage-of-Completion** | **Difference** |
| Year 1 $ 40,000 | $140,000 | $100,000 | |
| Year 2  160,000 | 280,000 | | 120,000 |
| Year 3  270,000 | 350,000 | | 80,000 |
| Year 4 | 360,000 | 490,000 | 130,000 |

The company used the completed-contract method in Years 1 thru 3 for both book purposes and tax purposes. In Year 4, the company changed to the percentage-of-completion method for book purposes only. The tax rate is 40% for all years.

## Instructions
(a) Indicate the amount of net income that should be reported in Year 4.
(b) Compute the effect of the change on periods prior to the change.
(c) Prepare the journal entry to record the accounting change in Year 4.
(d) Compute the effect of the change on the year of change.
(e) Assuming that in Year 4 comparative financial statements are prepared that include Years 3 and 4, explain whether financial statements of Year 3 are to be adjusted to reflect the period—specific effects of applying the new method. How are the effects on Years 1 and 2 to be reflected?

## Solution to Exercise 22-1

(a)  $294,000   Net income for Year 4

**Explanation:**
$490,000   Income before tax using percentage-of-completion method.
   60%   Net of tax rate (100% - tax rate of 40%)
$294,000

(b)     Total gross profit for Years 1, 2 and 3 using the new method     $770,000[1]
Total gross profit for Years 1, 2 and 3 using the old method   <u>470,000[2]</u>
Cumulative (total) effect on prior periods     300,000
Net-of-tax rate     <u>60%</u>
Cumulative effect on prior periods, net of tax     <u>$180,000</u>

    [1]$140,000 Year 1 + $280,000 Year 2 + $350,000 Year 3 = $770,000
    [2]$40,000 Year 1 + $160,000 Year 2 + $270,000 Year 3 = $470,000

(c)     Construction in Process .......................................................     300,000
    Deferred Tax Liability ($300,000 x 40%)............................     120,000
    Retained Earnings...............................................................     180,000

> **TIP:**   Follow the guidelines in **Illustration 22-2** in performing the computations and selecting the accounts involved in this journal entry.
>
> **TIP:**   The new method would have resulted in reporting higher net incomes if it had been used in prior periods; thus, the adjustment required to record the cumulative effect is a credit. Retrospective treatment is appropriate in this case; hence, the Retained Earnings account is used to record the catch-up adjustment for the impact on retained earnings of the change in accounting principle. If the new method had been used for book purposes in all prior periods, the Retained Earnings account would have been greater at the beginning of Year 4 by $180,000, the asset account maintained for the costs incurred and profit recognized on contracts would have been greater by $300,000, and deferred taxes would have been greater by $120,000.

(d)     Gross profit for Year 4 using the new method     $ 490,000
Gross profit for Year 4 using the old method     <u>360,000</u>
Increase in income before income taxes for Year 4     130,000
Net-of-tax rate     <u>60%</u>
Increase in net income for Year 4     <u>$ 78,000</u>

(e)     Yes, the financial statements are to be recast (adjusted) for all prior years presented (Year 3 in this case). A change in the method employed to account for long-term construction contracts constitutes a change in accounting principle; therefore, it is to receive retrospective treatment. Retrospective treatment requires: (1) recast the financial statements for each prior period presented to reflect the period-specific effects of applying the new accounting principle, and (2) record the total (cumulative) effect on prior periods as an adjustment directly to the Retained Earnings account; also, adjust asset and liability accounts to balances that would have been in those accounts if the new method had been used in all prior periods. The effects of the change on income of years prior to the years presented in this set of financial statements (Years 1 and 2 in this case) are to be reported as an adjustment to the beginning balance of retained earnings (as previously reported) on the retained earnings statement for the earliest period presented (Year 3 in this case). Thus, the net of tax effect on years prior to Year 3 (60% [($140,000 + $280,000) − ($40,000 + $160,000)] = $132,000 credit) would be shown as an addition to the beginning balance of retained earnings (as previously reported) on the retained earnings statement for Year 3 when it is presented in Year 4 in comparative financial statements.

## EXERCISE 22-2

**Purpose:**   (L. O. 3) This exercise provides an example of a change in accounting principle.

Pecota & Johnson Company began operations on January 1, 2008, and has used the FIFO cost method to price inventory since operations began. During 2011, management has indicated a desire to change to the LIFO inventory method. The following information is available for the years 2008-2010.

|  | **Net Income Computed Using:** | | |
|---|---|---|---|
|  | **FIFO Method** | **LIFO Method** | **Difference** |
| 2008 | $ 95,000 | $60,000 | $  35,000 |
| 2009 | 115,000 | 70,000 | 45,000 |
| 2010 | 125,000 | 85,000 | 40,000 |
|  |  |  | $120,000 |

## Instructions:
(Ignore all tax effects.)

(a)   Prepare the journal entry to record a change from the FIFO cost method to the LIFO cost method in 2011.
(b)   Assuming that the financial statements for 2011 include 2009 and 2010 for comparative purposes, determine the net income to be reported for the two prior years.
(c)   Indicate how to report the effect of the change on the year(s) prior to those presented on the comparative statements.

## SOLUTION TO EXERCISE 22-2

(a)   Retained Earnings............................................   120,000
         Inventory ...............................................          120,000

Inventory would have been less under the new method (LIFO); thus a credit to Inventory. Net incomes of the past would have been less under the use of the new method; thus, a debit to Retained Earnings is made to reduce Retained Earnings to the balance it would have had at the beginning of the year of change (2008) had the new method (LIFO) been used in all prior periods.

(b)   The statements of prior years are to be recast for a change in accounting principle; thus, the net income to show on the 2009 income statement is $70,000 and the net income to be reported for 2010 is $85,000 when these years are shown again in 2011 for comparative reports.

(c)   The effect of the change on periods prior to those presented (2008 is the only period prior to 2009 in this case) is $35,000 and should be shown as a subtraction from the opening balance of retained earnings on the retained earnings statement for 2009 when it is presented again in 2011 for comparative purposes. (The debit occurs because the new method would have given **less** income in the past than the old method.)

## ILLUSTRATION 22-3
## ACCOUNTING FOR A CHANGE IN ESTIMATE FOR A PLANT ASSET (L.O. 6)

Whenever there is a change in the estimate of service life or salvage value for a depreciable asset, the following format will aid in the computation of depreciation.

```
    Original Cost
-   Accumulated Depreciationᵃ
=   Book Value
+   Additional Expenditures Capitalized, If Anyᵇ
=   Revised Book Value
-   Current Estimate of Residual Value
=   Remaining Depreciable Cost to be Allocated Over Remaining Life of Asset
```

ᵃTotal depreciation taken prior to beginning of the year of change.

ᵇSometimes an extension of life is obtained by a major overhaul or other expenditure capitalized subsequent to the acquisition of the original asset.

> **TIP:**    If a change in estimate occurs during 2010, it does not matter whether the change occurs at the beginning or at the end of the year because the entry for depreciation is not made until the end of the year; that entry should reflect the change as if it occurred at the very beginning of the year of change.

## EXERCISE 22-3

**Purpose:**    (L.O. 5) This exercise will illustrate the following for a change in accounting estimate effected by a change in accounting principle.

The Spencer Corp. used the sum-of-the-years'-digits method for the first three years for both book and tax purposes to compute depreciation for its equipment. During the fourth year, the company changed to the straight-line method for book purposes for all assets held. The following facts pertain:

| | |
|---|---|
| Cost of equipment | $70,000 |
| Date acquired | January 1, Year 1 |
| Estimated service life | 10 years |
| Residual value | $15,000 |
| Tax rate | 40% |

## Instructions
(a)    Prepare the journal entry to record the accounting change.
(b)    Compute the depreciation expense for Year 4 and prepare the appropriate adjusting entry.

## Solution to Exercise 22-3

(a)   There is no catch-up adjustment (no cumulative effect on prior periods) to record because this situation (a change in accounting estimate effected by a change in accounting principle) is accounted for as a change in accounting estimate; thus, it is handled prospectively.

(b)   Depreciation Expense ...........................   6,142.86
            Accumulated Depreciation ...........                               6,142.86

Computations:

| | | |
|---|---|---|
| Asset cost | $70,000 | |
| Accumulated Depreciation | (27,000) | (See below) |
| Book Value | $43,000 | |
| Divided by remaining life | 7 years | |
| Depreciation for each remaining year | $6,142.86 | |

Accumulated Depreciation at the beginning of Year 4 is determined as follows:

| | Depreciation Using OLD (SYD) Method |
|---|---|
| Year 1 | $10,000[a] |
| Year 2 | 9,000[b] |
| Year 3 | 8,000[c] |
| | $27,000 |

[a]   $\dfrac{10}{\dfrac{10(10 + 1)}{2}}$ X ($70,000 - $15,000) = $10,000

[b]   $\dfrac{9}{\dfrac{10(10 + 1)}{2}}$ X ($70,000 - $15,000) = $9,000

[c]   $\dfrac{8}{\dfrac{10(10 + 1)}{2}}$ X ($70,000 - $15,000) = $8,000

---

**TIP:**   Take a few minutes to refresh your memory by reviewing the guidelines for computing depreciation using various methods. A quick review of the material in **Chapter 11** of your *Problem Solving Survival Guide* will enhance your recall of that subject and will improve your success rate on exam questions over this chapter.

## EXERCISE 22-4

**Purpose:**   (L.O. 5) This exercise will illustrate the proper accounting procedures for a change in an accounting estimate.

Mitzer Corporation acquired a plant asset costing $300,000 at the beginning of Year 1. After depreciating it for four years using the straight-line method, a ten-year service life and an expected residual value of $30,000, Mitzer estimated the asset would be useful for a total of twelve years and have a residual value of $20,000. The tax rate is 40% for all years.

## Instructions
(a)   Compute the depreciation expense to report for Year 5. Prepare the appropriate journal entry to record it.
(b)   Prepare the journal entry, if any, to record the accounting change. Also, explain the type of treatment to give this situation.
(c)   Compute the effect of the change on the year of change. Explain where it is to be reported.

## Solution to Exercise 22-4

(a)   **Approach:** Apply the format outlined in **Illustration 22-3** to compute depreciation where there has been a change in the estimate of service life and/or the estimate of salvage value for plant assets.

| | | |
|---|---:|---:|
| Original cost | | $ 300,000 |
| Accumulated depreciation | | (108,000)* |
| Book value, beginning Year 5 | 192,000 | |
| Additional costs capitalized | | -0- |
| Revised book value | | 192,000 |
| Current estimate of residual value | | (20,000) |
| Remaining depreciable cost | | 172,000 |
| Divide by the remaining life | | ÷      8** |
| Depreciation per year for Year 5 and subsequent years | | $   21,500 |

$$\frac{*\$300,000 \ - \ \$30,000}{10 \ \text{years}} = \$27,000 \text{ per year using old estimates}$$

   $27,000 x 4 years = $108,000

   **12 years total - 4 years gone = 8 years remaining

**Entry:**

Depreciation Expense.................................................................21,500
        Accumulated Depreciation ...................................................              21,500

> **TIP:**   An accounting change is always made as of the beginning of the year of change, even though it is not recorded until the end of the period of change.

(b)     **No entry.** There is no journal entry to record this change because a change in estimate is to receive prospective treatment. Therefore, there is no computation of the total effect on prior periods; there is no entry for the effect on prior periods. The total effect on the past is, in this case, spread over the current (Year 5) and future periods (Years 6 through 12).

(c)     Depreciation to be reported for Year 5 (part a)          $ 21,500
Depreciation for Year 5 if old estimate were used               27,000
Increase in income before income taxes for Year 5                5,500
Net-of-tax rate                                                     60%
Increase in net income for Year 5                               $  3,300

The $3,300 effect on the current year is to be disclosed in the footnotes.

## ILLUSTRATION 22-4
## COMMON RELATIONSHIPS AND ASSUMPTIONS INHERENT IN ERROR SITUATIONS (L.O. 7)

1.     An accrued expense that is **not** recorded at the end of one period is assumed to have been paid (and recorded as expense) in the following period.

2.     An accrued revenue that is **not** recorded at the end of one period is assumed to have been received (and recorded as revenue) in the following period.

3.     A prepaid expense that is omitted in Year 1 is assumed to have been recorded as expense in Year 1 when the cash was disbursed. Unless otherwise indicated, it is assumed to have become an expired cost in Year 2 (although not correctly recorded as such, due to the omission of the prepaid item at the end of Year 1).

4.     An unearned revenue that is omitted in Year 1 is assumed to have been recorded as revenue in Year 1 when the cash was received. Unless otherwise indicated, it is assumed to have become earned in Year 2 (although not correctly recorded as such, due to the omission of the unearned item at the end of Year 1).

5.     The ending inventory of one period is the beginning inventory of the following period.

6.     If purchases of inventory which are made near the end of Year 1 are not recorded and the merchandise is also omitted from the ending inventory for Year 1, there is no net effect on net income of Year 1 or Year 2.

7.     If the depreciation expense for Year 1 is omitted in Year 1, the depreciation expense for Year 2 is assumed to be recorded correctly in Year 2 (but only for the amount belonging in Year 2) unless otherwise mentioned.

**TIP:**    Most errors are **counterbalancing**. Therefore, if a counterbalancing error causes an understatement of net income in one period, the same error will cause an overstatement of net income in the immediately following period by the same amount. This type of error will effect two income statements and one balance sheet (the balance sheet at the end of the period in which the error occurred). The balance sheet at the end of the following period will not be affected as the error will have "offset" itself or counterbalanced by that date.

**TIP:**    Errors that are not counterbalancing will affect two or more income statements and two or more balance sheets. The error will "wash out" at some point in time, although it may take many years to do so. Conceivably, some may not "reverse" until a particular asset is disposed of, maybe at the point where a business ceases to exist. In the context of error analysis, the terms "offset," "reverse," "self-correct," and "wash out" are synonymous.

**TIP:**    If an error causes an **understatement** in revenue, it will cause an **understatement** of net income for that same year; however, if an error causes an **understatement** of expense, it will cause an **overstatement** of net income for that same year.

**TIP:**    All the error situations discussed in this chapter maintain balance in the basic accounting equation (often called the balance sheet equation). Thus, when you analyze the effects of these errors, always make sure your analysis maintains balance in the balance sheet equation (A = L + OE).

**TIP:**    Most of the errors illustrated in this chapter are the result of using the cash basis of accounting rather than the accrual basis of accounting.

## ILLUSTRATION 22-5
## GUIDE FOR PREPARING CORRECTING ENTRIES FOR ERRORS (L.O. 7)

**SHORT METHOD**

**Step 1:**    Adjust any current revenue and/or expense (or gain or loss) account affected by the error.

**Step 2:**    Adjust any asset and/or liability account to its proper balance, if needed.

**Step 3:**    Adjust revenue and/or expense items of prior periods by an entry to retained earnings.

**OR**

**LONG METHOD**

**Step 1:**    Reconstruct the erroneous entry that was actually made (sometimes no entry was made).

**Step 2:**    Reconstruct the entry that should have been made. Analyze it to determine the effects (what was understated, overstated, etc.). Remember: A = L + OE.

**Step 3:**    Make a correcting entry to bring accounts to the balances that should be shown at a current point in time. You can do so by "reversing" the entry that was made and by recording the entry that should have been made and by doing three additional steps:

   **Step 3(a):**    If any revenue or expense accounts of prior periods are involved, cross them out and replace them with Retained Earnings.

   **Step 3(b):**    Clean up the entry by combining like items.

   **Step 3(c):**    Make an adjusting entry for the current year, if necessary.

## EXERCISE 22-5

**Purpose:**    (L.O. 7) This exercise will provide examples of errors, their effects on net income, and their effects on the balance sheet.

The Kennedy Corporation discovered errors during a recent audit. The company has a calendar-year reporting period. The errors are as follows:

*Error 1*    Accrued interest on notes payable of $3,500 was omitted at the end of 2009.

*Error 2*    Prepaid insurance expense of $1,800 was overlooked at the end of 2009. (The premium paid in advance relates to coverage in 2010.)

*Error 3*    Accrued interest on investments of $5,100 was understated at the end of 2009.

*Error 4*    Unearned rent revenue of $4,500 was understated at the end of 2009.

*Error 5*    A truck with a cost of $10,000, a service life of four years, and a residual value of $4,000 was expensed when it was purchased at the beginning of 2009.

*Error 6*    Amortization of patent, $700, was omitted in 2009.

## Instructions

(a)   Assuming net income of $50,000 was reported for 2009, and net income of $72,000 was reported for 2010 (before discovery of the errors), compute the correct net income figures for 2009 and 2010.

(b)   For each error, describe the following:

1.   Effect on net income for 2009.

2.   Effect on the elements of the basic accounting equation at December 31, 2009.

3.   Effect on net income for 2010.

4.   Effect on the elements of the basic accounting equation at December 31, 2010.

(c)   Prepare the correcting entry for each error, assuming the errors are discovered at the end of 2010 before closing.

## Solution to Exercise 22-5

(a)

|  | | **2009** | **2010** |
|---|---|---|---|
| Net income as previously reported | $ 50,000 | $ 72,000 | |
| Failure to accrue interest expense in 2009 | (3,500) | 3,500 | |
| Failure to defer insurance expense in 2009 | 1,800 | (1,800) | |
| Failure to accrue interest revenue in 2009 | 5,100 | (5,100) | |
| Failure to defer rent revenue in 2009 | (4,500) | 4,500 | |
| Failure to capitalize truck in 2009 and depreciate | 8,500 | (1,500) | |
| Failure to amortize a patent in 2009 | (700) | 0 | |
| Net income, as corrected | $ 56,700 | $ 71,600 | |

> **TIP:**   To correct a net income figure that is understated, add the amount in error; to correct a net income figure that is overstated, deduct the amount in error.

(b) and (c)      The solution and explanation for each error is presented below:

> **TIP:**   Notice how the analysis of the effects of each error maintains balance in the basic accounting equation (A = L + OE).
>
> **TIP:**   When you are asked to describe the effects of an error, you are to describe the effects on all periods affected, assuming the error is allowed to run its course. Do not assume the error is corrected. To assume correction would mean there are no effects remaining.

**Approach to part (b):** Reconstruct what was done. Compare that with what should have been done. The effects of the error should then be readily determinable.

**Approach to part (c):** Follow the three easy steps in the "short method" in **Illustration 22-5** to prepare the correcting entries. Refer to the Explanation to part (b) of the Solution to analyze what corrections are needed.

## ERROR 1

(b) **Effects of Error 1:** Failure to accrue interest expense in 2009:

1. Net income for 2009 is overstated (because interest expense is understated).
2. Liabilities are understated, and owners' equity is overstated at 12/31/09.
3. Net income for 2010 is understated (because interest expense is overstated).
4. There is no effect on the balance sheet at 12/31/10.

> **TIP:** All income statement accounts are closed to owners' equity; therefore, if net income is affected in the year that an error originates, owners' equity is misstated in the same direction and by the same amount as net income.

**Explanation:**

| | *What Was Done* | | *What Should Have Been Done* | | |
|---|---|---|---|---|---|
| 12/31/09 | No Entry | | Interest Expense | 3,500 | |
| | | | Int. Payable | | 3,500 |
| | | | | | |
| During | Int. Expense | 3,500 | Interest Payable | 3,500 | |
| 2010 | Cash | 3,500 | Cash | | 3,500 |

An adjusting entry to record an accrued interest expense of $3,500 was omitted in 2009. The interest would, therefore, have been paid and recorded as an expense in 2010. The disbursement in 2010 should have been recorded as a reduction in a liability, but the liability was never reflected on the books.

> **TIP:** This is an example of a counterbalancing error. Therefore, two successive income statements and the balance sheet in between them are affected. The balance sheet at the end of the second period is unaffected because by that time the error has counterbalanced (or washed out).

(c) **Correcting entry for Error 1 at 12/31/10 before closing:**

Retained Earnings .................................................................3,500
    Interest Expense ...............................................................         3,500

**Error 1: Explanation for entry:**

*Step 1:*    Interest Expense in 2010 will be overstated unless a correcting entry is made; Interest Expense for 2010 is reduced by a credit.

*Step 2:*    No assets or liabilities are affected at 12/31/10.

*Step 3:*    Interest Expense for 2009 was understated. The Interest Expense for 2009 cannot be debited because all income statement amounts for 2009 have been closed to Retained Earnings. Therefore, debit Retained Earnings to correct for the error.

## ERROR 2

(b) **Effects of Error 2:** Failure to defer insurance expense in 2009:

1. Net income for 2009 is understated (because insurance expense is overstated).
2. Assets are understated, and owners' equity is understated at 12/31/09.
3. Net income for 2010 is overstated (because insurance expense is understated).
4. There is no effect on the balance sheet at 12/31/10.

**Explanation:**

| | *What Was Done* | *What Should Have Been Done* |
|---|---|---|
| 12/31/09 | No Entry | Prepaid Insurance   1,800 |
| | | Ins. Expense              1,800 |
| | | |
| 12/31/10 | No Entry | Insurance Expense   1,800 |
| | | Prepaid Ins.              1,800 |

In 2009, insurance premiums for 2010 were paid in advance. The payment must have been recorded by a charge to expense. An adjusting entry at the end of 2009 to record the deferral of a portion of the expense to a future period (2010) was omitted. The omission of that adjustment caused the failure to record any expense in 2010, even though some benefits were consumed in 2010.

**(c)     Correcting entry for Error 2 at 12/31/10 before closing:**

| | | |
|---|---|---|
| Insurance Expense | ...........................................................................1,800 | |
| Retained Earnings | ...................................................................... | 1,800 |

**Error 2: Explanation for entry:**

*Step 1:*    Insurance Expense in 2010 will be understated unless a correcting entry is made; Insurance Expense for 2010 is increased by a debit.

*Step 2:*    No assets or liabilities are affected at 12/31/10.

*Step 3:*    Insurance Expense for 2009 was overstated. The Insurance Expense account for 2009 cannot be credited because all income statement amounts for 2009 have been closed to Retained Earnings. Therefore, credit Retained Earnings to correct for the error.

**ERROR 3**

**(b)     Effects of Error 3:** Failure to accrue interest revenue in 2009:

1.    Net income for 2009 is understated (because interest revenue is understated).
2.    Assets are understated, and owners' equity is understated at 12/31/09.
3.    Net income for 2010 is overstated (because interest revenue is overstated).
4.    There is no effect on the balance sheet at 12/31/10.

**Explanation:**

| | *What Was Done* | | *What Should Have Been Done* | |
|---|---|---|---|---|
| 12/31/09 | No entry | | Interest Receivable   5,100 | |
| | | | Int. Revenue              5,100 | |
| | | | | |
| During | Cash | 5,100 | Cash | 5,100 |
| 2010 | Int. Revenue | 5,100 | Int. Receivable | 5,100 |

An adjusting entry to record accrued revenue of $5,100 was omitted in 2009. Therefore, the interest would have been received and recorded as a revenue in 2010. The receipt in 2010 should have been recorded as a reduction in a receivable, but the receivable was never reflected on the books.

(c)      **Correcting entry for Error 3 at 12/31/10 before closing:**

Interest Revenue      ........................................................................5,100

    Retained Earnings.................................................................      5,100

**Error 3: Explanation for entry:**

*Step 1:*      Interest Revenue in 2010 will be overstated unless a correcting entry is made; Interest Revenue for 2010 is reduced by a debit.

*Step 2:*      No assets or liabilities are affected at 12/31/10.

*Step 3:*      The Interest Revenue account for 2009 cannot be credited because all income statement amounts for 2009 have been closed to Retained Earnings. Therefore, credit Retained Earnings to correct for the error.

## ERROR 4

(b)      **Effects of Error 4:** Failure to defer rent revenue in 2009:

1.      Net income for 2009 is overstated (because rent revenue is overstated).

2.      Liabilities are understated and owners' equity is overstated at 12/31/09.

3.      Net income for 2010 is understated (because rent revenue is understated).

4.      There is no effect on the balance sheet at 12/31/10.

## Explanation:

|          | *What Was Done* | *What Should Have Been Done* | | |
|----------|-----------------|------------------------------|-------|-------|
| 12/31/09 | No Entry.       | Rent Revenue                 | 4,500 |       |
|          |                 |     Unearned Rent Revenue |       | 4,500 |
|          |                 |                              |       |       |
| 12/31/10 | No Entry.       | Unearned Rent Revenue        | 4,500 |       |
|          |                 |     Rent Revenue |       | 4,500 |

In 2009, rental receipts were collected in advance. The receipt must have been recorded by a credit to revenue. An adjusting entry at the end of 2009 to record the deferral of a portion of the revenue to a future period (2010) was omitted. The assumption is that the revenue was earned in 2010 or there would have been a description of another error.

(c)      **Correcting entry for Error 4 at 12/31/10 before closing:**

Retained Earnings      ..................................................................4,500

    Rent Revenue ....................................................................      4,500

**Error 4: Explanation for entry:**

*Step 1:*      Rent Revenue in 2010 will be understated unless a correcting entry is made; Rent Revenue is increased by a credit.

*Step 2:*      No assets or liabilities are affected at 12/31/10.

*Step 3:*      Rent Revenue for 2009 was overstated. The Rent Revenue account for 2009 cannot be debited because all income statement accounts for 2009 have been closed to Retained Earnings. Therefore, debit Retained Earnings in the correcting entry.

## ERROR 5

(b)    **Effects of Error 5:** Failure to capitalize a fixed asset in 2009 and depreciate:
1.    Net income for 2009 is understated by $8,500.
2.    Assets are understated by $8,500, and owners' equity is understated by $8,500 at 12/31/09.
3.    Net income for 2010 is overstated by $1,500.
4.    Assets are understated by $7,000, and owners' equity is understated by $7,000 at 12/31/10.

## Explanation:

|  | *What Was Done* | | *What Should Have Been Done* | |
|---|---|---|---|---|
| Beginning of 2009 | Truck Exp.  10,000 | | Truck            10,000 | |
|  |      Cash | 10,000 |      Cash | 10,000 |
| 12/31/09 | No Entry. | | Depreciation Exp.  1,500 | |
|  | | |      Accumulated | |
|  | | |           Dep. | 1,500 |
|  | | | [($10,000 - $4,000) ÷ 4 = $1,500] | |
| 12/31/10 | No Entry. | | Depreciation Exp.  1,500 | |
|  | | |      Accumulated | |
|  | | |           Dep. | 1,500 |

The acquisition of a truck in 2009 was incorrectly recorded as an expense of $10,000. The truck should have been depreciated by charging $1,500 to expense over each of four years, beginning with 2009. This means that the income statements for 2009, 2010, 2011, and 2012 will be affected by the error if it is not detected and corrected. The balance sheet at the end of each of those four years will also be in error. This error will turnaround or offset in the period of the disposal of the truck (a gain will be overstated in that period and only then will the error self-correct on the balance sheet).

**Effects:**    Truck Expense is overstated by $10,000 in 2009 and Depreciation Expense is understated by $1,500 in each year the truck is held. Therefore: Net income for 2009 is understated by $8,500; owners' equity at 12/31/09 is understated by $8,500; assets at 12/31/09 are understated by $8,500; net income for 2010 is overstated by $1,500; owners' equity at 12/31/10 is understated by $7,000; assets at 12/31/10 are understated by $7,000.

(c)    **Correcting entry for Error 5 at 12/31/10 before closing:**

| | | |
|---|---|---|
| Truck ................................................................................ | 10,000 | |
| Depreciation Expense............................................................... | 1,500 | |
|      Accumulated Depreciation ................................................. | | 3,000 |
|      Retained Earnings................................................................ | | 8,500 |

## Error 5: Explanation for entry:

*Step 1:*    Depreciation Expense in 2010 will be understated unless a correcting entry is made; Depreciation Expense of $1,500 is recorded by a debit.

*Step 2:*    The asset Truck will be understated at 12/31/10 by the cost of $10,000 unless a correcting entry is made. Likewise, Accumulated Depreciation will be understated by two years worth of depreciation unless a correcting entry is made. Therefore, debit Truck for $10,000 and credit Accumulated Depreciation for $3,000.

*Step 3:*    Truck Expense for 2009 was overstated by $10,000 and Depreciation Expense for 2009 was understated by $1,500. All income amounts for 2009 have been closed to Retained Earnings. Therefore, credit Retained Earnings for $8,500 (i.e., the amount by which Retained Earnings is understated at the beginning of the year in which the error is corrected).

## ERROR 6

(b)    **Effects of Error 6:** Failure to amortize an intangible asset in 2009:
1.    Net income for 2009 is overstated by $700 (because patent amortization is understated).
2.    Assets are overstated by $700 and owners' equity is overstated by $700 at 12/31/09.
3.    Net income for 2010 is not affected
4.    Assets are overstated by $700 and owners' equity is overstated by $700 at 12/31/10.

## Explanation:

|  | *What Was Done* | *What Should Have Been Done* | | |
|---|---|---|---|---|
| 12/31/09 | No Entry. | Patent Amortization Expense | 700 | |
|  |  | Patent | | 700 |

The failure to record amortization of a patent is **not** a counterbalancing error. This error will self-correct when the patent is fully amortized (it will be amortized one year after it should have been fully amortized) or when the patent is disposed of (through sale or writeoff). There is no mention of a similar omission in 2010 so the assumption is that the 2010 amortization was recorded properly. Therefore, this error will affect the income statement of 2009 and the income statement of the period of disposal (or of the last period amortized) and every balance sheet prepared between these two periods.

(c)    **Correcting entry for Error 6 at 12/31/10 before closing:**

| | | |
|---|---|---|
| Retained Earnings | ...................................................................700 | |
| Patent | .................................................................. | 700 |

## Error 6: Explanation for entry:
*Step 1:*    Amortization Expense for 2010 is apparently recorded correctly.
*Step 2:*    The asset Patent will be overstated at 12/31/10 unless a correcting entry is made. Therefore, credit Patent.
*Step 3:*    Amortization Expense for 2009 was understated. The Patent Amortization Expense account for 2009 cannot be debited because all income statement amounts have been closed to Retained Earnings. Therefore, debit Retained Earnings.

| | | | |
|---|---|---|---|
| **TIP:** | If the amortization expense or depreciation expense for 2009 is omitted in 2009, the amortization or depreciation expense for 2010 is assumed to be recorded correctly in 2010 unless otherwise indicated. Thus, the carrying value of the long-lived asset will remain overstated on the balance sheet until the asset is disposed of (thru sale or abandonment and written off) or completely depreciated. | | |
| **TIP:** | Very often students have a more detailed approach to correcting entries. The following pairs of entries are alternate answers to some of the correcting entries presented above. Both entries in each pair must be included to be equivalent to the entries shown above. | | |
| **Error 2:** | Prepaid Insurance ................................................... | 1,800 | |
| |     Retained Earnings ......................................... | | 1,800 |
| | Insurance Expense................................................ | 1,800 | |
| |     Prepaid Insurance......................................... | | 1,800 |
| **Error 4:** | Retained Earnings.................................................. | 4,500 | |
| |     Unearned Rent Revenue............................. | | 4,500 |
| | Unearned Rent Revenue........................................ | 4,500 | |
| |     Rent Revenue............................................... | | 4,500 |
| **Error 5:** | Truck. . . ........................................................ 10,000 | | |
| |     Accumulated Depreciation............................ | | 1,500 |
| |     Retained Earnings ......................................... | | 8,500 |
| | Depreciation Expense .............................................. | 1,500 | |
| |     Accumulated Depreciation............................ | | 1,500 |

# EXERCISE 22-6

**Purpose:**   (L.O. 7) This exercise will illustrate the effects of various errors involving purchases and ending inventory.

Surf & Turf Sports Equipment Company sells sporting goods. By taking a physical count and pricing its inventory using the FIFO cost method, inventory was determined to be $430,000 and $572,000 at December 31, 2009, and December 31, 2010, respectively. Net income was reported to be $200,000 and $218,000 for 2009 and 2010, respectively. The following errors occurred with regard to accounting for inventory transactions:

*Error 1:*   Purchases of $30,000 made near the end of 2009 were shipped f.o.b. shipping point by the vendor on December 29, 2009; they were not received by Surf & Turf until January 3, 2010. These purchases were omitted from the physical count at December 31, 2009, and were not recorded as purchases until January 3, 2010.

*Error 2:*   Merchandise costing $21,000 was on the premises but was overlooked during the physical inventory count at December 31, 2009.

*Error 3:*   Merchandise costing $32,000 was double counted during the physical inventory count at December 31, 2010.

**Error 4:** Sales made near the end of 2010 were shipped f.o.b. destination by Surf & Turf on December 28, 2010; they were not received by the customers until January 4, 2011. These items, costing $17,000, were omitted from the inventory sheets of the physical count taken on December 31, 2010, and were treated as sales for $28,500 in 2010.

## Instructions

Compute the correct net income amounts for 2009 and 2010.

## Solution to Exercise 22-6

|  | 2009 | 2010 |
|---|---|---|
| Net income as previously reported | $200,000 | $218,000 |
| Both purchases and ending inventory for 2009 understated | --- | --- |
| Ending inventory for 2009 understated | 21,000 | (21,000) |
| Ending inventory for 2010 overstated | --- | (32,000) |
| Sales for 2010 overstated | --- | (28,500) |
| Ending inventory for 2010 understated | --- | 17,000 |
|  | $221,000 | $153,500 |

**Explanation:** Analyses of effects of errors on cost of goods sold:

**Error 1:**

|  |  | 2009 | 2010 |
|---|---|---|---|
|  | Beginning inventory | No effect | Under $30,000 |
| + | Net cost of purchases | Under $30,000 | Over $30,000 |
| = | Goods available for sale | Under $30,000 | No effect |
| - | Ending inventory | Under $30,000 | No effect |
| = | Cost of goods sold expense | No effect | No effect |

**Error 2:**

|  |  | 2009 | 2010 |
|---|---|---|---|
|  | Beginning inventory | No effect | Under $21,000 |
| + | Net cost of purchases | No effect | No effect |
| = | Goods available for sale | No effect | Under $21,000 |
| - | Ending inventory | Under $21,000 | No effect |
| = | Cost of goods sold expense | Over $21,000 | Under $21,000 |

**Error 3:**

|  |  | 2009 | 2010 | 2011 |
|---|---|---|---|---|
|  | Beginning inventory | No effect | No effect | Over $32,000 |
| + | Net cost of purchases | No effect | No effect | No effect |
| = | Goods available for sale | No effect | No effect | Over $32,000 |
| - | Ending inventory | No effect | Over $32,000 | No effect |
| = | Cost of goods sold expense | No effect | Under $32,000 | Over $32,000 |

## Error 4:

| | 2009 | 2010 | 2011 |
|---|---|---|---|
| Beginning inventory | No effect | No effect | Under $17,000 |
| + Net cost of purchases | No effect | No effect | No effect |
| = Goods available for sale | No effect | No effect | Under $17,000 |
| - Ending inventory | No effect | Under $17,000 | No effect |
| = Cost of goods sold expense | No effect | Over $17,000 | Under $17,000 |
| **Also:** | | | |
| Sales revenue | No effect | Over $28,500 | Under $28,500 |

**TIP:** If you do not clearly recall how the shipping terms (f.o.b. shipping point and f.o.b. destination) effect inventory valuation, you can find that information in Chapter 8 of your *Problem Solving Survival Guide* It would be wise to review that material.

**TIP:** An error involving purchases and/or ending inventory and/or beginning inventory should be analyzed in terms of its effect on components of the cost of goods sold computation in order to then determine its effect on net income. That computation is:

> Beginning inventory
> + Net cost of purchases
> = Goods available for sale
> - Ending inventory
> = Cost of goods sold

**TIP:** The ending inventory for Year 1 is the beginning inventory for Year 2. Thus, when the ending inventory for Year 1 is overstated, it will cause an overstatement in the net income for Year 1 and an understatement in net income for Year 2. This error will cause retained earnings at the end of Year 1 to be overstated because net income for Year 1 (which is overstated) is closed into retained earnings. The balance of retained earnings at the end of Year 2 will be unaffected by this error because the net income for Year 2 (which is understated by the same amount as the overstatement in retained earnings at the end of Year 1) is closed into retained earnings; the error at this point counterbalances. Working capital at the end of Year 1 is overstated (because inventory is a current asset), but working capital at the end of Year 2 is unaffected because the inventory figure at the end of Year 2 is determined by a physical inventory counting and pricing procedure. No new error in this process is assumed unless otherwise indicated.

**TIP:** An understatement in ending inventory of Year 1 will cause an understatement in net income for Year 1 and overstatement in net income for Year 2. Thus, retained earnings and working capital at the end of Year 1 are understated. However, assuming no more errors are committed at the end of Year 2, retained earnings and working capital are not affected at the end of Year 2.

> **TIP:** If purchases for Year 1 are understated by the same amount as an understatement in inventory at the end of Year 1, there is no net effect on net income of Year 1 and no net effect on net income of Year 2. The balance sheet at the end of Year 1, however, has errors because assets (inventories) are understated and liabilities (accounts payable) are understated.
>
> **TIP:** When more than one error affects the net income amount for one year, analyze each error **separately** and write down its effects before you attempt to summarize all the effects on one given year.
>
> **TIP:** When analyzing an error situation involving inventory, assume a periodic inventory system is in use unless otherwise indicated.

## EXERCISE 22-7

**Purpose:**    (L.O. 7) This exercise will allow you to practice analyzing the effects of errors on income determination.

The Avery Corporation computed net income of $22,000 and $30,000 for Years 1 and 2, respectively. The following errors were later discovered:

*Error 1:*    Depreciation on computers was omitted in Year 1, $900.
*Error 2:*    Deferred (prepaid) expenses were understated at the end of Year 1, $400.
*Error 3:*    Accrued revenues were omitted at the end of Year 1, $600.
*Error 4:*    Deferred (unearned) revenues were understated at the end of Year 1, $980.
*Error 5:*    Accrued expenses were overlooked at the end of Year 1, $650.

## Instructions
Compute the corrected net income figures for Year 1 and Year 2.

## Solution to Exercise 22-7

|                                              | Year 1    | Year 2    |
|----------------------------------------------|-----------|-----------|
| Net income as previously reported            | $22,000   | $30,000   |
| Depreciation omitted—Year 1                  | (900)     | ---       |
| Deferred expenses understated—Year 1         | 400       | (400)     |
| Accrued revenues understated—Year 1          | 600       | (600)     |
| Deferred revenues understated—Year 1         | (980)     | 980       |
| Accrued expenses understated—Year 1          | (650)     | 650       |
| Corrected net income                         | $20,470   | $30,630   |

> **TIP:** The benefits from the prepaid expense (error 2) are assumed to be consumed in Year 2 and the unearned revenue (error 4) is assumed to be earned in Year 2 because there is no mention of similar errors existing at the end of Year 2.

# ANALYSIS OF MULTIPLE-CHOICE TYPE QUESTIONS

**QUESTION**

1.  (L.O. 3) A manufacturing company changes from the FIFO cost method to the average cost inventory pricing method for all inventories held. Which of the following describes the correct accounting treatment for the change?

| | **Include cumulative effect of a change in accounting principle in current income statement** | | **Recast prior years' statements** |
|---|---|---|---|
| a. | Yes | Yes | |
| b. | Yes | No | |
| c. | | No | No |
| d. | | No | Yes |

**Approach and Explanation:** Determine the type of accounting change that has occurred. It is a change in accounting principle. Determine the method of treatment to be accorded that type of change. The retrospective approach is applied to a change in principle. The retrospective treatment calls for reporting the cumulative effect of the change on prior periods as an adjustment to beginning retained earnings on the retained earnings statement of the earliest period presented. To restore comparability of the statements for successive periods, the financial statements of prior periods are formally recast (adjusted) to reflect application of the new method to all periods presented. (Solution = d.)

**QUESTION**

2.  (L.O. 3) A change from one generally accepted accounting method to another generally accepted accounting method is usually accounted for:
    a.  currently.
    b.  retrospectively.
    c.  prospectively.
    d.  as an initial adoption.

**Explanation:** A change from one generally accepted accounting method to another generally acceptable accounting method constitutes a change in accounting principle. The change is accounted for retrospectively. Prior period financial statements are to be adjusted. (Solution = b.)

**QUESTION**

3.  (L.O. 2, 7) A change from a nongenerally accepted accounting principle to a generally accepted accounting principle should be accounted for:
    a.  currently.
    b.  prospectively.
    c.  as an initial adoption.
    d.  as a prior period adjustment.

**Explanation:** A change from a non-GAAP method to one that is GAAP constitutes an error correction. The correction of an error is not an accounting change; it is a prior period adjustment. Prior period financial statements are to be restated. (Solution = d.)

**QUESTION**

4.  (L.O. 5) The Mercer Mayer Corporation purchased a computer system on January 1, 2008 for $210,000. The company used the sum-of-the-years'-digits method for accounting purposes and no salvage value to depreciate the asset for the first two years of its estimated six-year life. For tax purposes, Mercer Mayer has used and will continue to use the straight-line method. In 2010, Mercer Mayer changed to the straight-line depreciation method for this asset for accounting purposes. The following facts pertain:

|                              | **2008**  | **2009**  | **2010**  |
| ---------------------------- | --------- | --------- | --------- |
| Straight-line                | $35,000   | $35,000   | $35,000   |
| Sum-of-the-years'-digits     | 60,000    | 50,000    | 40,000    |

Mercer Mayer is subject to a 40% tax rate. In the journal entry to record the accounting change:

a.  Retained Earnings will be credited for $24,000.
b.  Retained Earnings will be debited for $24,000.
c.  Retained Earnings will be credited for $27,000.
d.  Retained Earnings will be debited for $27,000.
e.  There is no journal entry to record this accounting change.

**Approach and Explanation:** A change in depreciation method is an example of a change in accounting estimate effected by a change in accounting principle. The new depreciation method is adopted in partial or complete recognition of a change in the estimated future benefits inherent in the asset, the pattern of consumption of these benefits, or the information available to the entity about those benefits. The effect of the change in accounting principle, or the method of applying it, is inseparable from the effect of the change in accounting estimate. This situation is accounted for as a change in accounting estimate. There is no catch-up adjustment made; the change is give prospective treatment. (Solution = e.)

**QUESTION**

5.  (L.O. 5) Refer to the facts in **Question 4** above. The amount that Mercer Mayer should report for depreciation expense on its 2010 income statement is:

a.  $40,000.
b.  $35,000.
c.  $25,000.
d.  $24,000.
e.  $21,000.

**Approach and Explanation:** Calculate the depreciation for 2010 (the year of change) using the new method to spread the existing depreciable cost over the remaining life. The computation is:

| | |
| --- | ---: |
| Cost | $210,000 |
| Accumulated depreciation | (110,000)[a] |
| Book value | 100,000 |
| Current estimate of salvage | -0- |
| Remaining depreciable cost | 100,000 |
| Remaining years of useful life at 1/1/10 | ÷    4 [b] |
| Depreciation expense for 2010 | $ 25,000 |

[a]$60,000 + $50,000 = $110,000.
[b]6 years original life – 2 years used = 4 years remaining.          (Solution = c.)

**QUESTION**

6.  (L.O. 5) Refer to the facts of **Question 4** above. If Mercer Mayer prepares comparative financial statements in 2010, the income statement for 2009 included therein will reflect depreciation expense of:

a.  $50,000.
b.  $40,000.
c.  $35,000.
d.  $30,000.

**Explanation:** A change from one generally acceptable depreciation method to another generally acceptable depreciation method is treated as a change in accounting estimate that is to receive prospective treatment. Therefore, financial statements for prior periods are **not** to be recast if they are republished for comparative purposes. The depreciation expense for 2009 will appear in 2010 comparative reports as it originally appeared when the 2009 income statement was prepared in 2009. Therefore, it will be the amount computed under the sum-of-the-years'-digits method of $50,000. (Solution = a.)

## QUESTION
7.   (L.O. 3) A change from the LIFO inventory costing method to the FIFO inventory costing method is to be accounted for:
a.      currently.
b.      restrospectively.
c.      prospectively.
d.      as an initial adoption.

**Explanation:**  A change from LIFO to any other generally acceptable inventory costing (pricing) method constitutes a case of a change in accounting principle; thus, it is to be accounted for retrospectively. The financial statements of prior periods are to be adjusted when they are reported again for comparative purposes to reflect the period-specific aspects of applying the new accounting principle. (Solution = b.)

## QUESTION
8.   (L.O. 3) During 2010, a construction company changed from the completed-contract method to the percentage-of-completion method for accounting purposes but not for tax purposes. Gross-profit figures under both methods for the history of the company appear below:

|       | **Completed-Contract** | **Percentage-of-Completion** |
|-------|-------------------------|------------------------------|
| 2008  | $ 190,000               | $   320,000                  |
| 2009  | 250,000                 | 380,000                      |
| 2010  | 280,000                 | 410,000                      |
|       | $ 720,000               | $ 1,110,000                  |

Assuming an income tax rate of 40% for all years and only single period statements (no comparative reports) are presented, the effect of this accounting change on prior periods should be reported by a credit of:
a.      $156,000 on the 2010 income statement.
b.      $234,000 on the 2010 income statement.
c.      $156,000 on the 2010 retained earnings statement.
d.      $234,000 on the 2010 retained earnings statement.

**Approach and Explanation:** Identify the type of accounting change and the method of treatment. It is a change in accounting principle. It is to get retrospective treatment. Therefore, the total effect on prior periods (net of tax) is to be recorded as an adjustment to the beginning balance of retained earnings and reported on the retained earnings statement. Identify the prior years and the effect of the change on those prior years. (Solution = c.)

|                  | **Old Method** | **New Method** | **Difference** |
|------------------|----------------|----------------|----------------|
| 2008             | $ 190,000      | $ 320,000      | $ 130,000      |
| 2009             | 250,000        | 380,000        | 130,000        |
|                  | $ 440,000      | $ 700,000      | 260,000        |
| Net-of-tax rate  |                |                | 60%            |
| Effect net of tax|                |                | $ 156,000      |

**QUESTION**
9.   (L.O. 5) A change in accounting estimate should be accounted for:
     a.   as an adjustment to the beginning balance of retained earnings.
     b.   by restating the relevant amounts in the financial statements of prior periods.
     c.   in the period of change or in the period of change and future periods, if the change affects both.
     d.   by reporting pro-forma amounts for all periods presented.

**Approach and Explanation:** Think about the treatment to be accorded a change in accounting estimate before you read the answer selections. A change in accounting estimate receives prospective treatment; therefore, it is accounted for in the current period or in the current and future periods, whichever is applicable. (Solution = c.)

**QUESTION**
10.   (L.O. 5) When a change in estimate creates the need for a change in principle (such as when a manufacturing company changes from the policy of deferring and amortizing preproduction costs to the policy of expensing such costs because the estimate of the periods benefited has changed and any future benefits now appear doubtful), the change is accounted for:
a.   currently.
b.   retroactively.
c.   prospectively.

**Explanation:** A change in an accounting estimate that necessitates a change in an accounting principle is to be accounted for as a change in estimate. This situation is often referred to as a change in accounting estimate that is recognized in whole or in part by a change in accounting principle or a change in accounting estimate effected by a change in accounting principle. This situation receives prospective treatment because the effect of the change in principle cannot be separated from the effect of the change in estimate. (Solution = c.)

**QUESTION**
11.   (L. O. 5)  A machine was purchased at the beginning of 2007 for $68,000.  At the time of its purchase, the machine was estimated to have a useful life of six years and a salvage value of $8,000.  The machine was depreciated using the straight-line method of depreciation through 2009.  At the beginning of 2010, the estimate of useful life was revised to a total life of eight years and the expected salvage value was changed to $5,000.  The amount to be recorded for depreciation for 2010, reflecting these changes in estimates, is:
     a.   $7,875.
     b.   $7,600.
     c.   $6,600.
     d.   $4,125.

**Approach and Explanation:**  Write down the model to compute depreciation whenever there has been a change in the estimated service life and/or salvage value of a plant asset.  Fill in the data of the case at hand and solve:

| | |
|---|---|
| Cost $68,000 | |
| Accumulated depreciation | (30,000)[a] |
| Book value | 38,000 |
| Additional expenditure capitalized | -0- |
| Revised book value | 38,000 |
| Current estimate of salvage | (5,000) |
| Remaining depreciable cost | 33,000[b] |
| Remaining years of useful life at 1/1/10 | ÷   5 |
| Depreciation expense for 2010 | $  6,600    (Solution = c.) |

[a]Cost                                                  $68,000
  Original estimate of salvage                 (8,000)
  Original depreciable cost                      60,000
  Original service life in years                 ÷      6
  Original depreciation per year                 10,000
  Number of years used                                3
  Accumulated depreciation—1/1/10               $30,000

[b]Total life as revised                                      8
  Number of years used                              (3)
  Remaining part of useful life at 1/1/10             5

## QUESTION

12. (L.O. 6) Which of the following is an example of a change in reporting entity?
    - a. creation of a new business unit
    - b. purchase of a new subsidiary
    - c. disposition of a subsidiary
    - d. changing specific subsidiaries that constitute the group of companies for which consolidated financial statements are presented

**Approach and Explanation:** Mentally review the list of items that constitute a change in reporting entity and the items that do not result in a change in reporting entity.

Examples of a change in reporting entity are:
1. Presenting consolidated or combined statements in place of statements of individual companies.
2. Changing specific subsidiaries that constitute the group of companies for which consolidated financial statements are presented.
3. Changing the companies included in combined financial statements.
4. A change in the fair value, equity, or consolidation method of accounting for subsidiaries and investments. (This includes a change from the fair value method to the equity method or a change from the equity to the fair value method.)

A change in the reporting entity does **not** result from creation, cessation, purchase, or disposition of a subsidiary or other business unit. (Solution = d.)

## QUESTION

13. (L.O. 7) Merchandise inventory was overstated at December 31, 2009. How would this error affect earnings for 2009, earnings for 2010, working capital at December 31, 2009, and owners' equity at December 31, 2009?

|   | Earnings 2009 | Earnings 2010 | Working Capital 12/31/09 | Owners' Equity 12/31/09 |
|---|---|---|---|---|
| a. | Overstate | Understate | Overstate | Overstate |
| b. | Understate | Overstate | Understate | Understate |
| c. | Overstate | No effect | No effect | Overstate |
| d. | Overstate | Understate | Understate | Understate |

**Approach and Explanation:** This is a counterbalancing error. The overstatement of 2009 ending inventory will cause net income of 2009 to be overstated (because of the understatement of cost of goods sold) and net income of 2010 to be understated. The overstatement of 2009 net income will cause owners' equity to be overstated. Inventory is a current asset. Therefore, working capital at December 31, 2009 will be overstated. (Solution = a.)

> **TIP:**  **Earnings** is synonymous with **net income**.

## QUESTION

14.   (L.O. 7) Accrued interest expense of $7,500 was omitted at December 31, 2009. Accrued interest expense of $10,000 was omitted at December 31, 2010. The net effect of these errors on net income for 2010 is:
a.     overstatement of $10,000.
b.     understatement of $2,500.
c.     understatement of $7,500.
d.     overstatement of $2,500.
e.     none of the above.

**Approach and Explanation:** Handle each error separately. Fully describe the effects of each error. Write these effects down. Then summarize the effects. (If necessary, draft the entries that were made and the entries that should have been made to analyze the effects on interest expense.) (Solution = d.)

*Error 1:*         Interest expense for 2009 is understated by $7,500.
                      Net income for 2009 is overstated by $7,500.
                      Interest expense for 2010 is overstated by $7,500.
                      Net income for 2010 is understated by $7,500.

*Error 2:*         Interest expense for 2010 is understated by $10,000.
                      Net income for 2010 is overstated by $10,000.
                      Interest expense for 2011 is overstated by $10,000.
                      Net income for 2011 is understated by $10,000.

Net effects on 2010 net income:
    Understatement                    $  7,500
    Overstatement                        10,000
    Net overstatement                  $  2,500

**QUESTION**
15.   (L.O. 6, 10) Prior to the current year, Alexander Corporation owned 6% of Hough Corporation. During the current year, additional acquisitions of Hough Corporation common stock by Alexander brought Alexander's total holdings to 28%. Alexander appropriately changed from the fair value method to the equity method of accounting for this investment. This change in method is to be accounted for:
a.     currently.
b.     retrospectively.
c.     prospectively.

**Explanation:** This is one example of a change in reporting entity; a change in reporting entity is to receive retrospective treatment. (Solution = b.)

# CHAPTER 23

# STATEMENT OF CASH FLOWS

## OVERVIEW

A business enterprise that provides a set of financial statements that report both financial position and results of operations is also required to provide a statement of cash flows for each period for which results of operations are provided. The primary purpose of a statement of cash flows is to provide relevant information about the cash receipts and cash payments of an enterprise during a time period. The information provided in a statement of cash flows, if used with related disclosures and information in the other financial statements, should help investors, creditors, and others to (a) assess the enterprise's ability to generate positive future net cash flows; (b) assess the enterprise's ability to meet its obligations, its ability to pay dividends, and its needs for external financing; (c) assess the reasons for differences between net income and associated cash receipts and payments; and (d) assess the effects on an enterprise's financial position of both its cash and noncash investing and financing transactions during the period.

## SUMMARY OF LEARNING OBJECTIVES

1.  **Describe the purpose of the statement of cash flows.** The primary purpose of the statement of cash flows is to provide information about cash receipts and cash payments of an entity during a period. A secondary objective is to report the entity's operating, investing, and financing activities during the period.

2.  **Identify the major classifications of cash flows.** Companies classify cash flows as: (1) *Operating activities*—all transactions and events that are not defined as investing or financing activities; generally the cash effects of transactions and other events that enter into the determination of net income. (2) *Investing activities*—lending money and collecting on those loans, and acquiring and disposing of investments, plant assets, and intangible assets. (3) *Financing activities*—obtaining cash from creditors and repaying loans, issuing and reacquiring capital stock, and paying cash dividends.

3.  **Differentiate between net income and net cash flows from operating activities.** Companies must adjust net income on an accrual basis to determine net cash flow from operating activities because some expenses and losses do not cause cash outflows, and some revenues and gains do not provide cash inflows. Also, some gains and losses relate to transactions that are classified as investing or financing activities.

4.  **Contrast the direct and indirect methods of calculating net cash flow from operating activities.** Under the direct approach, major classes of operating cash receipts and cash disbursements are calculated and reported. Presentation of the direct approach of reporting net cash flow from operating activities takes the form of a condensed cash basis income statement. The indirect method adds back to net income the noncash expenses and losses and subtracts the noncash revenues and gains.

5.  **Determine net cash flows from investing and financing activities.** Once a company has computed the net cash flow from operating activities, the next step is to determine whether any other changes in balance sheet accounts caused an increase or decrease in cash. Net cash flows from investing and financing activities can generally be determined by examining the changes in noncurrent balance sheet accounts.

6.  **Prepare a statement of cash flows.** Preparing the statement of cash flows involves three major steps: (1) *Determine the change in cash.* This is the difference between the beginning and the ending cash balance shown on the comparative balance sheets. (2*) Determine the net cash flow from operating activities.* This procedure is complex; it involves analyzing not only the current year's income statement but also the comparative balance sheets and the selected transaction data. (3) *Determine cash flows from investing and financing activities.* Analyze all changes in all balance sheet accounts other than Cash to determine the effects on cash.

7.  **Identify sources of information for a statement of cash flows.** The information to prepare the statement usually comes from three sources: (1) *Comparative balance sheets*—information in these statements indicate the amount of the changes in assets, liabilities, and equities during the period. (2) *Current income statement*—information in this statement is used in determining the cash provided by operations during the period. (3) *Selected transaction data*—this information from the general ledger provides additional detail needed to determine how cash was provided or used during the period.

8.  **Identify special problems in preparing a statement of cash flows.** The special problems are: (1) adjustments similar to depreciation, (2) accounts receivable (net), (3) other working capital changes, (4) net losses, (5) gains, (6) stock options, (7) postretirement benefit costs, (8) extraordinary items, and (9) significant noncash transactions.

9.  **Explain the use of a work sheet in preparing a statement of cash flows.** When numerous adjustments are necessary or other complicating factors are present, companies often use a work sheet to assemble and classify the data that will appear on the statement of cash flows. The work sheet is merely a device that aids in the preparation of the statement; its use is optional.

## TIPS ON CHAPTER TOPICS

**TIP:** Homework and examination problems related to the subject of the statement of cash flows very often involve comparative balance sheet data. Although sometimes the older year's information is listed first so that the data is in chronological order, it is a more common practice to list the current year's data first. Before beginning to work a problem, carefully note the order of the data so that you properly interpret the changes in accounts as being increases or decreases. These comparative balance sheets are often accompanied by additional information. If no additional information is given about an account, but the account balance has changed, assume that (1) only one transaction is responsible for the change in the balance, (2) the most common transaction occurred to change that particular account balance, and (3) cash was involved in the transaction.

**TIP:** It is highly recommended that you review **Exercise 5-4, Exercise 5-5,** and **Exercise 5-6** in your *Problem Solving Survival Guide* before doing the exercises in this chapter. Those three exercises provide excellent coverage of the basic material pertaining to the statement of cash flows. A review of those simpler items will prepare you for the more complex work in this chapter. Also, a review of multiple choice **Questions 10-17** in **Chapter 5** will aid you in the comprehension of **Chapter 23** and will help you to prepare for examination questions over this topic.

**TIP:** In studying this chapter on the statement of cash flows and preparing homework assignments, you will encounter transactions for which you may not recall the proper accounting procedures. One of the challenging aspects about this chapter is that it draws on your knowledge of **all** of the chapters that precede it. Use this opportunity to look up the items you don't recall and refresh your memory. The procedures you review in this manner will likely be easier to recall the next time you need to use them.

**TIP:** Every transaction affecting the Cash account is to be reflected either as an inflow (receipt) or outflow (payment) on the statement of cash flows. Furthermore, the receipts and payments are to be classified by activity. The three activity classifications are: (1) operating, (2) investing, and (3) financing.

**TIP:** In determining if a cash transaction is related to an operating activity, investing activity, or financing activity, first see if it meets the definition of investing activities. If not, see if it meets the definition of financing activities. If not, then it is an operating activity. (Refer to **Illustration 23-1** for these definitions and examples.)

**TIP:** The statement of cash flows emphasizes reporting gross cash receipts and payments. Thus, if long-term debt is issued for $2,000,000 and payments of $300,000 on long-term debt occur during the same period, it is **not** permissible to just show the net inflow of $1,700,000. Rather, the inflow of $2,000,000 and the outflow of $300,000 must be separately shown in the financing activity section of the statement of cash flows. Similarly, if acquisitions and disposals of plant assets occur in the same period, the gross cash effects must be reported; they are **not** to be netted.

**TIP:** Generally, gross cash receipts and gross cash payments must be separately disclosed. However, for certain items, the turnover is quick, the amounts are large, and the maturities are short. Only net changes need be reported for these items. Examples include cash receipts and payments pertaining to (a) investments (other than cash equivalents); (b) loans receivable; and (c) debt, providing the original maturity of the asset or liability is three months or less. For this purpose, amounts due on demand are considered to have maturities of three months or less.

**TIP:** Cash equivalents may be combined with Cash for presentation on the balance sheet and for reporting cash flows on the statement of cash flows. **Cash** includes not only currency on hand but demand deposits with banks or other financial institutions. **Cash equivalents** are short-term highly liquid investments that are both (a) readily convertible to known amounts of cash, and (b) so near their maturity that they present insignificant risk of changes in value because of changes in interest rates. Generally, only investments with original maturities of three months or less qualify under that definition. Examples of items commonly considered to be cash equivalents are Treasury bills, commercial paper, and money market funds.

**TIP:** When a homework or exam problem requires use of the indirect method but does not give the net income figure, the amount of net income (or net loss) can usually be derived by analyzing the changes that took place in the balance of retained earnings.

**TIP:** Cash flows associated with the acquisition and disposition of investments in **trading securities** are classified as **operating activities.** Cash flows related to the acquisition and disposition of investments in **available-for-sale securities** are classified as **investing activities.**

## ILLUSTRATION 23-1
## OPERATING, INVESTING, AND FINANCING ACTIVITIES (L.O. 2)

**DEFINITIONS:**

**Operating Activities:** include all transactions and other events that are not defined as investing or financing activities. Operating activities generally involve producing and delivering goods and providing services. Cash flows from operating activities are generally the cash effects of transactions and other events that enter into the determination of net income.

**Investing Activities:** include (a) making and collecting loans; (b) acquiring and disposing of debt and equity instruments of other entities; and (c) acquiring and disposing of property, plant, and equipment and other productive assets.

**Financing Activities:** include (a) obtaining resources from owners and providing them with a return on and a return of their investment; (b) borrowing money and repaying the amounts borrowed, or otherwise settling the obligation; and (c) obtaining and paying for other resources obtained from creditors.

## ILLUSTRATION 23-1 (Continued)

### EXAMPLES:

**Operating Activities:**
**Cash inflows:**

From sales of goods or services (includes cash sales, collections on account, and collections in advance).

From returns on loans (interest received) and on equity securities (dividends received).

From other transactions, such as: Amounts received to settle lawsuits, refunds from suppliers, and some insurance settlements (such as business interruption claims).

**Cash outflows:**

To suppliers for inventory and other goods and services (includes cash purchases and payments on account).

To employees for services.

To government for taxes.

To lenders for interest.

To others for items such as: Payments to settle lawsuits, refunds to customers, and contributions to charities.

**Investing Activities:**
**Cash inflows:**

From sale of property, plant, and equipment and other productive assets.

From sale of debt or equity securities of other entities or return of investments in those instruments.

From collection of principal on loans to other entities or sale of loans made to others.

**Cash outflows:**

To purchase property, plant, and equipment (plant assets).[a]

To purchase debt or equity securities of other entities.

To make loans to other entities.

**Financing Activities:**
**Cash inflows:**

From sale of equity securities (company's own stock) and exercise of employee stock options.

From issuance of nontrade debt (bonds and notes).

**Cash outflows:**

To pay dividends to stockholders.

To reacquire capital stock.

To pay non-trade debt (both short-term and long-term).

[a]The cash outflows included in this category are payments at the time of purchase or soon before or after purchase to acquire property, plant, and equipment and other productive assets. Generally, only advance payments, the down payment, or other amounts paid at the time of purchase or soon before or after purchase of property, plant, and equipment and other productive assets are investing cash outflows. **Incurring directly related debt to the seller is a financing transaction and subsequent payments of principal on that debt thus are financing cash outflows.**

> **TIP:** The statement of cash flows summarizes all of the transactions occurring during a period that have an impact on the cash balance. The activity format is used whereby cash inflows and cash outflows are summarized by the three categories: operating, investing and financing.

## EXERCISE 23-1

**Purpose:** (L.O. 2) This exercise will give you practice in classifying transactions by activity.

The Wolfson Corporation had the following transactions during 2010:

1. Issued $100,000 par value common stock in exchange for cash.
2. Issued $22,000 par value common stock in exchange for equipment.
3. Sold services for $52,000 cash.
4. Purchased available-for-sale securities as a long-term investment for $18,000 cash.
5. Collected $9,000 of accounts receivable.
6. Paid $14,000 of accounts payable.
7. Declared and paid a cash dividend of $12,000.
8. Sold a long-term investment in available-for-sale securities with a cost of $18,000 for $18,000 cash.
9. Purchased a machine for $35,000 by giving a long-term note in exchange.
10. Exchanged land costing $20,000 for equipment costing $20,000.
11. Paid salaries of $6,000.
12. Paid $1,000 for advertising services.
13. Paid $8,000 for insurance coverage for a future period.
14. Borrowed $31,000 cash from the bank.
15. Paid $11,000 interest.
16. Paid $31,000 cash to the bank to repay loan principal.
17. Issued $40,000 par value common stock upon conversion of bonds payable having a face value of $40,000.
18. Paid utilities of $4,000.
19. Loaned a vendor $6,000 cash.
20. Collected interest of $2,000.
21. Collected $6,000 loan principal from borrower.
22. Purchased treasury stock for $4,000.
23. Sold treasury stock for $6,000 (cost was $4,000).
24. Paid taxes of $20,000.

**Instructions**
Analyze each transaction above and indicate whether it resulted in a(n):
(a) inflow of cash from operating activities,
(b) outflow of cash from operating activities,
(c) inflow of cash from investing activities,
(d) outflow of cash from investing activities,
(e) inflow of cash from financing activities,
(f) outflow of cash from financing activities, or
(g) noncash investing and/or financing activity.

## SOLUTION TO EXERCISE 23-1

| | | | | | | | | | |
|---|---|---|---|---|---|---|---|---|---|
| 1. | e | 6. | b | 11. | b | 16. | f | 21. | c |
| 2. | g | 7. | f | 12. | b | 17. | g | 22. | f |
| 3. | a | 8. | c | 13. | b | 18. | b | 23. | e |
| 4. | d | 9. | g | 14. | e | 19. | d | 24. | b |
| 5. | a | 10. | g | 15. | b | 20. | a | | |

**Approach:** Write down the definitions for investing activities, financing activities, and operating activities. (These definitions can be found in **Illustration 23-1**.) Analyze each transaction to see in which classification the transaction would be included. Watch for any transactions that do **not** result in a cash flow; they are noncash items. Most noncash items are to be included in the separate supplementary schedule of noncash investing and financing activities.

**Explanation:**
1.  Issuance of stock for cash results in a cash inflow from financing activities.
2.  Issuance of stock in exchange for plant assets does **not** involve any flow of cash; the issuance of stock is a financing activity and the acquisition of plant assets is an investing activity. The transaction is a noncash financing and investing activity.
3.  The sale of services is a revenue transaction. The sale of services for cash results in an inflow of cash from operating activities.
4.  The cash purchase of an available-for-sale security as an investment results in an outflow of cash from investing activities.
5.  The collection of accounts receivable constitutes a cash inflow from a customer for a prior revenue transaction. A collection of cash from a customer is an inflow of cash from operating activities.
6.  The payment of accounts payable constitutes a payment to a supplier for inventory or other goods or services. There will be a related expense transaction either before the cash payment or after the time of cash payment. A payment to a vendor is an outflow of cash from operating activities.
7.  The payment of cash dividends to stockholders is an outflow of cash from financing activities.
8.  The sale of an investment constitutes an inflow of cash from investing activities.
9.  The acquisition of a plant asset is an investing activity. The issuance of a debt instrument is a financing activity. The purchase of a plant asset by issuance of a note payable does **not** involve a cash flow. Hence, the transaction is a noncash financing and investing activity.
10. The acquisition of land (a plant asset) is an investing activity. The sale (disposal) of equipment (plant asset) is an investing activity. The exchange of one plant asset for another plant asset does **not** involve any flow of cash; the transaction is a noncash investing activity.
11. The payment of salaries is a payment to employees for services rendered; it results from an expense transaction. The payment to employees for services is a cash outflow from operating activities.
12. The payment for advertising services is an example of a payment to suppliers of goods and services used in operations; it is a cash outflow from operating activities.

13. The payment for insurance coverage is an example of a payment to suppliers of goods and services used in operations. There will be an expense recognized in a future period. It does not matter in what period the expense recognition takes place; the cash flow occurred in the current period and results in a cash outflow from operating activities.

14. The borrowing of cash from a bank causes an issuance of a debt instrument (i.e., note payable). The borrowing of cash is a cash inflow from financing activities.

15. The payment to lenders for interest will cause an expense to be recognized on the income statement in the period the interest is incurred. The payment of interest is a cash outflow for operating activities in the period the cash is paid.

16. The payment of a loan (debt) is a cash outflow from financing activities.

17. The issuance of common stock is a financing activity and the liquidation (redemption) of bonds payable is a financing activity. However, the redemption of bonds by issuance of stock is a **noncash** financing activity because no cash is received or given in the exchange.

18. The payment of utilities is a payment to a supplier for a service used in operations. The related expense will appear on the income statement in the period the services are consumed. The payment will appear on a statement of cash flows as an outflow of cash from operating activities in the period the cash payment is made.

19. The payment of cash to another entity in the form of a loan to that other entity is a cash outflow from investing activities.

20. The collection of cash for interest is a cash inflow from operating activities.

21. The collection of cash for the principal on a loan to another entity is a cash inflow from investing activities.

22. The cash payment to reacquire a company's own capital stock (treasury stock) is a cash outflow from financing activities.

23. The sale of treasury stock for cash results in a cash inflow from financing activities.

24. The payment of cash to the government for taxes is a cash outflow from operating activities.

---

**TIP:** In determining if a cash transaction is an operating activity, investing activity, or financing activity, it is usually helpful to reconstruct the journal entry used to record the transaction. The following observations are also helpful:

1. The journal entry to record a transaction that is an investing activity which results in a cash flow will generally involve: (1) Cash and (2) an asset account other than Cash, such as Investment (short-term or long-term), Land, Building, Equipment, Patent, etc.

2. The journal entry to record a transaction that is a financing activity which results in a cash flow will generally involve: (1) Cash and (2) a liability account or an owners' equity account such as Bonds Payable, Notes Payable, Dividends Payable, Common Stock, Paid-in Capital in Excess of Par, Treasury Stock, etc.

3. The journal entry to record a transaction that is an operating activity which results in a cash flow will generally involve: (1) Cash and (2) a revenue account or an expense account; or, a prepaid expense or an unearned revenue; or, a receivable or a payable account.

# EXERCISE 23-2

**Purpose:**    (L.O. 6)  This exercise will provide you with an opportunity to prepare a statement of cash flows using the indirect method.

A comparative balance sheet for Hernan Perez Pictures appears below:

|  | December 31 | | |
|---|---|---|---|
| **Assets** | **2010** | **2009** | **Change** |
| Cash | $ 61,000 | $ 35,000 | $ 26,000 |
| Accounts receivable | 66,000 | 50,000 | 16,000 |
| Inventory | 155,000 | 96,000 | 59,000 |
| Stock investments | 100,000 | 70,000 | 30,000 |
| Equipment | 170,000 | 100,000 | 70,000 |
| Accumulated depreciation | (31,000) | (20,000) | (11,000) |
|  | $521,000 | $331,000 | $190,000 |
|  |  |  |  |
| **Liabilities and Stockholders' Equity** |  |  |  |
| Accounts payable | $ 32,000 | $ 40,000 | $ (8,000) |
| Long-term note payable | 72,000 | 60,000 | 12,000 |
| Bonds payable | 100,000 | 0 | 100,000 |
| Common stock | 60,000 | 50,000 | 10,000 |
| Additional paid-in capital | 190,000 | 150,000 | 40,000 |
| Retained earnings | 67,000 | 31,000 | 36,000 |
|  | $521,000 | $331,000 | $190,000 |

Additional information:
1. New equipment costing $80,000 was purchased for cash.
2. Old equipment was sold at a loss of $4,500.
3. Bonds were issued for cash.
4. An investment costing $30,000 was acquired by issuing a long-term note payable.
5. Cash dividends of $14,000 were declared and paid during the year.
6. Depreciation expense for 2010 was $15,000.
7. Accounts Payable relate to operating expenses.
8. Stock investments are classified as available-for-sale securities.

**Instructions**
Prepare a statement of cash flows for 2010 using the indirect method.

| TIP: | In this exercise, you must analyze the changes in the Retained Earnings account balance to determine the net income figure for 2010. |
|---|---|

## SOLUTION TO EXERCISE 23-2

**HERNAN PEREZ PICTURES**
**Statement of Cash Flows**
**For the Year Ending December 31, 2010**

| | | |
|---|---:|---:|
| Cash flows from operating activities | | |
| Net income | | $ 50,000 |
| Adjustments to reconcile net income to net cash provided | | |
| by operating activities: | | |
| Increase in accounts receivable | $ (16,000) | |
| Increase in inventory | (59,000) | |
| Depreciation expense | 15,000 | |
| Loss on sale of equipment | 4,500 | |
| Decrease in accounts payable | (8,000) | (63,500) |
| Net cash used by operating activities | | (13,500) |
| Cash flows from investing activities | | |
| Purchase of equipment | (80,000) | |
| Sale of equipment | 1,500 | |
| Net cash used by investing activities | | (78,500) |
| Cash flows from financing activities | | |
| Payment on long-term note payable | (18,000) | |
| Issuance of bonds | 100,000 | |
| Issuance of stock | 50,000 | |
| Payment of dividends | (14,000) | |
| Net cash provided by financing activities | | 118,000 |
| Net increase in cash | | 26,000 |
| Cash at beginning of period | | 35,000 |
| Cash at end of period | | $ 61,000 |

**Noncash investing and financing activities**

| | |
|---|---:|
| Acquisition of investment in stock by issuance of long-term debt | $ 30,000 |

> **TIP:** Examine the statement and notice the major reasons for inflows and outflows of cash during the period.

**Approach:** Glance through the balance sheet data and additional information to get a feel for the facts given. Set up the format for the statement of cash flows by placing the major headings for the three activity classifications approximately where they go. Leave space to fill in the details later (allow about one-fourth page for investing activities, about one-fourth page for financing activities, and approximately one-half page for the operating activities section). Then take each fact in order and process it by placing it where it belongs on the statement of cash flows.

1. Find the net change in cash by comparing the balance of Cash at the end of the period with the balance of Cash at the beginning of the period. Use the net change in cash to reconcile beginning and ending cash balances.
2. Analyze every change in every balance sheet account other than Cash. Reconstruct the journal entries for the transactions that caused the balance sheet accounts to change. Examine each entry to identify if (a) there is an inflow of cash (debit to Cash) or an outflow

of cash (credit to Cash) or no effect on cash; (b) if the transaction involves an operating, investing, or financing activity, and (c) where it goes on the statement of cash flows.

3. To help identify the activity classification for each transaction, write down the definitions for investing activities, financing activities, and operating activities. Analyze each transaction to see if it meets one of these definitions. (Refer to **Illustration 23-1** for these definitions.)

4. To help identify investing activities, recall that transactions involving investing activities typically cause changes in noncurrent asset accounts (or changes in current asset accounts such as short-term investments and nontrade receivables).

5. To help identify financing activities, recall that transactions involving financing activities typically cause changes in noncurrent liability accounts or stockholders' equity accounts (or changes in current liability accounts such as short-term nontrade notes payable).

6. To help identify transactions involving operating activities, recall that operating activities typically result in recording revenues or expenses in some period of time. Thus, the journal entry to record the transaction either involves revenue earned, expense incurred, a receivable, a prepaid expense, a payable or an unearned revenue. When the indirect method is used, the net income figure is used as a starting point for the calculation of "net cash flows provided by operating activities." The net income figure must then be converted from the accrual basis to a cash basis amount. To help identify the transactions requiring an adjustment to net income, find the transactions whose journal entries involve an income statement account and a balance sheet account other than Cash (such as depreciation or amortization of a prepaid expense) or that involve Cash and accruals or deferrals of revenues or expenses (such as the entry to record the payment of expense in advance of its incurrence).

7. If the reasons for changes in balance sheet accounts are not fully explained in the additional information, assume the most common reason for a change. Assume purchases and sales of assets are for cash unless otherwise indicated.

8. When more than one transaction accounts for the net change in an account balance, it is wise to draw a T-account for the account in question and reflect all transactions occurring during the period.

## Explanation:

1. There was an increase of $26,000 in the Cash account. The net change goes near the bottom of the statement and reconciles the $35,000 beginning cash balance with the $61,000 ending cash balance.

2. The journal entry to record the increase in Accounts Receivable is reconstructed as follows:

| | | |
|---|---|---|
| Accounts Receivable............................................... | 16,000 | |
|     Sales................................................................ | | 16,000 |

Net income is increased but Cash is not increased; thus, using the indirect method, this increase in receivables is deducted from net income to arrive at the net cash provided by operating activities. An increase in accounts receivable indicates that sales revenue for the period exceeds the cash collections from customers during the period; therefore, net income is greater than net cash provided by operating activities.

3. The journal entry to record the increase in Inventory is reconstructed as follows:

| | | |
|---|---|---|
| Inventory............................................................. | 59,000 | |
|     Cash ................................................................ | | 59,000 |

Payments to suppliers are an operating outflow. This outflow is not reflected in the net income figure so, using the indirect method, the increase in inventory is deducted from net income to arrive at net cash provided by operating activities. An increase in inventory indicates that cost of goods sold expense is less than cash payments to suppliers; therefore, net income is greater than net cash provided by operating activities.

4. The journal entry to record the increase in Stock Investments is reconstructed as follows:

| | | |
|---|---|---|
| Stock Investments (Available-for-sale)............................. | 30,000 | |
| Long-term Note Payable............................................ | | 30,000 |

The acquisition of an available-for-sale security is an investing activity, and the issuance of debt is a financing activity; however, there is no effect on cash. This noncash investing and financing activity must be reported on a separate schedule to accompany the statement of cash flows. It is **not** to be reported in the body of the statement of cash flows.

5. The T-accounts for Equipment, Accumulated Depreciation, and Loss on the Sale of Equipment would appear as follows:

**Equipment**

| | | | |
|---|---|---|---|
| Jan. 1, 2010 Balance | 100,000 | Unexplained transaction | |
| Acquisition during 2010 | 80,000 | during 2010 | 10,000 |
| Dec. 31, 2010 Balance | 170,000 | | |

**Accumulated Depreciation**

| | | | |
|---|---|---|---|
| Unexplained transaction | | Jan. 1, 2010 Balance | 20,000 |
| during 2010 | 4,000 | Depreciation for 2010 | 15,000 |
| | | Dec. 31, 2010 Balance | 31,000 |

**Loss on Sale of Equipment**

| | |
|---|---|
| Sale of equipment during 2010 | 4,500 |

The problem states that Equipment costing $80,000 was purchased. Depreciation expense amounted to $15,000, and old equipment was sold at a loss of $4,500. We can solve for the missing data—an unexplained credit of $10,000 to Equipment and an unexplained debit of $4,000 to Accumulated Depreciation. The most common reason for a credit to the Equipment account is the disposal of an asset. That transaction also explains the $4,000 reduction in the Accumulated Depreciation account and the recording of a $4,500 loss. Thus, it appears that an asset with a cost of $10,000 and a book value of $6,000 ($10,000 - $4,000 = $6,000) was sold at a loss of $4,500. This means the cash proceeds amounted to $1,500 ($6,000 book value - $4,500 loss = $1,500 proceeds).

The journal entries to record the transactions mentioned above would be reconstructed as follows:

| | | |
|---|---|---|
| Equipment ............................................................ | 80,000 | |
| Cash ............................................................. | | 80,000 |

Cash decreased. The purchase of plant assets is an investing activity. Therefore, an outflow is reported in the investing section.

| | | |
|---|---|---|
| Depreciation Expense ......................................... | 15,000 | |
| Accumulated Depreciation......................................... | | 15,000 |

There is no effect on Cash but net income was reduced. Using the indirect method, depreciation expense is added to net income to compute the net cash provided by operating activities.

| | |
|---|---:|
| Cash.............................................................................. | 1,500 |
| Loss on Sale of Equipment ............................................. | 4,500 |
| Accumulated Depreciation ............................................... | 4,000 |
|     Equipment ............................................................ | 10,000 |

There is an inflow of $1,500 cash due to the disposal of plant assets which is an investing activity. When the indirect method is used, the loss must be added to net income; there was no corresponding outflow of cash.

6. The journal entry to record the decrease in Accounts Payable is reconstructed as follows:

| | | |
|---|---:|---:|
| Accounts Payable............................................................. | 8,000 | |
|     Cash ................................................................ | | 8,000 |

Payments to suppliers for goods and services consumed in operations is an operating activity. Using the indirect method, this decrease in Accounts Payable must be deducted from net income because a decrease in Accounts Payable indicates expenses incurred were less than cash payments to suppliers; hence, net income was more than the net cash provided by operating activities.

7. The T-account for Long-term Note Payable would appear as follows:

Long-term Note Payable

| | | | |
|---|---:|---|---:|
| Unexplained transaction | | Jan. 1, 2010 Balance | 60,000 |
| during 2010 | 18,000 | Issued for investment in 2010 | 30,000 |
| | | Dec. 31, 2010 Balance | 72,000 |

The most common reason for a debit to a liability account is a payment. The journal entries for the transactions affecting this account are reconstructed as follows:

| | | |
|---|---:|---:|
| Stock Investments (Available-for-sale).............................. | 30,000 | |
|     Long-term Note Payable............................................ | | 30,000 |

This transaction was analyzed and handled in point #4 above.

| | | |
|---|---:|---:|
| Long-term Note Payable ................................................. | 18,000 | |
|     Cash ................................................................ | | 18,000 |

This represents an $18,000 cash outflow due to the payment of a nontrade note payable which is a financing activity.

8. The journal entry to record the increase in Bonds Payable is reconstructed as follows:

| | | |
|---|---:|---:|
| Cash.............................................................................. | 100,000 | |
|     Bonds Payable ........................................................ | | 100,000 |

There is a cash inflow of $100,000 due to borrowing which is a financing activity.

9. The most common reason for an increase in the Common Stock account is the issuance of stock for cash. The journal entry to record that transaction is reconstructed as follows:

| | | |
|---|---:|---:|
| Cash.............................................................................. | 50,000 | |
|     Common Stock........................................................ | | 10,000 |
|     Paid-in Capital in Excess of Par ............................... | | 40,000 |

There is an inflow of cash of $50,000 due to the issuance of stock. Obtaining resources from owners is a financing activity.

> **TIP:** Notice that this transaction is reported by a single line item for $50,000 on the statement of cash flows even though it caused two stockholders' equity accounts to change—Common Stock increased $10,000 and Paid-in Capital in Excess of Par (an additional paid-in capital account) increased by $40,000.

10. The Retained Earnings T-account would appear as follows:

Retained Earnings

| Declaration of Cash Dividends during 2010 | 14,000 | Jan. 1, 2010 Balance | 31,000 |
|---|---|---|---|
| | | Unexplained transaction during 2010 | 50,000 |
| | | Dec. 31, 2010 Balance | 67,000 |

The most common reason for having a credit to Retained Earnings is net income. Because the indirect method is used, the net income figure is needed as the starting point for the computation of net cash provided by operating activities.

The journal entries to record the declaration and payment of cash dividends are reconstructed as follows:

| Retained Earnings | 14,000 | |
| Dividends Payable | | 14,000 |

| Dividends Payable | 14,000 | |
| Cash | | 14,000 |

Cash decreases by $14,000. Providing owners with a return on their investment constitutes a financing activity. The declaration of dividends has no effect on cash. The payment of a previously declared dividend reduces cash. The payment of cash dividends is to be reported as a financing outflow.

> **TIP:** The last step in the preparation of the statement of cash flows is to subtotal each of the three activity classifications. Inflows are shown as positive amounts; outflows are shown as negative amounts. An excess of inflows over outflows in a category results in a net inflow; an excess of outflows over inflows is captioned as a net outflow. The subtotals of the three activities are then summarized to determine the net change in cash during the year. This net change must agree with your analysis of the change in the Cash account balance (Step 1); otherwise, one or more errors exist and must be corrected to make the statement balance.

# CASE 23-1

**Purpose:**    (L.O. 2) This case will help you to classify transactions as being an operating activity, an investing activity, or a financing activity.

There are four situations described below:
1.    A company purchased a machine priced at $100,000 by issuing a check for $100,000.
2.    A company purchased a machine priced at $100,000 by giving a down payment of $20,000 and by issuing a note payable to the seller for $80,000. During the same year, the company made principal payments of $12,000 on the note and interest payments of $7,000.
3.    A company purchased a machine for $100,000. Of that amount, $80,000 was obtained by borrowing from a local bank. During the same year, principal payments of $12,000 and interest payments of $7,000 were made to the bank on this loan.
4.    A company acquired a machine by a capital lease agreement. The present value of the minimum lease payments at the inception date was $100,000. The first lease payment of $2,000 was made at the inception date. During the year, additional lease payments of $24,000 were made which included interest of $15,000.

## Instructions

For each situation above, explain how it would be reflected in a statement of cash flows. That is, indicate if it is reported in the operating, investing, or financing section of the statement of cash flows or in the schedule of noncash investing and financing activities. Also, indicate the amount reported and if it is a cash inflow or outflow.

## Solution to Case 23-1

1.    Investing outflow of $100,000

2.    Investing outflow of $20,000
Financing outflow of $12,000
Operating outflow of $7,000

    The schedule of noncash investing and financing activities would include the acquisition of machinery by issuance of note payable for $80,000.

3.    Financing inflow of $80,000
Investing outflow of $100,000
Financing outflow of $12,000
Operating outflow of $7,000

4.    Financing outflow of $11,000 ($2,000 + $24,000 - $15,000)
Operating outflow of $15,000

    The schedule of noncash investing and financing activities would include the acquisition of machinery by capital lease for $100,000.

**Approach:** Refer to **Illustration 23-1** for a description of the three classifications of activities.

---

**TIP:**    Note that all interest payments are classified as operating outflows. Also, note that in situations #2 and #4, all payments of principal on seller-financed debt are classified as financing outflows.

---

# ILLUSTRATION 23-2
# CONVERSION FROM ACCRUAL BASIS TO CASH BASIS (L.O. 3, 4)

| **ACCRUAL BASIS** | **CASH BASIS** |
|---|---|
| Revenues Earned | Cash Received from Operations |
| - <u>Expenses Incurred</u> | - <u>Cash Paid for Operations</u> |
| = Net Income | = Net Cash Provided by Operating Activities |

### DIRECT METHOD

**To Compute Net Cash Provided by Operating Activities:**

|   | |
|---|---|
|   | Cash Received From Customers |
| + | Interest and Dividends Received |
| + | Other Operating Cash Receipts |
| - | Cash Paid for Operating Expenses and Merchandise Inventory |
| - | Interest Paid |
| - | Income Taxes Paid |
| - | <u>Other Operating Cash Payments</u> |
| = | Net Cash Provided by Operating Activities |

**Explanation:** The major classes of cash receipts and cash payments from operating activities (for which selected computations are shown below) are listed and summarized on the face of the statement of cash flows when the direct method is used.

**To Convert Revenues Earned to Cash Received:**

|   | |
|---|---|
|   | Revenues Earned |
| - | Increase in Accounts Receivable |
| + | <u>Increase in Unearned Revenues</u> |
| = | Cash Received from Customers |

**Explanation:** An increase in accounts receivable from one balance sheet date to the next indicates that revenues earned exceed cash collections from customers; hence, subtract the increase in accounts receivable from sales revenue to obtain the amount of cash received from customers. (A decrease in receivables would indicate cash collections exceed revenues earned and would be added to revenues earned to compute cash collections.) An increase in unearned revenues indicates that cash collections from customers exceed revenues earned; hence, add the increase in unearned revenues to revenues earned to obtain the amount of cash received from customers. (A decrease in unearned revenue indicates opposite relationships.)

## ILLUSTRATION 23-2 (Continued)

### OR

| | Revenues Earned |
|---|---|
| + | Beginning Accounts Receivable |
| - | Ending Accounts Receivable |
| - | Beginning Unearned Revenues |
| + | <u>Ending Unearned Revenues</u> |
| = | Cash Received from Customers |

**Explanation:** The balance of accounts receivable at the beginning of the period represents revenues earned in a prior period that are collected in the current period; ending accounts receivable stem from revenues earned in the current period that are not yet collected. Beginning unearned revenues represent cash col-lections in a prior period (not the current period) that are for revenues earned in the current period. Ending unearned revenues come from collections during the current period that are not recognized as earned revenues.

**To Convert Cost of Goods Sold to Cash Paid:**

| | Cost of Goods Sold Expense |
|---|---|
| + | <u>Increase in Inventory</u> |
| = | Purchases |
| - | <u>Increase in Accounts Payable</u> |
| = | Cash Paid for Merchandise Inventory |

**Explanation:** An increase in inventory means purchases for the period exceed cost of goods sold. An increase in accounts payable indicates purchases exceed cash payments for merchandise. (Decreases indicate opposite relationships.)

### OR

| | Cost of Goods Sold Expense |
|---|---|
| - | Beginning Inventory |
| + | <u>Ending Inventory</u> |
| = | Purchases |
| + | Beginning Accounts Payable (for purchases of merchandise) |
| - | Ending Accounts Payable (for <u>purchases of merchandise)</u> |
| = | Cash Paid for Merchandise Inventory |

**Explanation:** Beginning inventory represents items purchased in a prior period that were consumed (sold) in the current year. Ending inventory represents items purchased in the current period that are not reported in the cost of goods sold expense (because they are on hand at the balance sheet date). Beginning accounts payable come from purchases of a prior period (as opposed to purchases of the current period) that require cash payment during the current period. The ending accounts payable balance stems from purchases in the current period that are not paid for in the current period.

**To Convert Operating Expenses to Cash Paid:**

| | Operating Expenses Incurred (**Excluding** Depreciation and Bad Debt Expense) |
|---|---|
| + | Increase in Prepaid Expenses |
| - | <u>Increase in Accrued Payables</u> |
| = | Cash Paid for Operating Expenses |

**Explanation:** An increase in a prepaid expense indicates expenses incurred are less than cash payments for those items. Therefore, the increase in the prepaid is added to the expense total to obtain the amount of related cash payments. An increase in accrued payables indicates the expense total exceeds the cash payments for these items; hence, the increase in accrued payables is deducted from the expense balance to arrive at cash payments. (A decrease is handled in the opposite manner.)

## ILLUSTRATION 23-2 (Continued)

### OR

Operating Expenses Incurred
(**Excluding** Depreciation and
Bad Debt Expense)
- Beginning Prepaid Expenses
+ Ending Prepaid Expenses
+ Beginning Accrued Payables
- Ending Accrued Payables
= Cash Paid for Operating
Expenses

**Explanation:** Beginning prepaid expenses represent amounts recognized as expense in the current period for which cash payments are not made in the current period. (The cash payments occurred in a prior period.) Ending prepaids stem from cash payments in the current period for expenses not recognized in the current period. (The expense recognition is being deferred to a future period.) Beginning accrued payables come from expenses recognized in a prior period (not the current year) that require cash payments during the current period. Ending accrued payables stem from expenses recognized during the current year that have not yet been paid.

**To Convert Interest Expense to Interest Paid:**
Interest Expense
- Increase in Interest Payable
- Amortization of Discount on Debt
+ Amortization of Premium on Debt
= Interest Paid

**Explanation:** An increase in an accrued payable indicates that expense exceeds the related cash payments. (A decrease in an accrued payable would indicate the opposite relationship—that expense is less than cash payments.) The amortization of discount on a debt increases total interest expense but does not cause a cash outlay; the amortization of premium on a debt instrument decreases total interest expense but does not reduce the cash outlay required for the interest.

### OR

Interest Expense
+ Beginning Interest Payable
- Ending Interest Payable
- Amortization of Discount on Debt
+ Amortization of Premium on Debt
= Interest Paid

**Explanation:** The balance of Interest Payable at the beginning of the period comes from interest expense accrued in a prior period. Therefore, that amount requires a cash outlay in the current period that relates to an expense of a prior period. The ending balance of Interest Payable comes about from interest accrued in the current period. Therefore, this amount is part of the total interest expense for the current period but it is not part of the cash paid for interest this period. The amortization of discount on a debt instrument increases total interest expense but does not cause a cash outlay; the amortization of premium on a debt instrument decreases total interest expense but does not decrease the corresponding cash outflow.

## ILLUSTRATION 23-2 (Continued)

**To Convert Income Tax Expense
to Income Taxes Paid:**

   Income Tax Expense
+  Increase in Prepaid Income Taxes
-  Increase in Income Tax Payable
+  Increase in Deferred Tax Asset
-  <u>Increase in Deferred Tax Liability</u>
=  Income Taxes Paid

**Explanation:** An increase in Prepaid Income Taxes and/or an increase in Deferred Tax Asset indicates that the amount of income tax expense is less than the amount paid for income taxes during the period. An increase in Income Tax Payable and/or an increase in Deferred Tax Liability indicates that the amount of income tax expense exceeds the amount paid for income taxes during the period.

**OR**

   Income Tax Expense
-  Beginning Prepaid Income Taxes
+  Ending Prepaid Income Taxes
+  Beginning Income Tax Payable
-  Ending Income Tax Payable
-  Beginning Deferred Tax Asset
+  Ending Deferred Tax Asset
+  Beginning Deferred Tax Liability
-  <u>Ending Deferred Tax Liability</u>
=  Income Taxes Paid

**Explanation:** A beginning prepaid income tax amount represents taxes recognized as expense in the current period for which a cash payment was made in a prior period. An ending prepaid income tax amount stems from cash payments in the current period for taxes to be expensed in a future period (rather than in the current period). A beginning income tax payable balance stems from income tax expense recognized in a prior period (not the current period) that requires cash payments during the current period. An ending balance in Income Tax Payable stems from income taxes recognized as expense in the current period that have not yet been paid. Changes in the balances of deferred tax assets or liabilities cause the income tax expense figure to change without a corresponding impact on cash. The treatment of the balance of Deferred Tax Asset in this reconciliation is the same as for Prepaid Income Taxes, and the treatment of the balance of Deferred Tax Liability is the same as for Income Tax Payable.

---

**TIP:**   For all of the items above, a **decrease** in an account balance will be handled in a manner **opposite** of the way an **increase** is to be treated.

---

## ILLUSTRATION 23-2 (Continued)

### INDIRECT METHOD

**To Compute Net Cash Provided
by Operating Activities:**

    Net income

Add noncash charges (such as depreciation
    expense, amortization of intangibles, and
    share-based compensation expense)

Add losses due to writedown of assets

Add losses on sale of assets, settlement of
    debt, and discontinued operations

Add (deduct) decrease (increase) in net
    accounts receivable

Add (deduct) decrease (increase) in accrued
    receivables

Add (deduct) decrease (increase) in
    inventory

Add (deduct) decrease (increase) in prepaid
    expenses

Add (deduct) decrease (increase) in deferred
    tax assets

Add (deduct) increase (decrease) in accounts
    payable

Add (deduct) increase (decrease) in accrued
    payables

Add (deduct) increase (decrease) in unearned
    revenues

Add (deduct) increase (decrease) in deferred
    tax liabilities

Add (deduct) difference between amount ex-
    pensed and amount funded for pension plan

Deduct noncash credits (such as amortization
    of premium on bonds payable and income
    recognized under equity method in excess
    of dividends received)

Deduct noncash gains (such as unrealized
    holding gain on investment in trading
    securities)

Deduct gains on sale of assets, settlement of
    of debt, and discontinued operations

=    Net cash provided by operating activities

**Explanation:** Noncash charges (such as depreciation and amortization) and losses due to writedown of assets are **added** to net income because they are expense or loss items that do not require an outlay of cash. Losses (or gains) from the sale of assets, settlement of debt, and discontinued operations are **added** to (or deducted from) net income because they relate to transactions for which the related cash flows are to be classified as investing or financing activities. An increase in receivables indicates that revenues earned **exceed** cash inflows; therefore, net income **exceeds** net cash provided by operating activities. An increase in inventory or prepaid expenses indicates that expenses are **less** than cash outflows; hence, net income is **more** than net cash provided by operating activities. Increases in accounts receivable, accrued receivables, inventory, and prepaid expenses must therefore be **deducted** from net income to obtain the amount of cash generated by operations. On the other hand, an increase in accounts payable or accrued payables indicates that expenses incurred **exceed** the amount of cash paid for merchandise inventory and operating expenses; hence, net income is **less** than net cash provided by operations. An increase in unearned revenues indicates that revenue earned is **less** than the cash received and net income is **less** than net cash generated by operations. Therefore, increases in accounts payable, accrued payables, and unearned revenues must be **added** to net income to compute the amount of cash generated by operations. Noncash credits (such as the recognition of income using the equity method) are **deducted** from net income because they increase net income without having a corresponding cash inflow.

## ILLUSTRATION 23-2 (Continued)

### SUMMARY OF TREATMENT FOR ACCRUALS AND DEFERRALS

The treatment of increases during the period for deferred revenues, deferred expenses, accrued expenses, and accrued revenues can be summarized for both the direct method and the indirect method as follows:

|  | Direct Method | | Indirect Method |
|---|---|---|---|
|  | **Revenues** | **Expenses** | **Net Income** |
| Increase in Unearned Revenues | + | | + |
| Increase in Prepaid Expenses | | + | - |
| Increase in Payables | | - | + |
| Increase in Receivables | - | | - |
|  | **Cash Received From Operations** | **Cash Paid For Operations** | **Net Cash Provided by Operating Activities** |

> **TIP:** In examining the summary above, notice the mathematical signs are the **same** for both the direct method and indirect method for handling a change in unearned revenues or a change in receivables. The reasons for this are (1) changes in unearned revenues and receivables are items which explain the difference between revenues earned during a period and cash received from operations; and (2) revenues earned are a **positive** component of net income, and cash received from operations is a **positive** component of net cash provided by operating activities.
>
> Also notice that the mathematical signs are **different** for the direct method and the indirect method for handling a change in prepaid expenses and payables. The reasons for this are (1) changes in prepaid expenses and payables are items which explain the difference between expenses incurred during a period and cash paid for operations; and (2) expenses incurred are a **negative** component of net income, and cash paid out for operations is a **negative** component of net cash provided by operating activities.
>
> **TIP:** "Cash provided by operating activities" (or "cash provided by operations") is another name for "net income on a cash basis."

## EXERCISE 23-3

**Purpose:** (L. O. 7)  This exercise will test your ability to convert accrual basis information to cash basis information.

The Tom Fuller Corporation reported the following on its income statement for 2010:

| | |
|---|---:|
| Sales revenue | $600,000 |
| Cost of goods sold | 400,000 |
| Salaries expense | 42,000 |
| Insurance expense | 3,000 |
| Depreciation expense | 50,000 |
| Other operating expenses | 60,000 |
| Income tax expense | 18,000 |
| Net income | 27,000 |

The comparative balance sheets reported the following selected information:

| | 12/31/10 | 12/31/09 | Increase (Decrease) |
|---|---:|---:|---:|
| Cash | $26,000 | $12,000 | $14,000 |
| Accounts Receivable | 37,000 | 41,000 | (4,000) |
| Inventory | 76,000 | 74,000 | 2,000 |
| Prepaid Insurance | 4,380 | 4,200 | 180 |
| Accounts Payable | 27,100 | 24,200 | 2,900 |
| Salaries Payable | 500 | 800 | (300) |
| Income Taxes Payable | 18,000 | 12,500 | 5,500 |
| Deferred Tax Liability | 5,400 | 5,000 | 400 |

All of the operating expenses reflected in the "other operating expenses" category were paid in cash during 2010.  Accounts payable relate to purchases of merchandise inventory.

**Instructions**
Compute the following amounts for 2010:
(a)  Cash collections from customers.
(b)  Cash payments for merchandise.
(c)  Cash payments to employees.
(d)  Cash payments for insurance.
(e)  Cash payments for income taxes.
(f)  Net cash provided by operating activities.

## SOLUTION TO EXERCISE 23-3

(a)

| Sales revenue | $600,000 |
|---|---|
| Decrease in accounts receivable | 4,000 |
| Cash collections from customers | $604,000 |

OR

| Sales revenue | $600,000 |
|---|---|
| Beginning accounts receivable | 41,000 |
| Ending accounts receivable | (37,000) |
| Cash collections from customers | $604,000 |

(b)

| Cost of goods sold expense | $400,000 |
|---|---|
| Increase in inventory | 2,000 |
| Purchases | 402,000 |
| Increase in accounts payable | (2,900) |
| Cash payments for merchandise | $399,100 |

OR

| Cost of goods sold expense | $400,000 |
|---|---|
| Beginning inventory | (74,000) |
| Ending inventory | 76,000 |
| Purchases | 402,000 |
| Beginning accounts payable | 24,200 |
| Ending accounts payable | (27,100) |
| Cash payments for merchandise | $399,100 |

(c)

| Salaries expense | $42,000 |
|---|---|
| Decrease in salaries payable | 300 |
| Cash payments to employees | $42,300 |

OR

| Salaries expense | $42,000 |
|---|---|
| Beginning salaries payable | 800 |
| Ending salaries payable | (500) |
| Cash payments to employees | $42,300 |

(d)

| Insurance expense | $3,000 |
|---|---|
| Increase in prepaid insurance | 180 |
| Cash payments for insurance | $3,180 |

OR

| Insurance expense | $3,000 |
|---|---|
| Beginning prepaid insurance | (4,200) |
| Ending prepaid insurance | 4,380 |
| Cash payments for insurance | $3,180 |

(e)

| Income tax expense | $18,000 |
|---|---|
| Increase in income taxes payable | (5,500) |
| Increase in deferred tax liability | (400) |
| Cash payments for income taxes | $12,100 |

**OR**

| | |
|---|---|
| Income tax expense | $18,000 |
| Beginning income taxes payable | 12,500 |
| Ending income taxes payable | (18,000) |
| Beginning deferred tax liability | 5,000 |
| Ending deferred tax liability | (5,400) |
| Cash payments for income taxes | $12,100 |

(f)

| | |
|---|---|
| Cash received from customers | $604,000 |
| Cash payments for merchandise | (399,100) |
| Cash payments to employees | (42,300) |
| Cash payments for insurance | (3,180) |
| Cash payments for income taxes | (12,100) |
| Cash payments for other operating expenses | (60,000) |
| Net cash provided by operating activities | $ 87,320 |

**TIP:** The change in the cash balance ($14,000 increase) had no effect on the computations requested. The net cash provided (used) by the total of the three activity classifications (operating, investing and financing) should net to this $14,000 increase.

**TIP:** Refer to **Illustration 23-2** for explanations to the above computations.

# EXERCISE 23-4

**Purpose**:    (L.O. 7)  This exercise will allow you to practice identifying how to classify transactions on a statement of cash flows using the direct method.

The J & M Salter Corporation uses the direct method for preparing the statement of cash flows. The following summarized transactions took place in 2010:

| | |
|---|---|
| Collected cash from customers on account | $ 75,000 |
| Paid interest on debt | 3,000 |
| Paid principal of note payable | 30,000 |
| Sold services for cash | 19,000 |
| Paid salaries and wages | 27,000 |
| Paid other operating expenses | 41,000 |
| Recorded depreciation expense | 7,000 |
| Paid dividends | 6,000 |
| Purchased machinery | 60,000 |
| Sold equipment for book value | 12,000 |
| Issued common stock in exchange for cash | 45,000 |
| Issued long-term debt | 52,000 |
| Amortized patents | 1,000 |
| Purchased treasury stock | 4,000 |
| Accrued salaries | 800 |
| Purchased an investment | 38,200 |
| Acquired a computer in exchange for J & M Salter common stock | 10,000 |
| Received dividends from investee | 700 |
| Paid income taxes | 6,500 |
| Sold an investment (and recognized a gain of $3,300) | 24,000 |

## Instructions

(a) Compute the following:
- (1) Net cash provided (used) by operating activities.
- (2) Net cash provided (used) by investing activities.
- (3) Net cash provided (used) by financing activities.
- (4) Net increase (decrease) in cash for the period.

(b) If any transactions are **not** used in the required computations in (a), explain why.

(c) Based on the information given, prepare a statement of cash flows using the direct method. Assume the cash balance at the beginning of the year was $23,000.

## SOLUTION TO EXERCISE 23-4

(a) (1)

| | |
|---|---:|
| Collected cash from customers on account | $75,000 |
| Sold services for cash | 19,000 |
| Received dividends from investee | 700 |
| Paid interest on debt | (3,000) |
| Paid salaries and wages | (27,000) |
| Paid other operating expenses | (41,000) |
| Paid income taxes | (6,500) |
| Net cash provided by operations | $17,200 |

(2)

| | |
|---|---:|
| Purchased machinery | $(60,000) |
| Sold equipment for book value | 12,000 |
| Purchased an investment | (38,200) |
| Sold an investment | 24,000 |
| Net cash used by investing activities | $(62,200) |

(3)

| | |
|---|---:|
| Paid principal of note payable | $(30,000) |
| Paid dividends | (6,000) |
| Issued common stock | 45,000 |
| Issued long-term debt | 52,000 |
| Purchased treasury stock | (4,000) |
| Net cash provided by financing activities | $57,000 |

(4)

| | |
|---|---:|
| Net cash provided by operating activities | $17,200 |
| Net cash used by investing activities | (62,200) |
| Net cash provided by financing activities | 57,000 |
| Net increase in cash | $12,000 |

(b) (1) Recorded depreciation expense, $7,000, was not used because it is a noncash charge to income. It is an expense which did not require a cash payment. (The cash outlay occurs at the date that payment is made to acquire the related depreciable assets.)

(2) Amortized patents, $1,000, was not used because it is a noncash charge against income. It is an expense which did not require a cash outlay this period. (The cash outlay occurs at the date that cash payment is made for the acquisition of related intangible assets.)

(3) Accrued salaries, $800, was not used because it relates to an expense recognized this period for which the related cash payment is being deferred until next period.

(4)  Acquired a computer in exchange for stock, $10,000, was not used because this is a noncash financing and investing activity.

---

**TIP:**  If the indirect method was used:  (1) the depreciation of $7,000 and the amortization of $1,000 would be added to net income, (2) an increase in the Salaries Payable account of $800 (due to the accrued salaries) would also be added to net income, and (3) the $3,300 gain on sale of investment would be deducted from net income in the process of reconciling net income to net cash provided from operations.

---

(c)

**J & M SALTER CORPORATION**
**Statement of Cash Flows**
**For the Year Ending December 31, 2010**
**(Direct Method)**

| | | |
|---|---:|---:|
| Cash flows from operating activities | | |
|     Cash receipts from customers | $94,000ᵃ | |
|     Dividends received from investee | 700 | |
|     Interest paid | (3,000) | |
|     Cash paid to employees | (27,000) | |
|     Cash paid for operating expenses | (41,000) | |
|     Income taxes paid | (6,500) | |
|       Net cash provided by operating activities | | $17,200 |
| Cash flows from investing activities | | |
|     Purchase of machinery | (60,000) | |
|     Sale of equipment | 12,000 | |
|     Purchase of investment | (38,200) | |
|     Sale of investment | 24,000 | |
|       Net cash used by investing activities | | (62,200) |
| Cash flows from financing activities | | |
|     Payment of note payable | (30,000) | |
|     Payment of dividends | (6,000) | |
|     Issuance of common stock | 45,000 | |
|     Issuance of long-term debt | 52,000 | |
|     Purchase of treasury stock | (4,000) | |
|       Net cash provided by financing activities | | 57,000 |
| Net increase in cash | | 12,000 |
| Cash at beginning of period | | 23,000 |
| Cash at end of period | | $35,000ᵇ |

**Noncash investing and financing activities**

| | |
|---|---:|
|     Acquired a computer in exchange for common stock | $10,000 |

ᵃ$75,000 + $19,000 = $94,000.
ᵇ$12,000 net increase in cash + $23,000 beginning cash balance = $35,000 ending cash balance.

---

**TIP:**  An additional schedule reconciling net income to net cash provided by operating activities should be presented as part of the statement of cash flows when using the direct method. The information with this exercise is insufficient to prepare that complete schedule.

---

## EXERCISE 23-5

**Purpose:**  (L.O. 6) This exercise will provide examples of transactions and their treatment on a statement of cash flows using the indirect method.

### CODE FOR FORMAT OF STATEMENT OF CASH FLOWS
### FOR USE WITH EXERCISE 23-2
(Read Instructions for use below)

| Code Items | Format of the Statement |
|---|---|
| | Cash flows from operating activities: |
| | Net income (loss). |
| A | Add noncash expenses (charges), losses, and changes in certain accounts needed to convert income to a cash basis. |
| D | Deduct noncash revenue (credits), gains, and changes in certain accounts needed to convert income to a cash basis. |
| | Net cash provided (used) by operating activities. |
| | |
| | Cash flows from investing activities: |
| II | Add amount for an **investing** activity that produced a cash **inflow**. |
| IO | Deduct amount for an **investing** activity that resulted in a cash **outflow**. |
| | Net cash provided (used) by investing activities. |
| | |
| | Cash flows from financing activities: |
| FI | Add amount for a **financing** activity that produced a cash **inflow**. |
| FO | Deduct amount for a **financing** activity that produced a cash **outflow**. |
| | Net cash provided (used) by financing activities. |
| | |
| | Net increase (decrease) in cash and cash equivalents. |
| | Cash and cash equivalents at beginning of year. |
| | Cash and cash equivalents at end of year. |

NI      Use this code for a transaction which is an operating activity and a component of net income. The transaction has the same effect (positive or negative) on cash as it has on the net income calculation (thus, it is part of net income and **no** adjustment to net income for this item is appropriate).

NC      Use this code for a noncash financing and/or investing activity to be reported on a separate schedule.

C       Use this code to refer to a transaction which only affects cash and cash equivalents.

X       Use this code for a transaction or event which is not reported or otherwise reflected on the statement of cash flows.

## Instructions

For each of the following transactions and events, indicate how it should be reported in a statement of cash flows using the indirect approach. Use the code from the format above for short-hand notations for your responses. Include the appropriate dollar amount with each code. A transaction or event may require more than one code for a complete answer.

_____ $_____     1.    Borrow $50,000 by issuance of a short-term note payable.

_____ $_____
_____ $_____     2.    Sell land used in operations: Selling price, $15,000; cost, $3,500.

_____ $_____
_____ $_____     3.    Exchange long-term mortgage note receivable for stock in another company: Carrying value of receivable, $38,000; fair value of the stock, $36,000. The shares of stock are to be classified as available-for-sale securities.

_____ $_____     4.    Repay short-term nontrade note payable, $5,100.

_____ $_____     5.    Declare and distribute 10% stock dividend: Par value, $10,000; market value, $18,000.

_____ $_____     6.    Pay administrative salaries for the current period, $56,000.

_____ $_____     7.    Accrue interest expense, $1,500.

_____ $_____     8.    Accrue rent revenue, $1,800.

_____ $_____     9.    Collect magazine subscription revenue in advance, $9,000.

_____ $_____
_____ $_____    10.    Recognize revenue of $5,000 from investment using the equity method of accounting. Collect $1,800 dividends from that investee.

_____ $_____    11.    Acquire machine by exchange of treasury stock: Par value, $10,000; cost of treasury stock, $18,000; market value of stock, $22,000.

_____ $_____    12.    Acquire machinery by issuance of long-term note payable to the seller: Face amount of note, $50,000; stated interest rate 2%; fair value of machinery, $40,000.

_____ $_____    13.    Amortize premium on bonds payable, $200.

_____ $_____    14.    Record increase in deferred income tax asset, $1,000.

_____ $_____    15.    Use $1,000 cash to purchase a 90-day certificate of deposit.

_____ $_____    16.    Record bad debt expense of $7,000.

_____ $_____    17.    Recognize $20,000 of compensation expense for stock options granted; none have been exercised.

_____ $_____
_____ $_____    18.    Settle long-term debt by transfer of a noncurrent investment: Carrying value of debt, $77,000; fair value of assets, $70,000; book value of assets, $70,000.

_____ $_____    19.    Amortize deferred service revenue of $600.

_____ $_____    20.    Sell a plant asset for $1,000: Cost, $7,000; accumulated
_____ $_____           depreciation, $4,000.

_____ $_____    21.    Exchange old truck for new truck and give boot of $11,000: Cost
_____ $_____           of old truck, $10,000; book value of old truck, $3,000; fair value
_____ $_____           of old truck, $2,200; list price of new truck, $14,500.

_____ $_____    22.    Recognize temporary decline of $7,000 in fair value of investment
                            in equity securities classified as trading securities.

_____ $_____    23.    Sell merchandise for $400 cash.

_____ $_____    24.    Pay advertising fees of $1,600 for the current period.

_____ $_____    25.    Purchase treasury stock: Cost, $7,500; par, $3,000; original
                            issuance price, $7,000; cost method is used.

_____ $_____    26.    Pay accounts payable, $5,700.

_____ $_____    27.    Acquire a machine by a capital lease: Present value of minimum
_____ $_____           lease payments at inception, $75,000; first annual payment made
                            at inception, $10,000.

_____ $_____    28.    Receive condemnation award of $88,000: Carrying value of
_____ $_____           condemned land, $78,000, tax rate is 40%.

## Solution to Exercise 23-5

| | | | | | |
|---|---|---|---|---|---|
| 1.FI | $50,000 | | 15. | C | $1,000 |
| 2. II | $15,000; & D $11,500 | | 16. | A | $7,000 |
| 3.NC | $36,000; & A $2,000 | | 17. | A | $20,000 |
| 4.FO | $5,100 18. | | NC | | $70,000; & D $7,000 |
| 5. X | $18,000 | | 19. | D | $600 |
| 6.NI | $56,000 | | 20. | II | $1,000; & A $2,000 |
| 7. A | $1,500 21. | | IO | | $11,000; & A $800; & NC $2,200 |
| 8. D | $1,800 22. | | A | | $7,000 |
| 9. A | $9,000 23. | | NI | | $400 |
| 10.D | $5,000; & A $1,800 | | 24. | NI | $1,600 |
| 11.NC | $22,000 | | 25. | FO | $7,500 |
| 12.NC | $40,000 | | 26. | D | $5,700 |
| 13.D | $200    27. | | NC | | $75,000; & FO $10,000 |
| 14.D | $1,000 28. | | II | | $88,000; & D $10,000 |

**Approach:**

1.    Reconstruct the journal entry for each transaction. Examine each entry to identify if there
      is an inflow of cash, an outflow of cash, or no effect on cash. Assume purchases and
      sales of items are for cash, unless otherwise indicated.

**TIP:**    The journal entry to record a transaction that is an investing activity which results
            in a cash flow will involve: (1) Cash and (2) an asset account other than Cash,

> such as Investment (short-term or long-term), Land, Building, Equipment, Patent, Franchise, etc.
>
> **TIP:** The journal entry to record a transaction that is a financing activity which results in a cash flow will involve: (1) Cash and (2) a liability account or an owners' equity account such as Bonds Payable, Notes Payable, Dividends Payable, Common Stock, Paid-in Capital in Excess of Par, Treasury Stock, etc.

2. Write down the definitions for investing activities and financing activities (see below). Analyze each transaction to see if it fits one of these definitions:

a) **Investing activities**: include (1) making and collecting loans; (2) acquiring and disposing of investments in debt and equity instruments; and (3) acquiring and disposing of property, plant, and equipment.

b) **Financing activities:** include (1) obtaining capital from owners and providing them with a return on and a return of their investment; (2) borrowing money and repaying the amounts borrowed, or otherwise settling the obligation; and (3) obtaining and paying for other resources obtained from creditors.

3. Identify the items requiring adjustments to net income to convert net income to net cash provided by operating activities by identifying the reconstructed journal entries that involve (a) an income statement account and a balance sheet account other than Cash (for example the entry to record depreciation), or (b) the Cash account and a noncash asset or liability account that relates to operating activity (accounts receivable, inventory, accounts payable, etc.) or (c) a gain or loss that has no cash effect or a gain or loss stemming from a transaction that is classified as an investing or financing activity.

4. Identify the items which are noncash financing and investing activities by identifying transactions which fit the definitions of investing activities and/or the definition of financing activities but do not affect Cash.

**Explanation:** The journal entries to record each transaction are reconstructed and analyzed below:

1. Cash.................................................................................... 50,000
   Short-term Note Payable (Nontrade) ........................................... 50,000

   There is an inflow of cash due to a financing activity.

2. Cash.................................................................................... 15,000
   Land ................................................................................. 3,500
   Gain on Sale of Land ............................................................. 11,500

   The cash proceeds from the sale of any asset are to be reflected as a cash inflow. Proceeds of $15,000 from the sale of a plant asset should be reported as an investing inflow. The proceeds of $15,000 represents a recovery of the asset's book value of $3,500 and a gain of $11,500. The gain of $11,500 is also a component of net income. When using the indirect method, the gain must be deducted from net income in reconciling net income with net cash from operating activities so that the $11,500 is not double counted.

3.       Available-for-Sale Securities ..................................................... 36,000
Loss on Disposal of Investment ................................................................. 2,000
      Investment in Mortgage Note Receivable .....................................           38,000

Cash is not affected. This exchange of one noncash asset for another noncash asset is an investing activity that must be disclosed. Regardless of whether this is a similar or dissimilar exchange of nonmonetary assets, a loss on the disposal of the receivable should be recognized on the income statement. That loss is added to net income when the indirect method is used for the statement of cash flows.

4.       Short-term Note Payable (Nontrade) .......................................... 5,100
      Cash   .................................................................................... 5,100

There is an outflow of cash due to a financing activity.

5.       Retained Earnings ..................................................................... 18,000
      Common Stock Dividend Distributable .........................................           10,000
      Paid-in Capital in Excess of Par ................................................           8,000

Common Stock Dividend Distributable .................................................... 10,000
      Common Stock ...........................................................................           10,000

Cash is not affected. There is no financing or investing or operating activity. This transaction is ignored in reporting the statement of cash flows. Other accounting requirements call for disclosure of this item in another financial statement or in the notes to financial statements because it changes stockholders' equity.

6.       Salaries Expense ....................................................................... 56,000
      Cash   .................................................................................... 56,000

There is a $56,000 decrease in cash due to an operating outflow. There is a reduction of $56,000 reflected in the net income figure due to the expense recognition. When the indirect method is used, no adjustment is needed because this transaction reduced both net income and cash.

7.       Interest Expense ....................................................................... 1,500
      Interest Payable .........................................................................           1,500

Net income is reduced but cash is not. This item is added to net income when the indirect method is used.

8.       Rent Receivable ......................................................................... 1,800
      Rent Revenue ............................................................................           1,800

Net income is increased but cash is not. This transaction caused an increase in rent receivable which must be deducted from net income when the indirect method is used.

9.       Cash ......................................................................................... 9,000
      Unearned Subscription Revenue .................................................           9,000

Cash is increased because of collections from customers; this is an operating activity. The inflow is not reflected in net income so the $9,000 increase in unearned revenue is added to net income when the indirect method is used.

| 10. | Investment in Affiliate | 5,000 | |
| | Revenue from Investment | | 5,000 |

| Cash | | 1,800 | |
| | Investment in Affiliate | | 1,800 |

There is a cash flow of $1,800; it is an operating inflow because all dividends received are operating inflows. The first entry increases revenue (and net income) but does not affect cash. The second entry increases cash but does not effect net income. Using the indirect method, the $5,000 credit to income which is not accompanied by a corresponding cash inflow is deducted from net income and the $1,800 cash receipt for dividends is added to net income. Thus, the net $3,200 undistributed earnings of investee is deducted from net income.

| 11. | Machinery | 22,000 | |
| | Treasury Stock | | 18,000 |
| | Paid-in Capital from Treasury Stock | | 4,000 |

Cash is not affected. This is a significant investing activity (acquisition of equipment) and financing activity (disposal of treasury stock) that must be disclosed outside the body of the statement of cash flows.

| 12. | Machinery | 40,000 | |
| Discount on Note Payable | | 10,000 | |
| | Long-term Note Payable | | 50,000 |

A note payable is issued at an unreasonably low interest rate for a noncash asset; it is to be recorded at the fair value of the asset received. Thus, a discount is established. Cash is not affected. This is a significant investing and financing activity that must be disclosed in the footnotes or in a schedule of noncash investing and financing activities.

| 13. | Premium on Bonds Payable | 200 | |
| | Interest Expense | | 200 |

There is an increase in net income without any corresponding cash inflow. Therefore, this credit to income is deducted from net income in the reconciliation of net income to net cash flow from operating activities.

| 14. | Deferred Tax Asset | 1,000 | |
| | Income Tax Expense | | 1,000 |

This entry causes net income to increase, but it does not affect cash. The increase in the deferred tax asset is deducted from net income when the indirect method is used.

| 15. | Certificate of Deposit—90 Day | 1,000 | |
| | Cash | 1,000 | |

There is a decrease in cash and an increase in cash equivalents. Therefore, there is no change in the total of cash and cash equivalents.

| 16. | Bad Debt Expense | 7,000 | |
| | Allowance for Doubtful Accounts | | 7,000 |

Net income decreases but cash does not. This noncash charge to income is added to net income when using the indirect method.

| 17. | Compensation Expense | 20,000 | |
| | Paid-in Capital—Stock Options | | 20,000 |

There is a decrease in net income, but no corresponding cash outflow. The $20,000 expense (or increase in Paid-in Capital—Stock Options) must be added to net income when using the indirect method.

| 18. | Long-term Debt | 77,000 | |
| | Long-term Investment | | 70,000 |
| | Gain on Settlement of Debt | | 7,000 |

Cash is not affected. This is a transaction that is a noncash financing and investing activity to be separately disclosed. When using the indirect method, the gain must be deducted from net income because the gain is a credit to net income that relates to a (noncash) financing activity.

| 19. | Unearned Service Revenue | 600 | |
| | Service Revenue | | 600 |

There is an increase in net income, but no corresponding cash inflow. The $600 decrease in Unearned Service Revenue must be deducted from net income when using the indirect method.

| 20. | Cash | 1,000 | |
| | Accumulated Depreciation | 4,000 | |
| | Loss on Disposal of Plant Asset | 2,000 | |
| | Plant Asset | | 7,000 |

There is a cash inflow of $1,000 related to an investing activity. When using the indirect method, the loss of $2,000 must be added back to net income because it is an effect of a transaction (sale of plant asset) that is an investing activity. That activity resulted in a cash inflow, not an outflow.

21.  Truck ($11,000 + $2,200).............................................................. 13,200
Accumulated Depreciation ($10,000 - $3,000) ............................................. 7,000
Loss on Disposal of Truck ($3,000 - $2,200)............................................. 800
     Truck  .......................................................................................... 10,000
     Cash  .......................................................................................... 11,000

There is an $11,000 cash outflow related to an investing activity (acquisition of property, plant and equipment). This exchange of similar productive assets results in a loss of $800 which must be added back to net income using the indirect method. The exchange of one noncash asset (book value of $2,200 after the write-down for impairment) for another must be disclosed as a noncash investing activity.

22.  Unrealized Holding Gain or Loss—Income ................................... 7,000
     Securities Fair Value Adjustment (Trading)................................... 7,000

There is a noncash charge to income. It is added to net income under the use of the indirect method.

> **TIP:** If the securities were classified as available-for-sale, there would be **no** impact on the statement of cash flows because the change in the fair value adjustment account for the available-for-sale category is **not** reported as a component of net income.

23.  Cash.................................................................................. 400
     Sales Revenue........................................................................ 400

There is an inflow of cash due to an operating activity. The effect on cash is the same as the effect on net income; no adjustment to net income is made.

24.  Advertising Expense ................................................................ 1,600
     Cash  .......................................................................................... 1,600

There is an outflow of cash due to an operating activity. The effect on cash is the same as the effect on net income; no adjustment to net income is made.

25.  Treasury Stock .......................................................................... 7,500
     Cash  .......................................................................................... 7,500

There is an outflow of cash for a financing activity (return of investment to owner).

26.  Accounts Payable (Trade)........................................................... 5,700
     Cash   ......................................................................... 5,700

The payment of a trade payable is an operating activity. The outflow is not reflected in net income. The $5,700 decrease in the accounts payable is, therefore, deducted from net income to compute net cash flow from operating activities.

27.  Machine Under Capital Lease...................................................... 75,000
     Obligation Under Capital Lease ................................................... 75,000

Obligation Under Capital Lease.............................................. 10,000
     Cash   ......................................................................... 10,000

The inception of the lease is a transaction that qualifies as a noncash investing and financing activity that requires disclosure. The first lease payment results in a cash outflow due to a financing activity.

28.  Cash   ....................................................................88,000
     Land   ......................................................................... 78,000
     Gain on Condemnation of Land (Extraordinary) .......................... 10,000

Gain on Condemnation of Land (Extraordinary) ...................................... 4,000
     Cash ($10,000 x 40%) ........................................................ 4,000

The receipt of $88,000 results in an inflow of cash from an investing activity. The extraordinary gain of $10,000 must be reported net of $4,000 tax on the income statement. However, all income taxes paid are to be classified on the statement of cash flows as operating cash outflows. Therefore, the **gross** gain of $10,000 must be deducted from net income when the indirect method is used for the statement of cash flows. The $88,000 receipt is shown as an investing inflow. The $4,000 payment of taxes is reflected as an outflow in the net cash flow from operating activities figure because a net gain of $6,000 is part of net income and the gross gain of $10,000 is deducted in the reconciliation of net income to net cash flow from operating activities.

> **TIP:** Transactions resulting in extraordinary gains and losses can be rather difficult to handle on the statement of cash flows.

## ANALYSIS OF MULTIPLE-CHOICE TYPE QUESTIONS

### QUESTION

1. (L.O. 2) At the end of 2010, a company acquired a hotel by paying a portion of the purchase price in cash and issuing a mortgage note payable to the seller for the balance. In a statement of cash flows for 2010, what amount is included in financing activities for this transaction?
a. Zero
b. Cash payment.
c. Mortgage amount.
d. Acquisition price.

**Explanation:** The portion of the building acquired by the cash down payment should be reported as a cash outflow due to an investing activity. The portion of the building acquired by the issuance of a mortgage note payable to the seller (i.e., a seller-financed debt) is a noncash investing and financing activity. The supplementary schedule of noncash investing and financing activities would include the acquisition of hotel by issuance of note payable; the amount shown in this schedule would be the mortgage amount. Payments of principal on the debt will be financing outflows; none have occured yet because the purchase happened at the end of the period. (Solution = a.)

### QUESTION

2.(L.O. 2, 5, 6) Xanthe Corporation had the following transactions occur in the current year:
1. Cash sale of merchandise inventory.
2. Sale of delivery truck at book value.
3. Sale of Xanthe common stock for cash.
4. Issuance of a note payable to a bank for cash.
5. Sale of a security held as an available-for-sale investment.
6. Collection of loan receivable.
7. Exercise of employee stock options.

Which of the above items will appear as a cash inflow from investing activities on a statement of cash flows for the current year?
a. Six items.
b. Five items.
c. Four items.
d. Three items.
e. Two items.

**Approach and Explanation:** Define investing activities. Compare each transaction above with the definition. Investing activities include (a) making and collecting loans; (b) acquiring and disposing of debt and equity instruments of other entities; and (c) acquiring and disposing of property, plant, and equipment and other productive assets. The sale of a delivery truck (regardless of the relationship of selling price and carrying value), the sale of an available-for-sale investment, and the collection of a loan receivable are three items that produce cash inflows from investing activities. The cash sale of merchandise inventory results in a cash inflow from operating activities. The sale of the corporation's own common stock, the issuance of the note payable, and the exercise of employee stock options all produce inflows of cash from financing activities. (Solution = d.)

| | |
|---|---|
| **TIP:** | Recall that transactions classified as investing activities involve assets (delivery equipment, available-for-sale investment, loan receivable, for the examples above) whereas transactions classified as financing activities involve liabilities (note payable, for example) or owners' equity (common stock, for example). |

**QUESTION**

3.   (L.O. 2, 5, 6) A corporation had the following transactions occur during the current year:

1.   Reclassification of debt from long-term liabilities to current liabilities.
2.   Payment of principal on mortgage note payable.
3.   Payment of interest on mortgage note payable.
4.   Purchase of treasury stock.
5.   Payment of cash dividend.
6.   Payment of property dividend.
7.   Distribution of stock dividend.

In a statement of cash flows, which of the above items is reported as a cash outflow from financing activities?

a.   Seven items.
b.   Six items.
c.   Five items.
d.   Four items.
e.   Three items.

**Explanation:** The payment of principal on a note payable, the purchase of treasury stock, and the payment of a cash dividend are the three items that will be reflected as cash outflows from financing activities. The reclassification of debt does not affect cash. It may be included in the schedule of noncash investing and financing activities. The payment of interest is to be reported as a cash outflow from operating activities. The payment of a property dividend is a noncash transaction to appear on the schedule of noncash investing and financing activities. Neither the declaration or distribution of a stock dividend affects cash. Because the declaration and distribution of a stock dividend is neither an investing or financing activity, a stock dividend is not reported anywhere on a statement of cash flows or in the supplementary disclosures related to that statement.  (Solution = e.)

**QUESTION**

4.   (L.O. 2, 5) During 2010, Pulido Inc. had the following activities related to its financial operations:

| | |
|---|---|
| Proceeds from the sale of treasury stock (on books at cost of $86,000) | $100,000 |
| Carrying value of convertible preferred stock in Pulido, converted into common shares of Pulido | 120,000 |
| Distribution in 2010 of cash dividend declared in 2009 to preferred shareholders | 62,000 |
| Payment for the early retirement of long-term bonds payable (carrying amount $740,000) | 750,000 |

The amount of net cash used in financing activities to appear in Pulido's statement of cash flows for 2010 should be:

a.   $716,000.
b.   $712,000.
c.   $592,000.
d.   $530,000.

**Explanation:** The net cash used in financing activities is computed as follows:

| | |
|---|---|
| Proceeds from sale of treasury stock | $100,000 |
| Payment of cash dividends | (62,000) |
| Retirement of bonds payable | (750,000) |
| Net cash flow from financing activities | (712,000) |

The conversion of preferred stock to common stock of $120,000 is a noncash transaction and would be shown in the supplementary schedule of noncash investing and financing activities. (Solution = b.)

> **TIP:**    The $10,000 loss on retirement of bonds payable ($750,000 retirement price exceeds carrying value of $740,000 by $10,000) would be a component of net income. If the indirect method is used to present the net cash provided (used) by operations, the $10,000 loss would be added to net income in this calculation.

## QUESTION

5.    (L.O. 2) During 2010, Jackson Montgomery Corporation had the following activities related to its financial operations:
    1.    Purchased equipment for cash which was borrowed from a bank.
    2.    Acquired treasury stock for cash.
    3.    Declared a cash dividend payable in 2011.
    4.    Reclassified long term debt to short term debt.
5.    Purchased a 2-month U.S. Treasury bill.
    6.    Acquired a 5-year certificate of deposit from a bank.
    7.    Made interest payments on bonds payable.
    8.    Converted preferred stock to common stock.
    9.    Received dividends from an investment in stock of another corporation.
    10.    Issued stock upon the exercise of employee stock options.

In a statement of cash flows, how many of the above transactions are reported as a cash **outflow** from investing activities?

a.    one
b.    two
c.    three
d.    four
e.    five
f.    six

**Approach and Explanation:** Identify each item as being reported as one of the following:
- A cash inflow from operating activities.
- A cash outflow from operating activities.
- A cash inflow from investing activities.
- A cash outflow from investing activities.
- A cash inflow from financing activities.
- A cash outflow from financing activities.
- An investing or financing activity not affecting cash.

Refer to the definitions in **Illustration 23-1** if you need to do so. Count the number that you identify to be reported as a cash outflow from investing activities.

Item 1:    The purchase of equipment for cash is an investing outflow. The borrowing of cash from a bank is a financing inflow.

Item 2:    The acquisition of treasury stock for cash is a financing outflow.

Item 3:    The declaration of a cash dividend is a transaction not affecting cash and does not get reported on a statement of cash flows. The subsequent payment of the cash dividend will be a financing outflow.

Item 4:    The reclassification of debt from long-term liabilities to short-term liabilities does not affect cash; it is not reported on a statement of cash flows.

Item 5:    The purchase of a 2-month U.S. Treasury Bill is a transaction where cash is exchanged for a cash equivalent. It is not reported on a statement of cash flows.

Item 6:    The acquisition of a 5-year certificate of deposit is an investing outflow.

Item 7:    Interest payments are an operating outflow.

Item 8:     The conversion of preferred stock to common stock is a financing activity that does not affect cash; this transaction is to be disclosed in the supplemental schedule of noncash investing and financing activities.

Item 9:     The receipt of dividends (and interest) are cash inflows from operating activities.

Item 10:   Exercise of employee stock options results in a cash inflow from financing activities.

Transactions 1 and 6 are reported as cash outflows from investing activities. (Solution = b.)

**QUESTION**

6.      (L.O. 2) Refer to the facts of **Question 5** above. In a statement of cash flows, how many of the transactions are reported as a cash **outflow** from financing activities?

a.      one
b.      two
c.      three
d.      four
e.      five
f.      six

**Approach and Explanation:** Refer to the Approach and Explanation for Question 5 above. Only Item 2 is reported as a cash outflow from financing activities. (Solution = a.)

**QUESTION**

7.      (L.O. 2, 6) Which of the following would be classified as a financing activity on a statement of cash flows?

a.      declaration and distribution of a stock dividend
b.      deposit to a bond sinking fund
c.      sale of a loan receivable
d.      payment of interest to a creditor

**Approach and Explanation:** Write down the definitions for investing, financing, and operating activities. Take each of the transactions and see if it meets the definition for a financing activity. Declaration and distribution of stock dividend does not meet any of the definitions. It is an example of an item that is not reported anywhere on a statement of cash flows or in supplementary disclosures related to that statement. Although the journal entry to record the deposit to a bond sinking fund results in an increase in the fund, which is often classified as a long-term investment, most accountants emphasize the purpose of the deposit, which is to ultimately pay for amounts borrowed; thus, it is usually classified as a financing activity. The sale of a loan receivable is clearly an investing activity, and the payment of interest to a creditor is an operating activity. (Solution = b.)

## QUESTION

8.  (L.O. 6) The following information was taken from the 2010 financial statements of the Laurel Banning Corporation:

|                                       |            |
| ------------------------------------- | ---------- |
| Bonds payable, January 1, 2010        | $ 100,000  |
| Bonds payable, December 31, 2010      | 400,000    |

**During 2010**

-   Bonds payable with a face amount of $40,000 were issued in exchange for equipment.
-   A $90,000 payment was made to retire bonds payable with a face amount of $100,000.

In its statement of cash flows for the year ended December 31, 2010, what amount should Laurel Banning report as proceeds from issuance of bonds payable?

a.  $300,000
b.  $360,000
c.  $160,000
d.  $340,000
e.  $170,000
f.  $240,000

**Approach and Explanation:** Draw a T-account for Bonds Payable. Enter the data given and solve for the unknown.

| Bonds Payable | | |
| --- | --- | --- |
| Retired | 100,000 | Bal., Jan. 1, 2010 |
| 100,000 | | |
| | 40,000 | Issued for equipment |
| | 360,000 | Issued for cash |
| | 400,000 | Bal., Dec. 31, 2010 |

(Solution = b.)

## QUESTION

9.  (L.O. 6) In a statement of cash flows, using the indirect method, which of the following are subtracted from net income to determine net cash provided by operating activities?

   I.   Amortization of premium on bonds payable.
   II.  Loss on sale of equipment.
   III. Depreciation expense.

a.  I only
b.  II only
c.  I and II
d.  I and III
e.  II and III
f.  I, II and III

**Approach and Explanation:** Think about how each item (1) affects net income and (2) affects cash. Then reason what is needed to reconcile net income to net cash provided by operating activities. The amortization of premium on bonds payable increases net income (because it reduces interest expense), but does not affect cash; thus it is deducted from net income in the reconciliation of net income to net cash provided by operating activities. The loss on sale of equipment reduces net income but does not affect cash; hence, it is added to net income in the reconciliation under discussion. Depreciation expense reduces net income but does not affect cash; thus, it is added to net income in this reconciliation. (Solution = a.)

## QUESTION

10.     (L.O. 6) Alley Cat Corporation had net income for 2010 of $5,000,000. Additional information is as follows:

| | |
|---|---|
| Depreciation of plant assets | $2,000,000 |
| Amortization of intangibles | $400,000 |
| Increase in accounts receivable | $700,000 |
| Increase in accounts payable | $900,000 |

Alley Cat's net cash provided by operating activities for 2010 was:
a.     $2,800,000.
b.     $7,200,000.
c.     $7,400,000.
d.     $7,600,000.

**Explanation:**  The depreciation and amortization amounts are items that reduce net income but do not cause a decrease in cash during the current period. The increase in accounts receivable indicates that sales revenue earned for the period exceeded the cash collections from customers, and therefore net income exceeded the net cash provided by operating activities. The increase in accounts payable indicates that expenses incurred exceeded cash payments for expense type items which caused net income to be less than net cash provided by operating activities. The solution is as follows:

| | |
|---|---|
| Net income | $5,000,000 |
| Depreciation of plant assets | 2,000,000 |
| Amortization of intangibles | 400,000 |
| Increase in accounts receivable | (700,000) |
| Increase in accounts payable | 900,000 |
| Net cash provided by operating activities | $7,600,000 |

(Solution = d.)

# QUESTION
11.     (L.O. 6) Net cash flow from operating activities for 2010 for Graham Corporation was $75,000. The following items are reported on the financial statements for 2010:

| | |
|---|---|
| Depreciation and amortization | 5,000 |
| Cash dividends paid on common stock | 3,000 |
| Increase in accrued receivables | 6,000 |

Based only on the information above, Graham's net income for 2010 was:
a.     $64,000.
b.     $66,000.
c.     $74,000.
d.     $76,000.
e.     none of the above.

**Approach and Explanation:** Write down the format for the reconciliation of net income to net cash flow from operating activities. Fill in the information given. Solve for the unknown.

| | |
|---|---|
| Net income | $     X |
| Depreciation and amortization | 5,000 |
| Increase in accrued receivables | (6,000) |
| Net cash flow from operating activities | $ 75,000 |

Solving for X, net income = $76,000.

Cash dividends paid on common stock have no effect on this computation because cash dividends paid are not a component of net income, and they are not an operating activity. They are a financing activity. (Solution = d.)

## QUESTION

12. (L.O. 8) A change in accounts receivable is used to convert sales revenue to cash receipts from customers when the direct method is used. A change in accounts receivable is also used to convert net income to net cash from operating activities when the indirect method is used. Do you use a change in gross accounts receivable or net accounts receivable?

|     | **Direct** | **Indirect** |
| --- | --- | --- |
| a. | Gross | Gross |
| b. | Net | Net |
| c. | Net | Gross |
| d. | Gross | Net |

**Explanation:** The change in net accounts receivable includes the change in the Accounts Receivable account and the change in the Allowance for Doubtful Accounts account. The Accounts Receivable account changes because of credit sales, write-offs of individual accounts, cash collections, and the reinstatement of accounts previously written off. The allowance account changes because of the recognition of bad debts expense, write-offs of individual accounts, and the reinstatement of accounts previously written off.

When the direct method is used, only the change in gross receivables is used to convert sales revenue to cash collections from customers. The change in the allowance account is not a factor in this conversion because the related bad debts expense has no impact on this calculation. When the indirect method is used, the change in net receivables is used to convert net income to net cash provided by operating activities because it reflects the bad debts expense (which does not require a cash outlay) as well as the difference between the accrual basis revenue amount and the cash collections from customers. (Solution = d.)

## QUESTION

13. (L.O. 6, 7) Donnegan Company reported salaries expense of $95,000 for 2010. The following data were extracted from the company's financial records:

|  | 12/31/09 | 12/31/10 |
| --- | --- | --- |
| Prepaid Salaries | $ 20,000 | $ 23,000 |
| Salaries Payable | 70,000 | 85,000 |

On a statement of cash flows for 2010, using the direct method, cash payments for salaries should be:

a. $77,000.
b. $83,000.
c. $107,000.
d. $113,000.

**Approach and Explanation:** Think of the relationship between salaries expense and cash payments for salaries when there is (1) an increase in prepaid salaries, and (2) an increase in salaries payable. Convert the expense amount to a cash paid figure.

| | |
| --- | --- |
| Salaries expense | $ 95,000 |
| Increase in prepaid salaries | 3,000 |
| Increase in salaries payable | (15,000) |
| Cash payments for salaries | $ 83,000 |

(Solution = b.)

**QUESTION**

14. (L.O. 6) The following information was taken from the 2010 financial statements of Jenny Gardner Corporation:

| | |
|---|---:|
| Inventory, January 1, 2010 | $ 30,000 |
| Inventory, December 31, 2010 | 40,000 |
| Accounts payable, January 1, 2010 | 25,000 |
| Accounts payable, December 31, 2010 | 40,000 |
| Sales | 200,000 |
| Cost of goods sold | 150,000 |

If the direct method is used in the 2010 statement of cash flows, what amount should Jenny Gardner report as cash payments for goods to be sold?

a. $175,000
b. $165,000
c. $155,000
d. $145,000
e. $125,000

**Approach and Explanation:** Draw T-accounts. Enter the information given.

| Cost of Goods Sold | Inventory | Accounts Payable |
|---|---|---|
| 150,000 | Beg. Bal. 30,000 / 150,000 CGS | 25,000 Beg. Bal. |
| | End. Bal. 40,000 | 40,000 End. Bal. |

Assume all purchases of inventory are on account. Solve for the amount of purchases. Then solve for the amount of cash payments for goods to be sold (assuming all accounts payable arise from purchases of inventory).

| Cost of Goods Sold | Inventory | Accounts Payable |
|---|---|---|
| 150,000 | Beg. Bal. 30,000 / 150,000 CGS | Cash Pay- / 25,000 Beg. Bal. |
| | Purchases 160,000 | ments 145,000 / 160,000 Purchases |
| | End. Bal. 40,000 | 40,000 End. Bal. |

(Solution = d.)

**QUESTION**

15. (L.O. 6, 7) Selected information for 2010 for the Truly Green Company follows:

| | |
|---|---:|
| Total operating expenses (accrual basis) | $200,000 |
| (includes depreciation and amortization) | |
| Beginning prepaid expenses | 10,000 |
| Ending prepaid expenses | 12,000 |
| Beginning accrued liabilities | 16,000 |
| Ending accrued liabilities | 19,000 |
| Depreciation of plant assets | 28,000 |
| Amortization of intangible assets | 7,500 |
| Payment of cash dividends | 5,000 |

The amount of cash payments made during 2010 for operating expenses is:
a. $234,500.
b. $165,500.
c. $163,500.
d. $160,500.
e. None of these.

**Approach and Explanation:**  Use one of the relevant formats in **Illustration 23-2** to convert operating expenses to cash paid.

| | |
|---|---:|
| Total operating expenses (accrual basis) | $200,000 |
| Increase in prepaid expenses | 2,000 |
| Increase in accrued liabilities | (3,000) |
| Depreciation of plant assets | (28,000) |
| Amortization of intangibles | (7,500) |
| Cash paid for operating expenses | $163,500  (Solution = c.) |

**TIP:**  Notice that the amount given in the question for "total operating expenses" includes depreciation and amortization whereas the format calls for exclusion of these items.  Depreciation and amortization are both expense items that do **not** require a cash outlay at the time the expense is recorded.  Thus, they are deducted from the operating expense total to arrive at the amount of cash paid for operating expense items this period.

**TIP:**  Dividends paid are neither an operating expense nor an operating activity.  Payment of dividends is a financing activity (outflow).  The receipt of dividends from an investee is an operating activity (inflow).

**QUESTION**

16.  (L.O. 6) The following information was taken from the 2010 financial statements of Greg Nelson Corporation:

| | |
|---|---:|
| Income tax payable, January 1, 2010 | $ 50,000 |
| Income tax payable, December 31, 2010 | 40,000 |
| Deferred tax liability, January 1, 2010 | 15,000 |
| Deferred tax liability, December 31, 2010 | 30,000 |
| Income tax expense | 200,000 |

If the direct method is used in the 2010 statement of cash flows, what amount should Greg Nelson report as cash payments for income taxes?

a.  $225,000
b.  $210,000
c.  $205,000
d.  $195,000
e.  $190,000
f.  $175,000

**Approach and Explanation:** Draw T-accounts. Enter the information given and solve for the missing amounts.

| Income Tax Expense | | |
|---|---|---|
| Curr. Tax Exp.[2] | | |
| 185,000 | | |
| Def. Tax Exp.[1] | 15,000 | |
| End. Bal. | 200,000 | |

| Income Tax Payable | | | |
|---|---|---|---|
| | | 50,000 | Beg. Bal. |
| Taxes Pd.[3] | 195,000 | 185,000 | Cur. Tax Exp.[2] |
| | | 40,000 | End. Bal. |

| Deferred Tax Liability | | |
|---|---|---|
| | 15,000 | Beg. Bal. |
| | 15,000 | Def. Tax Expense[1] |
| | 30,000 | End. Bal. |

[1]$30,000    Deferred tax liability, 12/31/10
(15,000)    Deferred tax liability, 1/1/10
$15,000    Deferred tax expense for 2010

[2]$200,000    Total income tax expense for 2010
(15,000)    Deferred tax expense for 2010
$185,000    Current tax expense for 2010

[3]$ 50,000    Income taxes payable, 1/1/10
185,000    Current tax expense for 2010
235,000
(40,000)    Income taxes payable, 12/31/10
$195,000    Income taxes paid in 2010          (Solution = d.)

**TIP:** The use of T-accounts is a good solutions approach because it requires only that you recall the normal balance of relevant accounts and the transactions that affect certain accounts. Picturing the accounts helps you to readily determine the amounts of any debits or credits that affected an account. Another approach that requires more analysis of the relationship of accounts appears as follows:

| | |
|---|---|
| Income tax expense for 2010 | $ 200,000 |
| Increase in deferred tax liability (deferred tax expense) | (15,000) |
| Current tax expense for 2010 | 185,000 |
| Decrease in income taxes payable | 10,000 |
| Income taxes paid during 2010 | $ 195,000 |

## QUESTION
17.(L.O. 7) The following facts are available for the Barbara Pace Company:

| | |
|---|---|
| Sales revenue for 2010 | $ 450,000 |
| Accounts receivable, January 1, 2010 | 35,000 |
| Accounts receivable, December 31, 2010 | 29,000 |
| Allowance for doubtful accounts, January 1, 2010 | 5,000 |
| Allowance for doubtful accounts, December 31, 2010 | 3,500 |
| Bad debt expense for 210 | 42,000 |
| Write-off of accounts receivable during 2010 | 43,500 |

The amount of cash collections from customers during 2010 was:
a.    $498,000.
b.    $496,500.
c.    $487,500.
d.    $412,500.
e.    none of the above.

**Explanation:** The computation for cash collections is as follows:

| | |
|---|---|
| Sales revenue | $ 450,000 |
| Decrease in accounts receivable | 6,000 |
| Write-off of accounts receivable | (43,500) |
| Cash collections from customers | $ 412,500 |

(Solution = d.)

**TIP:**    An alternative solution is as follows:

| | |
|---|---|
| Sales revenue | $ 450,000 |
| Decrease in accounts receivable | 6,000 |
| Decrease in allowance for doubtful accounts | (1,500) |
| Bad debt expense | (42,000) |
| Cash collections from customers | $ 412,500 |

**TIP:** Another way of solving for the above is as follows:

| | |
|---|---:|
| Sales revenue | $ 450,000 |
| Decrease in net accounts receivable | 4,500[a] |
| Bad debt expense | (42,000) |
| Cash collections from customers | $ 412,500 |

[a]$35,000 - $5,000 = $30,000 Beginning net receivables
$29,000 - $3,500 = $25,500 Ending net receivables
$30,000 - $25,500 = $4,500 Decrease in net receivables

**TIP:** You may also solve for the cash collections by drawing T-accounts for Sales Revenue, Accounts Receivable, Allowance for Doubtful Accounts, and Bad Debt Expense. Enter the information given and solve for the missing amount. The T-accounts would appear as follows:

| Sales Revenue | | | Accounts Receivable | | |
|---|---|---|---|---|---|
| | 450,000 | Beg. Bal. | 35,000 | | |
| | | | | 43,500 | Write-offs |
| | | Sales | 450,000 | | |
| | | | | 412,500 | Cash collections |
| | 450,000 | End. Bal. | 29,000 | | |

| Allowance for Doubtful Accounts | | | Bad Debt Expense | |
|---|---|---|---|---|
| | 5,000 | Beg. Bal. | 42,000 | |
| Write-offs 43,500 | 42,000 | Bad Debt Expense | | |
| | 3,500 | End. Bal. | 42,000 | |

**TIP:** Assume all sales were on account. Even if some sales were cash sales, the answer will be the same for total cash collections.

## QUESTION

18. (L.O. 8) When the indirect method is used for a statement of cash flows, should the gross amount or net-of-tax amount of an extraordinary gain be added to or deducted from net income in computing cash provided by operating activities?
a. Gross amount of an extraordinary gain should be added to net income.
b. Gross amount of an extraordinary gain should be deducted from net income.
c. Net-of-tax amount of an extraordinary gain should be added to net income.
d. Net-of-tax amount of an extraordinary gain should be deducted from net income.

**Explanation:** All income taxes paid are to be classified as operating cash outflows. No income taxes are to be allocated to investing and financing transactions. Assume an extraordinary gain from an investing activity is tax effected at 40%:

| | |
|---|---:|
| Cash received | $ 50,000 |
| Gain | 10,000 |
| Taxes paid | 4,000 |

Net income includes the net gain of $6,000 ($10,000 gain less income tax effect of $4,000). By deducting the gross gain of $10,000 from net income, an outflow of $4,000 (due to income taxes paid) is reflected in the operating activity section of the statement of cash flows. The $50,000 would be classified as an inflow in the investing activity section. (Solution = b.)

# CHAPTER 24

# FULL DISCLOSURE IN FINANCIAL REPORTING

## OVERVIEW

Financial statements often contain information for which more detail and/or explanation is desired by the users of the statements. Additional detail may be provided in the notes to the statements. Explanation of management's view may be included in the MD&A (management's discussion and analysis) section of the annual report. These and other subjects related to full disclosure in financial reporting are discussed in this chapter.

Now that you have learned about the content of financial statements, Appendix 24A will help you to interpret the information conveyed in the statements; this appendix covers basic financial analysis. Because a lot of companies are engaged in international business activities, the subject of international accounting standards is an increasingly important one and is the topic of Appendix 24B.

## SUMMARY OF LEARNING OBJECTIVES

1.  **Review the full disclosure principle and describe implementation problems.** The full disclosure principle calls for financial reporting of any financial facts significant enough to influence the judgment of an informed reader. Implementing the full disclosure principle is difficult, because the cost of disclosure can be substantial and the benefits difficult to assess. Disclosure requirements have increased because of (1) the growing complexity of the business environment, (2) the necessity for timely information, and (3) the use of accounting as a control and monitoring device.

2.  **Explain the use of notes in financial statement preparation.** Notes are the accountant's means of amplifying or explaining the items presented in the main body of the statements. Notes can explain in qualitative terms information pertinent to specific financial statement items, and can provide supplementary data of a quantitative nature. Common note disclosures relate to such items as the following: accounting policies; inventories; property, plant, and equipment; credit claims; contingencies and commitments; and subsequent events.

3.  **Describe the disclosure requirements for major business segments.** Aggregated figures hide much information about the composition of consolidated figures that is hidden in aggregated figures. There is no way to tell from the consolidated data the extent to which the differing product lines contribute to the company's profitability, risk, and growth potential. As a result, the profession requires segment information in certain situations.

4.  **Describe the accounting problems associated with interim reporting.** Interim reports cover periods of less than one year. Two viewpoints exist regarding interim reports. One view (**discrete view**) holds that each interim period should be treated as a separate accounting period. Another view (**integral view**) is that the interim report is an integral part of the annual report and that deferrals and accruals should take into consideration what will happen for the entire year.

Companies should use the same accounting principles for interim reports that they use for annual reports. A number of unique reporting problems develop related to the following items: (1) advertising and similar costs, (2) expenses subject to year-end adjustment, (3) income taxes, (4) extraordinary items, (5) earnings per share, and (6) seasonality.

5. **Identify the major disclosures found in the auditor's report.** The auditor expresses an unqualified opinion, if satisfied that the financial statements present the financial position, results of operations, and cash flows fairly in accordance with generally accepted accounting principles. A qualified opinion contains an exception to the standard opinion; ordinarily the exception is not of sufficient magnitude to invalidate the financial statements as a whole.

   An adverse opinion is required when the exceptions to fair presentation are so material that a qualified opinion is not justified. A disclaimer of an opinion is appropriate when the auditor has gathered so little information on the financial statements that no opinion can be expressed.

6. **Understand management's responsibilities for financial statements.** Management's discussion and analysis (MD & A) section covers three financial aspects of an enterprise's business: liquidity, capital resources, and results of operations. Management has primary responsibility for the financial statements and this responsibility is often indicated in a letter to stockholders in the annual report.

7. **Identify issues related to financial forecasts and projections.** The SEC has indicated that companies are permitted (not required) to include profit forecasts in reports filed with that agency. To encourage management to disclose this type of information, the SEC has issued a "safe harbor" rule. The safe harbor rule provides protection to an enterprise that presents an erroneous forecast, as long as the projection was prepared on a reasonable basis and was disclosed in good faith. However, the safe harbor rule has not worked well in practice.

8. **Describe the profession's response to fraudulent financial reporting.** Fraudulent financial reporting is intentional or reckless conduct, whether act or omission, that results in materially misleading financial statements. Fraudulent financial reporting usually occurs because of poor internal control, management's poor attitude toward ethics, poor performance, and so on. The Sarbanes-Oxley Act has numerous provisions intended to help prevent fraudulent financial reporting.

*9. **Understand the approach to financial statement analysis.** Basic financial statement analysis involves examining relationships between items on the financial statements (ratio and percentage analysis) and identifying trends in these relationships (comparative analysis). Analysis is used to predict the future, but it is limited because the data used are from the past. Also, ratio analysis identifies present strengths and weaknesses of a company, but it may not reveal why they exist. Although single ratios are helpful, they are not conclusive. For maximum usefulness, they must be compared with industry averages, previous periods, planned amounts, and the like.

   *This material is covered in Appendix 24A in the text.

*10. **Identify major analytic ratios and describe their calculations.** Ratios are classified as liquidity ratios, activity ratios, profitability ratios, and coverage ratios: (1) **Liquidity ratio analysis** measures the short-run ability of the enterprise to pay its currently maturing obligations. (2) **Activity ratio analysis** measures how effectively the enterprise is using its assets. (3) **Profitability ratio analysis** measures the degree of success or failure of a company to generate revenues adequate to cover its costs of operation and provide a return to the owners. (4) **Coverage ratio analysis** measures the degree of protection afforded long-term creditors and investors.

   *This material is covered in Appendix 24A in the text.

*11.　**Explain the limitations of ratio analysis.** Ratios are based on historical cost data, which can lead to distortions in measuring performance. Also, where estimated items (such as depreciation and amortization) are significant, income ratios lose some of their credibility. In addition, comparability problems exist because various companies use different accounting principles and procedures. Finally, analysts must recognize that a substantial amount of important information is not included in a company's financial statements.
　　　　*This material is covered in Appendix 24A in the text.

*12.　**Describe techniques of comparative analysis.** Companies present comparative data, which generally includes two years of balance sheet information and three years of income statement information. In addition, many companies include in their annual reports 5- to 10-year summaries of pertinent data that permit the reader to examine and analyze trends.
　　　　*This material is covered in Appendix 24A in the text.

*13.　**Describe techniques of percentage analysis.** Percentage analysis consists of reducing a series of related amounts to a series of percentages of a given base. Analysts use two approaches: **horizontal analysis** indicates the proportionate change in financial statement items over a period of time; such analysis is most helpful in evaluating trends. **Vertical analysis (common-size analysis)** is proportional expression of each item on the financial statements in a given period to a base amount. It analyzes the composition of each of the financial statements from different years (a) to detect trends not evident from the comparison of absolute amounts and (b) to make intercompany comparisons of different sized enterprises.
　　　　*This material is covered in Appendix 24A in the text.

**14.　**Describe the current international accounting environment.** Investors and creditors increasingly demand international accounting reports. The growth of multinational corporations, increased international mergers and acquisitions, and financial markets, all facilitated by technology, contributes to the demand for international accounting standards. Given these forces, many are working to establish a set of accounting principles that can be used worldwide. High-quality international standards: (1) permit **few alternative practices,** (2) are **clearly stated** to allow for easy interpretation and consistent application, (3) are **comprehensive,** covering the major transactions facing companies, (4) provide an **effective system** for responding to new transactions, and (5) provide **transparency of information** (full disclosure, understandability), to make that information relevant for making effective decisions.

　　The leading international accounting standard setter, the IASB, is working with the FASB to develop common high-quality accounting standards. The U.S. SEC may allow U.S. companies to use iGAAP.
　　　　**This material is covered in Appendix 24B in the text.

## TIPS ON CHAPTER TOPICS

**TIP:**    The initial note to the financial statements should be a **summary of significant accounting policies** adopted and followed by the reporting entity. This disclosure should identify principles applied by the entity that are: (a) selections from existing alternatives, (b) principles peculiar to a particular industry, or (c) unusual or innovative applications. This disclosure may precede the notes to the financial statements. It allows an analyst to determine whether a company is using conservative or liberal accounting practices.

**TIP:**    **Related party transactions** arise when a company engages in transactions in which one of the parties has the ability to significantly influence the policies of the other. They may occur also when a nontransacting party has the ability to influence the policies of the transacting parties. Related party transactions require separate disclosure because transactions involving related parties cannot be presumed to be carried out on an arms'-length basis; this is because the requisite conditions of competitive, free-market dealings may not exist. Transactions such as borrowing or lending money at abnormally low or high interest rates, real estate sales at amounts that differ significantly from appraisal value, exchanges of nonmonetary assets, and transactions involving enterprises that have no economic substance ("shell corporations") suggest that related parties may be involved. The **substance rather than the form** of these transactions should be reflected in the financial statements.

**TIP:**    Disclosure requirements are numerous, and they grow in volume and complexity as new standards come forth. Some people believe that small or nonpublic companies should not have to follow complex GAAP requirements such as those for deferred income taxes, leases, or pensions. This issue, often referred to as **"big GAAP versus little GAAP",** continues to be controversial. Although the FASB takes the position that there should be just one set of GAAP, except in unusual situations, the Board has eliminated reporting requirement for nonpublic enterprises in such areas as fair value of financial instruments and segment reporting.

**TIP:**    An interim report covers a period of time of less than one year. The most common period for which a company provides an interim report is a quarter (three months).

**TIP:**    The types of information included in the **MD&A (management's discussion and analysis)** section of the financial statements are not subject to FASB standards.

**TIP:**    The MD&A section of the annual financial report must provide information concerning the effects of inflation and changing prices if material to financial statement trends.

**TIP:**    A **financial forecast** and a **financial projection** are both prospective financial statements that present, to the best of the responsible party's knowledge and belief, an entity's financial position, results of operations, and cash flows for a future time. The difference between a financial forecast and a financial projection is that a **forecast** attempts to provide information on what is **expected to happen;** whereas, a **projection** may provide information on what is not necessarily expected to happen, but **what might take place.**

**TIP:**    To encourage management to disclose prospective financial information, the SEC has a **safe harbor rule.** It provides protection to a company that presents an erroneous forecast, as long as the company prepared the forecast on a reasonable basis and disclosed it in good faith. However, the rule is not working well in practice.

**TIP:**   **Internet reporting** allows users to take advantage of tools such as search engines and hyperlinks to quickly find information about the firm and, sometimes, to download the information into computer spreadsheets for analysis.

**TIP:**   Opportunities for fraudulent financial reporting are present in circumstances when the fraud is easy to commit and when detection is difficult. Frequently, these opportunities arise from:
1. The absence of a Board of Directors or audit committee.
2. Weak or nonexistent internal accounting controls.
3. Unusual or complex transactions.
4. Accounting estimates, requiring significant, subjective judgment.
5. Ineffective internal audit staffs.

Situational pressures that may lead to fraudulent reporting include:
1. Sudden decreases in revenue or market share for a single company or for an entire industry.
2. Unrealistic budget pressures.
3. Financial pressure from bonus plans that are based on performance.

The following **TIP** relates to the material covered in **Appendix 24B:**

**\*\*TIP:**   Most corporations are multinational corporations. With an increase in global affairs, many companies find it costly to comply with different reporting standards in different countries. Likewise, investors attempting to diversify their holdings and manage their risks have been interested in investing overseas. Having one common set of accounting standards will make it easier for international investors to compare the financial results of companies from different countries. For years the SEC required foreign companies that list on the U.S. exchanges to use U.S. GAAP or provide a reconciliation between international GAAP and U.S. GAAP. In 2007, the SEC eliminated this reconciliation in the name of convergence. In addition, the SEC has now proposed that U.S. companies be allowed to choose between using U.S. GAAP or iGAAP.

The independent objective standard setting body now in place, whose standards could meet the needs of the global capital markets, is the **International Accounting Standards Board** (IASB). The FASB and the IASB are working together toward the goal of a single set of high-quality accounting standards that will be used both domestically and internationally.

The following TIPS relate to the material covered in **Appendix 24-A:**

**\*TIP:**   The significance of a single absolute dollar amount reported in the general purpose financial statements for an entity is difficult to assess. To determine the meaningfulness of one amount, we must consider the significance of the amount when compared with other relevant amounts. Various techniques can be used to perform this analysis of financial statement data. Ratios developed for a particular company may be compared to industry averages to judge the solvency, strength, earning power, and growth potential of the company.

**\*TIP:**   A **ratio** is an expression of the relationship of one item (or group of items) to a second item (or group of items). It is determined by dividing the first item (amount) by the second item (amount).

**\*TIP:**   If A is $100,000 and B is $25,000, the ratio of A to B can be expressed in several ways, such as the following:

| A:B | A/B |
|-----|-----|
| 4:1 | 4.00 |
| 4 to 1 | $4.00 |
| 4 times | 400% |

The way in which the ratio is expressed depends on the particular ratio. If it is the current ratio or acid-test ratio, it would likely be expressed as a proportion (4:1 or 4 to 1) or as a rate (4 times). If it is the debt to stockholders' equity ratio, it would likely be expressed as a percentage (400%).

**\*TIP:**   The average number of days required to collect an account receivable (365 days divided by the receivables turnover) is not very meaningful until it is compared with the company's credit terms.

**\*TIP:**   When you are analyzing comparative data, carefully notice which information is for prior years and which is for the current year. On a comparative balance sheet, the current year data is typically placed in the first (inside) column. In some situations, however, the reverse may be found.

**\*TIP:**   The numerator of the current ratio includes total current assets; the numerator of the acid-test ratio includes only cash, marketable securities (short-term), and net receivables.

**\*TIP:**   The denominator of a turnover ratio (such as for receivables, inventory, or total assets) always involves an **average** balance. That average can be determined by adding the balance at the end of the period to the balance at the beginning of the period and dividing by 2. However, if seasonal variances are significant, the annual average should be determined by adding together the balances at the end of each month and dividing by 12.

**\*TIP:** If the return on common stockholders' equity is greater than the return on assets, the interest rate on the debt is less than the average return on total assets; hence, the entity is favorably trading on the equity. However, if the cost of debt exceeds the return on total assets, the return on common stockholders' equity will be less than the return on total assets; hence, the entity will be unfavorably trading on the equity.

**\*TIP:** A given piece of financial information which is reported on the financial statements may not be significant to a reader if the only information available is a given dollar amount. When an item for the current year is compared with the same item for the same company of the prior year (to determine the direction, dollar amount, and percent of change) or with other items on the same statement for the same year (to develop component percentages which may be compared to industry averages), the resulting relationship(s) may be more useful in determining the meaningfulness of the information being reported.

**\*TIP:** Although the average collection period for accounts receivable is to be computed by dividing 365 days by the receivables turnover ratio, 360 days is often used. Likewise, the average number of days' sales included in inventory is often determined by dividing 360 (rather than 365) days by the inventory turnover.

**\*TIP:** One problem with the asset turnover ratio is that it places a premium on using old assets because their book value is low (the lower the denominator of the ratio, the higher the ratio is). Another problem with the asset turnover ratio is that it is affected by the depreciation method employed by the company—the more accelerated the depreciation is, the higher the asset turnover will be.

**\*TIP:** The profit margin on sales ratio, combined with the asset turnover ratio, offers an interplay that leads to a rate of return on total assets.

$$\text{Profit margin on sales} = \frac{\text{Net income}}{\text{Net sales}} \qquad \text{Asset Turnover} = \frac{\text{Net sales}}{\text{Average total assets}}$$

Rate of return on assets = Profit margin on sales x Asset turnover

$$\text{Rate of return on assets} = \frac{\text{Net income}}{\text{Net sales}} \times \frac{\text{Net sales}}{\text{Average total assets}}$$

$$\text{Rate of return on assets} = \frac{\text{Net income}}{\text{Average total assets}}$$

The profit margin on sales does not answer the question of how profitable an enterprise was for a given period of time. Only by determining how many times the assets turned over during a period of time is it possible to ascertain the amount of net income earned on the total assets. Many enterprises have a small profit margin on sales and a high turnover (grocery and discount stores); whereas, other enterprises have a relatively high profit margin but a low inventory turnover (jewelry and furniture stores).

**\*TIP:** To compute the book value per share of common stock when there is preferred stock also outstanding, use the following steps:

**Step 1:** **Compute the total book value of preferred stock** by multiplying the book value per share of preferred stock by the number of preferred shares outstanding. The book value per share of preferred is one of the following (listed in order of preference):

a. Liquidation value of preferred plus dividends in arrears.
b. Call or redemption price of preferred plus dividends in arrears.
c. Par value of preferred plus dividends in arrears.

**Step 2:** **Compute the total book value of common stock** by deducting the total book value of preferred stock from total stockholders' equity.

**Step 3:** **Compute the book value per share of common stock** by dividing the total book value of common stock by the number of common stock shares outstanding.

**\*TIP:** Financial statements can be analyzed in percentage terms by using one of two basic approaches: horizontal analysis or vertical analysis.

**\*TIP:** **Horizontal analysis** involves the expression of dollar amounts of financial statement items in percentage terms of the dollar amounts for the same items in a prior year. There may be two or more years involved in the analysis. **Trend analysis** is a type of horizontal analysis that is prepared for more than two years.

**\*TIP:** In horizontal analysis, a base year (usually the earliest year being analyzed) is selected. Each dollar item on the statements is then divided by the dollar amount reported in the base year for the same item. For instance, if sales were $33,000 in Year 1, $46,000 in Year 2, and $50,000 in Year 3, horizontal analysis would yield percentages of 100% for Year 1, 139% for Year 2, and 152% for Year 3. The trend for sales is more clearly determined when expressed in percentage terms.

**\*TIP:** In **vertical analysis** (or the development of **common-size financial statements**), the relative importance of various items on a single financial statement is indicated by the relationships of these various items to some key figure on the same statement.

**\*TIP:** The key figure used for vertical analysis on the income statement is generally net sales, so every other item in the same statement for the same year is expressed in percentage terms of that key figure. This is accomplished by **dividing** every dollar item reported on the income statement by the dollar amount of net sales for the year to obtain the percentages.

**\*TIP:** The key figure (the 100% figure) used for vertical analysis of the balance sheet is generally the company's total assets. Each item on the balance sheet is then described as a percentage of the total asset figure.

## CASE 24-1

**Purpose:**    (L.O. 1 thru 8) This exercise will review the meaning or significance of a number of terms used in this chapter.

## Instructions

Select the letter of the item that most directly relates to the numbered statements. Use the letter of the item to identify your response.

A.   Summary of significant accounting policies.
B.   Related party transactions.
C.   Reporting of segment information.
D.   Subsequent events (post balance-sheet events)
E.   Errors.
F.   Fraudulent financial reporting.
G.   Full disclosure principle.
H.   Illegal acts.

I.   Interim reports.
J.   Notes to the financial statements.
K.   Auditor's report.
L.   Irregularities.
M.   Management's discussion and analysis.
N.   Financial forecast.
O.   Financial projection.

_____   1.   Calls for financial reporting of any financial facts significant enough to influence the judgment of an informed reader.

_____   2.   Information that is an integral part of the financial statements and serves as a means of amplifying or explaining the items presented in the body of the statements.

_____   3.   Disclosure of the accounting methods employed in the preparation of the financial statements.

_____   4.   A business enterprise engages in transactions in which one of the transacting parties has the ability to influence significantly the policies of the other, or in which a nontransacting party has the ability to influence the policies of the two transacting parties.

_____   5.   Unintentional mistakes.

_____   6.   Intentional distortions of financial statements.

_____   7.   Violations of laws and regulations, such as bribes and kickbacks.

_____   8.   Information related to revenues, operating profit or loss, and identifiable assets of different product lines of an entity.

_____   9.   Reports that cover periods of less than one year.

_____  10.   Section of an annual report that covers three financial aspects of an enterprise's business—liquidity, capital resources, and results of operations.

_____  11.   Transactions occurring after the balance sheet date that are disclosed in the notes because they have a material effect on the financial statements.

_____  12.   A report that states whether or not the financial statements are presented in accordance with generally accepted accounting principles.

_____  13.   Prospective financial statements based on a company's assumptions reflecting conditions it expects would exist in the future, given one or more hypothetical assumptions.

_____  14.   Prospective financial statements based on a company's assumptions reflecting conditions it expects will exist in the future and the course of action it expects to take.

_____  15.   Intentional or reckless conduct, whether act or omission, that results in materially misleading financial statements.

## Solution to Case 24-1

| 1. | G | 6. | L | 11. | D |
|----|---|----|---|-----|---|
| 2. | J | 7. | H | 12. | K |
| 3. | A | 8. | C | 13. | O |
| 4. | B | 9. | I | 14. | N |
| 5. | E | 10. | M | 15. | F |

## CASE 24-2

**Purpose:**     (L.O. 3) This case will review the tests applied in determining the reportable segments of an entity.

Many companies diversify their operations. The objective of reporting segmented financial data is to provide information about the different types of business activities in which an enterprise engages and the different economic environments in which it operates. Financial statements can be disaggregated in several ways, such as by products or services, by geography, by legal entity, or by type of customer. The method of segmenting chosen is referred to as the management approach—it reflects how management segments the company for making operating decisions. These components are called operating segments. Diversified Galore Inc. has several reportable industry segments that account for 80% of its operations.

### Instructions
(1)    Explain the term "operating segment" as it applies to an entity diversified in its operations.
(2)    Explain when the information about two or more operating segments may be aggregated.
(3)    Explain what criteria are to be used to determine Diversified's reportable segments.
(4)    Indicate what information is to be disclosed for each operating segment.

### Solution to Case 24-2

(1)    An **operating segment** is a component of an enterprise:
   (a)    That engages in business activities from which it earns revenues and incurs expenses.
   (b)    Whose operating results are regularly reviewed by the company's chief operating decision maker to assess segment performance and allocate resources to the segment.
   (c)    For which discrete financial information is available that is generated by or based on the internal financial reporting system.

(2)    Information about two or more operating segments may be aggregated only if the segments have the same basic characteristics in each of the following areas:
   (a)    The nature of the products and services provided.
   (b)    The nature of the production process.
   (c)    The type or class of customer.
   (d)    The methods of product or service distribution.
   (e)    If applicable, the nature of the regulatory environment.

(3)  After the company decides on the segments for possible disclosure, a quantitative materiality test is made to determine whether the segment is significant enough to warrant actual disclosure. An operating segment is regarded as significant and therefore identified as a reportable segment if it satisfies **one or more** of the following quantitative thresholds.

- Its **revenue** (including both sales to external customers and intersegment sales or transfers) is 10% or more of the combined revenue of all the enterprise's operating segments.
- The absolute amount of its **profit or loss** is 10% or more of the greater, in absolute amount, of
  - (a)  the combined operating profit of all operating segments that did not incur a loss, or
  - (b)  the combined loss of all operating segments that did report a loss.
- Its **identifiable assets** are 10% or more of the combined assets of all operating segments.

In applying these tests, two additional factors must be considered. First, segment data must explain a significant portion of the company's business. Specifically, the segmented results must equal or exceed 75% of the combined sales to unaffiliated customers for the entire enterprise. This test prevents a company from providing limited information on only a few segments and lumping all the rest into one category.

Second, the profession recognizes that reporting too many segments may overwhelm users with detailed information. The FASB decided that 10 is a reasonable upper limit for the number of segments that a company should be required to disclose.

(4)  The FASB now requires that an enterprise report:
- (a)  **General information about its operating segments.** This includes factors that management considers most significant in determining the company's operating segments, and the types of products and services from which each operating segment derives its revenues.
- (b)  **Segment profit and loss related information.** Specifically, the following information about each operating segment must be reported if the amounts are included in the determination of segment profit or loss:
  - Revenues from transactions with external customers.
  - Revenues from transactions with other operating segments of the same enterprise.
  - Interest revenue.
  - Interest expense.
  - Depreciation, depletion, and amortization expense.
  - Unusual items.
  - Equity in the net income of investees accounted for by the equity method.
  - Income tax expense or benefit.
  - Extraordinary items.
  - Significant noncash items other than depreciation, depletion, and amortization expense.
- (c)  **Segment assets.** An enterprise must report each operating segment's total assets.

(d)   **Reconciliation.** An enterprise must provide a reconciliation of the total of the segments' revenues to total revenues, a reconciliation of the total of the operating segments' profits and losses to its income before income taxes, and a reconciliation of the total of the operating segments' assets to total assets.

(e)   **Information about products and services and geographic areas.** For each operating segment that has not been determined based on geography, the enterprise must report (unless it is impracticable) [(a) in the enterprise's country of domicile and (b) in each other country if material]: (1) revenues from external customers, (2) long-lived assets, and (3) expenditures during the period for long-lived assets.

(f)   **Major customers.** If 10 percent or more of the revenues is derived from a single customer, the enterprise must disclose the total amount of revenues from each such customer by segment.


## CASE 24-3

**Purpose:**   (L.O. 4) This case will review the reporting requirements for interim financial statements.

Bon Jon Surf Shop is located in Daytona Beach, Florida. It sells surf boards, beach wear, and other related merchandise. Some shareholders have requested management to distribute quarterly financial statements to shareholders.

### Instructions
(a)   Discuss the accounting principles that should be employed for interim reports.
(b)   Indicate whether or not it is a requirement to include a statement of cash flows in an interim report. Also list the minimum data to be disclosed in an interim report.


### Solution to Case 24-3

(a)   **The profession indicates that, in general, the same accounting principles used for annual reports should be employed for interim reports.** Revenues should be recognized in interim periods on the same basis as they are for annual periods. Also, costs directly associated with revenues (product costs), such as materials, factory labor and related fringe benefits, and manufacturing overhead should be treated in the same manner for interim reports as for annual reports.

Companies generally should use the same inventory pricing methods (FIFO, LIFO, etc.) for interim reports that they use for annual reports. However, the following exceptions are appropriate at interim reporting periods:

1.   Companies may use the gross profit method at interim dates to estimate inventory and cost of goods sold, but disclosure of the method and adjustments to reconcile with annual inventory are necessary.

2.   When LIFO inventories are liquidated at an interim date and are expected to be replaced by year end, cost of goods sold should include the expected cost of replacing the liquidated LIFO base and not give effect to the interim liquidation.

3.   The use of lower of cost or market may result in inventory losses which should not be deferred beyond the interim period in which the decline occurs. Recoveries of these losses in subsequent periods should be recognized as gains, but only to

the extent of losses recognized in previous interim periods of the same fiscal year. Temporary market declines should not be recognized at the interim date since no loss is expected to be incurred in the fiscal year.

4. Planned variances under a standard cost system which are expected to be absorbed by year end ordinarily should be deferred.

Costs and expenses other than product costs, often referred to as period costs, are frequently charged to the interim period as incurred. But they may be allocated among interim periods on the basis of an estimate of time expired, benefit received, or activity associated with the periods. Considerable latitude is exercised in accounting for these costs in interim periods, and many believe more definitive guidelines are needed.

(b) The profession encourages but does not require companies to publish a balance sheet and a statement of cash flows in interim reports. When this information is not presented, significant changes in such items as liquid assets, net working capital, long-term liabilities, and stockholders' equity should be disclosed.

Regarding disclosure, the following interim data should be reported as a minimum:
1. Sales or gross revenues, provision for income taxes, extraordinary items, cumulative effect of a change in accounting principle, and net income.
2. Primary and fully diluted earnings per share where appropriate.
3. Seasonal revenue, cost, or expenses.
4. Significant changes in estimates or provisions for income taxes.
5. Disposal of a segment of a business and extraordinary, unusual, or infrequently occurring items.
6. Contingent items.
7. Changes in accounting principles or estimates.
8. Significant changes in financial position.

---

**TIP:** In general, the same accounting principles used for annual reports should be employed for interim reports. **An interim period is an integral part of an annual period.** Therefore, expectations for the annual report must be reflected in an interim report. Accruals, deferrals, and allocations are to be utilized.

**TIP:** Income taxes for an interim period are to be computed using an **estimated annual effective tax rate**. The estimated annual effective tax rate is to be applied to the year-to-date "ordinary" income at the end of each interim period to compute the year-to-date tax. The interim period tax related to "ordinary" income shall be the difference between the amount so computed and the amounts reported for previous interim periods of the fiscal year.

**TIP:**   Because of the short-term nature of the information in interim reports, there is considerable controversy as to the general approach companies should employ. One group, favoring the **discrete approach,** believes that a company should treat each interim period as a separate accounting period. Using that treatment, a company would apply the principles for accruals and deferrals used for annual reports; a company would report transactions as they occur and expense recognition should not change with the time period covered.

Another group, favoring the **integral approach,** believes that the interim report is an integral part of the annual report; thus, accruals and deferrals should take into consideration what will happen for the entire year. Using this approach, a company should assign estimated expenses to parts of a year on the basis of sales volume or some other activity base.

At present, many companies follow the discrete approach for certain types of expenses and the integral approach for others, because the standards currently have differing interpretations.

**TIP:**   For interim reporting purposes, extraordinary items are to be reported in the interim period in which they occur rather than arbitrarily allocated over multiple periods.

## ILLUSTRATION 24-1
## MAJOR DISCLOSURES IN FINANCIAL STATEMENT (L.O. 2)

Notes to the financial statements are sometimes called footnotes. They are an integral part of the financial statements. Notes are the means of amplifying or explaining the items presented in the main body of the statements. They can explain in qualitative terms information pertinent to specific financial statement items. In addition, they can provide supplementary data of a quantitative nature to expand the information in the financial statements. Notes can also explain restrictions imposed by financial arrangements or basic contractual agreements. Often the notes are very technical and difficult to understand because they deal with complicated issues.

Some of the more common disclosures follow:

*Inventory.* Companies should report the basis upon which inventory amounts are stated (lower of cost or market) and the method used in determining cost (LIFO, FIFO, average cost, etc.) . Manufacturers should report, either in the balance sheet or in a separate schedule in the notes, the inventory composition (finished goods, work in process, raw materials). Unusual or significant financing arrangements relating to inventories that may require disclosure include transactions with related parties, product financing arrangements, firm purchase commitments, involuntary liquidation of LIFO inventories, and pledging of inventories as collateral.

*Property, Plant, and Equipment.* Companies should state the basis of valuation for property, plant, and equipment. It is usually historical cost. Companies also should disclose pledges, liens, and other commitments related to these assets. In the presentation of depreciation, companies should disclose the following in the financial statements or in the notes: (1) depreciation expense for the period; (2) balances of major classes of depreciable assets, by nature and function, at the balance sheet date; (3) accumulated depreciation, either by major classes of depreciable assets or in total, at the balance sheet date; and (4) a general description of the method or methods used in computing depreciation with respect to major classes of depreciable assets. Finally, companies should explain any major impairments.

*Creditor Claims.* Investors normally find it extremely useful to understand the nature and cost of creditor claims. However, the liabilities section in the balance sheet can provide the major types of liabilities only in the aggregate. Note schedules regarding such obligations provide additional information about how a company is financing its operations, the costs that it will bear in future periods, and the timing of future cash outflows. Financial statements must disclose for each of the five years following the date of the statements the aggregate amount of maturities and sinking fund requirements for long-term borrowings.

*Equity Holders' Claims.* Many companies present in the body of the balance sheet information about equity securities: the number of shares authorized, issued, and outstanding and the par value for each type of security. Or, companies may present such data in a note. Beyond that, a common equity note disclosure relates to contracts and senior securities outstanding that might affect the various claims of the residual equity holders. An example would be the existence of outstanding stock options, outstanding convertible debt, redeemable preferred stock, and convertible preferred stock. In addition, it is necessary to disclose certain types of restrictions currently in force. Generally, these types of restrictions involve the amount of earnings available for dividend distribution.

*Contingencies and Commitments.* A company may have gain or loss contingencies that are not disclosed in the body of the financial statements. These contingencies include litigation, debt and other guarantees, possible tax assessments, renegotiation of government contracts, and sales of receivables with recourse. In addition, companies should disclose in the notes commitments that relate to dividend restrictions, purchase agreements (through-put and take-or-pay), hedge contracts, and employment contracts.

*Fair Values.* Companies that have assets or liabilities measured at fair value must disclose both the cost and fair value of all financial instruments in the notes to the financial statements. Fair value measurements may be used for many financial assets and liabilities, investments, impairments of long-lived assets, and some contingencies. Companies also provide disclosure of information that enables users to determine the extent of usage of fair value and the inputs used to implement fair value measurement. The fair value hierarchy identifies three broad levels related to the measurement of fair values (Levels, 1, 2, and 3). The levels indicate the reliability of the measurement of fair value information.

*Deferred Taxes, Pensions, and Leases.* The FASB also requires extensive disclosure in the areas of deferred taxes, pensions, and leases. Users of financial statements should carefully read notes to the financial statements for information about off-balance-sheet commitments, future financing needs, and the quality of a company's earnings.

*Changes in Accounting Principles.* The profession defines various types of accounting changes and establishes guides for reporting each type. Companies discuss, either in the summary of significant accounting policies or in the other notes, changes in accounting principles (as well as material changes in estimates and corrections of errors).

## CASE 24-4

Purpose:   (L.O. 5)  This case will discuss the auditor's report.

An auditor is an accounting professional who conducts an independent examination of a company's financial statements and the underlying data. An important source of information in a company's annual report is the auditor's report.

### Instructions
(a)   Describe the reporting standards to be followed by the auditor in preparing the auditor's report.
(b)   Differentiate between an unqualified opinion, qualified opinion, adverse opinion, and a disclaimer of opinion on the financial statements.
(c)   Assume an auditor is issuing an unqualified opinion. List three circumstances that may require the auditor to add an explanatory paragraph to the audit report.

## SOLUTION TO CASE 24-4

(a)   In preparing an audit report, the auditor follows these reporting standards:
1.   The report shall state whether the financial statements are presented in accordance with generally accepted accounting principles.
2.   The report shall identify those circumstances in which such principles have not been consistently observed in the current period in relation to the preceding period.
3.   Informative disclosures in the financial statements are to be regarded as reasonably adequate, unless otherwise stated in the report.
4.   The report shall contain either an expression of opinion regarding the financial statements taken as a whole or an assertion to the effect that an opinion cannot be expressed. When an overall opinion cannot be expressed, the reasons why should be stated. In all cases where an auditor's name is associated with financial statements, the report should contain a clear-cut indication of the character of the auditor's examination, if any, and the degree of responsibility being taken.

> **TIP:**   An audit of a public company is to be conducted in accordance with the standards of the Public Company Accounting Oversight Board (United States). Those standards require that the auditor plan and perform the audit to obtain reasonable assurance about whether the financial statements are free of material misstatement. An audit includes examining, on a test basis, evidence supporting the amounts and disclosures in the financial statements. An audit also includes assessing the principles used and significant estimates made by management, as well as evaluating the overall financial presentation. The standards also require the auditor to examine and evaluate the client's **system of internal control.**

(b)   In most cases, the auditor issues a standard **unqualified or clean opinion.** That is, the auditor expresses the opinion that the financial statements present fairly, in all material respects, the financial position, results of operations, and cash flows of the entity in conformity with generally accepted accounting principles.

A **qualified opinion** contains an exception to the standard opinion. A qualified opinion states that, except for the effects of the matter to which the qualification relates, the financial statements present fairly, in all material respects, the financial position, results of operations, and cash flows in conformity with GAAP. The usual circumstances in which the auditor may deviate from the standard unqualified short-form report are as follows:

1. The scope of the examination is limited or affected by conditions or restrictions.
2. The statements do not fairly present financial position or results of operations because of:
   (a) Lack of conformity with generally accepted accounting principles and standards.
   (b) Inadequate disclosure.

An **adverse opinion** is required in any report in which exceptions to fair presentation are so material that, in the independent auditor's judgment, a qualified opinion is not justified. An adverse opinion is an indication that the financial statements taken as a whole, are not presented in accordance with GAAP. An adverse opinion is rare to see because the SEC will not permit a company listed on an exchange to have an adverse opinion; therefore, most companies will make the necessary changes to avoid an adverse opinion. In fact, most will make the changes necessary to avoid even a qualified opinion.

A **disclaimer of an opinion** is appropriate when the auditor has gathered so little information about the financial statements that no opinion can be expressed.

**TIP:** An auditor must evaluate whether there is a substantial doubt about the entity's ability to continue as a going concern for a reasonable period of time; if there is substantial doubt, the auditor must add an explanatory note to the auditor's report describing the potential problem.

(c) Certain circumstances may require the auditor to add an explanatory paragraph to the auditor's report, although they do not affect the unqualified opinion. Some of the more important circumstances requiring further explanation include:

1. **Going concern.** If substantial doubt exists about the company continuing as a going concern, the auditor must add an explanatory note to the audit report describing the potential problem.

2. **Lack of consistency.** If a company has changed accounting principles or the method of their application in a way that has a material effect on the comparability of its financial statements, the auditor should refer to the change in an explanatory paragraph of the audit report.

   This paragraph should refer the reader to the note in the financial statements that **discuss the change in detail.**

3. **Emphasis of a matter.** The auditor may wish to emphasize a matter and will do so by presenting the explanatory information in a separate paragraph of the report. One example of such a matter is the occurrence of significant transactions with related parties.

## *ILLUSTRATION 24-2
## RATIOS: FORMULAS FOR COMPUTATIONS AND PURPOSES (L.O. 10)

| Ratio | Formula for Computation | Purpose and/or Comments |
|---|---|---|
| **I. Liquidity** | | |
| 1. Current ratio | $\dfrac{\text{Current assets}}{\text{Current liabilities}}$ | This ratio is an indication of a company's ability to meet its current liabilities with the cash flow that will result from its current assets. It is often called the working capital ratio. The higher the ratio, the greater the short-term solvency. |
| 2. Quick or acid-test ratio | $\dfrac{\text{Cash, marketable securities, and receivables}}{\text{Current liabilities}}$ | "Quick" assets are cash, marketable securities, and net receivables. The acid-test ratio (sometimes called the quick ratio) is a more severe test of short-run solvency than the current ratio. A large amount of inventory will cause an entity's acid-test ratio to be significantly less than its current ratio. |
| 3. Current cash debt ratio | $\dfrac{\text{Net cash provided by operating activities}}{\text{Average current liabilities}}$ | This ratio measures the company's ability to pay off its current liabilities out of its operations for a given year. |
| **II. Activity** | | |
| 4. Receivables turnover | $\dfrac{\text{Net sales}}{\text{Average trade receivables (net)}}$ | Theoretically, the numerator should include only net credit sales. Unless seasonal factors are significant, average trade receivables outstanding can be computed from the beginning and ending balance of net trade receivables. This ratio is another figure frequently used to measure the quality of the receivables and the efficiency and safety of a company's credit-granting activity. The higher the turnover, the shorter the time period necessary to collect the average account receivable. The receivables turnover is transformed to an average collection period by dividing 365 days by the receivables turnover. |
| 5. Inventory turnover | $\dfrac{\text{Cost of goods sold}}{\text{Average inventory}}$ | The inventory turnover ratio measures how quickly inventory is sold. Dividing 365 days by the inventory turnover indicates the average number of days it takes to sell inventory (or average number of days' sales for which inventory is on hand). This ratio is an indication of the efficiency of management in dealing with inventories. The greater the inventory turnover, the more liquid it is, and the lower the costs of storage, property taxes, maintenance costs, and so forth. The lower the turnover, the greater the chance of loss through obsolescence. |

## ILLUSTRATION 24-2 (Continued)

| Ratio | Formula for Computation | Purpose and/or Comments |
|---|---|---|
| 6. Asset turnover | $\dfrac{\text{Net sales}}{\text{Average total assets}}$ | This ratio supposedly indicates how efficiently the company utilizes its assets. If the asset turnover ratio is high, the implication is that the company is using its assets effectively to generate sales. If the turnover is low, the company either needs to use its assets more efficiently or dispose of them. |
| **III. Profitability** 7. Profit margin on sales | $\dfrac{\text{Net income}}{\text{Net sales}}$ | The ratio measures the profit on each sales dollar received. It provides some indication of the buffer available in case of higher costs or lower sales in the future. |
| 8. Rate of return on assets | $\dfrac{\text{Net income}}{\text{Average total assets}}$ | Some analysts modify this ratio by adding interest charges, net of tax effect, to the numerator because interest is a cost of securing additional assets and, therefore, should not be considered as a deduction in arriving at the amount of return on total assets. |
| 9. Rate of return on common stock equity | $\dfrac{\text{Net income minus preferred dividends}}{\text{Average common stockholders' equity}}$ | If this ratio is greater than the rate of return on total assets ratio, the company is using creditor sources and is favorably trading on the equity. Trading on the equity increases the company's financial risk, but it enhances residual earnings whenever the rate of return on assets exceeds the cost of debt capital. |
| 10. Earnings per share | $\dfrac{\text{Net income minus preferred dividends}}{\text{Weighted shares outstanding}}$ | The EPS figure is one of the most important ratios used by investment analysts, yet it is one of the most deceptive. A dual presentation is required for a complex capital structure. |
| 11. Price earnings ratio | $\dfrac{\text{Market price of stock}}{\text{Earnings per share}}$ | The P/E ratio is an oft-quoted statistic used by analysts in discussing the investment possibility of a given enterprise. The higher the market's perception of the company's growth potential, the higher the P/E ratio is likely to be. |
| 12. Payout ratio | $\dfrac{\text{Cash dividends}}{\text{Net income minus preferred dividends}}$ | Growth companies are characterized by low payout ratios because they reinvest most of their earnings. Another closely related ratio that is often used is the dividend yield—the cash dividend per share divided by the market price of the stock. |

## ILLUSTRATION 24-2 (Continued)

| Ratio | Formula for Computation | Purpose and/or Comments |
|---|---|---|
| **IV. Coverage** | | |
| 13. Debt to total assets | $\dfrac{\text{Debt}}{\text{Total assets or equities}}$ | This ratio provides creditors with some idea of the corporation's ability to withstand losses without impairing the interests of creditors. From a creditor's point of view, a low ratio of debt to total assets is desirable; the lower the ratio, the more "buffer" there is available to creditors before the corporation becomes insolvent. There are other similar ratios that are used for the same purpose, such as the ratio of debt to stockholders' equity or the ratio of stockholders' equity to the sum of debt and stockholders' equity. These ratios have a very definite effect on the company's ability to obtain additional financing. |
| 14. Times interest earned | $\dfrac{\text{Income before interest charges and taxes}}{\text{Interest charges}}$ | This ratio stresses the importance of a company being able to cover all interest charges. If a company pays preferred dividends, the number of times the preferred dividends were earned is computed by dividing the net income for the year by the annual preferred dividend requirement. |
| 15. Cash debt coverage ratio | $\dfrac{\text{Net cash provided by operating activities}}{\text{Average total liabilities}}$ | This ratio measures a company's ability to repay its total liabilities in a given year out of its operating cash flow. |
| 16. Book value per share of common stock | $\dfrac{\text{Common stockholders' equity}}{\text{Outstanding shares}}$ | Book value per common share of stock is the amount each common share would receive if the company were liquidated on the basis of amounts reported on the balance sheet. The figure loses much of its relevance if the valuations on the balance sheet do not approximate fair market value of the assets. When more than one class of stock is outstanding, stockholders' equity must be allocated among the various classes of stock and then expressed on a per share basis within each class. |

## *EXERCISE 24-1

**Purpose:**   (L.O. 10) This exercise will give you practice in developing key ratios.

The balance sheets at December 31, 2009 and December 31, 2010 and the income statement for 2010 for the Robert E. Busch, Jr. Corporation are presented below:

**Robert E. Busch, Jr. Corporation**
**COMPARATIVE BALANCE SHEET**
**December 31, 2009 and 2010**

|  | December 31 2009 | December 31 2010 |
|---|---|---|
| **Assets** | | |
| Cash | $ 50,000 | $ 40,000 |
| Marketable securities | 20,000 | 35,000 |
| Accounts receivable (net) | 60,000 | 85,000 |
| Inventory | 150,000 | 170,000 |
| Plant and equipment (net) | 500,000 | 470,000 |
| Total assets | $ 780,000 | $ 800,000 |
| **Liabilities and Stockholders' Equity** | | |
| Accounts payable | $ 130,000 | $ 95,000 |
| Accrued liabilities | 10,000 | 8,000 |
| 6% Bonds payable | 100,000 | 100,000 |
| Common stock, $10 par | 300,000 | 300,000 |
| Retained earnings | 240,000 | 297,000 |
| Total liabilities and stockholders' equity | $ 780,000 | $ 800,000 |

**Robert E. Busch, Jr. Corporation**
**INCOME STATEMENT**
**For the Year Ending December 31, 2010**

| | | |
|---|---|---|
| Net sales | | $ 900,000 |
| Cost of goods sold | | |
| Inventory, January 1, 2010 | $ 150,000 | |
| Purchases, net | 570,000 | |
| Goods available for sale | 720,000 | |
| Inventory, December 31, 2010 | 170,000 | 550,000 |
| Gross profit | | 350,000 |
| Operating expenses | | |
| Depreciation | 30,000 | |
| Other | 194,000 | 224,000 |
| Income from operations | | 126,000 |
| Bond interest expense | | 6,000 |
| Income before taxes | | 120,000 |
| Provision for income taxes | | 48,000 |
| Net income | | $ 72,000 |
| Earnings per share | | $ 2.40 |

**Additional information:** Dividends of $.50 per share were paid in 2010 to common stockholders. All sales during 2010 were on credit. The market value per share of common stock was $30 at December 31, 2010.  Cash provided by operating activities during 2010 was $20,000.

## Instructions

(a)    Fill in the blanks below with the appropriate amounts to develop ratios for the Robert E. Busch Jr. Corporation. (You do not have to compute the ratios, but a full solution is provided if you choose to do so.)

1.    The current ratio at the end of 2010 would be computed by dividing:
       $_____   by   $_____.

2.    The acid-test ratio at the end of 2010 would be computed by dividing:
       $_____   by   $_____.

3.    The ratio of debt to total assets at the end of 2010 would be computed by dividing:       $_

4.    The rate of return on common stockholders' equity for 2010 would be computed by dividing:   $_____         by   $_____.

5.    The debt to stockholders' equity ratio at the end of 2010 would be computed by dividing: $_

6.    The asset turnover ratio for 2010 would be computed by dividing:
       $_____   by   $_____.

7.    The number of times bond interest earned ratio for 2010 would be computed by dividing: $_

8.    The profit margin on sales for 2010 would be computed by dividing:
       $_____   by   $_____.

9.    The rate of return on assets for 2010 would be computed by dividing:
       $_____   by   $_____.

10.    The payout ratio for 2010 would be computed by dividing:
       $_____   by   $_____.

11.    The book value per common share at December 31, 2010 would be computed by dividing:       $_____         by   _____.

12.    The cash debt coverage ratio would be computed by dividing:
       $_____   by   _____.

13.     The receivables turnover for 2010 would be determined by dividing:
        $_____ by     $_____.
                The average number of days required to collect from a customer for a credit sale
                would be determined by dividing _____ by _____.

14.     The inventory turnover for 2010 would be determined by dividing:
        $_____ by     $_____.
                The average number of days sales included in inventory would be computed by
                dividing _____ by _____.

15.     Earnings per share for 2010 would be determined by dividing:
        $_____ by     _____.

16.     The price earnings ratio at the end of 2010 would be computed by dividing:
        $_____ by     $_____.

(b)     Which of the ratios in Part (a) above would be used to evaluate the company's financial
        strength and future solvency? Indicate your answers by use of the appropriate numbers.
(c)     Which of the ratios in Part (a) above would be used to evaluate the company's earning
        power and growth potential? Indicate your answers by use of the appropriate numbers.


# Solution to Exercise 24-1

(a)     1.      330,000; 103,000                    9.      72,000 (or 75,600); 790,000
        2.      160,000; 103,000            10.     15,000; 72,000
        3.      203,000; 800,000            11.     597,000; 30,000
        4.      72,000; 568,500             12.     20,000; 221,500
        5.      203,000; 597,000            13.     900,000; 72,500; 365 (or 360) days; 12.41
        6.      900,000; 790,000            14.     550,000; 160,000; 365 (or 360) days; 3.44
        7.      126,000; 6,000              15.     72,000; 30,000
        8.      72,000; 900,000             16.     30; 2.40

        **Approach and Explanation:** Write down the components of each ratio to be computed.
        (Refer to **Illustration 24-2** when needed.) Extract the pertinent data from the financial
        statements and "additional information."

        1.  Current ratio: $\dfrac{\text{Current assets}}{\text{Current liabilities}} = \dfrac{\$40,000 + \$35,000 + \$85,000 + \$170,000}{\$95,000 + \$8,000} = \dfrac{3.20}{\text{times}}$

        2.  Acid-test ratio: $\dfrac{\text{Quick assets}}{\text{Current liabilities}} = \dfrac{\$40,000 + \$35,000 + \$85,000}{\$95,000 + \$8,000} = 1.55 \text{ times}$

        3.  Debt to total assets: $\dfrac{\text{Total liabilities}}{\text{Total assets}} = \dfrac{\$95,000 + \$8,000 + \$100,000}{\$800,000} = 25.38\%$

4. Rate of return on common stockholders' equity:

$$\frac{\text{Net income}}{\text{Average common stockholders' equity}} = \frac{\$72,000}{1/2(\$597,000 + \$540,000)} = 12.66\%$$

5. Debt to stockholders' equity:

$$\frac{\text{Total debt}}{\text{Total stockholders' equity}} = \frac{\$95,000 + \$8,000 + \$100,000}{\$300,000 + \$297,000} = 34.0\% \text{ or } .34 \text{ to } 1.00$$

6. Asset turnover: $\dfrac{\text{Net sales}}{\text{Average total assets}} = \dfrac{\$900,000}{1/2(\$800,000 + \$780,000)} = 1.14 \text{ times}$

7. Number of times bond interest earned:

$$\frac{\text{Net income} + \text{interest} + \text{taxes}}{\text{Interest charges}} = \frac{\$72,000 + \$6,000 + \$48,000}{\$6,000} = 21 \text{ times}$$

8. Profit margin on sales: $\dfrac{\text{Net income}}{\text{Net sales}} = \dfrac{\$72,000}{\$900,000} = 8.0\%$

9. Rate of return on assets: $\dfrac{\text{Net income}}{\text{Average total assets}} = \dfrac{\$72,000}{1/2(\$800,000 + \$780,000)} = 9.11\%$

   **OR**

$$\frac{\text{Net income} + \text{interest expense} - \text{tax savings}}{\text{Average total assets}} = \frac{\$72,000 + \$6,000 - 40\% * (\$6,000)}{1/2(\$800,000 + \$780,000)} = 9.57\%$$

$$*\text{Tax rate} = \frac{\text{Income tax expense}}{\text{Income before taxes}} = \frac{\$48,000}{\$120,000} = 40\%$$

10. Payout ratio: $\dfrac{\text{Cash dividends}}{\text{Net income}} = \dfrac{\$.50(30,000 \text{ shares **})}{\$72,000} = 20.83\%$

    **Balance of common stock = $300,000; par = $10 per share; $300,000 ÷ $10 = 30,000 shares issued; there are no treasury shares, so outstanding shares = 30,000 shares.

11. Book value per common share: $\dfrac{\text{Common stockholders' equity}}{\text{Outstanding common shares}} = \dfrac{\$597,000}{30,000 **} = \$19.90$

    **See #10.

12. Cash debt coverage ratio:

$$\frac{\substack{\text{Net cash provided by} \\ \text{operating activities}}}{\text{Average total liabilities}} = \frac{\$20,000}{1/2(\$240,000 *** + \$203,000 ****)} = .09029$$

   *** = $130,000 + $10,000 + $100,000 = $240,000
   **** = $95,000 + $8,000 + $100,000 = $203,000

13. Receivables turnover:

$$\frac{\text{Net sales}}{\text{Average trade receivables (net)}} = \frac{\$900,000}{1/2(\$85,000 + \$60,000)} = 12.41 \text{ times}$$

Average number of days to collect an account receivable:

$$\frac{365 \text{ days}}{\text{Receivables turnover}} = \frac{365 \text{ days}}{12.41 \text{ times}} = 29.41 \text{ days}$$

14. Inventory turnover: $\dfrac{\text{Cost of goods sold}}{\text{Average inventory}} = \dfrac{\$550,000}{1/2(\$170,000 + \$150,000)} = 3.44 \text{ times}$

Average number of days' sales in inventory:

$$\frac{365 \text{ days}}{\text{Inventory turnover}} = \frac{365 \text{ days}}{3.44 \text{ times}} = 106.10 \text{ days}$$

15. Earnings per share: $\dfrac{\text{Net income minus preferred dividends}}{\text{Weighted shares outstanding}} = \dfrac{\$72,000 - \$0}{30,000} = \$2.40$

16. Price earnings ratio: $\dfrac{\text{Market price of stock}}{\text{Earnings per share}} = \dfrac{\$30.00}{\$2.40} = 12.5 \text{ times}$

(b)     1, 2, 3, 5, 7, 11, and 12.

(c)     4, 6, 8, 9, 10, 13, 14, 15, and 16.

# *EXERCISE 24-2

**Purpose:**     (L.O. 9, 10) This exercise points out the effects of various transactions on selected computations and ratios.

The following list of transactions relate to the Huseman Corporation for 2010. You are to analyze the transactions, assuming that on the date when each of the transactions occurred, the corporation's accounts showed only common stock (80,000 shares, $100 par) outstanding, a current ratio of 3.1 to 1 and a substantial net income for the year to date (before giving effect to the transactions concerned). On that date, the book value per share of common stock was $141.24. Each numbered transaction is to be considered completely **independent** of the others, and its related answer should be based on the effect(s) of that transaction alone. Assume all amounts are material and all transactions were recorded in accordance with generally accepted accounting principles.

## Instructions
For each of the transactions, indicate the effect (increase, decrease, or no effect) on each of the following:
(a)     The corporation's net income for 2010.
(b)     The corporation's current ratio
(c)     The book value per share of the corporation's common stock.

|  | | Effect on: | |
|---|---|---|---|
| **Transaction** | **(a)**<br>**Net Income**<br>**2010** | **(b)**<br>**Current**<br>**Ratio** | **(c)**<br>**Book Value**<br>**Per Share** |
| 1. The corporation declared a cash dividend of $1.00 per share. | _____ | _____ | _____ |
| 2. The corporation paid the cash dividend which had been recorded in the accounts at the time of declaration. | _____ | _____ | _____ |
| 3. The corporation purchased 100 shares of treasury stock for $150 per share. | _____ | _____ | _____ |
| 4. The corporation sold 100 shares of treasury stock for $145 per share; the shares had cost $150 per share. | _____ | _____ | _____ |
| 5. Huseman declared and paid a property dividend. The property used was a short-term investment which had a cost of $50,000 and a fair market value of $72,000. | _____ | _____ | _____ |
| 6. A loss of $20,000 was recognized due to an impairment in the value of equipment. | _____ | _____ | _____ |
| 7. Huseman sold a plot of land previously used in operations. The carrying value was $60,000 and the sales price was $50,000. | _____ | _____ | _____ |
| 8. A storm caused damage to a building. Repairs of $40,000 were completed, and payment was made. A pending insurance claim for $30,000 will partially cover the $40,000 loss. | _____ | _____ | _____ |
| 9. The corporation purchased equipment for $40,000 on account. | _____ | _____ | _____ |
| 10. The corporation collected $25,000 from a customer on account. | _____ | _____ | _____ |
| 11. Huseman wrote off a $10,000 account receivable. | _____ | _____ | _____ |
| 12. Huseman purchased short-term investments for $29,000. | _____ | _____ | _____ |
| 13. The corporation exchanged a $10,000 account payable for a $10,000 short-term note payable. | _____ | _____ | _____ |

| | Effect on: | | |
|---|---|---|---|
| **Transaction** | **(a)**<br>**Net Income**<br>**2010** | **(b)**<br>**Current**<br>**Ratio** | **(c)**<br>**Book Value**<br>**Per Share** |
| 14. Huseman provided services to customers for cash of $400,000. | _____ | _____ | _____ |
| 15. Huseman purchased $15,000 of inventory on account. | _____ | _____ | _____ |

## Solution to Exercise 24-2

| | (a) | (b) | (c) | | | (a) | (b) | (c) |
|---|---|---|---|---|---|---|---|---|
| 1. | No Effect | Decrease | Decrease | | 9. | No Effect | Decrease | No Effect |
| 2. | No Effect | Increase | No Effect | | 10. | No Effect | No Effect | No Effect |
| 3. | No Effect | Decrease | Decrease | | 11. | No Effect | No Effect | No Effect |
| 4. | No Effect | Increase | Increase | | 12. | No Effect | No Effect | No Effect |
| 5. | Increase | Decrease | Decrease | | 13. | No Effect | No Effect | No Effec |
| 6. | Decrease | No Effect | Decrease | | 14. | Increase | Increase | Increase |
| 7. | Decrease | Increase | Decrease | | 15. | No Effect | Decrease | No Effect |
| 8. | Decrease | Decrease | Decrease | | | | | |

**Approach and Explanation:** Write down the components of net income, the current ratio, and the book value per common share computations. Prepare the journal entry for each transaction. Analyze the accounts in each entry for their effects on the various components of the computations in question.

$$\text{Revenues} - \text{Expenses} = \text{Net income}$$

$$\frac{\text{Current assets}}{\text{Current liabilities}} = \text{Current ratio}$$

$$\frac{\text{Common stockholders ' equity}}{\text{Outstanding common shares}} = \text{Book value per common share}$$

| 1. | Retained Earnings............................................................. | 80,000 | |
|---|---|---|---|
| | Dividends Payable ............................................................ | | 80,000 |

(a)     Dividends are not a determinant of income; they are a distribution of income.
(b)     Current liabilities increase so the current ratio decreases.
(c)     Total stockholders' equity is reduced with no change in the number of shares outstanding; thus, book value per common share decreases.

2.      Dividends Payable ............................................................     80,000
        Cash     ...........................................................................80,000
        (a)     There is no income statement element affected by this transaction.
        (b)     Anytime the current ratio is greater than 1 to 1, a decrease in current liabilities accompanied by a decrease in current assets of the same magnitude will cause the current ratio to increase.
        (c)     There is no effect on stockholders' equity or the number of shares outstanding.

3.      Treasury Stock.................................................................     15,000
        Cash     ...........................................................................15,000
        (a)     There is no effect on net income.
        (b)     There is a reduction in current assets; hence, the current ratio is reduced.
        (c)     Total stockholders' equity and the total number of shares outstanding are reduced. Because the treasury shares are being purchased at a price ($150.00 per share) that exceeds the book value per share before that purchase ($141.24), the book value per outstanding share will decrease.

4.      Cash     ...........................................................................     14,500
Retained Earnings ..........................................................................     500
        Treasury Stock .................................................................          15,000
        (a)     There is no accounting gain or loss. This is a capital transaction.
        (b)     Current assets are increased; thus, the current ratio is increased.
        (c)     Total stockholders' equity and the total number of shares outstanding increase. Because the treasury shares are being sold at a price ($145.00) that exceeds the book value per share before that purchase ($141.24), the book value per outstanding share will increase.

5.      Short-term Investments.......................................................     22,000
        Gain on Appreciation of Investment .....................................          22,000

Retained Earnings ..........................................................................     72,000
        Property Dividend Payable.................................................          72,000

Property Dividend Payable ............................................................     72,000
        Short-term Investments.......................................................          72,000
        (a)     Net income is increased because of the gain of $22,000.
        (b)     There is a net decrease of $50,000 in current assets with no net change in current liabilities. Therefore, the declaration and payment of the property dividend causes a decrease in the current ratio.
        (c)     There is a net decrease of $50,000 in retained earnings and no effect on the number of shares of stock outstanding. Thus, the book value per share outstanding is decreased.

6.      Loss on Impairment of Equipment .......................................     20,000
        Accumulated Depreciation .................................................          20,000

(a)     Net income is reduced by $20,000.

(b)     The current ratio is not affected.

(c)     All income statement accounts are closed to retained earnings. Retained earnings is reduced; thus, total stockholders' equity is reduced. There is no effect on the number of shares outstanding. Book value per share, therefore, is decreased.

7.     Cash ............................................................................  50,000
Loss   ...................................................................................... 10,000
       Land   ...................................................................... 60,000
(a)     Net income is decreased because of the loss.
(b)     Current assets are increased; thus, the current ratio is increased.
(c)     Retained earnings are reduced because of the loss. There is no change in the outstanding shares. Book value per share is reduced.

8.     Insurance Claim Receivable .............................................  30,000
Loss   ...................................................................................... 10,000
       Cash   ...................................................................... 40,000
(a)     Net income is decreased by the $10,000 loss.
(b)     The current ratio is decreased because current assets are reduced by a net amount of $10,000.
(c)     The book value per share is reduced because total stockholders' equity is decreased by the amount of loss recognized. There is no change in the number of shares outstanding.

9.     Equipment ...................................................................  40,000
       Accounts Payable ..........................................................            40,000
(a)     There are no income statement accounts involved.
(b)     The current ratio is reduced because of the increase in current liabilities.
(c)     There is no effect on the elements of the book value per share computation.

10.    Cash ............................................................................  25,000
       Accounts Receivable ......................................................            25,000
(a)     There are no income statement accounts involved.
(b)     There is no net change in current assets and no effect on the current ratio.
(c)     There is no effect on the components of the book value per share ratio.

11.    Allowance for Doubtful Accounts .......................................  10,000
       Accounts Receivable ......................................................            10,000
(a)     There are no income statement accounts in the write-off entry when the allowance method is used to account for bad debts.
(b)     There is no net change in current assets and no effect on the current ratio.
(c)     There is no effect on the components of the book value per share ratio.

12.    Short-term Investments ....................................................  29,000
       Cash   ...................................................................... 29,000
(a)     There are no income statement accounts involved.
(b)     There is no net change in current assets and no effect on the current ratio.
(c)     There is no effect on the components of the book value per share ratio.

13.    Accounts Payable ...........................................................  10,000
       Short-term Note Payable ..................................................            10,000

(a)          There are no income statement accounts involved.
  (b)      There is no net change in current liabilities and no effect on the current ratio.
  (c)      There is no effect on the components of the book value per share ratio.

14.    Cash.................................................................................    400,000
         Services Revenue ............................................................                          400,000
         (a)     Net income is increased due to the revenue recognized.
         (b)     Current assets are increased so the current ratio is increased.
         (c)     Total stockholders' equity is increased (due to the increase in retained earnings)
                 which will cause the book value per share to increase.

15.    Inventory ........................................................................    15,000
         Accounts Payable ...........................................................                          15,000
         (a)     There is no effect on net income.
         (b)     Current liabilities are increased. Even though current assets increase by the
                 same amount, the current ratio will decrease. Anytime the current ratio is greater
                 than 1 to 1, an increase in current liabilities accompanied by an increase in
                 current assets of the same magnitude will cause a decrease in the current ratio.
         (c)     There is no effect on book value per share.


# *EXERCISE 24-3

**Purpose:**    (L.O. *9, *10, *12) This exercise will provide you with an example of how to interpret the meaning of ratios and trends.

Bandy Company is a wholesale distributor of professional exercise equipment and supplies. The company's sales have averaged about $900,000 annually for the three-year period 2008-2010. The firm's total assets at the end of 2010 amounted to $850,000. The president of Bandy Company has asked the controller to prepare a report that summarizes the financial aspects of the company's operations for the past three years. This report will be presented to the Board of Directors at their next meeting.

In addition to comparative financial statements, the controller has decided to present a number of relevant financial ratios which can assist in the identification and interpretation of trends. At the request of the controller, the accounting staff has calculated the following ratios for the three-year period 2008-2010:

|  | **2008** | **2009** | **2010** |
|---|---|---|---|
| Current ratio | 1.80 | 1.89 | 1.96 |
| Acid-test (quick) ratio | 1.04 | 0.99 | 0.87 |
| Accounts receivable turnover | 8.75 | 7.71 | 6.42 |
| Inventory turnover | 4.91 | 4.32 | 3.42 |
| Percent of total debt to total assets | 51.0% | 46.% | 41.0% |
| Percent of long-term debt to total assets | 31.0% | 27.0% | 24.0% |
| Sales to fixed assets (fixed asset turnover) | 1.58 | 1.69 | 1.79 |
| Sales as a percent of 2008 sales | 1.00 | 1.03 | 1.07 |
| Gross margin percentage | 36.0 | 35.1 | 34.6 |
| Net income to sales | 6.9% | 7.0% | 7.2% |
| Return on total assets | 7.7% | 7.7% | 7.8% |
| Return on stockholders' equity | 13.6% | 13.1% | 12.7% |

In the preparation of his report, the controller has decided first to examine the financial ratios independently of any other data to determine if the ratios themselves reveal any significant trends over the three-year period.

## Instructions

(a)    The current ratio is increasing while the acid-test (quick) ratio is decreasing. Using the ratios provided, identify and explain the contributing factor(s) for this apparently divergent trend.

(b)    In terms of the ratios provided, what conclusion(s) can be drawn regarding the company's use of financial leverage during the 2008-2010 period?

(c)    Using the ratios provided, what conclusion(s) can be drawn regarding the company's net investment in plant and equipment?                    (CMA adapted)

## Solution to Exercise 24-3

(a)    The acid-test ratio is the current ratio with the subtraction of inventory and prepaid expenses (generally insignificant relative to inventory) from current assets. Any divergence in trend between these two ratios would, therefore, be dependent upon the inventory account. Inventory turnover has declined sharply in the three-year period, from 4.91 to 3.42. During the same period, total sales have increased 7 percent. The decline in the inventory turnover is, therefore, not due to a decline in sales. The apparent cause is that investment in inventory has increased at a faster rate than sales, and this fact accounts for the divergence between the acid-test and current ratios.

(b)    Financial leverage has definitely declined during the three-year period. This is shown by the steady drop in the long-term-debt-to-total-assets ratio and the total-debt-to-total-assets ratio. Apparently the decline of debt as a percentage of this firm's capital structure is accounted for by a reduction in the long-term sector of the firm's indebtedness. This reduction of leverage accounts for the decrease in the return on stockholders' equity ratio. This conclusion is reinforced by the fact that net income to sales and return on total assets have both increased.

(c)    Bandy Company's net investment in plant and equipment has decreased during the three-year period 2008-2010. This conclusion is reached by using the sales-to-fixed-assets (fixed asset turnover) and sales-as-a-percent-of-2008-sales ratios.

Because sales have grown each year, the sales-to-fixed-assets could be expected to increase, unless fixed assets grew at a faster rate. The sales-to-fixed-asset ratio increased at a faster rate than the 3 percent annual growth in sales; therefore, net investment in plant and equipment must have declined.

## ANALYSIS OF MULTIPLE-CHOICE TYPE QUESTIONS

**QUESTION**

1.  (L.O. 2) Which of the following should be disclosed in the summary of significant accounting policies:

| | Depreciation Method | Composition of Property, Plant, & Equipment |
|---|---|---|
| a. | Yes | Yes |
| b. | Yes | No |
| c. | No | Yes |
| d. | No | No |

**Explanation:** The depreciation method for plant assets is a commonly required disclosure with respect to accounting policies. The composition of plant assets should **not** be in the summary of significant accounting policies because that information is required elsewhere in the statements. The accounting policy disclosures are **not** to duplicate information presented elsewhere in the financial statements.

Examples of accounting policies to be disclosed include:
a.      Consolidation method.
b.      Inventory pricing method.
c.      Depreciation method.
d.      Amortization method.
e.      Method of accounting for long-term contracts.
f.      Method of accounting for franchising and leasing activities.
g.      Criteria for determining which investments are treated as cash equivalents. (Solution = b.)

**QUESTION**

2.  (L.O. 3) Nickolodeon Corp. has six operating segments:

| Segments | Total Revenue (Unaffiliated) | Operating Profit (Loss) | Identifiable Assets |
|---|---|---|---|
| A | $ 30,000,000 | $ 5,250,000 | $ 60,000,000 |
| B | 24,000,000 | 4,200,000 | 52,500,000 |
| C | 18,000,000 | 3,600,000 | 37,500,000 |
| D | 9,000,000 | 1,650,000 | 22,500,000 |
| E | 12,750,000 | 2,025,000 | 21,000,000 |
| F | 4,500,000 | 675,000 | 9,000,000 |
| | $ 98,250,000 | $ 17,400,000 | $ 202,500,000 |

For which of the segments would information have to be disclosed in accordance with generally accepted accounting principles?
a.      segments A, B, C, and D
b.      segments, A, B, C, and E
c.      segments A, B, C, D, and E
d.      all six segments
e.      none of the segments

**Approach and Explanation:** Write down the criteria to be applied in determining reportable segments. Test each segment to see if it meets **one** of the criteria.

Criteria applied in determining reportable segments are:
1.      Operating segment revenue (from unaffiliated customers and other segments) is $\geq$ 10% of combined revenue of all operating segments.
2.      Operating segment's absolute operating profit/loss is $\geq$ 10% of the greater, in absolute amount, of:
(a)   Combined operating profit of all operating segments that did not incur a loss, or
(b)   Combined operating losses of all operating segments that did report a loss.

3. Operating segment's identifiable assets are ≥ 10% of the combined identifiable assets of all operating segments.

Segments A, B, C, and E pass the revenue and operating profit tests, but A, B, C, D, and E all pass the identifiable assets test. Since an operating segment only has to pass one of the three 10% tests to be considered a reportable segment, Nickolodeon has five reportable segments—A, B, C, D, and E. (Solution = c.)

**QUESTION**
3. (L.O. 4) Donnegan Manufacturing Company employs a standard cost system. A planned volume variance in the first quarter of 2010, which is expected to be absorbed by the end of the fiscal year, ordinarily should:
a. be deferred at the end of the first quarter, regardless of whether it is favorable or unfavorable.
b. never be deferred beyond the quarter in which it occurs.
c. be deferred at the end of the first quarter if it is favorable; unfavorable variances are to be recognized in the period incurred.
d. be deferred at the end of the first quarter if it is unfavorable; favorable variances are to be recognized in the period incurred.

**Explanation:** Companies generally should use the same inventory pricing methods and procedures for interim reports that they use for annual reports. One of a few exceptions, however, is that planned variances under a standard cost system which are expected to be absorbed by year end ordinarily should be deferred. (Solution = a.)

**QUESTION**
4. (L.O. 4) For interim financial reporting, a company's income tax expense for the second quarter should be computed by using the:
a. statutory tax rate for the year.
b. effective tax rate expected to be applicable for the second quarter.
c. effective tax rate expected to be applicable for the full year as estimated at the end of the first quarter.
d. effective tax rate expected to be applicable for the full year as estimated at the end of the second quarter.

**Explanation:** GAAP requires that, at the end of each interim period, an enterprise make its best estimate of the effective tax rate expected to be applicable for the full fiscal year. That rate should be used to determine income tax expense on a current year-to-date basis. (Solution = d.)

**QUESTION**
5. (L.O. 4) With regard to interim financial statements, the Accounting Principles Board concluded that interim reporting be viewed as:
a. reporting for a basic accounting period.
b. reporting for an integral part of an annual period.
c. a "special" type of reporting that need not conform to generally accepted accounting principles.
d. requiring a cash basis approach.

**Explanation:** GAAP views each interim period primarily as an integral part of an annual period. Generally, the preparation of interim reports should be based on the same accounting principles the enterprise uses in preparing annual financial statements. However, certain principles and practices used for annual reporting may require modification at interim dates so that interim reports may relate more closely to the results of operations for the annual period. (Solution = b.)
**QUESTION**

6.   (L.O. 4) For interim financial reporting, an extraordinary loss occurring in the second quarter should be:
a.   disclosed only in the footnotes in the second quarter.
b.   recognized in the second quarter.
c.   recognized ratably over the last three quarters.
d.   recognized ratably over all four quarters, with the first quarter being restated.

**Explanation:** GAAP requires that extraordinary items be disclosed separately and included in the determination of net income in the interim period in which they occur. Gains and losses that would not be deferred at year-end should not be deferred to later interim periods of the same year. Therefore, the extraordinary loss should not be prorated. (Solution = b.)

**QUESTION**
7.   (L.O. 2) Events that occur after the December 31, 2010 balance sheet date (but before the balance sheet is issued) and provide additional evidence about conditions that existed at the balance sheet date and affect the realizability of accounts receivable should be:
a.   discussed only in the MD&A (Management's Discussion and Analysis) section of the annual report.
b.   disclosed only in the Notes to the Financial Statements.
c.   used to record an adjustment to Bad Debt Expense for the year ending December 31, 2010.
d.   used to record an adjustment directly to the Retained Earnings account.

**Explanation:** Notes to the financial statements should explain any significant financial events that took place after the formal balance sheet date, but before it is finally issued. These events are referred to as **post-balance sheet events** or **subsequent events**. Two types of events or transactions occurring after the balance sheet date may have a material effect on the financial statements or may need to be considered to interpret these statements accurately:
1.   Events that provide additional evidence about conditions that existed at the balance sheet date, affect the estimates used in preparing financial statements, and, therefore, result in needed adjustments. Examples include a loss on an account receivable resulting from a customer's bankruptcy subsequent to the balance sheet when the bankruptcy stems from the customer's poor financial health existing at the balance sheet date.
2.   Events that provide evidence about conditions that did not exist at the balance sheet date but arose subsequent to that date and do not require adjustment of the financial statements. An example would be a loss resulting from a customer's fire or flood **after** the balance sheet date; it does not reflect conditions existing at that date.  (However, some of these events may have to be disclosed in the notes to keep the financial statements from being misleading. Examples of such events are sale of bonds or capital stock, stock splits, stock dividends, a pending business combination, loss of plant or inventories from a natural disaster occurring after the balance sheet date, gains or losses on certain marketable securities, settlement of litigation when the event giving rise to the claim took place subsequent to the balance sheet date, and losses on receivables resulting from conditions—such as customer's major casualty—arising subsequent to the balance sheet date).

The subsequent event described in the question encompasses information that would have been recorded in the accounts had it been available at the balance sheet date. This type of event requires adjustments to be made before the financial statements are issued. (Solution = c.)

**TIP:**   Many events or developments occurring subsequent to the balance sheet date do not require adjustment of or disclosure in the financial statements. Typically, these are nonaccounting events or conditions that management normally communicates by other means. These events include legislation, product changes, strikes, management changes, unionization, and loss of important customers.

**QUESTION**
8.   (L.O. 6) The MD&A section of an enterprise's annual report is to cover the following three items:
   a.   income statement, balance sheet, and statement of owners' equity.
   b.   income statement, balance sheet, and statement of cash flows.
   c.   liquidity, capital resources, and results of operations.
   d.   changes in the stock price, mergers, and acquisitions.

**Explanation:** Management's discussion and analysis (MD&A) section of the annual report covers three financial aspects of an enterprise's business—liquidity, capital resources, and results of operations. It requires management to highlight favorable or unfavorable trends and to identify significant events and uncertainties that affect these three factors. This approach obviously involves a number of subjective estimates, opinions, and soft data. However, the SEC, which has mandated this disclosure, believes the relevance of this information exceeds the potential lack of reliability. (Solution = c.)

**\*TIP:**     The following eleven questions are derived from the material in Appendix 24A in the text.

**QUESTION**
\*9.   (L.O. 10) The current ratio at any given date for a particular company is:
   a.   usually equal to the acid-test ratio at the same date.
   b.   usually smaller than the acid-test ratio at the same date.
   c.   usually larger than the acid-test ratio at the same date.
   d.   computed by dividing current liabilities by current assets.

**Approach and Explanation:** Write down the formulas for both the current ratio and the acid-test ratio. Notice what is similar and what is different about them. Think about how the difference will affect the relative results. The current ratio is calculated by dividing total current assets by total current liabilities; whereas, the acid-test ratio is calculated by dividing cash plus short-term investments plus current net receivables by total current liabilities. Current assets other than cash and short-term investments and short-term receivables would normally include inventory and prepaid expenses. Because the current ratio would normally have a larger numerator but the same denominator as the acid-test ratio, it would be larger than the acid-test ratio. (Solution = c.)

**QUESTION**
\*10.(L.O. 10) A company has a current ratio of 2:1 at December 31, 2010. Which of the following transactions would increase this ratio?
a.   purchase of merchandise on account
b.   sale of bonds payable at a discount
c.   payment of a 60-day note payable
d.   collection of an account receivable
e.   both "b" and "c"

**Approach and Explanation:** Set up an example of the situation described; assume current assets are $8,000 and current liabilities are $4,000. Prepare the journal entry for each of the transactions (assume the amount involved is $2,000) and analyze the effect of the entry on the components of the current ratio. The journal entries and analyses should appear as follows:

a.   Inventory.................................................................................     2,000
     Accounts Payable..............................................................................          2,000
     Current assets and current liabilities both increase by the same amount ($2,000); therefore, the current ratio will decrease. (The new ratio will be $10,000/$6,000, or 1.67:1 in this example.)

b.      Cash .................................................................................................... 2,000
Discount on Bonds Payable ................................................................................. 200
           Bonds Payable ........................................................................................                          2,200

Current assets increase with no change in current liabilities; therefore, the current ratio will increase. (The new ratio will be $10,000/$4,000, or 2.5:1 in this example.)

c.      Short-term Note Payable ..................................................................... 2,000
           Cash ......................................................................................................                2,000
Current assets and current liabilities both decrease by the same amount; therefore, the current ratio will increase because the ratio was something greater than 1:1 before the transaction. (The new ratio will be $6,000/$2,000, or 3:1 in this example.)

d.      Cash .................................................................................................... 2,000
           Accounts Receivable............................................................................                        2,000
Total current assets and total current liabilities both remain unchanged; therefore, there is no change in the current ratio.

e.      Both "b" and "c" cause an increase in the current ratio.                              (Solution = e.)

**QUESTION**
*11.    (L.O. 10) A company has a current ratio of 2:1 at December 31, 2010. Which of the following transactions will **not** cause a change in the current ratio?
a.      declaration of a 10% stock dividend
b.      purchase of short-term investments for cash
c.      payment of a long-term liability
d.      declaration of a cash dividend
e.      Both "a" and "b"
f.      Both "a" and "d"

**Approach and Explanation:** Set up an example of the situation described; assume current assets are $8,000 and current liabilities are $4,000. Prepare the journal entry for each of the transactions (assume the amount involved is $2,000) and analyze the effect of the entry on the components of the current ratio. The journal entries and analyses should appear as follows:

a.      Retained Earnings................................................................ 2,000
           Common Stock Dividend Distributable .............................................                  500
           Paid-in Capital in Excess of Par ........................................................               1,500
There is no effect on current assets, current liabilities, or the current ratio. (The par value of the dividend shares is an assumed amount here.)

b.      Short-term Investments ...................................................................... 2,000
           Cash ......................................................................................................   2,000
There is no effect on total current assets, current liabilities, or the current ratio.

c.      Long-term Liability ............................................................................... 2,000
           Cash ......................................................................................................   2,000
Current assets are reduced and, therefore, the current ratio is decreased. (The new ratio in this example is $6,000/$4,000, or 1.5:1.)

d.      Retained Earnings............................................................................... 2,000
           Dividends Payable.................................................................................                        2,000

Current liabilities are increased and, therefore, the current ratio is decreased. (The new ratio in this example is $8,000/$6,000, or 1.33:1.)

e.    Both "a" and "b" have no effect on the current ratio.

f.    Although "a" has no effect on the current ratio, "d" causes a decrease in the current ratio.(Solution = e.)

**QUESTION**
*12.   (L.O. 10) If the debt to stockholders' equity ratio is 150% and total assets are $500,000, which of the following is **false**?
a.    The ratio is favorable for obtaining additional loans because it is greater than 100%.
b.    Stockholders' equity totals $200,000.
c.    The ratio may be expressed as "3 to 2."
d.    The amount of total liabilities is 1.5 times the amount of total stockholders' equity.
e.    All of the above.

**Explanation:** The debt to stockholders' equity ratio is calculated by dividing total liabilities by total stockholders' equity. If X is total liabilities and Y is total stockholders' equity and X/Y = 150% and X + Y = $500,000, then:

$$\frac{X}{(\$500,000 - X)} = 1.5$$

**Solving for X:**   
X    =1.5($500,000 - X)
X    =$750,000 - 1.5X
X + 1.5X    =    $750,000
X    =$750,000 ÷ 2.5
X    =$300,000
Y    =$500,000 - $300,000  =  $200,000

Based on these calculations, selections "b," "c," and "d," are true. Selection "a" is false because creditors would rather see a debt to stockholders' equity ratio of less than 100%. Thus, potential creditors would not look favorably at a 150% debt to stockholders' equity ratio. (Solution = a.)

**QUESTION**
*13.   (L.O. 10) A company has total assets of $1,000,000. It has 6% bonds outstanding with a face value of $400,000. Income before income taxes for the current year is $110,000. The income tax rate is 40%. No preferred stock is outstanding. There are no liabilities other than the bonds. Which of the following is **true**?
a.    The rate of return on stockholders' equity exceeds the rate of return on total assets by 2%.
b.    The rate of return on total assets is 13.4%.
c.    The rate of return on stockholders' equity is 9%.
d.    The company is not favorably trading on the equity.

**Explanation:** Net income equals $110,000 - (40% x $110,000) = $66,000. The rate of return on total assets = net income plus interest expense divided by total assets. In this case, ($66,000 + $24,000) ÷ $1,000,000 = 9%. The rate of return on stockholders' equity equals net income divided by stockholders' equity. In this case, $66,000 ÷ $600,000 = 11%. Selection "a" is, therefore, a true statement, and selections "b" and "c" are not true statements. Selection "d" is not a true statement because the rate of return on stockholders' equity is greater than the return on total assets, which indicates a situation of favorable trading on the equity. (Solution = a.)

**QUESTION**

*14.    (L.O. 10) A corporation has two classes of stock outstanding. The return on common stockholders' equity is computed by dividing net income:

a.    minus preferred dividends by the number of common stock shares outstanding at the balance sheet date.

b.    plus interest expense by the average amount of total assets.

c.    by the number of common stock shares outstanding at the balance sheet date.

d.    minus preferred dividends by the average amount of common stock-holders' equity during the period.

**Explanation:** The return on common stockholders' equity is computed by dividing the amount of earnings applicable to the common stockholders' interest in the company by the average amount of common stockholders' equity during the period. The amount of earnings applicable to the common stockholders is the amount of net income for the period less the dividends declared on preferred stock during the period. (Solution = d.)

**QUESTION**

*15.(L.O. 10) Which of the following items would **not** be used in calculating the working capital ratio?

a.    accounts payable

b.    inventory

c.    accounts receivable

d.    furniture purchased during the current period

**Approach and Explanation:** Think about the working capital ratio and write down the formula to compute it. Then read the answer selections and determine which selection does not fit into the formula. The **working capital ratio** is another name for the **current ratio**. The current ratio is determined by dividing total current assets by total current liabilities at a point in time. Answer selection "d" would be classified under the property, plant, and equipment classification and would, therefore, not be included in the calculation of the working capital ratio. (Solution = d.)

**QUESTION**

*16.(L.O. 13) The base figure used for vertical analysis of the income statement is:

a.    net income.

b.    gross profit.

c.    income before income taxes.

d.    net sales revenue.

**Explanation:** On an income statement, net sales is the base amount for vertical analysis. All other items are then expressed as a percentage of that base amount. (Solution = d.)

**QUESTION**

*17.    (L.O. 13) The base figure used for vertical analysis of a corporate balance sheet is:

a.    total assets.

b.    current assets.

c.    property, plant, and equipment.

d.    stockholders' equity.

**Explanation:** In performing a vertical analysis of the balance sheet, total assets is the base figure. All other amounts are then expressed as a percentage of the total assets amount. (Solution = a.)

**QUESTION**
*18.    (L.O. 13) The Goodings Corporation reported sales of $80,000 in 2008, $96,000 in 2009, and $112,000 in 2010. In a trend analysis for these years, where 2008 is used as the base year, the respective sales percentages would be:
a.      100%; 120%; 137%.
b.      100%; 120%; 117%.
c.      100%; 120%; 140%.
d.      80%; 96%; 112%.

**Explanation:** Trend analysis is a type of horizontal analysis that is prepared for more than two years. In horizontal analysis, a base year (2008 in this case) is selected. Each item being analyzed is then divided by the amount reported for the base year for the same item. Thus, $80,000 is the 100% figure, $96,000 divided by $80,000 = 120%, and $112,000 divided by $80,000 = 140%. (Solution = c.)

**QUESTION**
*19.    (L.O. 13) An analyst is examining an income statement that shows only percentages; all items are expressed in terms of a percentage of net sales. This type of analysis is often called:
a.      common-size analysis.
b.      horizontal analysis.
c.      ratio analysis.
d.      multiple-step analysis.

**Explanation: Vertical analysis**, sometimes referred to as **common-size analysis**, is a technique for evaluating financial statement data that expresses each item within a financial statement in terms of a percent of a base amount. For an income statement, net sales is used as the base amount. (Solution = a.)

# NOTES

# NOTES

# NOTES

# NOTES

# NOTES